Grades 3–5

Lessons for Algebraic Thinking

Grades 3–5

Maryann Wickett

Katharine Kharas

Marilyn Burns

Lessons for Algebraic Thinking

$$y = 2x + 3$$

Math Solutions Publications
Sausalito, CA

Math Solutions Publications
A division of
Marilyn Burns Education Associates
150 Gate 5 Road, Suite 101
Sausalito, CA 94965
www.mathsolutions.com

Library of Congress Cataloging-in-Publication Data

Wickett, Maryann.
    Lessons for algebraic thinking. Grades 3–5 / Maryann Wickett,
Katharine Kharas, Marilyn Burns.
        p.   cm.—(Lessons for algebraic thinking series)
Includes index.
    ISBN 0-941355-48-9 (alk. paper)
    1. Algebra—Study and teaching (Elementary)   I. Kharas, Katharine.   II.
Burns, Marilyn, 1941–   III. Title.   IV. Series.
    QA159 .W53   2002
    372.7—dc21

                                                              2002011258

ISBN-10: 0-941355-48-9
ISBN-13: 978-0-941355-48-3

Editor: Toby Gordon
Production: Melissa L. Inglis
Cover & interior design: Catherine Hawkes/Cat & Mouse
Composition: Cape Cod Compositors, Inc.

Printed in the United States of America on acid-free paper
06   05   ML   4   5

A Message from Marilyn Burns

We at Math Solutions Professional Development believe that teaching math well calls for increasing our understanding of the math we teach, seeking deeper insights into how children learn mathematics, and refining our lessons to best promote students' learning.

Math Solutions Publications shares classroom-tested lessons and teaching expertise from our faculty of Math Solutions Inservice instructors as well as from other respected math educators. Our publications are part of the nationwide effort we've made since 1984 that now includes

- more than five hundred face-to-face inservice programs each year for teachers and administrators in districts across the country;
- annually publishing professional development books, now totaling more than fifty titles and spanning the teaching of all math topics in kindergarten through grade 8;
- four series of videotapes for teachers, plus a videotape for parents, that show math lessons taught in actual classrooms;
- on-site visits to schools to help refine teaching strategies and assess student learning; and
- free online support, including grade-level lessons, book reviews, inservice information, and district feedback, all in our quarterly *Math Solutions Online Newsletter*.

For information about all of the products and services we have available, please visit our Web site at *www.mathsolutions.com*. You can also contact us to discuss math professional development needs by calling (800) 868-9092 or by sending an e-mail to *info@mathsolutions.com*.

We're always eager for your feedback and interested in learning about your particular needs. We look forward to hearing from you.

SOLUTIONS® **Publications**

A DIVISION OF MARILYN BURNS EDUCATION ASSOCIATES

We dedicate this book in memory of Robert B. Davis, a mentor to us all, who for more than forty years guided our thinking about mathematics education in general and algebra for elementary students in particular. Without his influence, this book would never have been written.

Contents

Blackline Masters   299

Acknowledgments

We'd like to acknowledge the following California teachers and their students for allowing us to teach lessons in their classrooms and for providing useful feedback: Dee Uyeda and Danielle Ross, Park School, Mill Valley; Cathy Bullock, Capri School, Encinitas; Bill Wickett, Reynolds School, Oceanside; Carol Scurlock, Discovery School, San Marcos; and Linda Chick, Larry Dovenbarger, Eunice Hendrix-Martin, Kristin Kaufhold, Nicole McClymonds, Patti Reynolds, and Steve Musick, Carrillo School, San Marcos.

Introduction

To begin a lesson, I wrote *algebra* on the board and asked the class, "What do you know about algebra?" The students sat quietly. Slowly a few raised a hand to offer an idea.

Karena said, "My sister's taking it."

"It has letters instead of just numbers," Armando added.

"I think it's supposed to be hard," Paul added.

There were no other ideas. I turned and wrote the word *pattern* on the board. "Who knows something about patterns?" I asked. Now all hands flew into the air.

"I've been doing patterns since preschool," Kiko said.

"The multiplication facts are all patterns," Kurt said.

"Two, four, six, eight is a pattern," Rayna said. "It's adding two each time. It always does the same thing."

"There's patterns in spelling, too," Johanna commented.

"If you know how something is changing, you know the pattern and then you can predict, like scientists do," Chase said.

These responses were typical of students in all the classes in which we taught these lessons. Students in grades 3 through 5 generally have had little experience with algebra but are knowledgeable about and comfortable with patterns. This is good news. Understanding patterns is essential to algebraic thinking, and we know that children learn more easily when they can connect new experiences to what they already know. Also, teaching is more effective when it draws on experiences and contexts that are familiar to students, and patterns provide a useful foundation on which teachers can develop students' algebraic thinking.

The lessons in this book help teachers meet the challenge of making algebra an integral part of instruction in grades 3 through 5. The lessons not only make clear what to teach children about algebra, but also show how to teach the concepts and skills that build students' algebraic thinking. Key to children's learning about algebra in these grade levels is that they have experience creating, recognizing, and extending patterns; describing them verbally; and then representing the patterns symbolically in several ways—numerically on tables (often called T-charts), algebraically using equations with variables, and geometrically on graphs.

However, just as we know that children gain new knowledge when they are able to build new understanding on what they already know and can see the usefulness of the new ideas, the same is true for teachers learning to incorporate algebra into their mathematics teaching. The lessons in this book recognize that the main focus and teaching skill of teachers in the elementary grades is the development of children's number understanding and skills. Arithmetic is still the time-honored third R. Therefore, the lessons in this book help teachers see how instruction that supports algebraic thinking can not only build on the instruction they're already providing in the area of number and operations, but can also support, enhance, and extend children's arithmetic learning. In addition, the lessons also draw on and support students' understanding of geometry, helping students see arithmetic, geometry, and algebra as connected topics integral to the study of mathematics. Teaching the lessons is a win-win proposition. From these lessons, students' study of number and geometry is supported while they also receive preparation for their later, more formal study of algebra.

Teaching algebraic thinking in the elementary grades is a fairly new requirement in the mathematics curriculum. Algebra is no longer relegated to the high school math curriculum and available only to students judged to be capable of learning it. *Principles and Standards for School Mathematics*, published in 2000 by the National Council of Teachers of Mathematics, is the national guide for the mathematics education of students in prekindergarten through grade 12. The first five Standards in the document describe the content goals of the mathematics curriculum. Standard 1, Number and Operations, addresses the mainstay of the elementary mathematics curriculum and the cornerstone of the entire mathematics curriculum in all grades. Standard 2 is Algebra! The message of the document is clear: All students should learn algebra, from prekindergarten on up. The document makes the case: "By viewing algebra as a strand in the curriculum from prekindergarten on, teachers can help students build a solid foundation of understanding and experiences as preparation for more sophisticated work in algebra in the middle grades and high school."

The algebra to be taught to students in the elementary grades should not, however, be a watered-down version of the standard high school course that most of us took. The goal in grades 3 through 5 is to develop students' algebraic thinking, building a foundation of understanding and skills while they are young so that they can be successful in their later, more formal study of algebra.

We recognize that some elementary teachers don't feel comfortable with what they remember about algebra. We also believe that teachers can't teach effectively what they don't understand. Therefore, along with presenting classroom-tested lessons, we include a "Background" section for each that addresses the underlying mathematics. In addition, the "Mathematical Background" section in this Introduction provides explanations about some of the key ideas related to algebraic thinking. Also, the Glossary at the end of the book provides a reference of the algebraic terminology used in the book as well as other terminology that students will encounter later.

The Structure of the Lessons

The fourteen lessons in this book vary in several ways. Some require one class period; others take two, three, or four periods; and many of the lessons are suitable for repeat experiences throughout the year. Some incorporate manipulative materials, some make use of children's books, and some do both. To help you teach the lessons, each is organized into the following sections:

Overview This is a nutshell description of the mathematical focus of the lesson and what the students will be doing.

Background This section addresses the mathematics underlying the lesson and at times provides information about prior experiences or knowledge students need.

Vocabulary The algebraic terminology used in the lesson is listed alphabetically.

Materials This section lists the materials needed, along with quantities. Not included are regular classroom supplies such as paper and pencils. Worksheets required are included in the Blackline Masters section at the back of the book.

Time The number of class periods required is indicated, sometimes with a range allowing for different length periods and for differences among classes. Most lessons call for more than one class period.

The Lesson This section presents the heart of the lesson with a vignette that describes what occurred when the lesson was taught, providing the details needed for planning and teaching the lesson. Samples of student work are included.

Extensions This section is included for some lessons and offers follow-up suggestions.

The Content of the Lessons

We taught all fourteen lessons in third-, fourth-, and fifth-grade classes, and we taught most of them multiple times. In the vignettes, we purposely don't identify the grade level of the particular students described. We don't want to discourage you from considering a lesson because of the grade level of the students in the vignette. Rather, we encourage you to consider all of the lessons and, as you do with any instructional materials, make adjustments to fit your students' needs. This may entail moving more quickly through one section or spending more time on another. As you become more familiar and experienced with these lessons, you'll have a better feel for making appropriate adjustments. The lessons are organized into two sections within this book: "Part One: Getting Students Ready" and "Part Two: The Lessons."

Getting Students Ready

The five lessons in this section give students a foundation of experience on which the rest of the lessons build. Chapter 1, "Two of Everything," uses the context of a children's book to introduce a growth pattern that students learn to represent with words and then with equations using two variables. Chapter 2, "True, False, and Open Sentences," focuses students on equations using one variable. Chapters 3 and 4, "Introduction to Coordinate Graphing" and "Tic-Tac-Toe," teach students how to plot points on a coordinate grid; Chapter 3 also incorporates the use of a children's book. In Chapter 5, "Two of Everything Revisited," students return to the experience in Chapter 1 and apply the skills they learned in Chapters 3 and 4 to represent a growth pattern graphically. These five lessons require about ten days of instruction.

The Lessons

The nine lessons that follow build on the knowledge and skills in Part One, "Getting Students Ready." Chapter 10, "Guess My Rule," presents an experience similar to those in Chapters 1 and 5, using a different children's book as the context to provide a similar experience. In five other chapters, students interpret geometric patterns and use manipulative materials. In Chapters 6 and 12, "Iguanas" and "Table Patterns," students use pattern blocks; in Chapters 7, 11, and 13, "Letter Patterns," "Piles of Tiles," and "Amanda Bean," students use color tiles. Chapters 12 and 13 also use children's stories as the contexts for the investigations. All of these chapters are suitable for providing students with experience describing and extending growth patterns and representing them with equations and on graphs. The remaining three chapters in this section provide other experiences important to algebraic thinking. Chapter 8, "Pick a Number," gives students experience solving equations with one variable; Chapter 9, "Four Points," provides a problem-solving experience that helps reinforce the skill of plotting points; Chapter 14, "Identities," engages students in investigating properties of numbers, making generalizations, and describing them both with words and algebraic symbols.

Suggestions for Schoolwide Planning

To teach the lessons described in the fourteen chapters requires at least thirty-three days of instruction, plus additional time for extensions and repeat experiences, as suggested for some lessons. If you plan to teach all of the lessons in one school year, the order in which they appear is a suitable sequence.

The five lessons in Part One require a total of at least ten days of instruction and provide students with a beginning experience with algebraic thinking. Each of these lessons is appropriate for grades 3, 4, and 5. If this is the first time your school is focusing on algebraic thinking, it makes sense to teach these five lessons in all three grades.

If, however, students have had prior experience with algebraic thinking, then you may want to delegate specific lessons from the book to different grades. For example, you may decide that the initial five lessons are sufficient for providing third graders with a two-week unit on algebraic thinking.

Then, for fourth graders who experienced these five lessons the year before, substitute Chapter 6 for Chapters 1 and 2, which will give students a similar opportunity to think about growth patterns but in a fresh context. Chapters 4 and 9 will reinforce plotting points. And Chapters 7 and 10 provide further experiences. Teaching these chapters will provide students with at least two and a half weeks of algebra instruction.

For fifth graders, Chapter 8 will give experience solving equations with one variable; Chapters 11, 12, and 13 will continue their study of growth patterns; and Chapter 14 will engage them in investigating properties of numbers. Teaching these chapters provides students with about three weeks of algebra instruction.

In all grades, lessons don't have to be taught on consecutive days but can be spread throughout the year as support for your students' learning of arithmetic.

Mathematical Background

It's important to understand the math behind the math you teach. We recognize that some elementary teachers haven't thought a great deal about algebra since taking a course in high school or college and don't feel comfortable with what they remember about algebra. Therefore, following are descriptions of a few ideas that are key to algebraic thinking. These ideas are introduced in the lessons, but not with the formal language in the descriptions that follow. Therefore, please keep in mind that this is not information that your students are expected to learn, but background information to enhance your understanding. Also, descriptions of other ideas appear in the "Background" sections of individual lessons. We know how difficult it can be to learn mathematics from reading about it. If the information presented here is new for you, our suggestion is first to try the activities in the lessons and read the following descriptions after you've had some firsthand experience.

Patterns and Functions

(**Note:** Reading Chapter 1 first will provide you with a context for the information in this section.)

Patterns provide us with a way to recognize order and make sense of the world. The ability to create, recognize, and extend patterns is essential for making generalizations, seeing relationships, and understanding the order and logic of mathematics. The lessons in this book engage students in investigating both numerical and geometric patterns, building on what they have previously learned.

Students' observations of patterns that define how quantities relate to one another provide them with beginning experiences with functions. For example, we can look at the pattern of tricycles and wheels: one tricycle has three wheels, two tricycles have six wheels, three have nine wheels, and so on. To find the number of wheels for any number of tricycles, we multiply the number of tricycles by three. The pattern holds for any number of tricycles, and the relationship between these two quantities—the number of tricycles and the number of wheels—is called a *function*. We can represent a function symbolically in several ways. One way is to make a table, commonly called a *T-chart*.

# of tricycles	# of wheels
0	0
1	3
2	6
3	9
4	12
5	15
.	.
.	.
.	.

We can also represent a function as an equation using symbols for the changing quantities. In this case, one symbol would represent the number of tricycles and another would represent the number of wheels. We can use letters for symbols. For example, if we use *t* to represent the number of tricycles and *w* to represent the number of wheels, then we can represent the functional relationship of wheels to tricycles as $w = t \times 3$ or of tricycles to wheels as $t \times 3 = w$. Instead of using letters for the symbols, we can use shapes in which we can write numbers; for example, we can draw a box to represent the number of tricycles and a triangle to represent the number of wheels, so then $\triangle = \square \times 3$.

A third way to represent a function is to make a graph. Using the pairs of numbers from the T-chart as ordered pairs and plotting the points they represent produces the following graph:

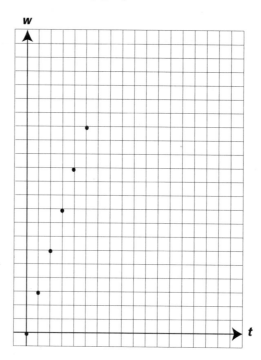

More formally, a function is a relationship between two variables in which the value of one variable, often called the *output*, depends on the value of the other, often called the *input*. An important characteristic of a function is that for every input, there is exactly one output. For example, if the rule for a function is to add two to the input number, and the input number is six, then eight is the only possible output number for that input. Using a triangle and a box as symbols to represent the variables, an equation to describe this function rule could be: $\triangle = \square + 2$. For every function presented in these lessons, it's possible for students to describe the pattern and identify a rule for determining the output value for any input value.

Variables

(**Note:** Reading Chapters 1 and 2 will provide you with an introduction to variables.)

Variables are letters, symbols, or other placeholders in mathematical expressions that can serve different purposes. They can represent an unknown value; for example, to make the equation $4x = 12$ true, x must represent the number 3. Variables can also represent the input and output values of a pattern that can be described as a function rule; for example, in $w = t \times 3$, the equation used to describe the function about tricycles and wheels, the letters w and t are variables, while 3 is a constant. Variables can represent quantities in formulas; for example, the l and w and A in $A = l \times w$ are variables. They can be used to represent a generalized numerical property; for example, in $\square + \triangle = \triangle + \square$, $\square$ and $\triangle$ are variables used to describe the commutative property of addition.

Graphing Functions

(**Note:** Reading Chapters 3 and 5 will provide you with an introduction to graphing.)

Most of the graphs in the lessons represent linear functions, which means that the points on the graphs lie on a straight line. (For a helpful way to remember this term, notice that the word *line* is contained in *linear*.) Also, most of the lines in the graphs go on a diagonal up to the right. The slant of the diagonal is referred to as the *slope* of the line, and the steeper the line, the higher the slope number. The slope is different for each of the three graphs shown here.

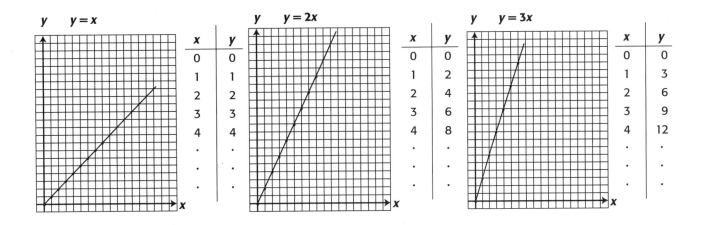

To figure the value of the slope of a line on a graph, examine a sequence of points that have been plotted with the input values in order—0, 1, 2, 3, 4, and so on. Start with any point, count one space to the right, and then see how many spaces you have to count up to reach the next point. For example, in the first graph above, to get from one point to the next, each time you count one to the right, you have to count up one to reach the next point. Therefore, the slope of the line on the first graph is 1. In the second graph, to get from one point to the next, you count up two spaces each time you go over one; therefore, the slope of the second line is 2. And, in the third graph, the slope is 3 because each time you go from one point to the next, you count over one and then up three. The larger the slope, the steeper the line is. For a line that is less steep than the line on the first graph, the slope has to be less than 1. For example, the line on the following graph has a slope of $\frac{1}{2}$; each time you count over one space from a point, you only have to go up half a space to get to the next point.

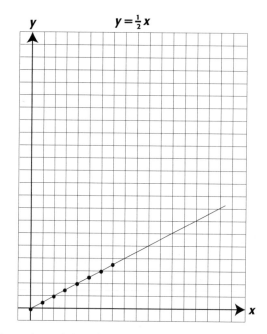

$$y = \tfrac{1}{2}x$$

x	y
0	0
1	$\frac{1}{2}$
2	1
3	$1\frac{1}{2}$
4	2
.	.
.	.
.	.

The value of the slope of a line is evident in the numerical information on the T-chart by examining the pattern of the output values when the inputs are listed in order—0, 1, 2, 3, 4, and so on. For the first graph on the preceeding page, the output numbers increase by the same value of one each time; in the second graph, they increase by two; in the third graph, they increase by three. For the graph above with a slope of $\frac{1}{2}$, the output values increase by one-half each time. When the increase of successive output values is a constant, as it is on the T-charts for each of these graphs, the increase is the slope. If the increase in the output values on a T-chart isn't constant, but changes, that indicates that graphing the ordered pairs won't produce points in a straight line but, instead, on a curve. However, for this introductory experience, the points on all of the graphs the students will investigate in Part One go in straight lines and the graphs are, therefore, linear.

The patterns of the points in graphs connect to the algebraic equations that represent the patterns. Notice that the slope for each of the graphs shown above is the same number that is multiplied by the input variable in the equation. For example, for the middle graph above, the equation is $y = 2x$ or $\triangle = 2 \times \square$, and the slope is 2. (For a slope of 1, the multiplication isn't indicated in the equation since multiplying by one doesn't change the value of a number. However, we could write the equation as $y = 1x$ or $\triangle = 1 \times \square$.)

The four graphs shown above each pass through the origin of the coordinate grid. That's because the ordered pair (0, 0) fits each pattern. This isn't always true. For example, if the rule for a pattern is that the output value is equal to two times the input value plus one, the equation would be $y = 2x + 1$ or $\triangle = 2 \times \square + 1$. (Check the pattern in the output values on the T-chart and the pattern of successive points on the graph to verify that the slope of this graph is 2.) For this pattern, the input value of zero produces one, which means that the ordered pair for the input value of zero is (0, 1). If you graph the pairs of numbers for the T-chart, as shown on the next page, the line doesn't go through the origin. It crosses the vertical axis at one space above the origin, and this information is also contained in the equation; the + 1 in the rule tells that the line will intercept the vertical axis at one above the origin.

For the first four previous graphs, there is no "plus" number in the rule or in the equation. If we wanted to have a "plus" number and still have the same equation, we would have to use + 0 in each equation so that the values of the

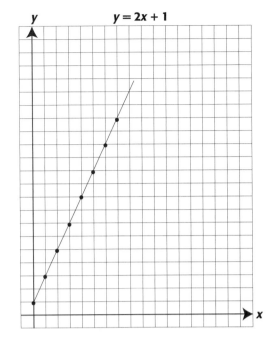

$y = 2x + 1$

x	y
0	1
1	3
2	5
3	7
4	9
.	.
.	.
.	.

output numbers would stay the same. So, for example, the middle equation above could be written as $y = 2x + 0$ or $\triangle = 2 \times \square + 0$, and the zero would indicate where on the vertical axis the line would hit, which is the origin.

If you're not familiar with this aspect of mathematics, investigate the graphs for other equations and see if you can figure out how to predict for any linear equation what the slope of the line will be and where the line will intercept the vertical axis. While this knowledge isn't a goal for the lessons in this book, it's helpful background information for teaching the lessons effectively.

More About Linear Functions

(**Note:** The following information extends the previous information about linear functions and offers you background information beyond the mathematics presented in the lessons.)

It's valuable to look for connections among ideas in mathematics. Making connections strengthens understanding and helps us see mathematics in a cohesive way. In this light, it's helpful to think about connections among the three representations for a function—a T-chart, an equation using variables, and a graph.

In the previous section, "Graphing Functions," connections were made between the equation and the graph that represent a function. One connection is that the slope of the line on a graph is the same as the number that is multiplied by the input variable in the equation. Another connection is that the point where the line intercepts the vertical axis on the graph is the number that is added in the equation. For example, a rule that is presented in Chapter 10 is that the number that comes out of the machine is always equal to two times the number that is put into the machine, plus one. The number put into the machine is the input value; the number that comes out is the output value. For an input of three, for example, the machine multiplies two times three to get six and then adds one, producing an output value of seven. For an input of zero, multiplying two by zero results in zero and adding one produces an output value of one. Algebraically, using y for the output value and x for the input value, the function rule can be written as $y = 2 \cdot x + 1$. The multiplier of x in the equation, 2, is the slope of the graph; that is, when you go over from one point to the next on the graph, you go up two. Also, the number added in the equation is 1; on the graph, the line of points intercepts the vertical axis at

(0, 1), which is one space above the origin. This information about the equation and the graph also connects to the numerical information on a T-chart. Following is the T-chart for the rule:

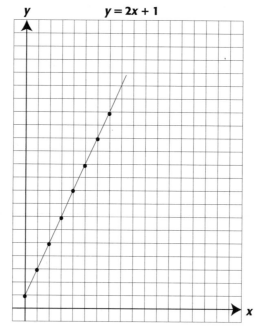

x	y
0	1
1	3
2	5
3	7
4	9
.	.
.	.
.	.

Notice that the difference between the output numbers on the T-chart is two. This is the multiplier of the input number in the equation, and it's also the slope of the graph! Also notice that the output value for the input of zero is one. This relates to the number added in the equation and also to where the line crosses the vertical axis on the graph!

When you understand these connections, if you see the T-chart or the equation of a function, you'll be able to visualize its graph. Also, if you see a graph, you'll be able to write the equation and create the T-chart. And if you see only the equation, you can construct the T-chart and make a graph. They're all connected!

In high school algebra books, you'll often see a generalized equation for linear functions written as $y = mx + b$. In our rule above, $y = 2 \cdot x + 1$, $m = 2$, and $b = 1$. There is nothing magical about the choice of m and b in the general equation; they're arbitrary choices for letters that have become one of the symbolic conventions of mathematics. What's important to know is that on a graph of a function, m represents the slope and b represents where the line crosses the vertical axis. Also, on a T-chart representing the function, m is the difference between numbers in the output column and b is the output value when zero is the input value. A part of understanding mathematics is bringing meaning to the symbols we use to represent ideas.

Algebra I students in middle or high school traditionally haven't previously encountered many of the ideas in this book. They are expected to assimilate algebraic concepts and skills in a very short time and often end up with incomplete understandings. Introducing students to algebraic reasoning in the elementary grades provides a valuable foundation for their later, more formal experiences. Many elementary students will enthusiastically discover the relationships among T-charts, functional equations, and graphs if given the opportunity. While understanding the ideas in this section isn't the focus of any of the lessons in the book, the ideas are valuable background knowledge for your understanding of algebraic thinking. If you haven't yet explored this aspect of mathematics, we encourage you to do so.

## PART ONE

Getting Students Ready

As stated in the Introduction, the five lessons in this section give students a foundation of experience on which the rest of the lessons build. Chapter 1, "Two of Everything," uses the context of a children's book to introduce a growth pattern that students learn to represent with words and then with equations using two variables. Chapter 2, "True, False, and Open Sentences," focuses students on equations using one variable. Chapters 3 and 4, "Introduction to Coordinate Graphing" and "Tic-Tac-Toe," teach students how to plot points on a coordinate grid; Chapter 3 also incorporates the use of a children's book. In Chapter 5, "Two of Everything Revisited," students return to the experience in Chapter 1 and apply the skills they learned in Chapters 3 and 4 to represent a growth pattern graphically. These five lessons require about ten days of instruction.

The section in the Introduction titled "Suggestions for Schoolwide Planning" offers guidance for choosing and sequencing lessons that are appropriate for your class.

Two of Everything

A First Experience with Growth Patterns

OVERVIEW

The children's book *Two of Everything*, by Lily Toy Hong, tells the story of a magical brass pot that doubles whatever is put into it. The story is an engaging context for providing students with a beginning experience with examining a growth pattern, recording and extending data on a T-chart, and representing the pattern algebraically with an equation. The experience is then extended by changing the doubling rule of the pot to other rules for the children to figure out. The students use T-charts to represent what goes into and comes out of the pot and describe the patterns with both words and equations. Students also create rules of their own for others to guess.

BACKGROUND

Two of Everything, by Lily Toy Hong, is a Chinese folktale about an elderly couple, Mr. and Mrs. Haktak, who find magic in an ancient brass pot. Mr. Haktak discovers the pot while digging in his garden, and he puts his coin purse into it for safekeeping. When he brings the pot into the house for Mrs. Haktak, she accidentally drops her hairpin into the pot. When she reaches in to get it, she pulls out two hairpins and two coin purses! Mr. and Mrs. Haktak realize their good luck and get to work doubling their possessions. The story takes a hilarious turn when Mrs. Haktak loses her balance and falls into the pot.

This lesson uses the model of the magical pot to introduce students to the idea of functions. A function is a relationship between two variables in which the value of one variable, often called the *output*, depends on the value of the other, often called the *input*. An important characteristic of a function is that for every input, there is exactly one output. When the students identify a number that is an input value, the rule for the function pairs that number with exactly one other number, the output value.

For example, if a function rule is to add two to the input number, and the input number is six, then eight is the only possible output number for that input. Using a triangle, $\triangle$, and a box, $\square$, as symbols to represent the variables, an equation to describe this function rule could be $\triangle = \square + 2$. In this lesson, the students use boxes and triangles as the variables to describe the patterns they investigate. In other lessons, they use other variables as well; for example, the equation $\triangle = \square + 2$ can also be written in others ways and using other variables: $O = I + 2$, $x + 2 = y$, $y = x + 2$, and so on. Over time, students become comfortable with different algebraic representations and learn how these representations connect to their related T-charts.

In later grades, students study functions in more depth. In grades 3–5, however, our goal is introductory and, therefore, we don't identify the activity to the class as an investigation of functions or present a formal definition of *function* to the students. Rather, we keep the focus of the lesson on having students create and interpret rules, represent them numerically on a T-chart, and describe them first with words and then algebraically with equations.

If you're not familiar with functions, check the Introduction for background information about the mathematics.

VOCABULARY

equation, input value, output value, T-chart, variable

MATERIALS

- *Two of Everything*, by Lily Toy Hong (Morton Grove, IL: Albert Whitman & Company, 1993)

TIME

- at least three class periods

The Lesson

Day 1

"Today I'd like to share a book with you written by Lily Toy Hong," I said. "It's called *Two of Everything.*"

"We read that book last year," Michael said. "It was funny." Several others nodded their heads, indicating their agreement with Michael.

"How many of you have heard the story before?" I asked. Several students raised their hands. "Do you recommend it for other students?"

"Yes!" they chorused.

I read the story aloud. The class giggled when Mrs. Haktak fell into the pot and became two Mrs. Haktaks rather than one. Sam said, "I don't think my dad would want two wives!"

Audrey commented, "I wonder what Mr. Haktak will do."

I continued reading, and when Mr. Haktak also fell into the pot, Karly squealed, "Oh no! Now what?"

James said, "Each Mr. Haktak can have a Mrs. Haktak!"

When I finished reading the story, Andrea said, "It's neat the way the pot gave Mr. and Mrs. Haktak friends and everything everybody needed."

I then drew a T-chart on the board and labeled the columns *In* and *Out*. "Here's a way we can keep track of what goes into and comes out of the pot," I explained to the students. I wrote *5* about halfway down the In column of the T-chart, leaving room to record 1, 2, 3, and 4 above it.

"Suppose we put five coins in the pot. How many would come out?" I asked.

"Ten," Audrey replied.

"How do you know?" I asked. I always encourage the students to explain how they arrived at their answer.

"In the story, things that fell into the pot doubled," Audrey explained. "If five coins went in, then five would double, which is five plus five. That makes ten coins." The other students nodded their agreement with Audrey.

"Does anyone have something to add?" I asked. No one did. I wrote *10* on the T-chart in the right column next to the *5*.

In	Out
5	10

"What about four coins? If we put in four coins, how many would come out?" The students raised their hands immediately. "Use your fingers to show me how many coins would come out." The students quickly showed eight fingers.

"Can I share how I got it?" Annie asked. I nodded.

"I know you could just add four and four, but I did four times two and got eight," Annie shared. I added *4* and *8* to the T-chart above where I had recorded *5* and *10*.

"What if we put in three coins?" I continued, writing *3* above the 4 in the In column. "What is the output value if the input value is three?" I used the terminology *output value* and *input value* in this instance to help the children become familiar with this alternative terminology for *in* and *out*, and I used the terminology interchangeably throughout the lesson.

"Six," the class responded. I added *6* to the chart.

I then asked the children a question that required them to think differently about the information we were collecting. "What if four coins came out of the pot? How many coins would we have to put in so that four coins would come out?"

Armando said, "If four came out, then two went in. Two plus two equals four. It works!"

"Or you could do times to check instead of addition," Brianna added. "Two times two is like two plus two, and it equals four." I added *2* and *4* to the T-chart.

In order to emphasize that doubling a number can be interpreted both as multiplying it by two and as adding it to itself, I said, "I agree with Brianna that we can use either multiplication or addition to think about the number of coins. Why is that?"

Rick said. "Sometimes multiplication can be used as a shorter way to add, like when all the numbers to be added are the same."

"Would someone else like to share their thoughts?" I asked.

"Doubling is like adding the same number twice or multiplying a number by two, right?" James asked to clarify his own understanding. I nodded. No one had anything else to add.

I returned to the T-chart and said, "If the input is one coin, how many coins will come out?"

"Two," the class responded. I added *1* and *2* to the chart.

In	Out
1	2
2	4
3	6
4	8
5	10

Discussing the Patterns in the T-Chart   James, a student who loved to look for patterns, commented on the T-chart. "I see a pattern," he said. "The In numbers are going up by one each time—one, two, three, four, five. And the Out numbers are counting by twos—two, four, six, eight, ten." (If James hadn't made his comment, I would have initiated a discussion at this point in the lesson by asking the students what patterns they noticed in the columns of numbers.)

"Oh yeah," a few students added softly.

I wrote James's idea on the board. Recording students' ideas not only validates their thinking but also provides the others with a reference of their classmates' ideas. In addition, taking the time to record James's idea gave the other students the opportunity to consider what he said.

James
The In numbers go up by ones (1, 2, 3) and the Out numbers count by twos (2, 4, 6).

"Does everyone agree with James's pattern?" I asked. The students indicated they did. "Who sees a different pattern?"

"If you multiply the In number by two, you get the Out number," Brianna shared. "One times two is two, two times two is four, three times two is six."

I recorded Brianna's pattern on the board:

Brianna
1 × 2 = 2
2 × 2 = 4
3 × 2 = 6

"If you agree with Brianna's pattern please put your thumb up, if you disagree put your thumb down, and if you're not sure put your thumb sideways," I said. The students indicated their agreement by putting their thumbs up.

"Does anyone see another pattern?" I asked. Nina raised her hand.

"I noticed something," Nina began. "You add the In number to itself, and it gives the Out number. One plus one is two, two plus two is four, three plus three is six." I recorded Nina's idea on the board as she explained it:

Nina
1 + 1 = 2
2 + 2 = 4
3 + 3 = 6

"What would come next in Nina's pattern?" I asked.

"Four plus four is eight," Beatriz said.

"Next?" I asked after adding Beatriz's idea to Nina's pattern.

"Five plus five equals ten," David answered.

"I know the next one," Andrea said. "Six plus six equals twelve." I added David's and Andrea's contributions to Nina's pattern:

Nina
1 + 1 = 2
2 + 2 = 4
3 + 3 = 6
4 + 4 = 8
5 + 5 = 10
6 + 6 = 12

"And what if we put ten coins into the pot?" I asked.

"I know the answer," Beatriz said. "It's twenty because ten plus ten is twenty."

"Who agrees?" I asked the class. All hands went up.

"I thought of it differently, though," David said. "I did ten times two, and that's twenty."

"That's like Brianna's pattern," Karly noticed.

"Anyone think of it differently?" I asked.

"I think it could be two times ten," Annie said.

"Let's see what we have so far," I said. As I wrote on the board, I explained, "Here's how Beatriz, David, and Annie thought of it."

10 + 10 = 20   *Beatriz*
10 × 2 = 20   *David*
2 × 10 = 20   *Annie*

"David's and Annie's ways are the same," James said.

"No, they aren't," Armando answered. "They equal the same amount of things, but they don't look the same."

"I don't get it," Kris said.

"Well, two groups of ten look different than ten groups of two," Armando explained.

"Oh, I get it now," Kris said.

"I agree with Armando," I said. "The answer is the same, but they do look different. Let's look back at the chart." As the children watched, I added *10* to the In column of the T-chart, leaving some space so that I could later fill in the numbers from 6 through 9. I also wrote *20* in the Out column.

"It's missing some numbers," Andrea noticed.

"It is," I agreed. "Let's fill in those numbers together." I wrote *6, 7, 8,* and *9* in the In column and then had children tell me what to write in the

Out column for each. When we had filled in the T-chart up to 10, I wrote three dots following the last number in each column and then wrote *100* in the In column.

In	Out
1	2
2	4
3	6
4	8
5	10
6	12
7	14
8	16
9	18
10	20
.	.
.	.
.	.
100	

"The dots mean that I've purposely skipped some numbers," I explained. "What is the output value if the In column says we put one hundred coins into the pot?"

"Two hundred," Rick said.

"How did you figure that?" I asked.

"I multiplied one hundred times two and that's two hundred," Rick explained. I wrote on the board:

Rick
$100 \times 2 = 200$

"I did it differently," Andrea said. "I did one hundred plus one hundred equals two hundred."

I wrote on the board:

Andrea
$100 + 100 = 200$

"You can do the multiplication the other way, so it's two times one hundred," Beatriz said. I wrote Beatriz's idea on the board:

Beatriz
$2 \times 100 = 200$

No one had anything else to say. I added *200* to the T-chart and asked, "Suppose one hundred coins came out of the pot. How many coins went in?"

"Fifty!" Audrey said.

"Fifty!" Cami agreed.

"Does anyone have a different answer?" I asked. No one did.

"Cami, can you explain?" I asked.

"You have to take one-half of the Out number to find the In number," Cami explained.

"I already knew that fifty plus fifty is one hundred," Nina said.

"Hey, taking half of something is making it into two equal groups. If you add those two equal groups, it's like doubling," Sam said with surprise. "It's, like, all connected together!" Sam's delighted surprise reminded me that children need many opportunities to make connections among ideas.

Generalizing from the T-Chart I redirected the students' attention to Nina's pattern, which was still recorded on the board:

Nina
1 + 1 = 2
2 + 2 = 4
3 + 3 = 6
4 + 4 = 8
5 + 5 = 10
6 + 6 = 12

"Who can describe Nina's pattern for figuring out the output when you know the number of coins put into the pot?" I asked.

"Take one number and add two of the number," Armando said.

"What number?" I pushed.

"The In number," Armando added.

"And what do I add to the In number?" I pushed further.

"Itself," Armando said. I wrote Armando's idea on the board as follows:

The Out number is equal to the In number added to itself.

While Armando didn't offer a complete sentence, I used a complete sentence to record his idea. The students would soon translate the sentences to equations, so complete sentences were necessary.

"You could say it another way," Annie suggested. "You could say In plus In equals Out." I recorded Annie's suggestion.

In plus In equals Out.

"Does anyone have another idea?" I asked. No one did, so I said, "It looks like we have two different ways to describe Nina's pattern."

I then pointed to Brianna's pattern on the board and said, "What about Brianna's pattern? How could you describe Brianna's pattern?"

Brianna
1 × 2 = 2
2 × 2 = 4
3 × 2 = 6

"Brianna's way is to times the In number by two," Sam said.

"So to get the Out number, you do the In number times two?" I asked. Sam nodded. I wrote on the board:

The Out number is equal to the In number times two.

I then said to the class, "A shortcut way to describe these patterns is to use symbols in place of the words. Instead of the word In, we'll use a box to represent whatever number of coins we put into the pot. And instead of the word Out, we'll use a triangle to stand for the number of coins that comes out of the pot." Above the word *In* on the T-chart I drew a box, and above the word *Out* I drew a triangle.

□	△
In	**Out**
1	2
2	4
3	6
4	8
5	10
6	12
7	14
8	16
9	18
10	20
.	.
.	.
.	.
100	200

I pointed to the sentence that was Armando's idea: *The Out number is equal to the In number added to itself.* I asked, "What symbol did I suggest for the Out number?"

"A triangle," Rick said. I drew a triangle on the board under Armando's sentence, large enough for a number to be written inside it.

"What's the next part of Armando's sentence?" I asked.

"Is equal to," Audrey answered. I added an equal sign:

$$\triangle =$$

"Now what?" I asked.

"You write a box for the In number," Nina said.

"And then plus another box," Armando added. I did as they suggested:

$$\triangle = \square + \square$$

"Triangle equals box plus box," I read. I pointed next to the sentence that was Annie's idea: *In plus In equals Out.* "Now let's use symbols to represent Annie's idea. How should I start?"

"Use a box for In," Beatriz said. I drew a box below the first *In* in the sentence.

"And then?" I asked.

"The plus sign," James said.

"I know what goes next," Cami said. "The next word is *In*, so I think a box goes next." Several students nodded. I added the plus sign and another box.

"You can use the equals sign for the word *equals*," Jaime said.

"What should I write after the equals sign?" I asked.

"A triangle because the Out column has the triangle symbol," David said.

I completed writing the equation:

In plus In equals Out.

$$\square + \square = \triangle$$

I said, "So this equation is 'Box plus box equals triangle.' Whose pattern does this equation describe?" I used the word *equation* without defining it, but referring to what I had just written. Using new terminology in the context of an activity is an effective way to introduce it.

"Nina's," Michael said. "It adds itself twice, and that's what Nina's pattern said to do."

"Let's think about Brianna's pattern that Sam described," I said, pointing to the board where I had written *The Out number is equal to the In number times two.*

"Brianna multiplies instead of adding," Andrea said.

"How can we write an equation using a box and a triangle for Brianna's pattern?" I asked, again using the word *equation*. Several hands went up, as students were eager to help.

"You use a triangle for the Out number," Kris said. I drew a triangle under the part of the sentence that said *The Out number*.

"Now what?" I asked the class.

"The equals sign comes next," Audrey suggested. I followed her suggestion.

"Then write a box for the In number and then 'times two,'" Jaime added. I finished writing the equation below the sentence:

The Out number is equal to the In number times two.

$$\triangle = \square \times 2$$

"Does anyone know what symbols like the box and triangle are called when they're used in equations like this?" I asked, pointing to the box and the triangle. No one seemed to know.

"They're called *variables*," I said, introducing the class to the correct terminology. "That's because the numbers they represent can vary. In this case, the number of coins that come out of the pot depends on the number of coins that go into the pot. You can put any number in the box and then you can figure out the number that belongs in the triangle." I ended class with this simple explanation of a very complex idea.

Day 2

In this part of the lesson, students build on the experience from the day before and explore what happens if the pot does something other than double what's put into it. To begin the lesson, I held up the book and pointed to the pot on the cover. I asked, "Who would like to tell what the pot does in the story?" Almost all hands were immediately in the air.

"It doubles," Beatriz said.

"It multiplies by two," Andrea added.

No one had any other ideas to add. Adam raised his hand. "I was absent and I don't know the story," he said.

I quickly retold the story of Mr. and Mrs. Haktak and the discovery of their magic doubling pot. I ended my retelling by showing the class the last few pages so that Adam could see how the pot had doubled everything, including Mr. and Mrs. Haktak.

I said, "Instead of doubling, today the pot is going to do something different. As Mr. and Mrs. Haktak did, you'll have to figure out what the pot is doing. We'll use a T-chart as a way of keeping track of the information to help us figure out the pot's rule." I quickly drew a T-chart on the board and labeled the left column *In* and the right column *Out*. As I had done the day before, I drew a box above *In* and a triangle above *Out*.

I continued with the directions, "I'll start by giving you a clue about what the pot is doing by writing on the T-chart what happens when one coin is put into the pot. Then I'll call on someone to guess the output value when two coins are put in. When I call on you, tell me what you think the Out number is, but don't say the rule for what the pot is doing. If you're right, I'll record your guess. If you're not right, then I'll record the correct answer, and then you'll have more information for your next guess." The rule I had chosen was to multiply the number of coins put in by three. I wrote *1* and *3* on the T-chart, and then wrote a *2* underneath the 1.

□	△
In	**Out**
1	3
2	

"Raise your hand if you'd like to guess the next Out number." All students were eager and had raised a hand. I called on Karly.

"Four comes out," Karly said. Karly's incorrect guess was a typical one. Some children reason that I added two to the 1 to get the first output of 3, and they then add two to the new input of 2 to get 4. Others look at the 3 in the Out column and increase it by one to get 4, seeing that I had increased the 1 in the In column by one to enter the next number of 2.

"Your Out number makes sense, Karly, but it isn't the pot's rule," I replied as I wrote *6* in the Out column. Some students were surprised, while others had their thinking confirmed. I wrote *3* in the In column.

"Who would like to guess the output value for three?" I asked. I called on Michael.

□	△
In	**Out**
1	3
2	6
3	

"Nine," Michael said. "Can I tell what it's doing?"

"No, not just yet," I said. "When four different students have made correct guesses, then someone can describe what the pot is doing. For now, you can just give output values for the input values. So far, that's one correct guess." Limiting the students to guessing outputs and not telling the rule before four correct guesses have been made provides a way to keep the students involved and thinking. I recorded 9 in the Out column and then wrote 4 in the In column. Hands were waving. I called on Sam.

"Twelve," he said with confidence. I nodded and recorded the 12, and then a 5 in the In column.

□	△
In	**Out**
1	3
2	6
3	9
4	12
5	

"That makes two correct guesses," I said. Practically all hands were raised now and I called on Audrey. She gave the correct output value of 15 for 5, and then Brianna gave the correct output value of 18 for 6. Brianna's was the fourth correct answer.

□	△
In	**Out**
1	3
2	6
3	9
4	12
5	15
6	18

"That's four correct guesses," I said. "Who would like to share what you think the pot's rule is?" Almost all hands were up, accompanied by pleading looks. I called on Adam.

"They go by threes," he said.

"Which number are you talking about?" I asked.

"The Out numbers; they count by threes—three, six, nine, twelve, fifteen, eighteen," Adam said.

I wrote 7 in the In column and asked, "Can you figure out how many coins come out if I put seven coins into the pot?"

He nodded and said, "Twenty-one." I recorded *21* in the Out column.

□	△
In	**Out**
1	3
2	6
3	9
4	12
5	15
6	18
7	21

It's typical for students to focus on the pattern of the numbers in the Out column. While this way of thinking is useful for predicting what comes next, it isn't practical for predicting output values when input values aren't offered in sequence. For example, figuring the output value for 25 or 37 calls for a different approach. However, this pattern is a starting place for students and it's important to value this thinking. I recorded Adam's idea on the board:

The Out numbers count by 3s.   Adam

"Does anyone have another way to describe what the pot is doing?" I asked. I called on Cami.

"The pot is multiplying what goes in by three," she explained.

"If we use your rule, would you get the same output value for seven as Adam did with his pattern?" I asked.

Cami replied, "Yes, seven times three is twenty-one. It works." In contrast to Adam's rule, Cami's rule is useful for figuring out the output value for any input value. I wrote a sentence starter on the board:

The Out number equals

I said to Cami, "Can you say your rule again using this sentence starter I wrote on the board?" I used this structure so that translating to equations would result in equations that followed the standard algebraic form, with the output variable first.

Cami said, "The Out number equals what goes in times three." I recorded on the board:

The Out number equals what goes in times three.   Cami

Two of
Everything

15

"I know a shorter way from before to write it," Michael said.

"Share your idea with us, Michael," I said.

"Couldn't you just save time and write 'triangle equals box times three'?" Michael asked. He continued, "The triangle means the Out number and the box means the In number." I recorded on the board under Cami's statement:

$$\triangle = \square \times 3 \quad \textit{Michael}$$

"Mathematicians call this an *equation*," I reminded the class. "The box and the triangle are variables because the numbers they represent can vary, depending on the number of coins that are put into the pot. You can put any number in the box and then figure out the number that belongs in the triangle." I had planned to ask the children to shorten the description by writing an equation, and I was pleased that the suggestion came from Michael instead.

A Second Rule   I said, "I'm now going to think of a new rule for the pot. Would you like it to be harder or easier?"

"Harder!" the class eagerly responded.

I left the first T-chart on the board and drew a new one beside it. I wrote *1* under the In column and *3* under the Out column. The rule I used was "The Out number equals two times the In number plus one."

There were several responses from the students. "It's the same as last time."

"It can't be, that would be too easy."

"She said she would make it hard!"

"Remember just to guess. If you think you know the rule, don't say it until it's time," I reminded the class as I wrote *2* in the In column. I called on Audrey.

□ In	△ Out
1	3
2	

"Four," she responded.

"That output value doesn't follow the pot's rule," I replied. I recorded *5* next to the 2 and then wrote a *3* in the In column.

□ In	△ Out
1	3
2	5
3	

Elisa said, "It really is a hard one."

"I'm confused," Audrey said.

"Talk this over with your neighbor and see if you can figure out what the pot is doing," I suggested. After the students talked for a few moments, I asked for their attention.

"Who would like to guess for three?" I asked.

"Eight," Jaime guessed.

"No, that doesn't follow the rule," I responded. Other hands shot up to give a different answer, but I followed the procedure I had begun. I wrote the correct answer of 7, giving the class more correct information, and then wrote the next input value of 4. Now all hands were up.

□	△
In	**Out**
1	3
2	5
3	7
4	

I called on Elisa. "Nine," she said with confidence.

"You're right. That's one correct guess," I said, recording the 9 and extending the In column to 5. There were lots of comments from the others. "I get it now."

"It's easy."

"I know the answer for five."

"I know the rule."

Brianna, Gary, and Andrea correctly guessed for the next three input values, bringing the total to four correct guesses.

□	△
In	**Out**
1	3
2	5
3	7
4	9
5	11
6	13
7	15

"Before we talk about the rule," I said, "I want to give you an output value and see if you can guess the input value." I wrote *41* under the Out column, putting three dots after *15* to indicate that I was skipping some numbers.

□	△
In	**Out**
1	3
2	5
3	7
4	9
5	11
6	13
7	15
.	.
.	.
.	.
	41

The students thought for a few moments and then hands began to go up. Some students were writing on their papers. I know that some students are initially only comfortable following the pattern of the output numbers, looking down the numbers in the Out column. They haven't yet figured out how to get to an output value from an input value, or vice versa. At this time, some students were writing down the pattern of odd numbers to 39. Then they counted down to figure the corresponding input number. While this strategy works and is typical when students first explore patterns like these, it limits students' thinking for generalizing a pattern. However, with more experience, students learn how to identify output values from input values. When more than half the students had a hand raised, I called on Kris.

"I think the In number could be twenty," Kris said with uncertainty.

"That's what I got!" "Me, too!" were some of the responses of the other students. I wrote *20* under the In column and the class cheered. Kris looked especially pleased for answering correctly.

"What's the pot's rule?" I asked. "Remember to state the rule starting with 'The Out number equals.'"

"The Out number equals the In number plus the In number then plus one," Rick said.

I wrote on the board above the T-chart:

The Out number equals the In number plus the In number plus one.   *Rick*

"Let's try Rick's idea," I said. "If we use the In number of seven, then seven plus seven is fourteen, and fourteen plus one is fifteen. Is fifteen the output value for the input of seven?"

"Yes, it works!" James exclaimed, then apologized for blurting out. "Seven plus seven is fourteen and one more is fifteen."

"It works for six," Brianna added. "Six plus six equals twelve, plus one is thirteen. It checks."

"Can I tell a shorter way to write it?" Annie asked. I nodded. "Triangle equals box plus box plus one," she said.

I wrote on the board under Rick's sentence:

$$\triangle = \square + \square + 1 \quad \textit{Annie}$$

"I have a different idea," Nina said. "Instead of 'box plus box,' couldn't you write 'two times box'?"

I nodded and then said, "First, tell me in a sentence what you think the rule is. Use the sentence starter I wrote on the board."

Nina said, "The Out number equals two times the In number plus one." I wrote on the board above Rick's idea:

The Out number equals two times the In number plus one.   Nina

"Is what I wrote what you were thinking?" I asked Nina. She nodded.

"I also know how to write it a shorter way," Nina added. "It would be 'triangle equals two times box plus one.' "

Under Nina's sentence I wrote the equation:

$$\triangle = 2 \times \square + 1$$

"Let's try Nina's idea and see if it works," I said. "Let's use the In number three and its Out number, seven. Is the Out number the box or the triangle?"

"Triangle," the students chorused.

I wrote the 7 in the triangle and the 3 in the box and read, " 'Seven equals two times three plus one.' Is that true?" I asked the class. "Thumbs up if you think it's true, thumbs down if you think it's false, and put your thumb sideways if you're not sure." All thumbs were up.

Rick explained, "Two times three is six, and then if you add one to six then that's seven, and that's what we're supposed to get."

"Can I try it with the Out number eleven for five?" David asked. "I think it works." I nodded and replaced the 7 and 3 in the triangle and box with *11* and *5*.

David said, "Eleven is the same as five times two, which is ten, and then add one and it makes eleven. See, it works!" There were no other comments.

I asked, "Does it surprise you that two different equations work to give the same numbers on the T-chart?" A few hands went up. "Talk with your neighbor about this," I said. After a few moments I asked for their attention.

Armando shared, "Sam and I talked and we don't think it's weird or anything that two rules work. We had two yesterday when the pot was doubling."

Cami said, "Multiplication is another way of writing addition. Nina just thought of Rick's way with multiplication instead of addition." Several others nodded.

I added, "Multiplication is another way of writing addition when all the groups are the same size or you have to add the same number several times."

A Third Rule   "This time, I'd like to have one of you choose the rule for the pot," I said. I paused and gave the students a few moments to consider what rule they could suggest for the pot. I called on Andrea and asked her to come to the front of the room and whisper her rule into my ear.

She whispered, "Do two times the In number minus three." I agreed. I drew a third T-chart beside the first two, and wrote *1* in the In column.

"Do you know what the output value is for one?" I whispered back to Andrea.

She nodded and with a giggle whispered back, "Do negative one for the Out number." I mentally checked Andrea's arithmetic and wrote *–1* in the Out column. I've found that many children can figure this out without having had formal instruction about calculating with negative numbers. Those who couldn't, however, would still be able to figure out the rule from the other pairs of numbers on the T-chart.

I asked Andrea to return to her seat and I repeated the procedure of waiting for four correct guesses before asking someone to explain what the pot was doing. It took eight guesses after the clue for the students to correctly guess the Out number four times.

□	△
In	**Out**
1	–1
2	1
3	3
4	5
5	7
6	9
7	11
8	13
9	15

Jaime said, "Hey, the numbers are the same as the last T-chart, just pushed down."

"But my rule is different," Andrea said.

Michael then correctly stated the rule: "Andrea's rule is 'The Out number equals the In number plus the In number minus three.' " I wrote on the board above the T-chart for Andrea's rule:

The Out number equals the In number plus the In number minus three.
Michael

Sam pointed out that Michael's rule could also be written using multiplication. He said, "The Out number equals the In number times two minus three." I wrote on the board:

The Out number equals the In number times two minus three.   Sam

"Would anyone like to write an equation for Michael's rule?" I asked.

"You can write 'triangle equals box plus box minus three,' " Audrey said. I asked Audrey to come to the board and write her equation under Michael's sentence. She wrote:

$$\triangle = \square + \square - 3$$

"What equation can we write for Sam's sentence?" I asked. Most hands were up quickly. I called on Cami, who suggested, "Triangle equals two times box minus three." She came to the board and wrote:

$$\triangle = 2 \times \square - 3$$

A Fourth Rule "Who would like to pick the next rule for the pot?" I asked. I called on Kris. He came up and whispered his rule in my ear: "The Out number equals the In number divided by two plus one." When I drew the T-chart, Kris said, "The first clue is one and one and a half." I recorded these numbers and wrote the next input value of 2.

$\square$	$\triangle$
In	**Out**
1	$1\frac{1}{2}$
2	

The fractions presented a complication for the students. However, some were able to use the increasing pattern of the output numbers to make correct guesses. After the input value of 9, they had made four correct guesses.

$\square$	$\triangle$
In	**Out**
1	$1\frac{1}{2}$
2	2
3	$2\frac{1}{2}$
4	3
5	$3\frac{1}{2}$
6	4
7	$4\frac{1}{2}$
8	5
9	$5\frac{1}{2}$

No one, however, was willing to state the rule. I asked, "Who notices how this T-chart is different from the others?"

"There are fractions," Brianna said.

Rick said, "Some of the Out numbers are smaller than the In numbers, and on most of the other charts, the Out numbers are bigger than the In numbers." There were no other comments.

"What operation causes whole numbers to get smaller?" I asked.

"Subtraction," James said.

"I agree," I responded. "What's another operation that causes whole numbers to get smaller?"

"Division," several students said. I nodded my agreement.

I said, "Here's a hint: Kris's rule has two steps. The first step is to divide by some number, and the second step is to add the number one. Talk with your neighbor. Use the information I gave you to figure what number Kris's rule divides by."

The discussions were animated as students grappled with the rule. When students thought they had a rule, I asked them to test it for the numbers on the T-chart. After a few minutes, I called for the students' attention.

"I think Kris's rule divides by two," Armando said. "I thought this because you can divide any even number by two with no leftovers. On the T-chart, none of the even numbers had leftovers."

Karly added, "If you divide an odd number by two, you could have a remainder of one or one-half. It depends on what you're dividing. If you're dividing cookies, then you could have one-half. If you're dividing bicycles, you'd have remainder one."

Brianna explained, "We got stuck on the 'plus one' part. We tried a bunch of different numbers on the T-chart and sometimes we added one and sometimes we subtracted one. If you start with the In number, then after you divide by two, you add one. If you start with the Out number, you subtract one and then multiply what you have left by two to get the In number."

"Who can state Kris's rule?" I asked. Most students were eager to do so. I called on James.

James said, "The Out number equals the In number divided by two plus one." I wrote this on the board above the T-chart. Annie came to the board and wrote the equation:

$$\triangle = \square \div 2 + 1$$

Annie's equation made sense mathematically, but it didn't follow standard algebraic form. I wanted both to honor Annie's contribution and to introduce the students to another way to write the equation. I said, with a light touch, "And here's another way to write Annie's equation." I wrote on the board:

$$\triangle = \frac{\square}{2} + 1$$

I explained, "In this form, it's as if I've replaced the two dots in the division sign with the box and the two. It's another mathematical shortcut, and you'll usually see algebra equations written like this when division is involved." These students hadn't studied fractions in depth and most weren't comfortable yet seeing how division and fractions related, so I left my comment at that. Time was up, and I ended the class.

Day 3

I began the lesson by asking the class, "What are some other rules the pot might follow?" My plan was to have students work in pairs to choose a rule, write it as an equation, and generate a T-chart for it. A difficulty that sometimes arises when students create their own rules is that they make the rules too hard. By brainstorming a list, I have some control over the diffi-culty of the rules. Also, creating a list gives support to students who might have difficulty deciding on a rule on their own.

Cami suggested, "The pot could double and then subtract five."

Sam said, "It could multiply whatever goes in by four and subtract two."

"My idea is a little different," Armando said. "Maybe the pot could add fifteen and subtract three."

As the students made their suggestions, I listed them on the board.

Double and subtract 5.
Multiply by 4 and subtract 2.
Add 15 and subtract 3.

"So far all of you have suggested rules that take two steps. Could the pot do just one thing?" I wanted to make sure that there were some simpler rules for students to choose from.

Michael nodded and said, "Maybe the pot just multiplies everything by ten."

"Maybe it could just add nine every time," Annie said.

"The pot could divide everything that goes in by two," David said.

"Or maybe it could divide everything by two and then multiply by two," Brianna said. I added these ideas to the list:

Multiply by 10.
Add 9.
Divide by 2.
Divide by 2 and then multiply by 2.

When I had a dozen ideas listed on the board, I gave directions to the class: "You're going to work with the person sitting beside you and together choose a rule. You may pick a rule from the list on the board or you may make up one of your own. Be careful that you can figure out the In and Out numbers for the rule you choose. On the back of a sheet of paper, write your names and also write the rule as an equation. Then, on the front of the sheet, draw a T-chart. Label the columns as I've done and write seven or eight pairs of numbers on it."

I had given quite a few directions, so I asked the class, "Who can tell me what to do first?"

David said, "Choose a rule. We can get it from the board or make it up."

Brianna continued, "Get a sheet of paper and write our names and our rule."

"Where do you write your names and your rule?" I asked.

"On the back," the class replied in unison.

Beatriz said next, "Make a T-chart using your rule on the plain paper."

"How many pairs of numbers should you have on your T-chart?" I asked.

"Seven or eight," Nina said. I wrote the directions on the board as the students gave them.

1. *Choose a rule from the board or make it up.*
2. *Write your names and rule on the back of a sheet of paper.*
3. *Make a T-chart on the front of the paper with 7 or 8 pairs of numbers.*

There were no questions and the students got to work. Most chose rules from the board, but some made up their own. Elisa and Michael chose the rule from the board of adding nine to the In number. Brianna and David made up their own rule of adding five to the In number and then subtracting three. These two pairs worked quickly and were done before many of the other students. I asked each pair to write their T-chart on an overhead transparency.

As I was circulating and observing the students at work, Kris and Annie called me over. Their rule was to add two and subtract five. "We're stuck," Annie said. "We figured out the Out number for three. Three plus two equals five and then subtract five and that's zero. But we can't figure out the Out number for one."

Kris added, "If we do the rule to two, it's two plus two, which is four. But then when we subtract five, we run out of numbers."

"Can we use negative numbers?" Annie asked. I nodded.

"That's easy, then," Kris said, looking relieved. "The Out number for two would be negative one."

"And the Out number for one would be negative two," Annie said. They completed their T-chart. (See Figure 1–1.)

Most of the students were close to finishing and I gave a one-minute signal. Then I asked for the students' attention.

FIGURE 1–1   Kris and Annie's rule resulted in negative Out numbers for the In numbers 1 and 2.

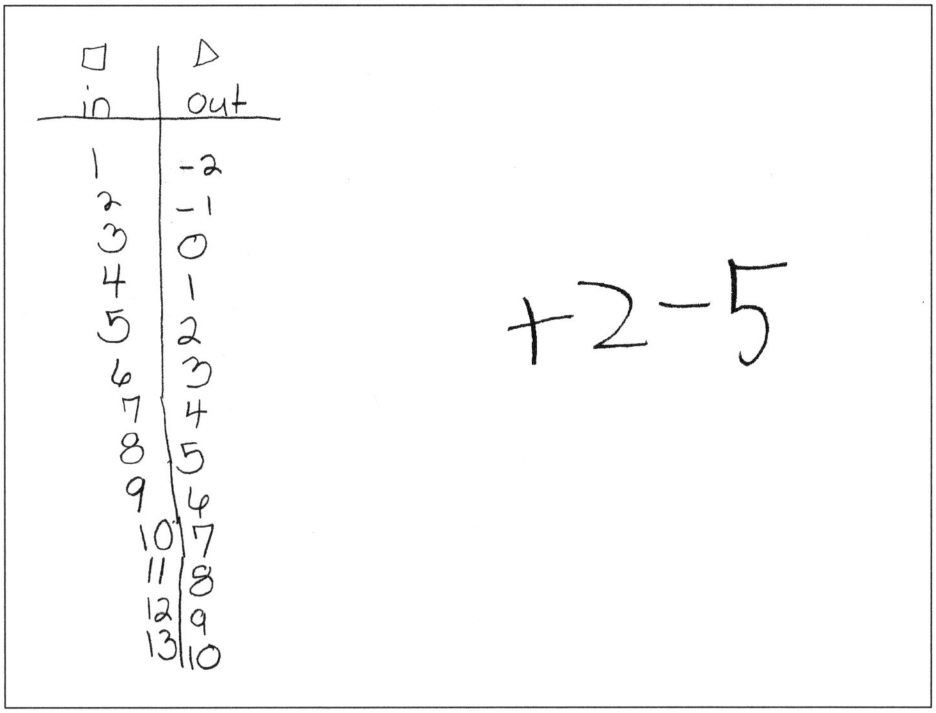

A Class Discussion   To begin a discussion, I said, "I asked Brianna and David and Elisa and Michael to write their T-charts on overhead transparencies. Let's start with Elisa and Michael's." I projected their T-chart and said to the class, "Take a moment to study their T-chart quietly." (See Figure 1–2.)

When a moment had passed I added, "Talk with your neighbor about

FIGURE 1-2 Elisa and Michael's rule was *Out = In + 9.*

in	out
1	10
2	11
3	12
4	13
5	14
6	15
7	16

$$Out = in + 9$$

what you think the rule is and why. Be sure both of you have the opportunity to talk." After a few more moments, I called for the students' attention once again. The students were eager to share. The rule Elisa and Michael chose was simple for the others to figure out: "The Out number equals the In number plus nine."

I asked, "Using the sentence starter 'The Out number equals,' who would like to share what you think the rule is?"

Beatriz volunteered, "The Out number equals the In number plus nine." The rest of the students showed their agreement with thumbs up.

"Who knows what the equation could be?" I asked.

Gary said, "Triangle equals box plus nine." I recorded on the board:

$$\triangle = \square + 9$$

We checked the rule for several pairs of numbers from the T-chart, writing the numbers in the triangle and the box and doing the arithmetic mentally.

Then I projected Brianna and David's T-chart. (See Figure 1–3.) I repeated the process I had used with Elisa and Michael's T-chart, asking students first to study the T-chart by themselves and then to talk with their partners. Many students were interested in telling the rule. I called on Sam.

"The Out number equals the In number plus two," Sam said. "It's 'triangle equals box plus two.'" Most of the others showed their agreement with thumbs up.

"That's not it," David said, with a sly smile. The others were shocked.

"It has to be!" James protested.

"No, it's not right," Brianna insisted. Conversation broke out across the room. I called the class to order.

"Tell me again what you think the equation is, Sam, so I can write it on the board," I said. Sam repeated his idea and I recorded:

$$\triangle = \square + 2$$

Nina said, "But it works for all of the numbers on the chart."

"I agree," I responded, "but I also know that Brianna and David have a different rule in mind that also works for all of the pairs of inputs and outputs on the chart." The class was stumped.

"How about we give them a hint?" I asked Brianna and David. They agreed.

I said to the class, "Brianna and David have a two-step rule." The class remained silent. Then Jaime's hand shot up.

"I know," he said. "They added one and then they added one again. It would be 'triangle equals box plus one plus one.' " Brianna and David giggled and shook their heads "no." I recorded on the board below Sam's idea:

$$\triangle = \square + 1 + 1$$

The class was quiet again, so I gave another hint. "They used addition and subtraction in their rule," I said. Audrey wanted to make a guess.

"Is it 'triangle equals box plus four minus two'?" she asked. Brianna and David again giggled and shook their heads as I recorded below Jaime's idea:

$$\triangle = \square + 4 - 2$$

"Tell the class your rule," I then said to Brianna and David. As they reported, I recorded their rule underneath the others:

$$\triangle = \square + 2$$
$$\triangle = \square + 1 + 1$$
$$\triangle = \square + 4 - 2$$
$$\triangle = \square + 5 - 3$$

"That's not fair," Rick said. "It's just another way of writing the first one."

"Why do you say that?" I asked.

"Because five minus three is two," Rick said. "It's just another way to write two."

"So is four minus two," Audrey added.

"All of these equations work for Brianna and David's T-chart," I said. "They all produce the same output number for an input number. Equations like these are called *equivalent equations*. Mathematically, they're all correct, but they are different ways to describe the T-chart. Your job is to find any equation that works."

For the rest of the class, other pairs of students came up and recorded their T-charts on transparencies. As we did for the others, first the other students thought quietly, then they talked with their partners, and finally I called on someone to tell a rule and then someone else to tell an equation.

Time ran out before all of the students could present their rules, and some were disappointed. "You'll all have a chance to do so on other days," I reassured the students.

"Can we do a different rule?" Audrey asked.

I responded, "Yes, if you'd like you can do another, but you won't be able to share it until everyone has had a chance to share one rule."

I collected their papers and saved them for a later activity, when the students would make graphs of their patterns. Over the next few days, the rest of the students had the chance to present their T-charts for the others to guess their rules. Figure 1–4 shows one more pair's T-chart.

FIGURE 1–4 Rick and Audrey's rule was *In* × 5 − 2 = *Out.*

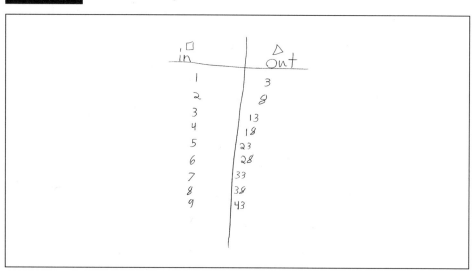

True, False, and Open Sentences

## CHAPTER 2

OVERVIEW

In this lesson, students first consider arithmetic sentences to decide if they are true or false. The lesson then introduces students to sentences that are neither true nor false but are algebraic equations, also called *open sentences*, such as $x + 3 = 7$ or $2 \times \square = 12$. Students learn to write equations using different variables and to figure out what numbers the variables represent in order to make the open sentences true.

BACKGROUND

Equations are mathematical sentences with equals signs. In an equation, the expressions on either side of the equals sign name the same quantity. Following are examples of arithmetic equations:

$$3 + 4 = 7$$
$$6 \times 7 = 42$$
$$9 + 7 = 10 + 6$$
$$3 \times 8 = 32 - 8$$
$$\tfrac{2}{3} + \tfrac{1}{2} = \tfrac{7}{6}$$
$$10 - 6.5 = 3.5$$

It's typical to talk about equations such as those listed as "math sentences" or "arithmetic sentences." This terminology is fine. However, it's beneficial to use "equation" interchangeably with "math sentence" and "arithmetic sentence" so that students become comfortable with this algebraic terminology as well.

In the elementary grades, students also have experience with sentences that use inequality signs, including $\neq$, $>$, $<$, $\geq$, and $\leq$. The following are true mathematical sentences:

$$3 + 9 \neq 10$$

$$7 \times 4 > 8 \times 3$$

$$3 + 4 < 3 + 5$$

Because they don't have an equals sign, these math sentences are *inequalities*, not equations. It's important to keep in mind that a math sentence must contain an equals sign in order to be called an equation. The focus of this chapter is on equations, not on inequalities.

Working with sentences in which the arithmetic is easy for students is helpful for introducing common mathematical conventions. For example, parentheses are useful punctuation to clarify equations, and this convention is introduced to students in the context of this lesson. In the following two sentences, the numbers and operations on the left side of the equals sign are the same, but the quantities on the right side are different:

$$(5 \times 2) + 6 = 16$$

$$5 \times (2 + 6) = 40$$

The parentheses used in math sentences indicate that you should perform the operations within the parentheses first. If no parentheses are included, however, then the mathematical convention called "order of operations" must be applied. This convention says to first perform all multiplication and division in order from left to right, and then to perform all addition and subtraction in order from left to right. Check the following equations written without parentheses to see how the order of operations convention has been applied:

$$3 + 2 \times 5 = 13$$

$$2 + 6 \times 6 \div 2 = 20$$

While parentheses aren't necessary in these equations for students who understand the convention for the order of operations, they are useful to include for clarity:

$$3 + (2 \times 5) = 13$$

$$2 + (6 \times 6 \div 2) = 20$$

But if the parentheses were placed differently in these equations, the quantities on the right side of the equals sign would change. For example:

$$(3 + 2) \times 5 = 25$$

$$(2 + 6) \times 6 \div 2 = 24$$

Another mathematical convention that's useful for students to learn is to use a dot to represent multiplication. For example, another way to write 5×3 is $5 \cdot 3$. Using the dot is especially helpful with algebraic equations to avoid confusing an x used as a variable with an $\times$ used to indicate multiplication. This convention is also presented in the lesson.

A difference between arithmetic equations and algebraic equations is that arithmetic equations are either true or false. Algebraic equations, however, involve variables, and therefore aren't true or false. An equation such as $x + 3 = 5$, for example, becomes true if you replace the variable, x, with 2. Equations like this are also called open sentences, since they're open to a decision about whether they're true or false until you decide on the value for the variable. In this lesson, we use the term *open sentence* interchangeably with an *equation* with a variable. (Keep in mind that it's also correct to use *open sentence* to refer to algebraic inequalities, such as $\square + 3 < 5$ or $6 - x \geq 1$.)

In this lesson, we introduce various symbols for the variables in algebraic equations, but we mostly use boxes and triangles. These symbols are useful because you can write numbers in them and then do the arithmetic to see if the sentence is true or false. We also introduce the convention of using the same variable more than once in an open sentence, such as $\square + \square = 10$. When a variable appears more than once in an equation, it must represent the same number. Therefore, in $\square + \square = 10$, you must follow the convention and write the same number in both boxes. In order to make $\square + \square = 10$ true, you have to put 5 in both boxes. When an equation uses two different variables, however, such as $\square + \triangle = 10$, the variables can represent different numbers. In order to make $\square + \triangle = 10$ true, for example, you can put a 6 in the box and a 4 in the triangle, or a 2 in the box and an 8 in the triangle, or a 3 in the box and a 7 in the triangle, and so on. However, it's also OK for two different variables, such as the box and the triangle, to represent the same number; therefore, you can also make $\square + \triangle = 10$ true by writing 5 in both the box and the triangle.

All of these conventions are presented in the lesson in the context of the activities used to engage students. The emphasis is not on defining the conventions but on using them.

VOCABULARY

equation, open sentence, variable

MATERIALS

- 3"-by-3" sticky notes

TIME

- at least two class periods

Day 1 | **The Lesson**

To begin class, I wrote the following mathematical sentences on the board:

$8 + 4 = 5 + 7$
$5 = 4 + 1$
$6 \cdot 0 = 6$

I read the first sentence aloud: "Eight plus four equals five plus seven." I then asked, "Is this true or false?" I paused just a moment and added, "Tell me in a whisper voice."

"True," the class whispered.

"Who would like to explain your thinking?" I continued. Most students put their hands up quickly. I called on Cameron.

"Eight plus four is twelve and so is five and seven," Cameron said. Several other students nodded their agreement.

"Does someone have a different idea?" I asked.

"Well," Dana said pensively, "another way of thinking about it is that if you take one away from the eight, then that is seven. If you put the one you took away from the eight with the four, then that's five. You can change eight plus four to seven plus five by just moving one from the eight to the four." No one had anything else to add.

"What do you think about the second equation?" I asked. "Is it true or false that five is equal to four plus one?"

"I think it's false," Marvin blurted out. "You can't put the answer at the beginning like that."

"What do the rest of you think?" I asked. I paused to give the students time to consider Marvin's point. It was early in the school year and I was still learning about my students' mathematical understanding. While Marvin's comment surprised me, it let me know that I needed to provide students with experiences involving different ways of writing mathematical sentences. A typical misconception that students have is to see the equals sign as an indicator that "the answer is coming" instead of as a symbol that indicates a relationship of equality.

"I think you can write it with the answer first," Rayna said.

"Please tell us more about your thinking," I encouraged.

"The equals sign means that both sides have to equal the same amount," Rayna explained. "Four plus one does equal five, so I think it's OK to write it the way it is on the board."

"I was thinking of it with candy bars," Jessie said. "You could have a group of five candy bars. You could split that group into a group with four and a group with one and it would still be five candy bars." Several students nodded as Jessie explained her idea. No one had anything else to add.

I then said, "It may look a bit strange to some of you, but it's mathematically OK to write an equation with the answer first. Is this second equation true or false?"

"True," the class responded.

"How do you read the third mathematical sentence?" I asked. Few students put their hands up. I suspected that the students were unfamiliar with using a dot to indicate multiplication. This convention is useful for students to learn and I've found it effective to introduce a new symbol like this one in the context of an activity when students are expected to make sense of and explain their reasoning.

"What does the dot mean?" I asked.

"It's a decimal point," Truc said.

"You could use it in money to separate dollars and cents," Carmen added.

"Those are both good ideas," I responded as I wrote *$1.25* on the board. "This is one way to write one dollar and twenty-five cents. What do you see that's different about the dot in one dollar and twenty-five cents and the dot in the third mathematical sentence?"

"In money, the dot is called a decimal point," Joshua said.

"That's correct," I responded. "What else do you notice?"

"The decimal point is lower in money than in the third problem," Jazmin said. "In the third problem the dot's in the middle and there's space between the dot and the numbers, so it looks like two numbers instead of one number like with money."

I responded, "Yes, Jazmin, the dot is in the middle. When you write a dot like that, it isn't a decimal point. It means multiplication. You can use a dot in this way instead of the times sign that you usually use for multiplication."

"I know about the third problem now," Tawny said. "You read it 'Six times zero equals six,' and that's false."

"I agree," Diego added. "Zero times anything is zero because zero groups of anything is zero, or a million groups of zero is still zero."

"At first I thought the dot was the middle of the plus sign and it meant plus," Tony said. "If it did mean plus, then it would be true because six plus zero is six."

"Show me using your thumb if you think the third mathematical sentence is true or false," I said. "If you think it is true put your thumb up, if you think it's false put your thumb down, and if you're not sure put your thumb sideways." Most students put their thumbs down. I didn't worry about the students who were unsure or who responded incorrectly because in a moment, all of the students would have the chance to think of sentences that were true and false. Then I'd be able to check on students who hadn't been sure about the last sentence.

A Class Assignment   I then said, "With your partner, take the next few minutes to think of at least one example of an equation that's true and at least one example of one that's false. Write them on a sheet of paper so you don't forget them, and then some of you will have the chance to share your ideas." I circulated, listening to students and observing what they were writing. When most pairs had at least one true and one false mathematical sentence, I asked for their attention.

"In just a moment I'm going to give you a chance to share your ideas," I said. "I'm going to make two columns on the board, one for true mathematical sentences and a second for false mathematical sentences." As I explained this to the students, I drew two columns on the board, labeling one *True* and the other *False*. "When I call on you, just read us your mathematical sentence. Don't tell if you think it is true or false. We'll guess and see if you agree with our guess." I called on Tony and Lucy.

"Three times four," Tony said.

"That's only part of a mathematical sentence," I said. "You need to complete it."

"Oh, three times four equals twelve," Tony corrected himself.

"Thumbs up if you think Tony and Lucy's sentence is true, thumbs down if you think it is false, and put your thumb sideways if you aren't sure," I said. All thumbs were up. "Do you agree, Tony and Lucy?" They nodded. I wrote their equation in the True column and asked, "Who has another?"

"Ours is sort of tricky," Rayna began. "You multiply six times three and divide that by two. Then comes the equals sign. On the other side you do four plus five."

I paused to give students time to think. I noticed some seemed confused, so I asked Rayna to repeat herself. There was a mix of responses, with some students indicating their agreement, others their disagreement, and some not sure.

"It looks to me like some students think it's true, some think it's false, and a few aren't sure," I said. "Let's see if we can figure it out together. Rayna, please come up and write your mathematical sentence up to the equals sign."

Rayna came to the board and wrote:

$6 \times 3 \div 2$

After they had a few moments to think about what Rayna wrote, several students raised a hand. "Please call on someone to figure out how much this is worth," I said. Rayna called on Terry.

"It's nine," Terry said. "Six times three is eighteen, and eighteen divided by two is nine."

"I agree!" Rayna said.

"What's the rest of your mathematical sentence?" I asked.

"Equals four plus five," Rayna replied. She completed her sentence on the board:

$6 \times 3 \div 2 = 4 + 5$

"Show me using your fingers how much four plus five is," I instructed the class. The students quickly put up nine fingers. Rayna nodded her head, indicating that she agreed. "Both sides of the equation are worth nine. Is Rayna's mathematical sentence true or false?" I asked.

"True," the class chorused. I added her equation to the list under True.

"Who has a mathematical sentence or equation that you think is false?" I asked. I called on Jazmin.

"Six plus one is equal to six minus one," Jazmin said.

"False," the class responded.

"It has to be false because six is the same on both sides and if you add one on one side and take away one on the other, automatically it has to be false," Carmen said with conviction. I recorded Jazmin's equation on the chart under False.

"Who else would like to share?" I asked. I called on Tawny.

"One times one equals one plus one," Tawny said.

"Show me with your thumb if you think it is true, false, or you're not sure," I said. Thumbs went down.

"Why do you think it's false?" I asked.

"Easy!" Pablo said. "One times one is one. One plus one is two. One doesn't equal two." No one else had anything to add. I added Tawny's sentence to the chart under False.

True	False
$3 \times 4 = 12$	$6 + 1 = 6 - 1$
$6 \times 3 \div 2 = 4 + 5$	$1 \times 1 = 1 + 1$

We processed several more equations in the same way. Kiko offered $12 \cdot 4 = 24 + 24$, Cameron shared $15 \div 3 = 3$, and then Joshua shared $4 + 1 = 10 - 4$. For each, students decided if they were true or false and explained their reasoning.

True	False
$3 \times 4 = 12$	$6 + 1 = 6 - 1$
$6 \times 3 \div 2 = 5 + 4$	$1 \times 1 = 1 + 1$
$12 \cdot 4 = 24 + 24$	$15 \div 3 = 3$
	$4 + 1 = 10 - 4$

Introducing Open Sentences   I knew that more of the students wanted to share their equations, but I wanted to move on with the lesson. Also, I wanted to give the students who hadn't had a chance to share an opportunity to do so. I said, "I know many of you still have equations you'd like to share. Later, I'll give you each a sticky note and you can write an equation on it and post it on the chart in the appropriate column." Then, as the students watched, I wrote the following on the board:

$5 + \square = 13$

"Is this equation true or false?" I asked. The class was quiet. Finally a few hands went up. I waited a moment more to give the students a chance to think, and then I called on Jazmin.

"It could be either," Jazmin said. "We don't know what the box is, so we don't know if it's true or false."

"That's what I think, too," Garrett said.

"How could we make it true?" I asked.

"Change the box to eight," Jeremy suggested.

"Or just write eight in the box because five and eight equals thirteen," Lizzie said.

"I'll write eight in the box," I said. "Your idea is fine, Jeremy, but if I write an eight in the box, then we'll still have a record of the original open sentence." I wrote *8* in the box:

$5 + \boxed{8} = 13$

"Is there any other number I could write in the box that will make the sentence true?" I asked.

"I don't think so," Truc said thoughtfully. "All the other numbers make it wrong. Like, seven is wrong and so is nine. I think the only way to make it true is to put eight in the box." Several other students nodded as they listened to Truc explain his thinking.

Elyssa had a different idea. "You could write 'four plus four' in the box and that would make it true," she said. "Four plus four is the same as eight."

"Yes," I responded, "four plus four is another name for eight, and there are many different ways we can write eight. But is there anything that isn't worth eight that we can write in the box to make the open sentence true?"

"I think you could make it work by fractions," Chase said. "You could put sixteen over two as the answer and that would make it true." As I wrote $\frac{16}{2}$ on the board, several hands went up.

"Sixteen over two looks different, but it's really the same amount," Jessie said.

"It's still eight," Tina added.

I replied, "The equation would be true as long as whatever we put in the box is equivalent to eight." No one had any further comments.

"Mathematical sentences like this one are called *open sentences*," I said. "They're neither true nor false because there's a part of the sentence—the box in my equation—that isn't a number. The box is called a *variable*, because you can vary what number you put into it or use to replace it." I wrote *open sentence* and *variable* on the board. I planned to use this vocabulary regularly to help students become familiar and comfortable with it, just as periodically throughout the lesson I used the word *equation* rather than *mathematical sentence*.

"Would 'seven times six equals box' be an open sentence?" Jazmin asked. I wrote on the board:

$$7 \cdot 6 = \square$$

"Does someone have a thought they'd like to share about Jazmin's question?" I responded as some students raised their hands. Allowing students to respond to one another in this kind of situation helps build confidence and can increase understanding. I called on Rayna.

She explained, "I think it's an open sentence because you can't tell whether the mathematical sentence is true or false. It depends on what goes in the box. It could be true, but you could also make it be false."

Lucy added, "Forty-two should go in the box if you want the problem to be true. If you put thirty-nine in the box instead, then it's false."

"There are lots of ways to make it false," Tony said.

"What about 'four plus box equals twelve'?" Joshua asked. I wrote on the board:

$$4 + \square = 12$$

"Joshua wants to know if this is an open sentence," I said. "Put your thumb up if you think it is, put your thumb down if you think it isn't, and put your thumb sideways if you're not sure." All thumbs went up immediately.

"I agree that it's an open sentence," I said. "Why is it?"

"I know," Turner said, clearly excited. "Because whether or not it's true or false depends on what goes in the box."

"What would make it true?" I asked. "Show me with your fingers." The students put up eight fingers.

"What would make it false?" I asked.

"Anything would make it false except for what makes it true!" Terry said. The class giggled. "Well, anything would make it false except for eight, so all other numbers make it false."

When I've taught this in other classes, students don't always suggest open sentences, as Jazmin and Joshua did. In those situations, I write open sentences on the board and ask the students questions as I did for the open sentences that Jazmin and Joshua offered.

I then said to the class, "Work with your partner for a few minutes to come up with some other open sentences." A class discussion allows only some of the students to contribute. Having students work in pairs gives all of them a chance to take an active role. After a few minutes, I noticed that all of the students had written at least three open sentences, and I asked for the class's attention. I called on Lizzie to share first.

"How about 'fifteen thousand plus one equals box'?" Lizzie said.

I wrote on the board:

15,000 + 1 = ☐

"Use your thumb to show me what you think," I said. "If you agree that Lizzie's equation is an open sentence put your thumb up, if you disagree put your thumb down, if you aren't sure put your thumb sideways." All thumbs were up, showing agreement with Lizzie.

"Who has an idea about what number to write in the box to make Lizzie's open sentence true?" I asked. Practically all of the hands went up. I called on Diego.

"Fifteen thousand and one," he said.

"Who would like to come up to the board and write fifteen thousand one?" I asked. Fewer hands were raised now. Some children weren't sure that they could write the number correctly. I called on Keith.

"But it won't fit in the box," he said.

"I can make the box bigger," I responded. I did so and Keith came to the board and correctly wrote *15,001*.

Introducing Other Variables   I then called on Kenny to give another open sentence. "Triangle minus four equals three," Kenny said.

I wrote on the board:

$$\triangle - 4 = 3$$

"Show me what you think with your thumbs," I said. The students indicated with their thumbs that they thought Kenny's mathematical sentence was an open sentence.

"Who knows what number to put into the triangle to make the open sentence true?" I asked.

"Seven," Dana said. The others agreed.

It's important for students to learn that we can use different symbols for variables. I was pleased that Kenny had volunteered the use of a triangle. If no student had, however, I would have written an open sentence as Kenny did, talked about it with the students, and then introduced other symbols as well. Since Kenny made his suggestion, I built on it at this time. Underneath Kenny's equation, I wrote:

$$\square - 4 = 3$$

I said, "I think that my open sentence is the same as Kenny's in one way and different in another way. Who thinks they know what I'm thinking?" Hands shot up.

"You used a box instead of a triangle," Tawny said.

"Yes, I used a box for the variable and Kenny used a triangle for the variable," I said, taking the opportunity to use the word *variable*.

"But the numbers are the same," Terry said. I then wrote on the board:

$$x - 4 = 3$$

"What about this equation?" I asked. The class was quiet so I asked, "Is it an open sentence?" Some thought it was and others weren't sure.

"Who would like to use your own words to explain what an open sentence is?" Several hands went up. I called on Tony.

"It's a sentence that has a box or something that stands for a number,"

Tony explained. "It depends on what number you put in whether or not it's true."

"Is there something anyone else would like to add to what Tony said?" I asked. No one had another idea to share.

"So what do you think about the sentence I wrote with the x instead of a box or a triangle? If you think it's an open sentence, show thumbs up; show thumbs down if you think it isn't an open sentence; and thumbs sideways if you're not sure." Three students showed their thumbs sideways and the rest showed thumbs up.

"Who would like to explain why you think it's an open sentence?" I said. I called on Terry.

He said, "It's like Tony said—it has something that stands for a number that's missing. I think you can use whatever you want. An x is OK, so is a box, so is a triangle."

"I agree with Terry," I said.

"Can you use any letter?" Lucy asked.

"Yes," I replied. "Actually, you could use any symbol you'd like. But mostly we see boxes, triangles, and letters used for variables in equations." I then asked, "Who else would like to give an open sentence?" I called on Dana.

"I have one with fractions," she said. " 'Box plus one-half is equal to one.' I know what to put into the box. It has to be one-half because one-half plus one-half is one."

I wrote on the board:

$$\square + \tfrac{1}{2} = 1$$

"I agree that putting one-half in the box makes the open sentence true," I said. "Is Dana's equation an open sentence?" Thumbs were up.

Introducing Other Algebraic Conventions Before class was over, I wanted to introduce to the students the idea that when a variable is used more than once in an equation, it represents the same number. I wrote on the board:

$$\square + \square = 10$$

"Who notices how this open sentence is different from the others we've been talking about?" I asked.

The class was silent for a moment. Then Steve's hand flew up and, at the same time, he blurted out, "There are two boxes!" A murmur rippled through the classroom as the others acknowledged Steve's discovery.

"Can you do that?" Lucy wanted to know. "I mean, is it still an open sentence?"

"Yes," I replied. "It's fine to have more than one box in a sentence, or more than one triangle or more than one x, or even some of each."

"There are lots of numbers that work," Terry said.

"Tell me more about what you're thinking," I said.

"It could be ten plus zero, or six plus four, or five plus five, like that," he explained.

"I agree that there are different combinations that add to ten," I said, "but there's an important rule for equations like this one that we have to follow. When a variable appears more than once in an open sentence, then it must represent the same number everywhere it's used in that problem.

That means that in the open sentence I just wrote, both boxes have to stand for the same number. Your arithmetic figuring was correct, Terry, but in this open sentence, whatever I put in one box I must put in the other. How can we make this open sentence true and follow this rule?"

"So it has to be five?" Terry said.

I wrote *5* in each box, saying as I did so, "If I put a five in this box, then I have to put it in the other box, too. So now the equation says, 'Five plus five equals ten,' and that's true."

$$\boxed{5} + \boxed{5} = 10$$

"What number could I write in the boxes to make this equation false?" I asked. Hands went up and I called on Scott.

"Six, or seven, or any other number will make it false," he said.

I then wrote on the board:

$$\square \times \square = 16$$

"How can I make this open sentence false and also follow the rule that the box stands for the same number each time it appears?" I asked. Hands flew up.

"Put fives in the boxes," Pablo said. As I wrote *5* in the boxes, Pablo added, "Five times five is twenty-five, not sixteen."

"What about making the open sentence true?" I asked.

"Put four in the boxes," Rayna said. I erased the 5s and wrote *4* in the boxes. The class agreed that the sentence was now true and followed the rule.

I had time for one more sentence. To introduce the idea of using two different variables in the same equation, I wrote on the board:

$$\square + \triangle = 10$$

"Hey, can you have a box and a triangle in the same sentence?" Kenny asked.

"Yes, you can," I answered. "Talk with your neighbor about how to make this sentence true."

This typically causes a little confusion. Because the variables are different, you don't have to put the same numbers in them. Therefore, there are several different ways to make the equation true, as Terry had suggested earlier when I wrote $\square + \square = 10$ on the board. But it's also possible for the different variables to represent the same numbers, so it's also correct to write 5 in both the box and the triangle. I wanted to explain this convention to the students. I called them back to attention and called on Carmen.

She said, "We think there are all the different ways to add numbers to ten, like Terry said before, but you can't do five and five because the box and triangle are different."

"You're almost completely right," I responded to Carmen. "It's OK to put different numbers in the box and triangle because they are different symbols, but it's also OK to put five in both the box and the triangle. If the variables are the same, the numbers they represent have to be the same. If the variables are different, they can be anything, which includes also being the same number. This is another bit of information about algebra that's important to remember."

"So five and five is OK?" Jazmin asked.

"Yes," I said.

It was now the end of the period. I gave an assignment. "For homework, make up five open sentences and figure out how to make them true."

"Do we have to use boxes?" Dana asked.

"You can use boxes, triangles, or any letter, as long as each of your open sentences has at least one variable," I responded. I then wrote an example on the board to model for the students how to record:

$(2 \times \square) + 7 = 15$

"Is this an open sentence?" I asked the class.

Lucy explained, "Yes; you can't tell if it's true or false because it has a box."

"I put the parentheses in so that you would be sure to multiply the two by the box first before adding on the seven," I said. It isn't necessary to use parentheses since the convention is always to multiply first before adding, but it's OK to include them for clarity.

"What number do I have to put into the box to make the open sentence true?" I asked. "Raise your hand when you've figured this out." I waited until most hands were up. I then asked the students to say the number in a whisper voice. Most students said, "Four," but I heard a few other numbers, too.

"Let's test to be sure that four makes the sentence true," I said and wrote 4 in the box.

Carmen explained, "Two times four is eight, and eight plus seven is fifteen. So four is right."

"Yes, four makes the open sentence true," I said. I wrote on the board:

$(2 \times \square) + 7 = 15 \qquad \square = 4$

"Can we make them hard?" Tony asked.

I said, "As long as you can figure out how to make your equations true, you can make them as hard as you like. My goal is to be sure that you know how to write an open sentence. I'll be checking that each of your mathematical sentences is complete with an equals sign and that each contains at least one variable."

At the end of class, I distributed sticky notes to students who wanted to record their true or false sentences. I planned to start each math class over the next few days with analyzing whether the equations posted were true or false.

Day 2

At the beginning of class, after talking about three of the equations on sticky notes and categorizing them as true or false, I gave the students directions about what to do with their homework from the night before. "Please share your paper with the person sitting next to you. When you look at your partner's paper, your job is to check that he or she has written five open sentences. You don't have to figure out what makes them true; just verify that they are complete open sentences. If you have any questions, talk with your partner. If you both can't resolve your issue, then raise your hands."

I gave the students a few minutes to check each other's papers. A few pairs called me over to ask about putting in parentheses, and a few found arithmetic errors, but their discussions went smoothly. Figures 2–1 through 2–3 show three students' homework.

FIGURE 2–1 Steve liked using large numbers in his open sentences but had incorrect solutions for equations three and five.

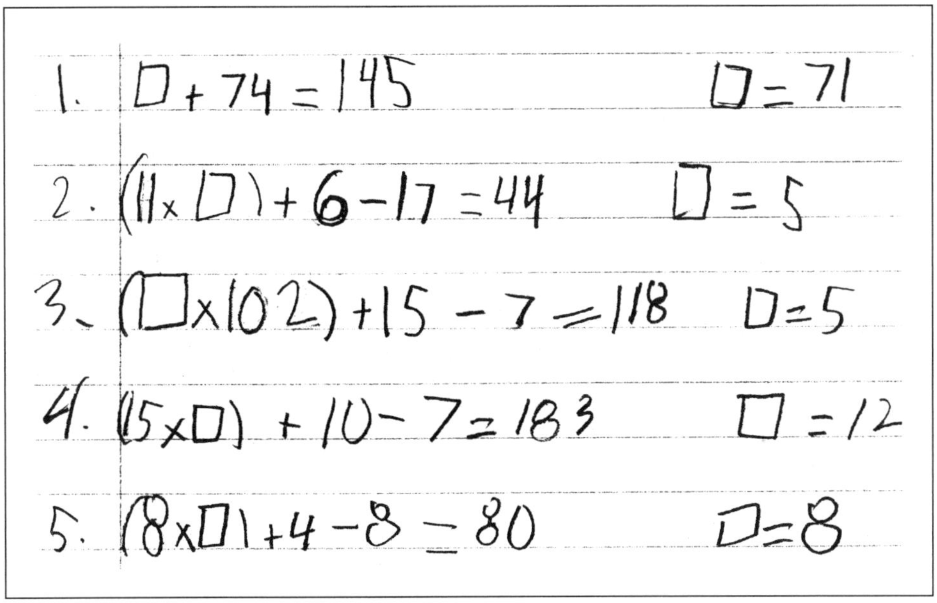

1. $\square + 74 = 145$ $\square = 71$

2. $(11 \times \square) + 6 - 17 = 44$ $\square = 5$

3. $(\square \times 102) + 15 - 7 = 118$ $\square = 5$

4. $(5 \times \square) + 10 - 7 = 183$ $\square = 12$

5. $(8 \times \square) + 4 - 8 = 80$ $\square = 8$

FIGURE 2–2 Justin helped Matt add parentheses to his sixth equation, but neither boy noticed the error in the first equation.

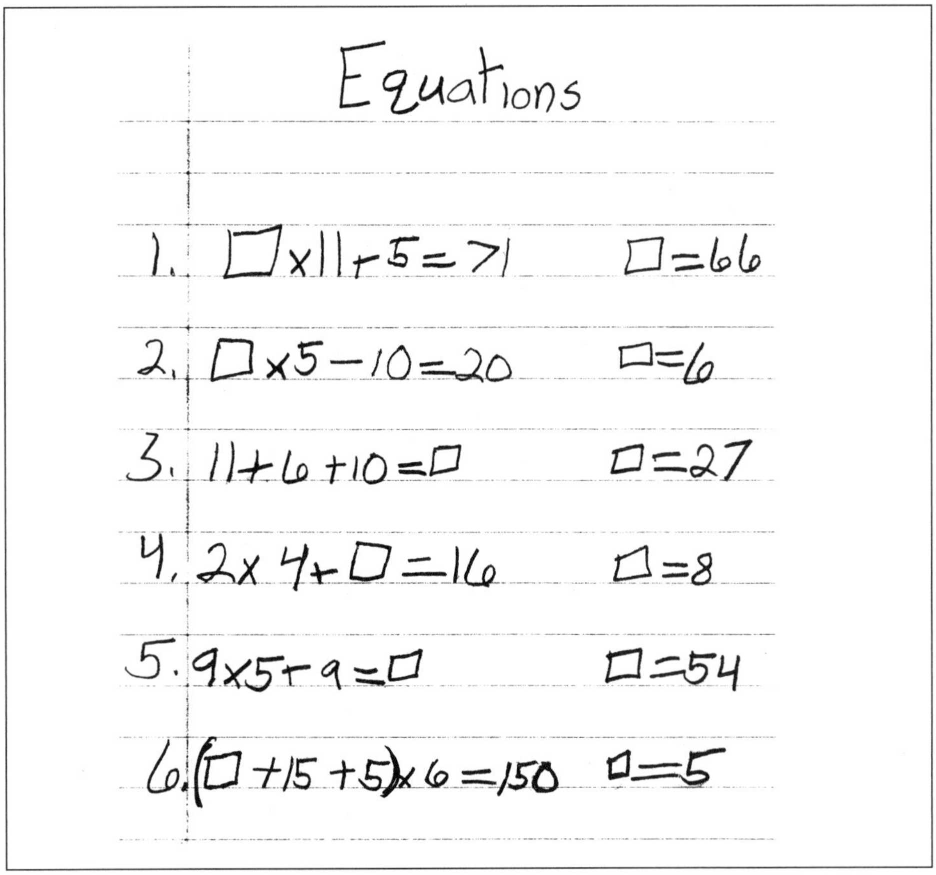

Equations

1. $\square \times 11 + 5 = 71$ $\square = 66$

2. $\square \times 5 - 10 = 20$ $\square = 6$

3. $11 + 6 + 10 = \square$ $\square = 27$

4. $2 \times 4 + \square = 16$ $\square = 8$

5. $9 \times 5 + 9 = \square$ $\square = 54$

6. $(\square + 15 + 5) \times 6 = 150$ $\square = 5$

FIGURE 2–3 Tessa used multiplication, addition, and subtraction in each of her equations.

1. $\square \times 10 - 30 + 5 = 15$ $\square = 4$

2. $\square \times 6 + 4 - 10 + 5 = 35$ $\square = 6$

3. $\square \times 12 + 2 - 3 = 107$ $\square = 9$

4. $\square \times 7 - 3 + 15 = 75$ $\square = 9$

5. $8 \times 6 - \square + 10 = 52$ $\square = 6$

Bonus: $\square \times 2 + 5 = 11$ $\square = 3$

I then called the class to order and said, "Each of you should choose one of your open sentences to present to the class. You'll tell it to me, I'll write it on the board, and then the rest of the class will try to figure out what makes it true." Cameron went first. I recorded her equation on the board:

$72 + \square = 100$

After giving the class a chance to think, I called on Chase. "I think it's twenty-eight," he said. Cameron nodded.

"How did you figure that out?" I asked Chase.

Chase explained clearly, "First I thought that seventy-two plus eight made eighty, and then I knew I needed twenty more to get to one hundred. So eight and twenty is twenty-eight, so seventy-two plus twenty-eight makes one hundred." I recorded Chase's thinking on the board:

$72 + 8 = 80$
$80 + 20 = 100$
$8 + 20 = 28$
$72 + 28 = 100$

I wrote Chase's answer on the board next to Cameron's open sentence:

$72 + \square = 100 \qquad \square = 28$

Next Lizzie gave her open sentence and I recorded it on the board:

$(\square \times 5) + 3 - 20 = 8$

"Try to figure out what number to write in the box to make Lizzie's open sentence true," I said. I gave the students a few moments to think. Most were trying different numbers, and this guess-and-check approach gave the students useful practice with mental computation. I called on Pablo.

"Write five in the box," he said, and then explained how he calculated. "Five times five is twenty-five, plus three is twenty-eight, and twenty-eight minus twenty is eight."

We continued for the rest of the period with students presenting their open sentences for others to solve. Several times, a student presented an equation for which he or she had an incorrect solution. In those instances, I asked the student to rethink the work by either revising the equation or the number he or she had identified to make it true. For example, Steve's third equation, $(\square \times 102) + 15 - 7 = 118$, stumped the class. When Steve revealed his answer of 5, others disagreed and convinced Steve that 5 didn't make the equation true. I asked the class to help Steve correct his work and gave them several minutes to work in pairs. When I called the class to attention, I gave Steve the first chance to report. He had revised his equation so that 1 was the correct answer: $(\square \times 102) + 15 - 7 = 110$. Lucy, however, had another suggestion. She said, "Change the multiplication sign to an addition sign and then 8 works." We tried Lucy's suggestion and found that for her revised equation, $\square + 102 + 15 - 7 = 118$, the number 8 made it true.

After about half of the students had had a turn, Nick asked, "Can we show more than one?"

I answered, "Right now, I'm going to be sure that everyone who wants to has a chance to present one open sentence. Then we'll see if there's time for repeats."

"Do we have to use the ones on our sheets or can we think of other ones?" Carmen asked. She hadn't yet presented an equation.

"You can think of other ones if you'd like," I answered.

Over the next several days, every student had a chance to present at least one open sentence.

Introduction to Coordinate Graphing

## CHAPTER 3

OVERVIEW

In this lesson, students learn how to use ordered pairs of numbers, called *coordinates*, to plot points on a coordinate grid. The mathematical convention for plotting points is fairly easy to explain to students. However, along with teaching the skill, this lesson helps students understand the underlying structure of the system and see how axes—intersecting perpendicular number lines—make it possible to locate points anywhere on a plane.

BACKGROUND

The system we use in this book to graph points is a mathematical invention attributed to René Descartes (1596–1650), a French mathematician, philosopher, and scientist who is sometimes called "the father of modern mathematics." Descartes's most important contribution to mathematics was his invention of analytic geometry, a way of connecting algebra and geometry that enabled mathematicians to display an equation as a set of points on a graph. Analytic geometry does more than connect algebra and geometry; that had been done by Archimedes and many others and had become the usual method of procedure in the works of the mathematicians of the sixteenth century. The great advance made by Descartes was that he saw that a point in a plane could be exactly located if its distances, say x and y, were given from two fixed lines drawn at right angles in the plane. The values of these two distances, the coordinates of a point—(x, y)—determine its location. For an equation such as $y = x + 3$, the number of solutions is infinite, and each is a pair of numbers for x and y. For example, if $x = 1$, then $y = 4$, a solution that we can represent as $(1, 4)$. Other solutions include $(2, 5)$, $(3, 6)$, $(5, 8)$, and so on. Descartes learned that when he used the solutions from equations like this one as coordinates and graphed the points, the points formed a straight line. He also discovered that when an equation involved a squared term, for example $y = x^2 + 3$, the points formed a curve. Also, for some equations containing two squared terms, for example $x^2 + y^2 = 25$, the points made a circle. From his investigations, Descartes discovered that the higher the degree of the equation (that is, the larger the exponents), the more complex the curve of its graph.

As an introductory lesson to graphing based on Descartes's work, this lesson only introduces students to the system Descartes invented for locating points on a plane. Along with teaching students how to use ordered pairs of numbers as coordinates to locate points, the lesson gives students a background in how Descartes thought about the system.

To end the lesson, we suggest that you read aloud to the class *The Fly on the Ceiling, A Math Myth,* by Julie Glass. The story introduces René Descartes not only as a great thinker but also as a person so messy that he couldn't find a thing in his house. The story goes on to spin a yarn about how Descartes figured out his system of locating points on a coordinate grid to bring some order to his messiness. While this is an easy reader geared for grades 2–3, we found that fourth and fifth graders were completely engaged in the story and delighted by it. Our recommendation is that you read this story after the students have learned about plotting points so that the skill they've learned provides a context for enjoying the story.

To provide your students with additional practice plotting points, see Chapter 4, "Tic-Tac-Toe: Practice with Plotting Points," and Chapter 9, "Four Points: Investigating Patterns in Coordinates."

VOCABULARY

axes, axis, coordinates, graph, horizontal, intersect, number line, ordered pair, origin, plane, point, vertical

MATERIALS

- lined notebook paper, 1 sheet per student
- half-inch graph paper, 1 sheet per student (see Blackline Masters)
- *The Fly on the Ceiling, A Math Myth,* by Julie Glass (New York: Random House, 1998)
- optional: overhead transparency of lined notebook paper
- optional: overhead transparency of half-inch graph paper

TIME

- one class period

The Lesson

"How many of you sometimes wonder about things and how they came to be?" I asked the class. Several hands went up.

I continued, "I sometimes wonder, too. One thing I've wondered about is why someone invented paper with lines arranged in this way." I held up a sheet of half-inch graph paper for the class to see.

"I'm not sure why someone did it, but I know what that kind of paper is called," Brianna said. "It's graph paper."

"I've heard it called that," I said. "Has anyone heard it called other names?"

"It can be called grid paper," Jaime said.

"It's squared paper," Michael added. No one else had an idea.

"I've heard it called all those things," I said.

I then distributed lined notebook paper with a red margin ruled down the left side of the page, one sheet to each student. I said, "When I thought about paper like this, I thought about one reason that graph paper came to be. First I remembered that we can locate numbers on a number line."

On a projected overhead transparency of the lined paper, I darkened the fifth line from the bottom by tracing over it. Also, I drew an arrow at the right end of the line to indicate that it could be extended. I said, "The darkened line will be my number line."

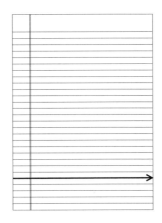

"I can locate any number on it," I continued.

"What about a million?" Gary asked.

"Yes, I could locate one million," I said. "The arrow I drew on the end of the line means that the line goes on and on. The point for one million might be out in the parking lot."

"That's cool!" Kris said.

I said, "Darken a line near the bottom of your paper as I did on mine." I wanted the students to construct their own number lines rather than merely watch me demonstrate. Firsthand experience helps develop students' understanding and increases the likelihood that they'll remember what they've learned. I circulated and made a quick check around the room to see that all students had done as I had asked.

"I'm marking a point on my number line," I said as I marked a point along the darkened line about one line space away from the red margin line. "Please mark a point on your paper at approximately the same spot."

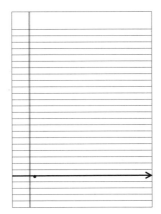

"Like this?" Audrey asked. I nodded and quickly made a visual check of the rest of the students' papers. All did it correctly except for Taylor, who put the point one line space from the left edge of the paper, not from the red margin line. I pointed this out quietly and he quickly corrected it.

"The point I just marked is where I've located the number one," I said as I labeled it.

"Should we label ours too?" Sam wanted to know. I nodded.

"Now I'm going to move just a bit to the right on the line and mark another point," I said. "Don't mark your paper yet—just watch. I'll label the point *two*." I marked a point that was as far from the first point as the first point was from the red margin line. Then I marked another point one space to the right of the 2 and asked, "What number do you think I should use to label this point?"

Hands went up immediately. "Tell me in a whisper voice," I said.

"Three," the class responded. I labeled the point.

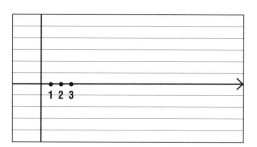

"What do you notice about how I marked the points on the number line?" I asked.

"They're not at the beginning of the line," Annie said.

"They're before the middle, but sort of in the middle," Armando added.

"The numbers go up by one," James shared.

"I spaced the points in a particular way," I said. "Who thinks you know how I spaced them?"

"Oh," Brianna said, "the space between one and two is about the same amount as the space between two and three."

"Yes, that's how I tried to space them," I confirmed." I wanted the students to be aware that the spaces between consecutive numbers should be equal. If no student had made this observation, I would have pointed it out. I then marked a point on the darkened line near the right edge of the transparency and said, "I don't think that it would be right to label this point with the number four. Who can explain why I think this?" Several children had ideas.

"It's too far over," Gary said.

"Why do you think that?" I probed.

"Because one, two, and three come one right after the other, and you put four way down the line. It doesn't look right."

"I think it should go the same amount over," Karly said. "Then you would go one, two, three, four, all in a row." Others nodded their agreement. I erased the point I had marked on the far right.

"You're both right," I responded. "It's important on a number line for the points for numbers that go in order, like one, two, three, and four, to be the same distance from each other. When numbers are the same distance from one another, the points that represent them should be the same distance apart, too. Keep this in mind and mark points on your line for the numbers two and three, and label them as you did for the number one." As the students did this, I circulated through the class, checking their work.

"I'm using my baby finger to make the spaces about the same," Cami commented as she worked. She had accurately marked and labeled the points on her paper.

"That's a good idea," Kris said. "I have to keep erasing because the spaces aren't the same." Cami smiled as Kris used her idea to complete his number line.

I noticed that Audrey was having difficulty with the spaces on her number line and suggested she use Cami's method.

I returned to the overhead projector. After the point for the number 3 on my number line, I marked two more points, spaced the same as the first three. I pointed to the last point I marked and asked, "What shall I label this point?"

"Five," the students responded. I wrote *5* and then asked about the point before it.

"Four," the class said.

"It has to be four because the mark is about halfway between three and five and four is halfway between three and five," Michael said.

"Please mark and label points for the numbers four and five on your number line," I instructed. The students did this easily.

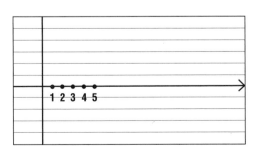

I then marked the point where the number line crossed the red margin. "What number should I use to label this point?" I asked.

"Zero," the class responded. I labeled the point and asked the students to mark and label *0* on their number lines.

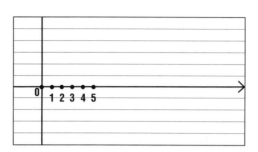

"I can explain why it's zero," Sam said. "It's zero because it comes before one, and so does the mark we just made on the number line."

I then gave the students some historical background. "René Descartes is sometimes called 'the father of modern mathematics.' He was a mathematician who was born in France more than four hundred years ago." I stopped to write on the board:

Descartes (1596–1650)

"How old was Descartes when he died?" I asked, taking a small diversion to ask the students to calculate mentally. I waited until about two-thirds of the students had raised a hand. Then I called on Jaime.

"Fifty-four," he answered. Others agreed.

"How did you figure?" I asked.

Jaime explained, "Well, I know it was fifty years from 1600 to 1650, so I added on the four extra years from 1596 to 1600."

I then continued by giving the class information about Descartes. I said, "One of Descartes's mathematical inventions was to figure out a way of locating points anywhere on a plane, which is a flat surface like a piece of paper lying on your desk. Descartes's idea was to use two number lines, one going horizontally, like the one you've just made, and another going vertically. Then you use two numbers to locate a point, one telling how far to go over on the horizontal number line and the other telling how far to go up or down on the vertical number line. Every point on the plane or paper can be located exactly with two numbers. Just as an address tells exactly where you live so that the mail carrier can deliver your mail, each point on a plane in Descartes's system has an address, and each address is a pair of numbers."

"How are we going to make another number line?" Beatriz asked.

"On this paper, we'll use the red margin for a vertical number line," I said as I modeled this on the overhead transparency, drawing over the margin with a red marker. "The handy thing about lined paper is the lines are spaced equally so we can label the points where the red margin and blue lines meet, or *intersect*. Let's label some of the points on this vertical number line. I'll go up from where the two heavy lines intersect to where the next blue line intersects the margin line, and I'll label that point *one*." I did this and waited for the children to do the same on their papers. *Intersect* was probably a new word for some of the students, but I didn't stop to define it. I find that children learn what a word means from hearing it used in context. I was careful to use *intersect*, *meet*, and *cross* interchangeably.

"Then we can write two, three, four, and five going up, can't we?" Annie asked. I nodded, labeled those points on the overhead transparency, and directed the children to do the same.

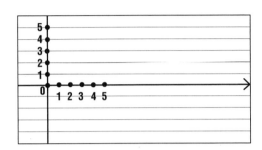

"What about this point, where the two number lines cross?" I asked, pointing to the intersection of my two number lines.

"It's zero, just like on the other line," Sam said.

"Yes," I confirmed and then added, "This point where the two number lines meet has a special name. It's called the *origin*. We use this intersection as our starting place when we locate points. Since it's located at zero on both number lines, its address is (zero, zero)." I stopped to write *origin* on the board. Beside it I wrote *(0, 0)* to model for the students how to write the coordinates in parentheses.

I then marked the point (2, 1) on the overhead transparency. "If I start at the origin and want to locate this point, how far over to the right do I need to go and then how far up?"

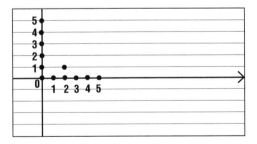

"It looks like you go two over," Audrey said. I placed my marker at the origin and counted two over.

"And how far up?" I asked.

"One," Jaime said. I counted one up and landed on the point I had marked.

"The address for this point is (two, one)," I said. On the board, I wrote *(2, 1)*.

"Oh, I know!" Cami said. "If you go to the point you made on the graph and put your two fingers on it and then move your fingers to the heavy lines, your fingers will come to two on the horizontal number line and one on the vertical number line." I did as Cami suggested and showed my fingers crossing the horizontal axis at 2 and the vertical axis at 1. There were several "oohs" and "ahhs" as I did this. Cami was pleased with herself.

I said, "Cami's idea is one way to show why the point is located at (two, one). Watch as I show you another way to check." I put my marker on the origin and explained, "I start where the two number lines intersect, the origin. Then I count two over and one up, and I land on the point I marked." I did this, counting aloud as I moved my marker. "The point's address, (two, one), tells exactly how to get there from the origin."

"Can we mark it on our papers?" Karly asked. I nodded and checked that all of the students did this correctly.

"Here's another point," I said as I marked a point at (3, 2) on the coordinate graph. "Who knows its address?"

"(Two, three)," David said.

"I think it's (three, two)," Armando disagreed. There were no other suggestions.

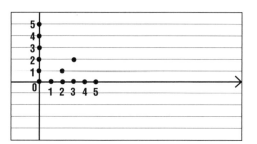

"(Two, three) and (three, two) will get us to two different places on the graph," I said. "Let's check (two, three) first to see where that gets us. We start at the origin, count over to the right two, and then up three," I said as I modeled counting over two and up three on my overhead transparency. "Did we land on my point?"

"No," the class responded.

"(Two, three) didn't work, so let's try (three, two)," I suggested. "Start at the origin and count to the right three and up two."

"It worked!" several children responded.

Michael was gazing at the graph and slowly raised a hand. "I think something different," he said. "I think it's over three and up three. Can I come up and show?" I nodded and Michael came to the front of the room, put his finger on the origin where it appeared on the screen, and said, "First you count over three." He counted correctly three to the right on the horizontal axis. "Then you count up." This time, Michael made an error, leaving his finger on the horizontal axis as he said, "One," and then moving up to the point as he counted, "Two, three." Michael's error is a common one that students make when learning to plot points: counting the number line as one instead of zero.

Audrey raised a hand. "You said one, but you didn't go up. See, the point is across from the two on the number line, not the three." Audrey was referring to the vertical axis. Michael was confused.

"You started correctly," I said to Michael. "Let's do it again. Start by putting your finger back on the origin." This time Michael counted over three and up two correctly, landing on the point.

"Hey, I got two up this time," he said, confused.

I replied, "Last time you didn't move up a space when you said 'one.' You stayed at zero." Michael returned to his seat. I made a note to myself to be sure to check back with him later. On the board I wrote *(3, 2)* and asked the students to mark the point on their papers. I checked to see that the students marked (3, 2) correctly. All but two did. I helped Natalie, and Blake got help from his neighbor, Gary.

"The order of the numbers is very important," I said. "These number pairs have a special name, *ordered pairs*, because the order is important." Under where I had written *origin* on the board, I wrote *ordered pair*. Then, underneath, I wrote *coordinates*. I explained, "*Coordinates* is another name for the pair of numbers. Each of the numbers in the pair is called a *coordinate*, and every point has two coordinates." I didn't expect children to learn these terms immediately, but I planned to use them as we continued our study. Using new terms in the context of activities is an effective way for children to learn what they mean and become comfortable using them.

I then wrote *(3, 5)* on the board. "Watch and listen to what I do as I use these coordinates to mark the next point," I said. "I start at the origin where the two number lines cross and count first to the right—one, two, three. Now I'll count up—one, two, three, four, five. Then I mark the point. This point is located at (three, five)." The students marked their papers.

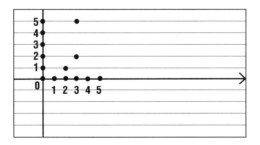

I then marked the point (0, 2). "Who knows the coordinates for this point?" I asked. Hands flew up and I called on Andrew.

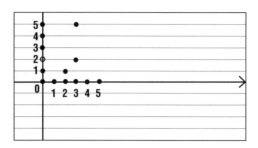

"It's nothing over and just two up," he said.

"How shall I write that?" I asked.

"Zero, comma, two," Andrew said.

I recorded *(0, 2)* and said, "We usually write the coordinates in parentheses, like this. Mark the point for (zero, two) on your paper."

I then marked a point three spaces to the right of the origin and one space down. "What do you think are the coordinates for this point?" I asked.

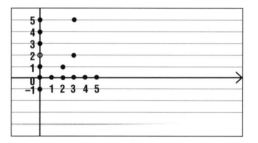

We hadn't studied negative numbers, but some children had heard about them and most had thought about negative numbers on thermometers. I've found that in every class in which I've done this activity, from third grade on up, there is always at least one child who has an idea about negative, or "minus," numbers. In this class, several were eager to report.

"It's three and minus one," Sam said. I recorded *(3, –1)* on the board.

"You could also say, '(Three, negative one),' " I commented. "You'll learn more about negative numbers in middle school and high school." I didn't plan to do more at this time other than establish the existence of negative numbers.

Using Graph Paper   To bring the students' attention back to the usefulness of graph paper, I said, "After thinking about Descartes's system for locating points on a sheet of paper, I realized that it's much easier to plot points on graph paper than on notebook paper. Who has an idea about why this is so?" I said. Several hands went up.

Brianna said, "It was hard to keep straight on the lined paper. With the graph paper, you have the lines going both ways."

Andrew added, "The vertical lines would really help."

Michael said, "It's hard to be exactly sure where the point is on the lined paper. You can be exact on the grid paper."

I then removed the overhead transparency of the lined paper and replaced it with a transparency of half-inch squares. "When you use graph paper to plot points, first you have to draw number lines so that you know where the origin is," I said, darkening a horizontal and a vertical line. "Each number line is called an *axis*. You have to draw the two axes." I wrote *axis* and *axes* on the board.

I pointed to the (3, 5) I had written on the board and said, "Who would like to come up and locate the point for (three, five)?" Armando came up, placed the marker at the origin, counted over three, then up five, and placed a point.

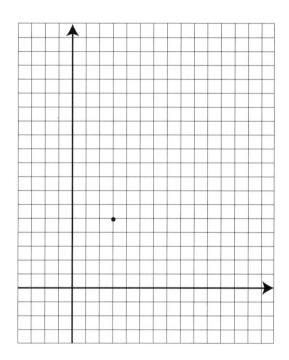

"Why does graph paper make it easier?" I asked.

"You know they're spaced right," James said.

"What's spaced right?" I asked.

"Counting over on the horizontal line. You don't have to guess," he answered.

"And it's easier to count up straight," Brianna added.

I then distributed a sheet of half-inch graph paper to each student. "First draw your two axes," I said.

"Do we write the numbers in?" Nina wanted to know.

"You don't need to," I said. "You can count fairly easily." When all of the students had drawn axes, I gave them practice plotting points. I'd write an ordered pair on the board, ask the students to plot the point on their graph paper, and then have one student come up and mark the point on the transparency. After doing this for several points, I varied the practice by marking a point on the transparency and asking the students to identify its coordinates.

Reading the Story   I left time at the end of class to gather the students and read aloud *The Fly on the Ceiling,* by Julie Glass. The students were engaged and delighted by the book, and their experience learning how to plot points made the story even more enjoyable than it otherwise would have been.

Tic-Tac-Toe
Practice with Plotting Points

OVERVIEW

In this lesson, students practice plotting points by playing a game similar to tic-tac-toe. In this game, however, students play on a coordinate grid. Also, in order to win, they must get four Xs or Os in a row horizontally, vertically, or diagonally. While providing practice with plotting points, the game also encourages students to think strategically.

BACKGROUND

This graphing version of tic-tac-toe engages students' interest, making it an ideal activity for providing practice with plotting points on a coordinate grid and introducing or reinforcing the standard terminology of graphing. The game also promotes strategic thinking, giving a problem-solving aspect to practicing a skill.

When introducing the game, draw a small grid so that (5, 5) is the largest pair of coordinates that will locate a point that fits. This keeps the playing area small enough so that you can complete a game fairly quickly. When using a larger grid, such as an entire sheet of graph paper, some students, especially younger ones, mark their points far from their opponents' moves; the smaller playing area forces more interaction between the two teams' moves, pushing students to think strategically.

It makes sense in an introductory game for the teacher to mark the Xs and Os, modeling for the students how to use coordinates to locate points. However, after a first game, it's valuable to have students come up and mark the points they identify so that you can assess their ability to do so.

After the students are proficient with marking points, you may want to introduce them to plotting points that are below and to the left of the origin, when one or both of the coordinates are negative numbers. Learning about negative numbers isn't a focus in grades 3–5, but this version of tic-tac-toe provides a context for introducing the children to numbers less than zero. See this chapter's "Extensions" section for a suggestion about doing this.

While this lesson can be taught as a first experience with plotting points, it's also suitable as a follow-up to the lesson presented in Chapter 3, "Introduction to Coordinate Graphing." Check the "Background" section of that chapter for additional information about graphing points on a coordinate grid. Also, to provide additional experience with plotting points, refer to Chapter 9, "Four Points: Investigating Patterns in Coordinates."

VOCABULARY

axes, axis, coordinates, diagonal, horizontal, ordered pairs, origin, vertical

MATERIALS

- *Tic-Tac-Toe* game grids, several per student (see Blackline Masters)
- optional: overhead transparency of *Tic-Tac-Toe* gameboard (see Blackline Masters)

TIME

- one class period to introduce, plus additional time for playing and describing strategies

The Lesson

To begin the lesson, I drew on the chalkboard a playing board as shown, ruling six vertical and six horizontal intersecting lines and marking the axes. (If you prefer, project an overhead transparency of the grid.)

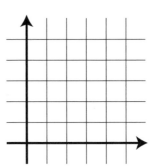

I said to the class, "I'm going to teach you a game that's like the game of tic-tac-toe that you all know how to play. One thing that's different about this game is that we play on a grid like this. Another thing that's different is that you put your X or O at the points where lines cross, not in the spaces as you do in regular tic-tac-toe. Also, in order to win this game, you must get four of your Xs or Os in a row, not three. Your four Xs or Os can be vertical, horizontal, or on a diagonal." I motioned with my hand up and down when I said "vertical," back and forth sideways when I said "horizontal," and in both diagonal directions when I said "diagonal." I then wrote on the board:

Seeing words helps some children more easily learn and remember terminology that may be new to them. Also, when they write about their strategies later, the words can be a useful reference.

I then said, "For a first game, I'm going to play against the class. I'll give you time before each of your turns to talk with your table group about what you think is a good next move. Also, choose someone who will report the move for your table. Then I'll call on a table, and the person you've chosen will tell me what point to mark. It's important to talk with your table group so that all of you know and agree on what you think is the best point to mark. You'll have fifteen seconds to decide. Do you have questions?"

"Only one table group gets to tell the turn for the whole class?" Beatriz asked.

"For this first game, that's correct," I said.

"Can we talk with other table groups?" Rick asked.

"No, you'll talk just with your own group," I explained.

"What if the table group you call on makes a mistake?" Annie asked.

"Hopefully that won't happen, since all members of the group will have discussed the move and agreed that it's a good one," I said. "Besides, typically there's more than one move that's a good play."

There were no more questions so I continued with instructions. "When you tell me what point to mark, you have to give me two numbers, and I'll use them as the coordinates to mark the point." I added *coordinates* to the list on the board. "It's important to talk with your table group so all of you know and agree on the coordinates for your move. Would you like to go first, or would you like to have me go first?"

"Us," the class said.

I responded, "OK, talk with your table group to figure out what you think would be a good move for your first turn. I'll time fifteen seconds." The class broke into excited discussion. Students usually get excited when playing this game, and I've found that the system I impose—for them to confer at their tables for fifteen seconds and then for me to call on one table for a move—is effective for managing the game. Having the students discuss moves at their tables keeps all students involved, and having table groups agree on moves avoids putting any one student on the spot. In some classes, I don't use fifteen-second time limits but instead call the class to order after I sense that they've had enough time to discuss. However, the extra structure is particularly useful when a class is a rambunctious group, like this one was. I timed the students for fifteen seconds using the second hand on the classroom clock. Then I called them to order and chose a table.

"Who is reporting for your table?" I asked.

"Oops," Kris said. "We didn't pick." I gave them a moment to do so.

"I'll do it," Karly announced.

"What coordinates did your table choose?" I asked, using correct terminology to reinforce it.

"(Two, two)," Karly reported.

"Would you like to be X or O?" I asked.

"X," Karly replied. Before placing Karly's point, I recorded the coordinates. I ruled two columns on the board and labeled them *X* and *O*. Under the X, I wrote *(2, 2)*. Then I located the point, saying as I did so, "I start at the origin where the axes cross and count over to the right two and up two." As I had done before, I emphasized "over" and "up," and marked an X. Also, I added *origin* and *axes* to the list on the board.

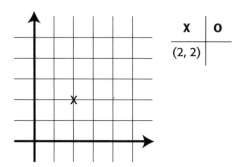

I then said to the students, "Please time me for fifteen seconds." I waited until they reported that fifteen seconds had passed, then announced, "I'd like the point (three, four)." I wrote *(3, 4)* under the O, then placed the marker on the origin and moved it as I explained, "Starting at the origin, I count over to the right three and up four. I'm O, so that's where I'll put my O. Does everyone agree I'm in the right spot?" The students nodded.

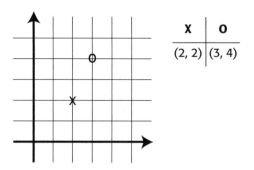

"Your turn. Fifteen seconds," I said. When time was up, I called on a different table.

"We want (two, three)," Rick said, and his table partners gave him high fives to show their support and agreement. I wrote *(2, 3)* on the board under the X.

"Starting where the axes intersect, I count over on the horizontal axis to the right two and up three," I said, and marked the point with an X. I stopped to add *axis* to the list on the board, explaining, "*Axis* is singular. It means just one of the heavy number lines. We have two axes, a horizontal axis and a vertical axis."

The students then timed me for fifteen seconds. "I'll play at (two, four)," I said. I recorded the coordinates and marked an O.

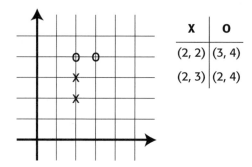

After I timed fifteen seconds, Nina announced her table's move. "(Two, one)," she said. I recorded the coordinates and marked an X.

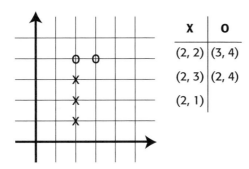

X	O
(2, 2)	(3, 4)
(2, 3)	(2, 4)
(2, 1)	

After the class timed fifteen seconds, I said, "I guess I had better block. I'll play (two, zero)." I recorded the coordinates and marked my O, saying as I did so, "I had to play my O on the horizontal axis to block you."

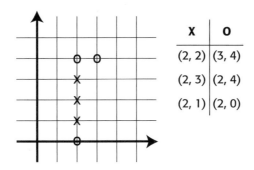

X	O
(2, 2)	(3, 4)
(2, 3)	(2, 4)
(2, 1)	(2, 0)

For their next move, Gary reported for his table and asked for (3, 2). Some students complained. I recorded the coordinates and pointed out, "(Three, two) is the reverse of (two, three) that you played before. The order of the coordinates matter. We also call them *ordered pairs*." I added *ordered pair* to the list of terminology.

"You should have done (four, four) to block her," James said.

"No, this way we have Xs going in two ways," Sam defended his table's move. I placed the X for (3, 2).

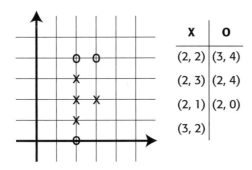

X	O
(2, 2)	(3, 4)
(2, 3)	(2, 4)
(2, 1)	(2, 0)
(3, 2)	

I waited for them to call "time" and then said, "I'll play (one, four)." I recorded the ordered pair and marked the O.

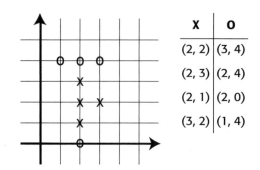

X	O
(2, 2)	(3, 4)
(2, 3)	(2, 4)
(2, 1)	(2, 0)
(3, 2)	(1, 4)

"She blocked us," Jaime said.

"Yes," I confirmed. "You had two Xs going in a diagonal, so I played my O to block you." I timed fifteen seconds for them to talk about their next move.

James was looking at the board while his tablemates talked. "Now we're sunk!" James exclaimed. Others weren't as alarmed.

"We're sunk!" James said again.

"No, we can block her at (four, four)," Michael said.

"But that's not enough," Brianna said.

"Shh, let's not tell her more," Cami said in a loud whisper.

"Decide at your tables where you'd like to move next," I said. I timed fifteen seconds and then called on a table. Armando said, "(Four, four)," as Michael had suggested.

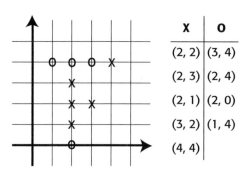

X	O
(2, 2)	(3, 4)
(2, 3)	(2, 4)
(2, 1)	(2, 0)
(3, 2)	(1, 4)
(4, 4)	

"Look, we blocked her!" Rick said.

"I tell you, we're sunk!" James said once more.

"I'll play (zero, four)," I said after the class had timed fifteen seconds. I recorded the coordinates and placed my O.

"You win," Annie said.

"Yes, I have four in a row horizontally," I said.

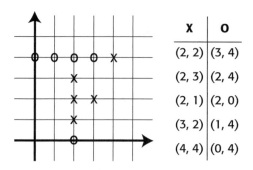

X	O
(2, 2)	(3, 4)
(2, 3)	(2, 4)
(2, 1)	(2, 0)
(3, 2)	(1, 4)
(4, 4)	(0, 4)

Playing a Second Game "Would you like to play again?" I asked. There was a resounding "Yes!" I erased the game, redrew a grid, and marked the axes.

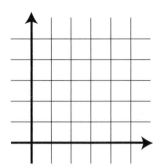

"This time, I'll divide the class into two teams so that the tables on the right side of the room play against the tables on the left side." I identified the tables for each team.

I explained, "As you did before, you'll talk at your tables for fifteen seconds about the move you'd like to make. I'll call first on a table group from the right side of the room, then one from the left side."

I erased the coordinates I had listed in two columns and said, "For this game, I'd like one person from each team to come up and record the coordinates for each of your team's turns. Who would like to do this?" There were several volunteers and I chose Nina for the X team and Gary for the O team. Having students record the coordinates helps establish a way that the class can play the game independently. Also, the students who record benefit from the practice of writing ordered pairs.

I gave the tables time to discuss possible moves. After fifteen seconds, I said to Nina, "Call on a table from your team."

Nina identified a table and Cami gave the coordinates. "We think (three, three)," she said. Nina wrote *3, 3* on the board under the X. I reminded her, "We always put parentheses around coordinates and separate the two numbers with a comma." Nina made the correction.

Instead of locating the X myself, I held the marker out to Cami and said, "Come up and mark your X." It's important to have the students come up to plot points. It not only helps them be more actively involved, but also gives me a way to check on their understanding of the skill.

As Cami came up to the overhead projector, I said, "Please count out loud and show how you're plotting the point." Cami put the marker at the origin, counted over three and up three, and marked an X.

I again timed fifteen seconds and then asked Gary to choose a table. Jaime reported. "(Four, three)," he called out confidently. Gary recorded the pair and Jaime came up to place the O.

Play continued in this way. A few of the students had difficulty placing their point, still needing practice. The most common error was to start counting before they moved to the right or up, forgetting that the point on the axis was 0, not 1. But I've learned that with practice, students soon stop making this error and become proficient with plotting points.

We had time for one more game before class time ran out. Over the next few days, we played a game each day until I felt sure that all of the students could use coordinates to plot points correctly and with confidence. Also, I transferred the words from the board to chart paper to post for their reference.

Playing in Pairs   Playing *Tic-Tac-Toe* then became an option for choice time for students to play in pairs. I duplicated *Tic-Tac-Toe* grids, two on a page. These grids were larger than I had used for the whole-class games and gave students more playing room. When they played, they first had to draw the axes. They also had to keep track of their moves, as we had done on the board. However, when playing in pairs, the students didn't have to use the fifteen-second rule. Interest in the game continued for several weeks. Figures 4–1 and 4–2 show two pairs' games.

FIGURE 4–1   Kris won the first game with four Os on a diagonal, and Jaime won the second game with four vertical Xs.

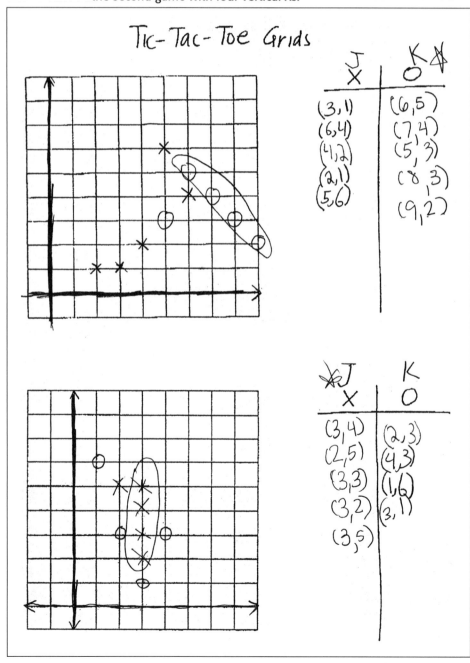

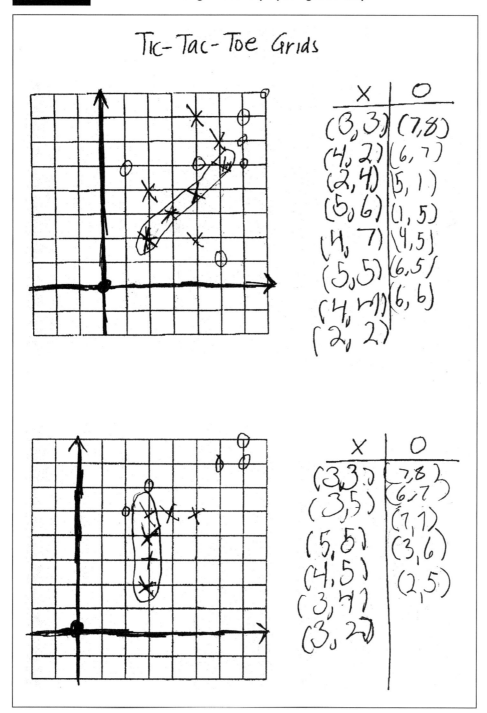

Extensions

1. After students have played for a while, ask them to write about the strategies they use when playing the game. Encourage them to use as many words as possible from the list posted. For example, Luis wrote: *My strategy is that I think it's easier to go diagnol because I won all the games using diagnol stradegys. All my coordinates were close. I kept them in a group.* Lisa wrote: *I started with a right angle with my X's. I could go diangle, horizontal, and* *vertical. If he blocked me one way I could move the next.* (See Figure 4–3.) Sam wrote: *A good strategy could be to go in the center of the box. Then you could go vertical, diagonal, and horizontal.* Figures 4–4 through 4–7 show other students' strategies.

FIGURE 4–3 Lisa explained her strategy of placing three Xs to make a right angle.

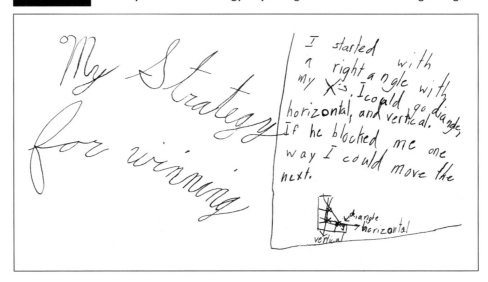

FIGURE 4–4 Shea explained the two strategies that he used and included a drawing to illustrate his second idea.

FIGURE 4–5 Kalli illustrated her two strategies with sample games.

Tic-Tac-Toe **65**

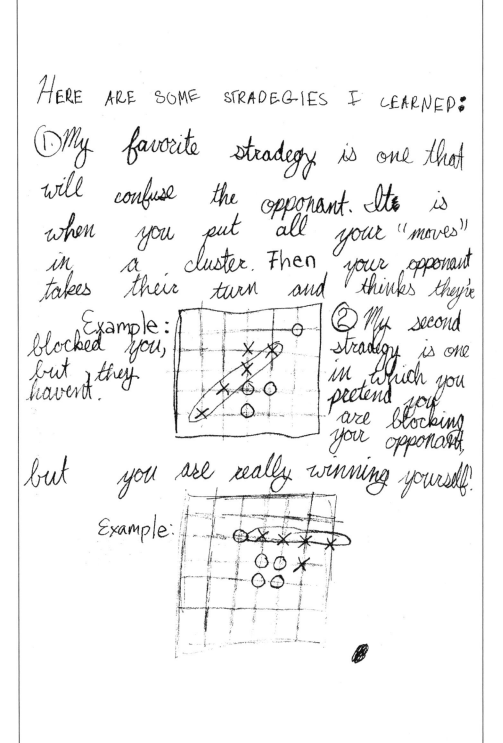

HERE ARE SOME STRADEGIES I LEARNED:

① My favorite stradegy is one that will confuse the opponant. It is when you put all your "moves" in a cluster. Then your opponant takes their turn and thinks they're blocked you, but they havent.

Example:

② My second stradegy is one in which you pretend you are blocking your opponant, but you are really winning yourself!

Example:

FIGURE 4–6 In his strategies, Eli tried to use all of the words from the vocabulary list.

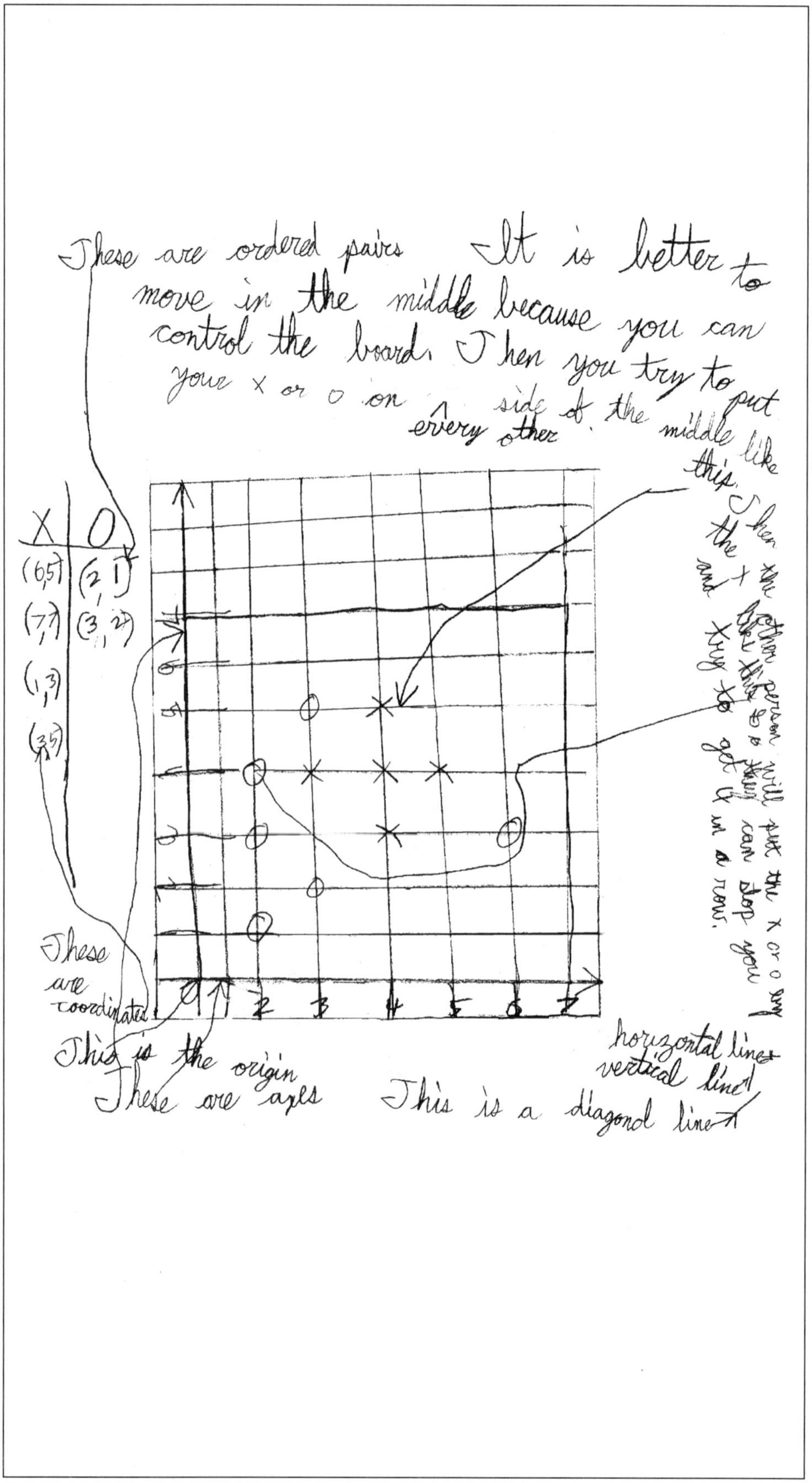
These are ordered pairs
It is better to move in the middle because you can control the board. Then you try to put your x or o on every other side of the middle like this.
Then the other person will put the x or o by the + and this so they can stop you and try to get it in a row.
X
O
(6,5)
(2,1)
(7,7)
(3,2)
(1,3)
(3,5)
These are coordinates
This is the origin
These are axes
This is a diagonal line
horizontal line
vertical line
2
3
4
5
6
7

FIGURE 4–7 Katia's strategy was to place three Xs or Os in a diagonal row with two open spaces on both sides.

Tic-Tac-Toe **67**

My Stategies

My Strategy is you make 3 0's or x's going diagnoly with two spaces on both sides then if your opponet goes on one side the you go on the other you win! That is what my strategies mathematics tic - tac - toe.

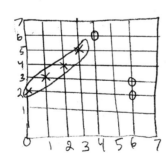

X	O
(2,4)	(6,2)
(3,5)	(4,3)
(1,3)	(4,6)
(0,2)	

2. For a homework assignment, ask students to play the game with someone at home.

3. Introduce students to plotting points below and to the left of the origin by redefining the playing area for a game of *Tic-Tac-Toe* to include more than just the upper right quadrant. Mark an X as shown:

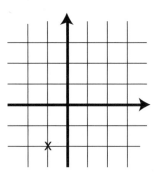

Ask students what the ordered pair might be to locate the point you marked. You may want to refer to a thermometer as a model of a number line that has numbers below zero. Typically, some student in the class comes up with a suggestion, and often the suggestion is to use a "minus" number. The thinking is correct, but the correct terminology for numbers less than zero is *negative numbers*. The coordinates for the point shown above are (–1, –2), read as "negative one, negative two." If no student suggests these coordinates, then it's appropriate to explain this mathematical convention by introducing the language, showing how to write the numbers, and modeling how to use negative numbers to plot points. Some students will choose to use negative numbers in their own games. (See Figure 4–8 [below] and Figure 4–9 on the following page.)

FIGURE 4–8   Torin and Emma used both positive and negative coordinates in their game.

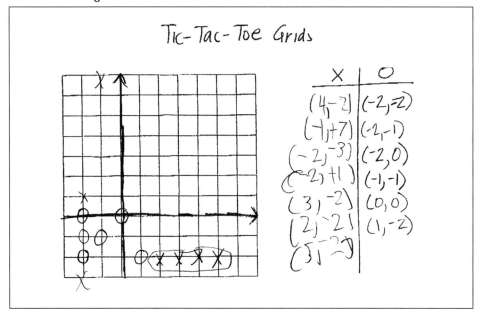

FIGURE 4–9 Karly and Armando used only positive coordinates in their first game but then used negative coordinates in their second game.

Tic-Tac-Toe   **69**

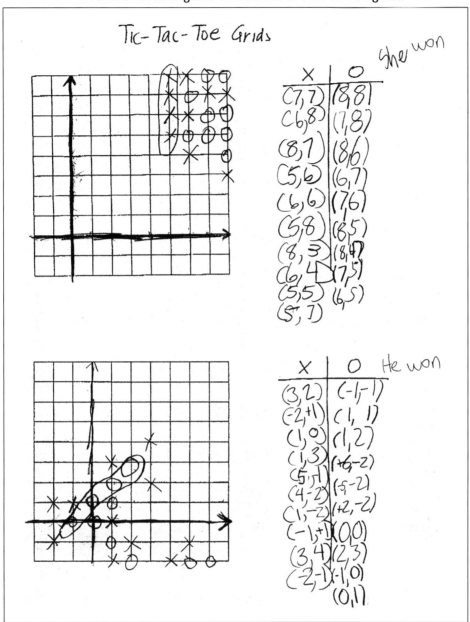

4. One day, Amy, James, and Sam asked if they could play together. I agreed, and they used Xs, Os, and Ss. (Sam used the Ss.) Figure 4–10 on page 70 shows two of their games.

Others tried playing in groups of three as well. "You have a longer game that way," Rick said.

"And it's easier to sneak a move that your opponent doesn't notice," Armando said.

FIGURE 4-10 When Amy (X), James (O), and Sam (S) played together, Sam won the first game and Amy won the second game. They used negative coordinates in both games.

Tic-Tac-Toe Grids

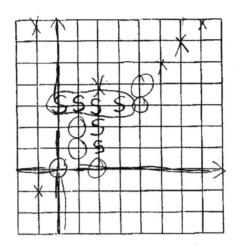

X	O	S
(6,6)	(0,0)	(3,3)
(-1,7)	(1, 1)	(2,2)
(5, 5)	(1, 2)	(2,1)
(7,7)	(4, 4)	(2, 3)
(2,4)	(2,0)	(1, 3)
(-1,+7)	(4,3)	(0, 3)

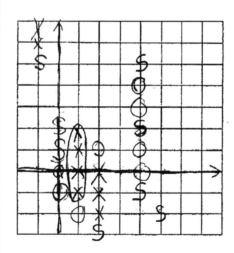

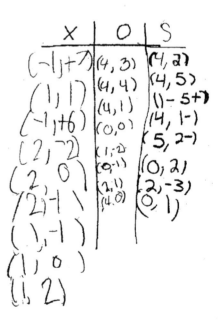

X	O	S
(-1,+7)	(4, 3)	(4, 2)
(1,1)	(4, 4)	(4, 5)
(-1,+6)	(4,1)	(1,-5+)
(2,-2)	(0,0)	(4, 1-)
(2, 0)	(1,2)	(5, 2-)
(2,-1)	(0,-1)	(0, 2)
(1,-1)	(1,1)	(2, -3)
(1, 0)	(4,0)	(0, 1)
(1, 2)		

## CHAPTER 5

Two of Everything Revisited

Graphing Growth Patterns

OVERVIEW

This lesson builds on students' previous experience with representing the *Two of Everything* doubling pattern numerically on a T-chart, describing the pattern in words, and then writing an algebraic equation to represent the pattern (see Chaper 1). The previous lesson provides a springboard for introducing students to connecting patterns to graphs. Students see how plotting points on a coordinate grid using the ordered pairs on the T-chart from the *Two of Everything* investigation produces a graph of the pattern. Students extend this experience by graphing other patterns from the *Two of Everything* lesson and investigating how graphs relate to the equations they represent.

BACKGROUND

This lesson is appropriate after students have had experience with patterns that grow, as described in the *Two of Everything* lesson (see Chapter 1), and are able to plot points on a coordinate grid (see Chapters 3 and 4). This introductory lesson about graphing lays the foundation for the subsequent experiences with graphing presented in the other lessons throughout the book. From cumulative experiences over time, students become familiar with making graphs and seeing connections among T-charts, equations, and their graphical representations.

All of the graphs in this lesson represent linear equations, which means that the points on the graphs lie on straight lines. (Notice the word *line* in *linear*.) Also, all of the lines in this introductory lesson go on a diagonal up to the right. The slant of the diagonal is referred to as the *slope* of the line, and the steeper the line, the higher the slope numbers. If you're not familiar with linear graphs, check the Introduction for background information about the mathematics.

VOCABULARY

axes, axis, equation, graph, input value, linear graph, ordered pair, origin, output value, plot, point, T-chart, variable

MATERIALS

■ centimeter graph paper, several sheets per student (see Blackline Masters)

TIME

■ two class periods

The Lesson

Day 1

To begin the class, I projected an overhead transparency of centimeter graph paper with axes drawn.

"Are we going to play *Tic-Tac-Toe*?" Armando asked. This class had learned how to plot points on a coordinate grid, then had practiced the skill by playing *Tic-Tac-Toe*. (See Chapters 3 and 4.)

"Not today," I said. "*Tic-Tac-Toe* is a good way to practice locating points and thinking strategically. But mathematicians figured out some other things they could do with coordinates. Let's think back to the story we read called *Two of Everything*. We found a pattern for what happened when something went into the pot and came back out. What was it?"

"Do you mean in the story or the ones we made up?" Armando asked.

"In the story," I answered.

"Something went into the pot, like Mrs. Haktak's hairpin, and two came out," Brianna explained.

"That happened whenever one of something went in—then two came out," Armando said.

"What about if five coins went in?" I asked. "Do you remember how many coins would come out?"

"Ten," the class chorused.

"What if four coins went in?" I asked.

"Eight would come out," Rick said.

"What if six coins came out? How many went in?" I continued.

"Three," Cami replied. "If six came out, then what went in was half, and half of six is three."

"If four came out, how many went in?" I asked. "Show me with your fingers." The students put up two fingers.

"One is easy," Elisa said. "One goes in and two come out."

"If seven go in, how many come out?" I asked.

"Fourteen," Michael said. "You double it to get the number that comes out. Seven and seven is fourteen."

"We made a T-chart to record data about the coins," I reminded the students. On the board, I drew a T-chart, labeled the columns, and, with the students' help, recorded information on it for inputs from 1 to 7.

□ In	△ Out
1	2
2	4
3	6
4	8
5	10
6	12
7	14

I pointed to the numbers on the T-chart as I said, "The T-chart shows the numbers as input and output pairs—one goes with two, two goes with four, three goes with six, and so on. Just as when we played *Tic-Tac-Toe*, we can use each pair of numbers to locate a point on graph paper. For example, we could take the numbers in the first pair, one coin in and two coins out, and use them as coordinates to mark a point. Who would like to explain how to do this?" I paused to give the students a few moments to think and then I called on Karly.

"I think for one coin in and two coins out, you start where the heavy lines cross and count going right one and up two," Karly said.

"Did anyone else have the same idea as Karly?" I asked. Several students raised a hand.

"I think that makes sense because in *Tic-Tac-Toe* you always went across for the first number and up for the second number, and that's what Karly did," Brianna said. There were no more comments.

"Karly's idea is correct," I said. "To plot the point for one coin in and two coins out, we start at the origin and count one over and two up." I used the words *plot* and *origin* to reinforce the correct terminology. I marked the point for (1, 2) on the overhead transparency.

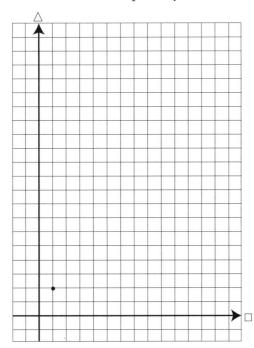

"What about the second pair of numbers, (two, four)? Would someone like to come up and mark the point for (two, four)?" Most students were eager to do this. I called on Rick.

When Rick came to the overhead, he made a common mistake. He counted the origin as one rather than zero and consequently marked the wrong spot. The class showed some thumbs up and some thumbs down. I said to the class, "Let's check to be sure Rick's point is marked correctly. Starting at the origin where the axes cross, I move across the horizontal axis, one, two."

Rick interrupted me as I was counting. "Oh no! I counted the origin as one! Can I fix it?" I nodded and Rick quickly made the correction.

"Now put your thumb up if you agree with where Rick marked the point, thumb down if you disagree, or thumb sideways if you aren't certain," I said. All thumbs were up.

"Where would the point be for three coins in and six coins out?" I called on Nina, who came to the overhead and correctly marked the point.

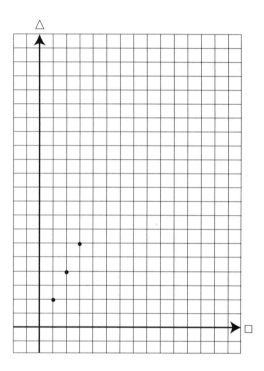

"I see a pattern," James announced. "You can go from one dot to the next by starting at the last dot and going to the right one and up two." I recorded James's idea on the board:

Start at the last dot and go to the right one and up two.   James

"Let's try that idea," I said. "James, how about coming up and putting another point where you think it should go?"

James came up to the overhead projector, put the overhead marker on the point (3, 6), counted over one space to the right and then up two spaces, and marked a new point. "I think that's right," he said, and then he sat down.

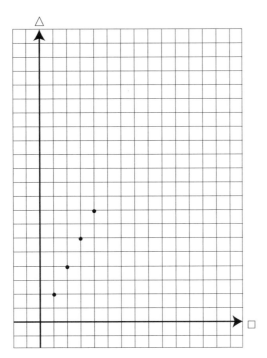

"Who can tell me the pair of numbers that would get us to the point that James just marked?" I asked. It was hard for some of the students to count from their seats, but those nearest to the front of the room were able to do so. I called on Beatriz.

"It's (four, eight)," she said. I placed the overhead marker on the origin and counted four over to the right and then eight up, verifying that (4, 8) were the coordinates of the point James marked.

"Does the ordered pair of (four, eight) belong in the *Two of Everything* pattern?" I asked. The children agreed that it did.

"Who can explain why?" I asked. It's important to emphasize the connection between the coordinates of a point, the information on the T-chart, and the context of the investigation that produced the ordered pairs.

"It's on the chart," Rick said.

"And why does it make sense for the ordered pair of (four, eight) to be on the T-chart?" I probed.

Elisa answered, "If you put four coins into the pot, then eight come out. That's how those numbers got up on the T-chart."

Armando added, "It works backwards, too. If eight coins came out, that means four went in."

"Could I write the numbers backward on the T-chart?" I asked. The students seemed confused by my question, so I rephrased it. "Could I switch two numbers around and write, for example, eight in the In column and four in the Out column?" I wrote the numbers this way at the bottom of the T-chart. Several students protested, but others didn't seem sure.

Julian said, "If you put eight in, you'd get sixteen out, not four."

"You can't switch the numbers around," Annie said. "It doesn't work."

"They won't match the pattern," Gary added.

"Oh, I get it," Kris said. He hadn't been sure a moment ago.

I said, "We call these pairs of numbers *ordered pairs* because the order matters. If you switch the numbers around, they won't follow the same pattern. Also, watch as I plot the point for the switched-around pair of (eight, four).” I put the overhead marker on the origin of the graph, counted eight over to the right, then four up, and then marked a point.

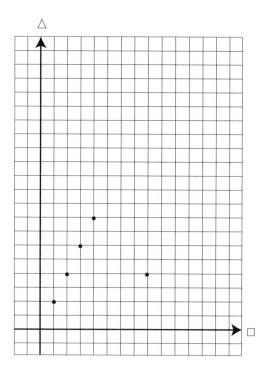

“That’s way off!” James said.

“It doesn’t fit the pattern of the other dots,” Beatriz said.

“Yes, I agree,” I said. “The point for (eight, four) doesn’t seem to follow the pattern of the other points.” I paraphrased Beatriz’s comment to model the correct terminology of *point*, not *dot*. Discussing the result of reversing the numbers had been sparked by Armando’s comment and was useful for reinforcing the importance of the order of coordinates. I made a note to myself that when I taught the lesson again, even if a student didn’t make a comment like Armando’s, I would raise the issue of switching the numbers.

I erased the point at (8, 4) and then asked, “Who can describe the pattern of points on this graph?”

“They go in a diagonal,” Cami shared. “You can sort of tell just by looking where the next point should be.” I recorded Cami’s idea on the board:

The points go in a diagonal. Cami

Brianna also had an idea. “This one is sort of weird,” she said. “The In side of the T-chart goes up by one and you always go by ones on the horizontal number line, and the Out side of the T-chart goes up by twos and you always go up two more each time.”

I thought about Brianna’s comment for a moment and then said, “Hmmm, that’s a lot of words to write. How about if I write this?” I wrote on the board:

The In numbers go by ones and the Out numbers go by twos.
The points go horizontally over one and vertically up two. Brianna

"Is this OK to explain your idea?" I asked Brianna. She nodded.

"That seems right because the numbers are telling you where to put the points on the graph," Beatriz said with some uncertainty. The students were making connections that would become clearer as they had additional opportunities to explore patterns, T-charts, graphs, and the relationships among them.

"What if zero coins went in—how many coins would come out?" I asked.

"Zero," the students replied.

"Why would zero coins come out?" I asked.

"How can nothing double?" Annie responded. "Zero plus zero is zero. Zero times zero is zero. You can't make something when nothing goes in." The other students nodded.

"What about zero times two?" I asked. "When we double, we multiply by two."

Armando said, "Zero times two is still zero, because zero times anything is zero."

"So if I put zero on the chart on the left side, what number will it pair with on the right side?" I asked. I wrote _0_ in the left column of the T-chart, above the 1. "What number shall I write in the right column for zero?" I asked. This seemed to help with the confusion, and hands went up.

"Let's say the number together in a whisper voice," I said. I heard a chorus of "zero" and wrote the _0_ on the chart.

□	△
In	**Out**
0	0
1	2
2	4
3	6
4	8
5	10
6	12
7	14

I said, "I don't think we have a point on the graph for this pair of numbers. Who would like to come up and plot (zero, zero)?"

Nina came to the overhead projector and marked the point correctly. "It's (zero, zero), so you don't go anywhere," she explained.

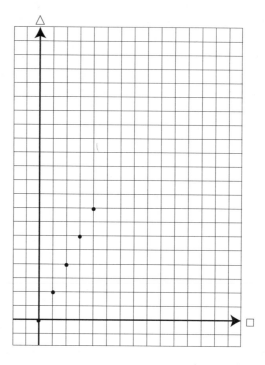

"The point (zero, zero) is located right at the origin," I said, using the terminology *origin* in the context of what we were doing.

"Do you think any more points belong on this graph?" I asked. I posed this question to focus the class on looking at the graph and predicting how to extend it to include other points. Just as when they extend numerical patterns on T-charts, looking at the pattern of points on a graph gives students experience with extending patterns to make predictions beyond the information currently available, this time using a visual pattern.

"There are lots more," Kris said. "You just keep going up on the diagonal."

"Would you like to come up and show us your idea by putting some more points on the graph?" I asked. Kris nodded, came up, and marked all the rest of the points that could fit on the transparency.

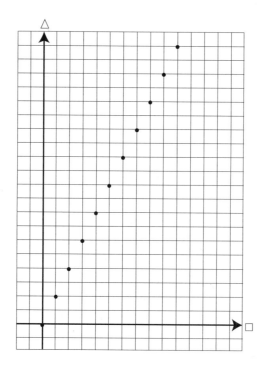

□	△
In	**Out**
0	0
1	2
2	4
3	6
4	8
5	10
6	12
7	14
8	16
9	18
10	20

I commented, "These points all look right, but I think it's always a good idea to check our mathematical ideas in another way. Let's figure out what the coordinates are for each of these new points and be sure that they fit the *Two of Everything* pattern." As students identified the coordinates for each new point, we talked about why they fit the pattern. I recorded (8, 16), (9, 18), and (10, 20) on the T-chart.

Connecting the Graph to the Pattern   I then changed the direction of the conversation to focus on the rule for the *Two of Everything* pattern that the students had discussed when they first encountered it. "Who can describe the rule we came up with for the *Two of Everything* pattern?" I asked. More than half of the students raised a hand.

"It's a doubling pattern," Jaime explained. "You add the In number to itself and that's the Out number."

"I know another way," Armando said. "You can multiply the In number by two and that will make the Out number."

There were no other ideas, so I asked, "How do the T-chart and the graph show these ideas of doubling by adding the In number to itself, or multiplying the In number by two?" Some children seemed confused, so I rephrased my question. "How do the numbers on the T-chart show a doubling pattern? And how do the locations of the points on the graph show a doubling pattern? Talk with your partner about these questions."

When I called the class back to attention, I asked who wanted to share. About half of the students raised a hand. I called on Rick.

He said, "It's easy to see the doubling pattern on the T-chart. Every number doubles to the number next to it." There were lots of nods.

"Does anyone want to explain this pattern another way?" I asked.

Beatriz said, "When you have an input number, you double it by either adding it to itself or timesing it by two and you get the number in the Out column." Again there were nods of agreement.

James added, "And it works the other way, too. If you take a number in the Out column and take half of it, you get the number in the In column. Taking half is like the opposite of doubling." A buzz broke out in the room. This idea was novel for some of the students, but it seemed to make sense to them.

"Did anyone have an idea about how the points on the graph show the doubling pattern?" I asked. Only about half a dozen hands were raised. I called on Annie.

She said, "I think it's like what Brianna said before. The In numbers go up by ones, but the Out numbers go up by twos, and that means that when you go over one, the point goes up double." Annie seemed to understand her idea, but others weren't clear.

"Could you come up and show the class on the graph what you mean?" I asked. Annie came up and put her finger on one of the points. "See, you have to go up two spaces to the next point, but only over one space. Two spaces is the double of one space."

"That's like what James said," Michael said.

"Do you agree, James?" I asked. "Is Annie's idea similar to the pattern you saw earlier?"

James nodded. "It's always one over and two up to get to the next point. That's the doubling part."

Connecting the Graph to the Equation   I said to the class, "When we discussed the *Two of Everything* pattern, after we wrote the rule in words, we wrote an equation using symbols. Who remembers how we did that?" Many hands went up and I called on David.

"We wrote 'triangle equals box times two,' " David said. I wrote on the board:

$$\triangle = \square \times 2$$

"We did it another way, too," Elisa said. "We did 'triangle equals box plus box.' " I also recorded this version of the equation on the board:

$$\triangle = \square + \square$$

I said, "We've now shown the *Two of Everything* pattern in three different ways: as a T-chart, as points on a graph, and as an equation written in two different ways. The T-chart is a list of the pairs of numbers, the graph is a picture of the numbers on a coordinate grid, and the equation is a mathematical shortcut that describes the pattern algebraically."

Introducing Another Graph   I projected a clean transparency of centimeter graph paper, drew axes on it, and said to the class, "Now we're going to plot the ordered pairs from another pattern we investigated with the magic pot." On the board, I drew a T-chart and entered the numbers for the second pattern we had investigated. The rule for this pattern was "The output number is equal to the input number times three."

$\square$	$\triangle$
In	**Out**
1	3
2	6
3	9
4	12
5	15
6	18
7	21

I continued, "Raise your hand if you'd like to come to the overhead and mark a point on the graph from the T-chart. When you come up, first check off on the board the ordered pair you plan to plot. Then, on the overhead transparency, mark the point on the graph. The rest of you should watch carefully and then show with your thumb whether or not you agree with the location of the point."

Brianna came up first. She checked the ordered pair (3, 9) and then marked the point on the graph. All of the students showed thumbs up. Other students followed and soon all of the points from the T-chart were marked.

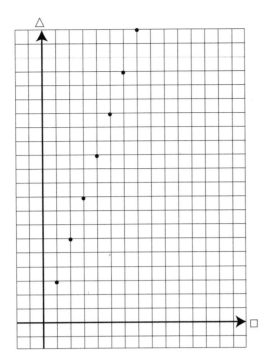

"They go in a line again," Rick said.

"The line is on a diagonal again," Annie added.

Cami said, "It's a stair-step pattern like the other one, but different, too. Can I come up and show?" I agreed. Cami came up and showed how she saw that you go over one and up three to get from one point to the next.

"Or you could come down the stairs by going to the left one and down three," Michael added.

"What if we had an input value of zero?" I asked, squeezing in a *0* at the top of the In column of the T-chart.

"Zero would come out," James said.

"How do you know?" I asked.

"Well, the pattern is times three, and zero times three is zero," James answered. Others nodded their agreement. I recorded a *0* in the output column and marked a point at the origin for (0, 0).

"Does anyone remember the equation for this pattern?" I asked. About a third of the children raised a hand. I called on Adam.

He said, "It's 'triangle equals three times box.' " I recorded on the board above the T-chart:

$$\triangle = 3 \times \square$$

"So this graph is another way to represent the T-chart and the equation," I said. "Like the other graph, the points on this graph also go in a straight line. When the points go in a line, a graph is called a *linear graph*." I wrote *linear* on the board and underlined *line*:

<u>line</u>ar

I pointed out to the class, "The word *line* is in the word *linear*, and that can help you remember what linear means."

"Do they always go in a line?" Sam wanted to know.

"No, not all graphs are linear," I answered, "but most of the ones we'll be exploring for a while are."

I ended the lesson by saying, "Tomorrow you'll have a chance to graph your own rules for patterns for the magic pot, and you'll see what pattern of points you get."

Day 2

At the beginning of class, I handed back to the students their papers for the rules they had chosen the week before in the *Two of Everything* lesson. On these papers, they had written their names and the rule they used on one side, and a T-chart with seven or eight pairs of numbers on the other side. All of the students had had a chance to present their patterns to the class for others to guess.

"Today you'll make a graph of your pattern," I said. "Use centimeter graph paper and on the back of the paper, as you did before, write your names and the rule. Then, on the other side, draw axes and plot the points from your T-chart."

"Does it matter where we draw the axes?" Michael asked.

"You can draw them anywhere you'd like, but it makes sense to choose a location that allows you to plot as many of your points as possible," I answered.

"If we want, can we do Xs instead of dots?" Elisa asked.

"When we make graphs like these, we generally mark points, so please don't use Xs or Os or any other marks," I answered. There were no more questions and the students got to work.

Kris and Annie called me over. Their rule was to add two and then subtract five from the input number. Two of the pairs of numbers on their T-chart included negative numbers and they weren't sure how to plot the points. The ordered pairs were (1, –2) and (2, –1).

Annie said, "I think you have to go down for the negative numbers, but Kris doesn't agree."

"What's your idea, Kris?" I asked.

"I don't know," he said.

"Well, it turns out that Annie's idea is correct," I said. "The second number in the ordered pair tells us where to go on the vertical number line, the vertical axis." I pointed to the vertical axis on their paper as I said this. "You generally go up from the origin, but if the second coordinate is negative, then you go down from the origin."

"Oh, OK," Kris said.

"How about you each mark one of those points," I said. "Then you'll both have practice plotting a point with a negative coordinate." (See Figure 5–1.)

None of the other students had problems. I gave each of the first three pairs of students who finished an overhead transparency of centimeter graph paper and asked them to reproduce their graphs. I also asked them each to write their T-charts on the board. My plan was to project one of their graphs and see if the other students could figure out which T-chart it represented. I gave a one-minute warning to the class.

FIGURE 5–1   Kris and Annie's rule, input number plus 2 minus 5 equals output number, can be written as either $\triangle = \square + 2 - 5$ or $\triangle = \square - 3$.

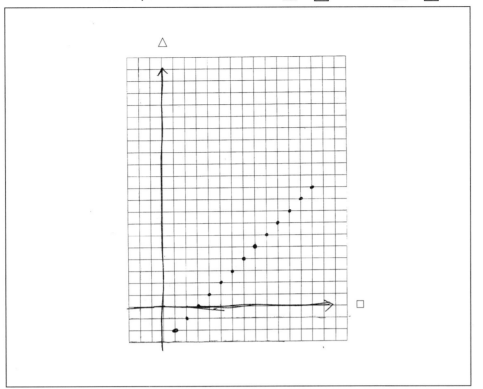

A Class Discussion   When I called the class to order, I projected Rick and Cami's graph. (See Figure 5–2.)

FIGURE 5–2   Rick and Cami's graph represents their rule of multiplying by 2 and adding 5. They wrote their rule as $\square \times 2 + 3 = \triangle$.

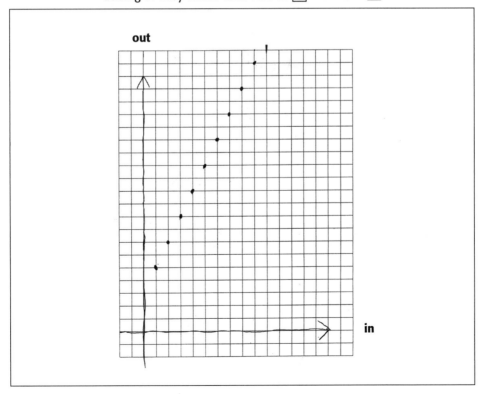

"Which of the T-charts on the board do you think this graph represents?" I asked. I labeled the T-charts *A*, *B*, and *C* so that we could talk about them more easily. (See Figures 5–3 through 5–5.)

FIGURES 5-3, 5-4, 5-5 These T-charts were done by Kris and Annie, James and Armando, and Rick and Cami.

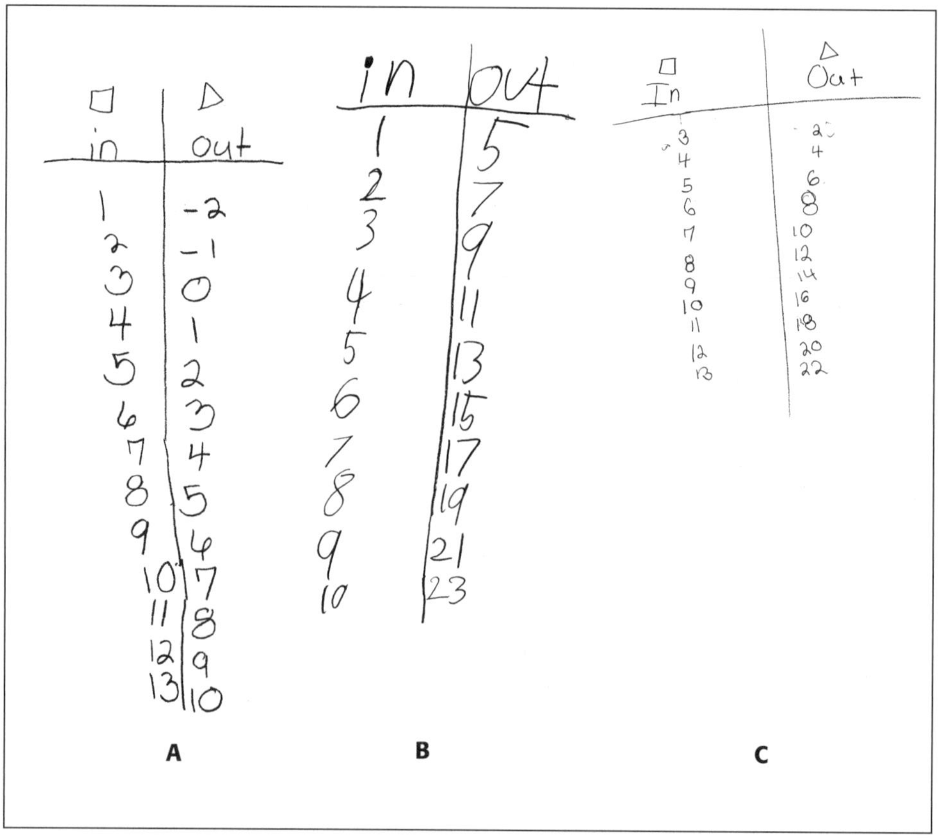

□ in	△ out
1	-2
2	-1
3	0
4	1
5	2
6	3
7	4
8	5
9	6
10	7
11	8
12	9
13	10

A

in	out
1	5
2	7
3	9
4	11
5	13
6	15
7	17
8	19
9	21
10	23

B

□ In	△ Out
3	2
4	4
5	6
6	8
7	10
8	12
9	14
10	16
11	18
12	20
13	22

C

"Talk with your partner and see if you can decide," I said. The discussions in the class were lively and soon most hands were in the air.

Before I asked children to share, I called for a show of hands for each of the charts. Most students indicated that they thought the graph matched the T-chart labeled B, but some students raised a hand for each of the others. "Who would like to explain your choice?" I asked. I called on Karly.

"I think it can't be A. The points would have to be lower on the graph where the negative numbers go," Karly said. Several students nodded their agreement. Next I called on David.

"It has to be B," he said. "The first point is at (one, five), and that's on the chart." No one had anything else to share. I showed the students the graph for another of the T-charts. (See Figure 5–6.) Again, I asked the students to talk in pairs about which T-chart it represented.

Again the discussions were animated. When I called the class to attention, I called on Brianna. She said, "It can't be B because the other one was, and it can't be A because, like Karly said, the points don't go down enough. I vote for C." Others agreed but no one had anything to add.

FIGURE 5–6 James and Armando's rule was $\triangle = 2 \times \square - 4$.

Two of Everything Revisited

85

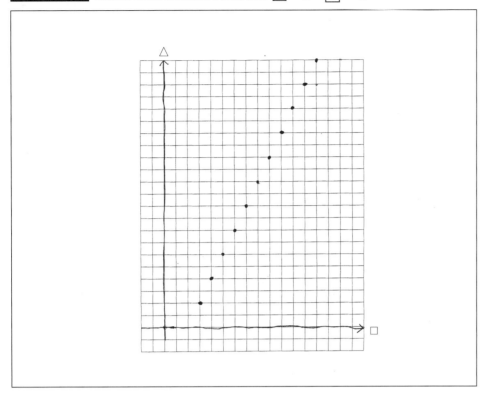

"Let's check one of the points and see if it's on the T-chart," I said. Michael identified the coordinates of the lowest point as (3, 2).

"It checks; it's on the chart," Audrey said.

When I presented the third graph, the answer was obvious. "But who can explain why you're sure it represents the T-chart labeled A?" I asked.

"It has negative numbers," James said.

I then asked the students, "What do you notice was the same and what was different about the three graphs?"

"They all go diagonal in a straight line," Rick said.

"One was steeper than the others," Gary observed.

"Our graph went in a diagonal like those did," David said. "I wonder if they all do."

"Did anyone make a graph that didn't go in a diagonal straight line?" I asked. No one had a graph that didn't make a diagonal straight line.

"How come that happens?" Karly asked.

"Is there a way to make it go diagonally the other way?" David wondered.

"Can it just go straight across or straight up and down?" Brianna asked.

"Those are excellent questions, and we'll explore many of them during the year," I said as I ended the lesson. Over the next several days, I planned to have the other pairs draw their graphs on overhead transparencies. Then, as we did today, I'd ask three pairs to write their T-charts on the board, then I'd project their graphs one by one and ask the students to figure out which T-chart each matched (see Figures 5–7 through 5–10).

FIGURE 5–7 Brianna and Beatriz used □ + 4 = △ as their rule.

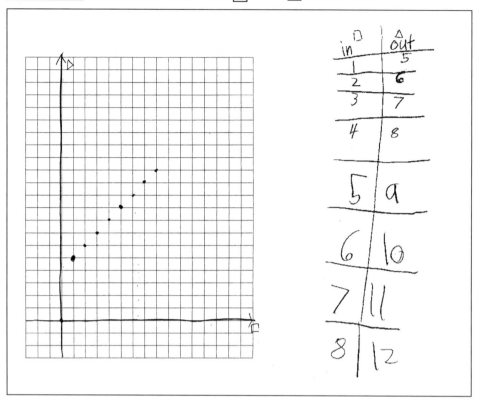

FIGURE 5–8 Adam and Sam made a T-chart and graph for the rule
□ × 2 + 9 = △.

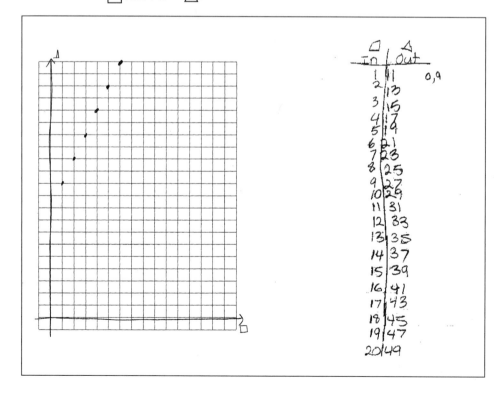

FIGURE 5-9 Jaime and Julian chose for their rule $\square \times 4 - 3 = \triangle$.

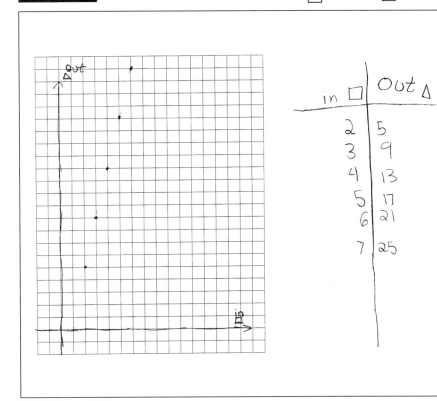

FIGURE 5-10 Nina and Audrey's rule was $\square \times 3 = \triangle$.

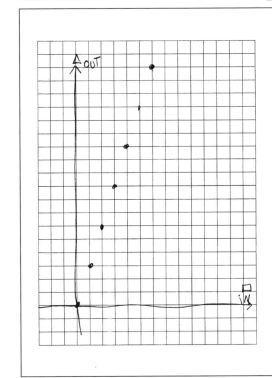

## PART TWO

The Lessons

As stated in the Introduction, the nine lessons that follow build on the knowledge and skills in Part One, "Getting Students Ready." Chapter 10, "Guess My Rule," presents an experience similar to those in Chapters 1 and 5, using a different children's book as the context. In five other chapters, students interpret geometric patterns and use manipulative materials. In Chapters 6 and 12, "Iguanas" and "Table Patterns," students use pattern blocks; in Chapters 7, 11, and 13, "Letter Patterns," "Piles of Tiles," and "Amanda Bean," students use color tiles. Chapters 12 and 13 also use children's stories as the contexts for the investigations. All of these chapters are suitable for providing students with experience describing and extending growth patterns and representing them with equations and on graphs. The remaining three chapters in this section provide other experiences important to algebraic thinking. Chapter 8, "Pick a Number," gives students with experience solving equations with one variable; Chapter 9, "Four Points," provides a problem-solving experience that helps reinforce the skill of plotting points; Chapter 14, "Identities," engages students in investigating properties of numbers, making generalizations about them, and describing them with both words and algebraic symbols.

The section in the Introduction called "Suggestions for Schoolwide Planning" offers guidance for choosing and sequencing lessons that are appropriate for your class.

## CHAPTER 6

Iguanas
Building with Pattern Blocks

OVERVIEW

This lesson gives students experience with building, extending, and describing growth patterns. To begin, the students are introduced to a Stage 1 "iguana" built from pattern blocks. They predict what a Stage 2 iguana might look like and then extend the pattern to Stage 3 and Stage 4 iguanas. They record the information on a chart, look for patterns, and extend the patterns to predict the number of blocks needed for Stage 10 and Stage 100 iguanas. They repeat the experience for two other investigations with pattern blocks.

BACKGROUND

This lesson engages students in investigating growth patterns using a concrete material. The pattern blocks provide the concrete experience for the lesson, and the iguanas provide a context that helps students relate to the exploration. The focus of the lesson is on having students figure out patterns and then use them to make predictions beyond the information available to them.

The lesson described in this chapter wasn't extended to include either writing equations or making graphs to describe the patterns. However, it's possible to do both. For example, for the first iguana pattern, the total number of blocks used to build any iguana is equal to 4 (the number of blocks in the body) plus the stage number (the number of blocks in the tail). It's possible to write this relationship as an equation. Using t for the total number of blocks and s for the stage number, the equation could be $t = 4 + s$. Using other variables would result in other equations, such as $\triangle = 4 + \square$ or $y = 4 + x$. Also, plotting ordered pairs with the first number representing the stage number and the second the total number of blocks—(s, t), $(\square, \triangle)$, or (x, y)—would produce a graph of the relationship. If you're interested in including these two aspects, follow the procedures used in Chapters 1 and 5, in which students write equations and graph growth patterns for the *Two of Everything* exploration.

VOCABULARY

column, constant, variable, vary

MATERIALS

■ pattern blocks, 1 bucket or plastic sandwich bag per table group

■ optional: overhead pattern blocks

TIME

■ three class periods

The Lesson

Day 1

"For this lesson, you'll need to use your imagination and try to figure out the pattern I have in my mind," I began as I carefully built a design on the overhead projector using overhead pattern blocks.

"It looks like a cat," Juan said.

"I think it looks like someone running with a kite in their hand," Karena suggested.

"It could be a puppy," Joanna said.

"Those are clever ideas, but I think my design is an iguana," I said.

"Oh yeah," Pete said, "I see the tail and the feet and the head."

"I have an iguana," Nancy said, "but its tail is really long."

On the overhead, I labeled the design *Stage 1* and asked, "If this is a Stage One iguana, think about what the next iguana, a Stage Two iguana, would look like." I waited to give students time to think and then called on Issac.

"It could have two squares for the head, a hexagon body, two triangle feet and one block for the tail," Issac suggested. I built his suggestion on the overhead underneath the first iguana.

"Like this?" I asked Issac. He nodded.

"That's a good idea for a Stage Two iguana," I said, "but it isn't what the Stage Two iguana in my mind looks like."

"Maybe it has two bodies and two heads and four feet and two tails," Tomas thought. "Every part would double." I changed what I had built for Issac's suggestion and confirmed with Tomas that I had represented his idea accurately.

"That's another good idea," I said, "but it's not the Stage Two iguana that I'm thinking of."

Jasmine had a different idea. She said, "Maybe it would be the same as Stage One only there would be four feet."

"Where would the two extra feet go?" I asked as I removed the blocks I had used to build Tomas's suggestion.

"Underneath the other feet," Jasmine said. "It will be taller." I built Jasmine's idea and she nodded her agreement.

I said, "That's not it, either."

"I think since it's an iguana that the tail is what will grow," Brad said.

"Tell me how to build a Stage Two iguana using your idea, Brad," I said.

"The head and body and feet would all be the same and the tail would grow with another block," Brad explained. "Iguanas can have really long tails, so that's what I think." I changed Jasmine's iguana to reflect Brad's idea and labeled it *Stage 2*.

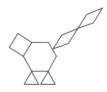

"This is exactly what my Stage Two iguana looks like," I said. "The other ideas were all possible, but this is the idea that I had."

To be sure that all of the students were following this discussion, I asked, "What's the same about the Stage One and Stage Two iguanas and what's different? Talk with your table group about the two iguanas I built." The students talked quietly with their partners and after a few moments I asked for their attention. Several hands were up. I called on Pete.

"The heads are both the same in Stage One and Stage Two. They're both orange cubes," Pete explained.

"The heads are orange squares in both Stage One and Stage Two?" I asked, correcting Pete's use of the word *cubes* for *squares*. Pete nodded his agreement.

"The body is the same, too," Nina added.

"So are the feet," Wanda added.

"And what's different?" I asked. Most students raised a hand.

"The tails are different," Karena said. "In Stage One the iguana has one block in its tail, and in Stage Two it has two blocks. Other than that everything is the same."

"Your idea is that the body remains the same and one block is added to the tail?" I asked to be sure I understood what Karena had explained. Karena nodded her agreement. "Put your thumb up if you agree with Karena, down if you disagree, and sideways if you're not sure," I said. Most students quickly put their thumbs up to indicate their agreement.

"So the only thing that varied from Stage One to Stage Two was the block that was added to the tail," I said. "What do you think the third-stage iguana will look like? Talk it over with your table group." I used the word *varied* because I thought that if children weren't familiar with it, they could figure out its meaning from the context of the sentence. Also, I planned to use the words *vary* and *variable* to describe the changing part of the pattern. After a few moments I asked for the students' attention.

"I think Stage Three will have two orange squares for heads, one hexagon for the body, two triangles for feet, and two white diamonds for the tail," Kasey explained. There wasn't room to build Kasey's idea on the overhead, so I drew his suggestion on the board.

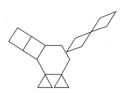

"Please explain why you think that," I said to Kasey.

"Well," Kasey said and paused for a moment, "I think the tail will increase one time and then the head the next time."

Joanna had another idea. She said, "I think Stage Three will be the same as Stage One and Two except you add one more white diamond for the tail. The pattern seems to be about the tail, not some other part." I drew Joanna's suggestion on the board next to Kasey's.

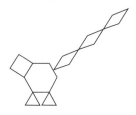

I said, "Kasey and Joanna have two different ideas, and both are possible. It's hard to read my mind and figure out my pattern for changing a design when you only have a little bit of information."

"What does your Stage Three iguana look like?" Jess asked.

"My idea is the same as Joanna's," I responded. A buzz of conversation broke out in the room.

"That's like I thought!" Issac said with excitement.

"I was right," Turner added. Other students commented, too.

After settling the class, I said, "Kasey, your idea is really interesting to me and a possibility that I haven't ever thought of. Thanks for giving me another way to think about making patterns grow. But for now, we'll continue with the idea I had in mind." I erased Kasey's idea and asked, "What changed or varied to make Stage Three in my pattern?" again deliberately using the word *varied*.

"The tail," the students responded.

"What remained the same, or constant?" I asked, laying the foundation for the terminology *constant*.

"The body," the class said.

"And how many blocks are in the body?" I asked. I gave them a moment to count.

Nancy answered, "There are four—one yellow, two green, and an orange square for the head." In some lessons, I push students to use the correct geometric names of the blocks, but in this lesson, since I was more concerned with the number of blocks, not their shapes, I accepted Nancy's answer.

Extending the Iguana Pattern   "In a moment, you'll send one person from your group to get a container of pattern blocks," I said, pointing to where they were located on a table. "Listen to what you'll do with them. With your table group, build what you think Stage Four of my pattern will look like." There were no questions. As the students gathered their materials, I drew the first two stages on the board to the left of where I had drawn the third stage so that the students had all three together for their reference.

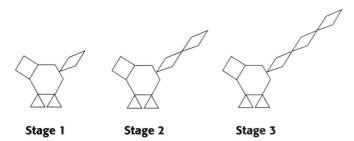

Stage 1   **Stage 2**   **Stage 3**

Then I circulated through the class, answering some students' questions, asking questions of others, observing, and listening to conversations as the students worked. I watched Josh and Damon working. Both boys seemed to be creating patterns of their own rather than trying to build the fourth stage of my pattern.

"Tell me about your pattern," I said.

"It's a pattern where the body is growing," Josh said.

"In my pattern, what part is growing?" I asked.

"The tail," Josh responded. "I have to make your pattern?"

"My instruction was to build the fourth stage of my pattern," I said.

"Oh." Josh paused. Then he and Damon began to talk quietly between themselves. Damon commented that in my pattern the body stayed the same and maybe the body should be the same for the fourth stage, too. Josh agreed. The boys built the body and then looked to me for approval.

"Tell me what you're thinking," I said.

"Well, the body didn't change before, so it should probably stay the same for Stage Four, too," Josh said.

"But the tail should grow one more," Damon said.

"If the tail should grow one more, how many blocks should the iguana have for Stage Four altogether?" I asked.

"Eight," both boys replied in unison. I quickly looked around the class and saw that by this time, almost all of the students had built the fourth stage correctly. I called the class back to attention.

"Who can describe how to build the fourth stage?" I asked.

"Build the body the same as the other three, and then add four white diamonds for the tail," Pete explained.

I built Stage 4 on the overhead and verified with Pete that I had built it the way he thought it should look. He indicated I had. As I looked around the room at what the children had built, I could see quickly that the others agreed.

"It looks to me that you all built Stage Four the same way as Pete," I said. "Now work with your table group to build Stage Five of my pattern." The students went to work immediately as I drew Stage 4 next to the other three stages I had drawn on the board. By the time I turned around, most students had finished. Issac explained how to build the Stage 5 iguana, and I drew it on the board as well.

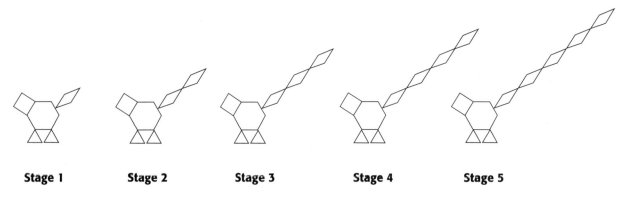

Stage 1   **Stage 2**   **Stage 3**   **Stage 4**   **Stage 5**

"I noticed something," Brad said.

"I told you," Joanna said in a stage whisper, concerned that Brad was going to share her idea.

"No, I figured it out before you said it," Brad responded to Joanna.

"What did the two of you notice?" I asked.

"We noticed that the stage number and the number of blocks in the tail is the same," Joanna explained. Brad nodded his agreement.

"We noticed that at our table, too," Nina said. "The body part is always the same and the tail part matches the stage number." This discovery is key to the lesson. If Joanna and Brad hadn't offered it, I would have asked the class to count the number of blocks in the tail in each stage and compare it with the stage number.

I then said to the class, "The blocks in the body are always the same, or constant. But in each stage, the length of the tail varies, and the number of blocks in the tail is always the same as the stage number." I again used the terminology *constant* and *varies*.

"Oh, I get it," Nancy said with some surprise. "In Stage One the tail had one block, in Stage Two it had two blocks, Stage Three was three blocks, Stage Four has four blocks, and Stage Five has five blocks! That's cool!"

Recording the Information   I then shifted the conversation by telling a story. I said, "Every day before I come to school in the morning, I have to visit the pattern block maker. He's a strange-looking little creature who enjoys thinking about most things. His job is to make and give out pattern blocks, but he sometimes gets tired of thinking about how many pattern blocks to give and gets headaches. Too much thinking about pattern blocks causes them, he claims. When he has a headache, he's really grumpy. So maybe he would have fewer headaches and be less grouchy if we could tell him the number of blocks we need for the bodies and tails of iguanas so he doesn't have to figure it out. How many blocks do we need for the body and tail of a Stage One iguana?" I asked. Hands danced in the air as students waited to share their ideas. I called on Gary.

"For Stage One you need five blocks," Gary said.

"Explain how you know," I pushed.

"I counted them," Gary replied.

"How many blocks are needed just for the body?" I asked.

"I know," Karena said. I reminded Karena not to blurt out. Gary wasn't sure, so I asked if he would like to call on someone else to help him out. He called on Tomas.

"There are five blocks," Tomas said.

"I agree there are five blocks altogether to make the Stage One iguana," I said. "But how many are needed for just the body?"

"Oh, that would be four," Tomas said. "I included the tail."

"There are four blocks in the body and one in the tail, and if you add them together then you'll know the total of blocks to tell the pattern block maker," Pete summarized.

"If I add four blocks for the body and one for the tail, what's the total number of blocks needed for Stage One?" I asked.

"Five," replied the class. I ruled lines on the board to make a chart with three columns. I labeled them *Stage #*, *Body + Tail*, and *Total # of Blocks*, filled in the chart for a Stage One iguana, and then wrote a *2* in the Stage # column.

Stage #	Body + Tail	Total # of Blocks
1	4 + 1	5
2		

"How many blocks are in the body of a Stage Two iguana?" I asked. Hands went up. I called on Gary, now eager to answer.

"It's four again; it stays the same," Gary said.

"And in the tail?" I asked. "Let's say it together in a whisper voice."

"Two," the class answered.

"And the total number of blocks?" I asked.

"Six," the class whispered, and I recorded this on the chart.

Stage #	Body + Tail	Total # of Blocks
1	4 + 1	5
2	4 + 2	6

We continued filling in the chart for Stages 3, 4, and 5. When I got to Stage 4, we filled in the first two columns together. Then I asked the students to show with their fingers the total number of blocks needed to build Stage 4. About half of the students held up four fingers on one hand and four on the other, while the rest showed five fingers and three fingers.

"Some of you are showing four fingers and four fingers, while some of you are showing five fingers and three fingers," I said. "What do you think about this?"

"I think the right way would be four fingers and four fingers because that shows what's on the chart," Joanna said.

"I think five fingers and three fingers could also be right," Karena said. "The question is how many blocks altogether, and the answer is eight. Five and three is eight."

"They both equal the same number," Bianca said. "I think both ways are right."

"If the problem says four and four, then I think you should have four fingers and four fingers," Josh added.

"I agree with Bianca," Nina said. "It's sort of like money. You could have eight cents by having a nickel and three pennies, or eight pennies. It's worth the same amount either way."

I pointed to the third column and said, "For this column, we're interested in the total number of blocks, and both ways give this information."

Stage #	Body + Tail	Total # of Blocks
1	4 + 1	5
2	4 + 2	6
3	4 + 3	7
4	4 + 4	8
5	4 + 5	9

"What do you notice about the numbers under the column that says Body Plus Tail?" I asked.

"The body always stays the same," Nina said.

"The four goes on and on and on," Damon said.

"Mathematicians would say that the four is the *constant* part of the pattern," I said. "When something is always the same, we can describe it as constant. In this case, the number of blocks for the iguana body is always constant, or the same." On the chart, I wrote *Constant* above Body.

"Oh, I get it," Turner said. "My mom says my room is a constant mess. She thinks it's always messy."

"My mom says she has to constantly tell me to take out the trash!" Haley added. The students giggled when Haley and Turner related the meaning of *constant* to their own lives.

To change the direction of the conversation, I asked, "What do you notice about the tail numbers?"

"They change," Stacy said.

"They aren't constant," Jess added. "They must be unconstant!"

"The tail numbers always add one," Issac said.

"Like Brad and I said before, the tail numbers are the same as the stage number," Joanna reminded us.

"Numbers like the tail numbers that change, or vary, are the variable part of the pattern," I explained and added the word *Variable* above the Tail column.

Stage #	Constant Variable Body + Tail	Total # of Blocks
1	4 + 1	5
2	4 + 2	6
3	4 + 3	7
4	4 + 4	8
5	4 + 5	9

"The temperature varies," Jess noted. "Today it's really hot, hotter than usual!" The other students nodded their agreement with Jess.

I then asked, "What do you think a Stage Ten iguana would look like? How many blocks would I need to get from the block maker?" I gave the students a moment to think about this and then hands started going up quickly. To give as many students as possible the opportunity to talk about the question, I asked the students to talk in pairs, first giving one person thirty seconds to speak without interruption, then giving the second person the same opportunity. I wrote the following on the board to help keep the students focused:

1. *What will a Stage 10 iguana look like?*
2. *How many blocks do I need to get from the block maker to build a Stage 10 iguana?*

After a minute had passed, I asked for the students' attention once again. Hands were up, as students were eager to share. I called on Paul.

"It would have four blocks to make the body and then ten blocks for the tail," Paul explained. The others showed thumbs up to indicate their agreement.

I said, "That describes what it would look like. What about my second question? How many blocks will it take to make a Stage Ten iguana?"

Again there were many hands in the air, so I asked the students to respond in a whisper voice. "Fourteen!" they answered.

"Why fourteen?" I asked.

"Ten for the tail and four for the body is fourteen," Bianca explained.

An Individual Assignment "Here's my next challenge," I continued. The students were excited and eager to hear what I had to say. "What about the hundredth-stage iguana?"

"Wow! That's hard!" Issac said.

"No, not really, Issac," Gary said. The other students were starting to talk among themselves and many hands were going up.

"This time, I'm going to give you a sheet of paper and ask you to write your thoughts about these two questions," I explained, pointing to the two questions on the board we had used to think about the tenth stage. I changed *10* to *100* in the questions.

1. *What will a Stage 100 iguana look like?*
2. *How many blocks do I need to get from the block maker to build a Stage 100 iguana?*

I then said, "For the hundredth stage, describe what it will look like and how many blocks we need from the block maker."

"Hey, we can't make it with the blocks," Jess noticed. "There aren't enough!"

"That's right," I responded. "What are some other ways you could think about it?"

"Use the patterns from the chart," Karena suggested.

"Oh yeah!" Jess replied with a giggle.

The students were eager to get to work. I quickly distributed paper and observed carefully as the students worked. As I glanced over shoulders to read what they were writing, I noticed some students using the new words that I had introduced as part of the lesson.

After a few moments, Nancy called me over. "I don't know what to put," she said with some frustration.

"Let's back up and see if I can ask you some questions that might help you figure it out," I responded. "What's the problem you're trying to solve?"

"I have to describe what the hundredth stage will look like and how many blocks it will take to build it," Nancy said.

"OK, I can tell you understand the problem," I said. "Let's go back to the first stage. Tell me what the first stage looked like."

"It had four blocks to make the body and one block to make the tail," Nancy explained.

"How many blocks altogether?" I asked.

"Five," Nancy replied.

"For the first stage, you just described what it would look like and how many blocks you would need to build it," I explained. "What about the third stage? Can you describe it and tell how many blocks would be needed to build it?"

"Oh, I'm starting to get it," Nancy said. "The third stage would have four blocks for the body and three blocks for the tail. Four and three would be seven, so you would need seven blocks. OK, I know what to do now for the hundredth stage."

After talking with Nancy I circulated through the class, noting differences in the students' papers. Some students replicated a chart like the one written on the board, while others just wrote about how they reasoned. (See Figures 6–1 through 6–3.) When they were finished, I led a class discussion about what they found out about the hundredth-stage iguana.

FIGURE 6–1   Tomas described the specific block shapes needed to build a Stage 100 iguana, as well as the total number of blocks.

It will have 1 Square head, 1 Hexagon for a body, 2 triangle feet and 100 Rhombuses for a tail

total blocks 104

FIGURE 6-2 Nina's chart was modeled after the one on the board.

Iguanas   **101**

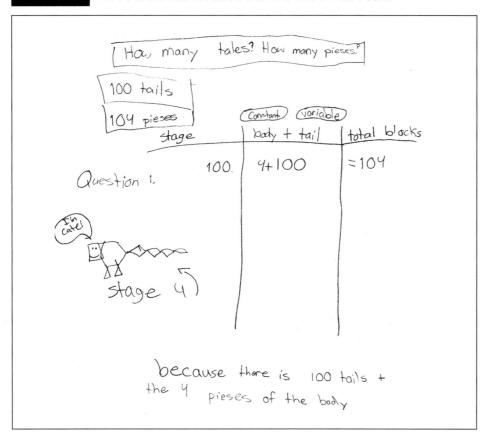

FIGURE 6-3 Jess included a note to the pattern block maker.

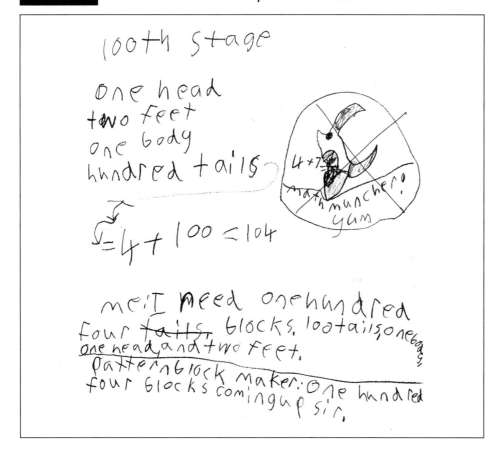

"At first I thought one hundred might be hard," Wanda began. "But after I thought for a minute, it came to me! The number of blocks in the tail is the same as the stage number, and then add four. One hundred plus four is one hundred four."

"That's what I think too," Brad agreed.

"How many thought the way Wanda and Brad did?" I asked. Most students raised a hand.

"Mine is mostly like Wanda's, but just a little different," Turner said. "I thought of the body parts in pieces, like one head and two feet, like that. It's still four blocks for the body."

"That's what I did, too," Jess said. No one had anything else to add.

Generalizing the Pattern   "I now have another question for you to answer on your papers. How would you figure out the number of blocks needed for any stage?" I asked.

"I don't think I get it," Karena said. No one else had an idea, either.

"Let me see if I can help you understand what I'm asking," I said. I thought giving the students several stage numbers and asking them to figure the total blocks needed for each might help them think about what to do for any stage number.

"What about Stage Twenty-Five—how many blocks would we need?" I asked. Hands shot into the air. "Tell me in a whisper voice," I said.

"Twenty-nine," responded the students. I added this information to the chart already on the board.

"How about Stage Fifty? How many blocks would we need?" I continued.

"Fifty-four," the students replied.

"What about Stage Thirty-Seven?" I asked, choosing a less familiar number.

"Forty-one," the students said. I added to the chart the information about these two stages.

"Oh, I noticed what I was doing," Alyssa said. "I was adding four to the stage number."

"I get it now," Tomas replied and started writing on his paper, as did many other students.

"If you're still not certain what to do," I said to the few students still looking puzzled, "study the information on the chart. See if you can figure out what we did over and over again, no matter what the stage number was."

"Oh, you always add the body and the tail," Pete said. "The body stays the same and the tail changes." Pete's explanation seemed to make sense to the remaining students, and they got to work writing their thoughts on their papers.

As I circulated among the students, watching them work, I encouraged them to include examples to support their written explanations. (See Figures 6–4 and 6–5 for two students' writing.)

When I called the students back to attention, I asked, "Who would like to share?" I called on Joanna.

"For whatever number you have, you just add four," Joanna said. "Whatever stage you have is the number in the tail and the four is the body."

I recorded Joanna's idea on the board:

I called on Karena next. "All you do is plus four to the stage number," she said. I recorded her idea on the board under Joanna's, changing *plus* to *add*:

All you do is add four to the stage number. Karena

"If the stage number is one thousand, you'll need one thousand four blocks," Pete said. I recorded Pete's idea:

If the stage number is 1,000, you need 1,004 blocks. Pete

FIGURE 6–4 Brad's explanation and examples.

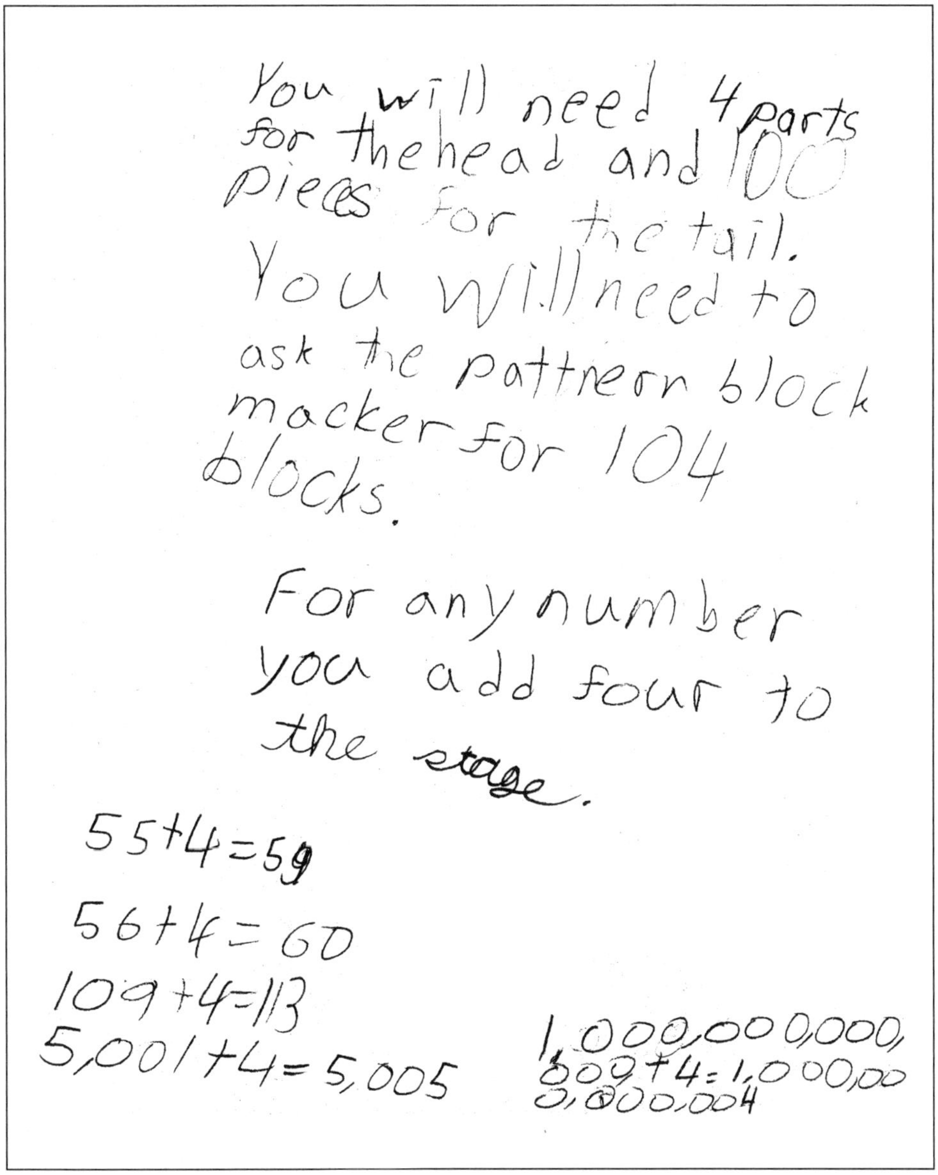

> You will need 4 parts for the head and 100 pieces for the tail. You will need to ask the pattreon block macker for 104 blocks.
>
> For any number you add four to the stage.
>
> 55 + 4 = 59
> 56 + 4 = 60
> 109 + 4 = 113
> 5,001 + 4 = 5,005
>
> 1,000,000,000,000 + 4 = 1,000,000,000,004

FIGURE 6–5   Karena understood how to figure out the total number of blocks for any stage iguana, although she made an error in her last example.

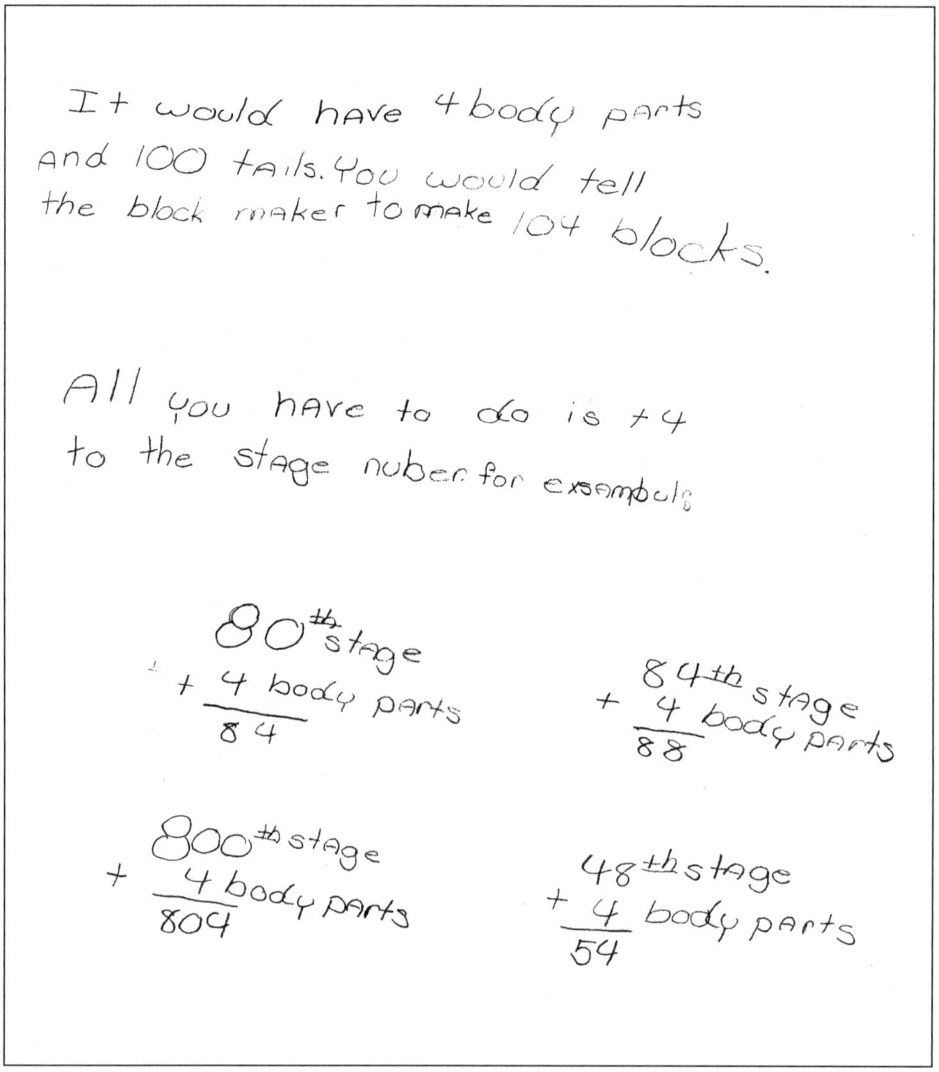

It would have 4 body parts and 100 tails. You would tell the block maker to make 104 blocks.

All you have to do is +4 to the stage nuber for exampule:

$$\begin{array}{r} 80^{th} stage \\ + \;\; 4 \;\; body \;\; parts \\ \hline 84 \end{array}$$

$$\begin{array}{r} 84^{th} stage \\ + \;\; 4 \;\; body \;\; parts \\ \hline 88 \end{array}$$

$$\begin{array}{r} 800^{th} stage \\ + \;\; 4 \;\; body \;\; parts \\ \hline 804 \end{array}$$

$$\begin{array}{r} 48^{th} stage \\ + \;\; 4 \;\; body \;\; parts \\ \hline 54 \end{array}$$

"Aren't they all saying the same thing but with different words?" Nina asked.

"What do the rest of you think?" I asked the class. "Talk it over with your neighbor." After a short time I asked for the students' attention.

"Alyssa and I think it's the same because in all the examples, the body is four and you're adding the four to the tail or stage number," Jasmine said.

"Juan and I think the same thing," Avery shared. "Pete's idea is an example of what Joanna and Karena said."

"If you think all three statements on the board mean the same thing put your thumb up, if you disagree put your thumb down, and if you aren't sure put your thumb sideways," I said. The students indicated their agreement that the three statements were saying essentially the same thing by putting their thumbs up.

"There sure are a lot of ways to say the same thing!" Issac said. With Issac's comment, I ended the class.

Before class, I drew on the board the first three stages of the Iguana Pattern from the day before.

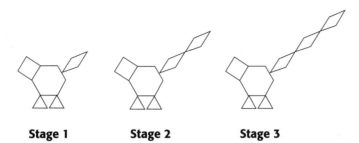

Stage 1   **Stage 2**   **Stage 3**

"What do you remember about this pattern?" I asked.

"Those are iguanas," Jess said.

Joanna added, "The Stage One iguana needed five blocks from the block maker, the Stage Two iguana needed six blocks, and the Stage Three iguana needed seven blocks."

"How did we figure out the number of blocks needed?" I asked.

Wanda answered, "Well, the body was always four blocks and then the stage number was the same as the number of blocks in the tail. Add them up, and that's how many blocks altogether."

"I remember something else," Nina said. "The four was always the same so we called it a consonant . . . or something like that."

"I think you mean a constant," I said.

"Oh yeah." Nina giggled. "A consonant is a kind of letter, like B or D.

"The four represented the part of each stage that stayed the same, and that's why we call it a constant," I repeated. "What part of the iguana did the four represent?"

"The body," Nancy said. "It had a hexagon, a square, and two triangles; that's four blocks."

"The other part of the iguana was the tail," Pete said.

"The number of blocks in the tail was the same as the number of the stage," Brad said.

"Today we are going to look at a different pattern," I explained. "Here's Stage One." On the overhead projector using overhead pattern blocks, I built a new design and labeled it *Stage 1*.

Stage 1

"What's your pattern supposed to be today?" Gary asked.

"Today it's a caterpillar," I explained.

"It's a short caterpillar right now!" Alyssa said.

I then asked, "What do you think Stage Two might look like? Think about it by yourself for a bit. Then I'll build it and you can see how close your thinking was to mine." After a few moments, I built the second stage on the overhead and labeled it *Stage 2*.

Stage 2

"That's what I was thinking!" Jess said.

"Me, too!" several other students chorused.

"How many of you were thinking of Stage Two the way I was?" I asked. Many hands went up.

"Who would like to share an idea that was different from mine?" I asked.

"After the iguanas, I sort of thought it might be like what you did, but I also thought it might be different. Like maybe you might make two neck parts, or something like that," Karena said. "There really wasn't any way to know because we only had Stage One to think about."

"I agree with Karena," I said. "There really wasn't much information and my new caterpillar pattern could have grown several different ways. But now that we know what two stages of the caterpillar look like, what do you think the third stage will look like?"

"This reminds me of yesterday," Nina said.

"Tell me more about what you are thinking, Nina," I encouraged.

"For Stage One of the iguanas, it took five blocks to make it," Nina explained. "That's the same with the caterpillar. Stage One takes five blocks. Then for Stage Two of the iguana pattern, it took six blocks. Look at the caterpillar pattern; it takes six blocks for Stage Two, too. I think it's the same number pattern."

"Let's make a chart and see if what Nina is saying makes sense," I said.

"I think it does," Turner added. "You can think of the caterpillar in two parts, the head and the body. You can put that on the middle column of the chart."

"The head part is the constant," Kurt said.

"Yeah, the head part is the constant because it always stays the same," Turner continued. "The body part changes."

I drew a three-column chart, as I had done the day before, and labeled the columns.

"I know what to put for Stage One," Jasmine said. "Under the Stage column, write one, then in the middle column put four for the head, then a one for the body part. In the last column, put a five because that's how many blocks there are altogether."

Stage #	Head + Body	Total # of Blocks
1	4 + 1	5

"I know what Stage Two is," Stacy said. Stacy had been very quiet for the two days of this lesson, so I was very interested to hear what she had to say. "You put a two in the first column because this is Stage Two. Then you put a four for the number to make the head part of the caterpillar and a two to make the body part. It's like the Iguana Pattern. The stage number and the number in the body are the same. Then add those up, and you get four plus two, which is six." I recorded her numbers on the chart.

Stage #	Head + Body	Total # of Blocks
1	4 + 1	5
2	4 + 2	6

"I think I'm right," Nina said with a grin. "I think this is the same chart as with the iguanas. It's working so far."

"That's really cool!" Kurt said.

"I think it's working, too," Pete commented. "I already figured out Stage Three in my head and it's the same as Stage Three for the Iguana Pattern. The constant part is four, the variable part is three, and the total blocks is seven, just like with the iguanas."

I then asked the students to finish the investigation on their own. I posed questions similar to those I had posed the day before, writing them on the board.

1. *Describe what the caterpillar will look like at Stage 10, and explain how many blocks are needed.*
2. *Repeat Step 1 for Stage 100.*
3. *Repeat Step 1 for any stage.*

"We did this before," Gary complained. "Why do we have to do it again?"

"Yes, you did do this before," I explained. "You did it with a lot of help from me. I think you understand this pretty well now, and by asking you to do this independently, I'll know more clearly what you each understand."

"I guess that means our answers should be really complete," Gary commented.

"It's important that your answers be as complete and well explained as possible so I have the best idea possible about what you understand," I said. This seemed to satisfy Gary and the others, and they took their work very seriously.

Some students wrote explanations about how they figured out the number of blocks needed for the tenth stage, for the hundredth stage, and for any stage. Others showed their thinking numerically, labeling what the numbers represented. Some incorporated a chart in their work. (See Figures 6–6 through 6–8 on the following pages.)

FIGURE 6-6   Joanna did a sketch of the caterpillar and explained how she figured out the number of blocks needed for any stage.

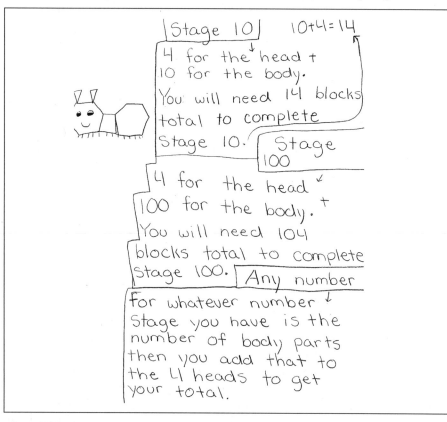

FIGURE 6-7   Turner's paper included explanations and an example.

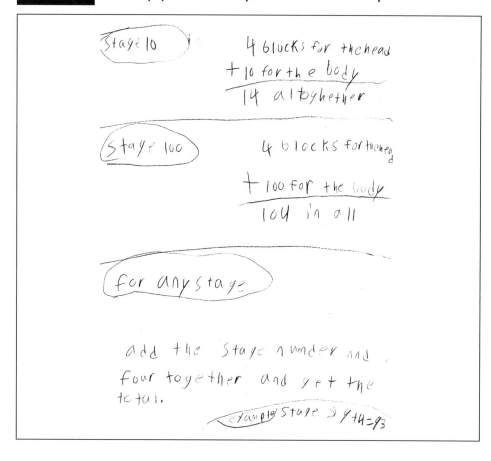

FIGURE 6-8 Tomas's paper included a chart and explanations.

Iguanas   **109**

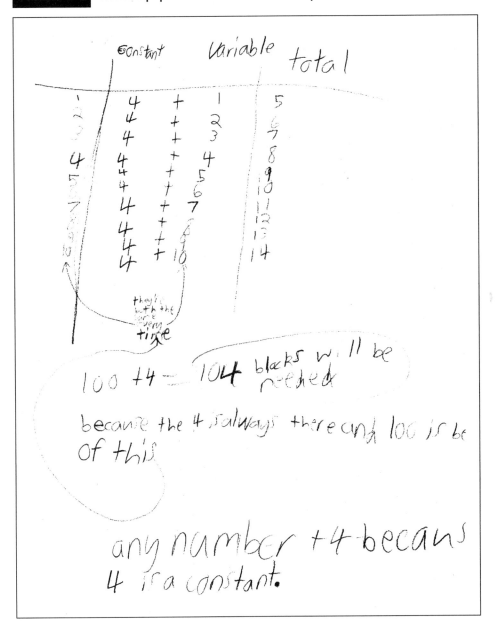

Day 3

"I'm going to ask you to consider a new pattern today," I said. I built the original Iguana Pattern on the overhead as the students watched.

"It's the first pattern we did," Haley said.

"That's correct," I replied. "Watch what I do next." I added a triangle to the head so it looked like a hat, and I added a white parallelogram to the tail so the tail now had two blocks rather than one.

"What's different?" I asked.

"It looks like a rhino," Juan said.

"Why is that?" I asked.

"The triangle you added looks like a rhino horn," Juan explained.

"So one thing that's different is the triangle?" I asked, redirecting to my question about what was different.

"Yep," Juan replied.

"I see something else that's different," Issac said. "You added a white block to the tail." The others nodded. No one had anything else to add.

"This is Stage One of my new pattern," I said as I labeled it *Stage 1* on the overhead. "Think about what Stage Two could look like." After a few moments, hands started to go up. I called on Avery.

"I think it will have another tail," Avery suggested.

"So now Stage Two has two tails?" I asked, not sure what Avery meant.

"No, that's not what I mean," Avery said. "The body will stay the same and one more white block will be added to the tail."

"Oh, I think I understand better now," I responded. "The tail will have three white parallelograms." As I said this, I built Stage Two on the overhead as Avery had suggested.

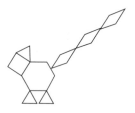

"That's it," Avery confirmed.

"And that's the idea I had, too," I said. Avery grinned, showing his pleasure with himself.

"What's the constant part of the pattern?" I asked.

"The body," Joanna replied.

"Joanna says the body is the constant part," I continued. "If you agree with that put your thumb up, if you disagree put your thumb down, and if you are not certain put your thumb sideways." All the students put their thumbs up, indicating their agreement with Joanna.

"How many blocks are needed to build the body?" I asked.

"I think five or six," Joanna said. "I'm not sure because I don't know about the tail."

"I think the constant is six," Nancy said. "It takes six for the body."

"When you say it takes six for the body, are you including the first block for the tail?" Joanna asked Nancy. "That's what I wasn't sure about."

"Yeah, the first block would be part of the constant," Nancy confirmed. "If you do that, then the tail number will be the same as the stage number."

"I disagree," Karena said. "The variable part doesn't always have to be the same as the stage number. I think the constant could be five, because it takes five blocks to make the body and then the variable is the number of blocks in the tail."

"This is very interesting," I said. "Nancy's thinking makes sense to me, and so does Karena's."

"Does the stage number have to be the same as the variable?" Conner asked.

"No, it doesn't," I said. "In the first Iguana Pattern it was, but it doesn't have to be." The students started talking among themselves about this latest information and about Nancy's and Karena's ideas. I let this discussion continue a few moments before asking for their attention once again.

"Maybe it would help us think more about this if we built Stage Three," I suggested. "Talk with your partner about what Stage Three would look like. First one of you shares while the other listens without interrupting, then after thirty seconds I'll tell you to switch and the first listener will get to share while the first talker gets to listen." The room broke out in animated discussion. After thirty seconds I asked the students to switch roles. After another thirty seconds I asked for the students' attention.

"Who would like to share?" I asked. All hands were up. I called on Nina.

"Stage Three is where the body stays the same, but we have to add one more tail block," Nina explained.

"If I add one more white parallelogram to the tail, how many tail blocks will that be?" I asked.

"Four," Nina said. "Stage Three has four white parallelograms for the tail."

"How many blocks are needed to make Stage Three?" I asked.

"Nine," the students replied.

There wasn't room on the overhead projector, so I said, "Let me draw all three stages on the board."

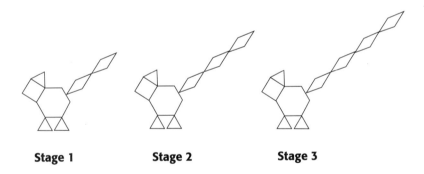

Stage 1   **Stage 2**   **Stage 3**

"Based on what we know so far, can you predict the number of blocks needed for Stage Ten?" I asked. "Talk it over with your table group." As I listened to the students' conversations, I expected to hear them grappling with the issue of whether the constant was five or six. This is exactly what happened. The constant could be either, depending on how one looked at the pattern. Karena's way could be represented with the equation $y = 5 + (x + 1)$, where y is the total number of blocks and x is the stage number. Nancy's thinking could be represented by $y = 6 + x$. These equations are equivalent. After a few moments, I asked for the students' attention.

"How many blocks do we need for Stage Ten?" I asked.

"I think it depends on the constant," Bianca said. "We weren't sure."

"That was our problem, too," Jess said.

"Let's make a chart, as we have done before, to help us figure out what we know," I suggested. I drew a three-column chart on the board, labeled the columns, and titled the chart *Nancy's Way*.

Nancy's Way

Stage #	Body + Tail	Total # of Blocks

"If we use Nancy's way of thinking, that the constant is equal to six, what shall I write in the other columns for Stage One?" I asked, writing a *1* in the first column.

"The total is seven," Karena responded. I recorded the information on the chart.

"And what about the middle column?" I asked.

"It's six for the body and one for the tail," Pete said. I added this information to the chart and added a *2* to the first column.

"What about Stage Two?" I asked.

"You need eight blocks for Stage Two," Conner said. "The constant is six and then two more blocks for the tail." I wrote the information Conner gave on the chart and added a *3* to the first column.

"What about Stage Three?" I continued.

"The constant is six and you need three for the tail," Alyssa explained. "Six and three is nine. You need nine blocks." I added this to the chart.

Nancy's Way

Stage #	Body + Tail	Total # of Blocks
1	6 + 1	7
2	6 + 2	8
3	6 + 3	9

"We now have information about Nancy's way," I said. "Let's gather the same information about Karena's way on another chart and see what we notice." I drew another chart on the board next to the first one and labeled it *Karena's Way*.

"Karena suggested the constant could be five rather than six," I began. "If the constant is five, what part of the pattern does that represent?"

"I think it's just the body with no tail blocks," Gary said.

"Do you agree with that, Karena?" I asked. She nodded her head.

"So if the body part made of five blocks is the constant, what varies according to Karena's way?" I asked.

"The whole tail grows, the body doesn't," Jasmine said. Again, Karena nodded her agreement.

"For Stage One, how many blocks would I need altogether?" I asked.

"Seven," the class responded. I wrote this information on the chart.

"I know what goes in the middle column," Alyssa said. "The constant is five and the variable is two, and that's what goes in the middle column."

"What about Stage Two?" I asked.

"You need five for the body and three for the tail," Turner said. "I just noticed something. The variable part is one more than the stage number. For Stage One it was two, and for Stage Two it was three."

Karena's Way

Stage #	Body + Tail	Total # of Blocks
1	5 + 2	7
2	5 + 3	8

"Hey, that's cool," Juan said.

"In Nancy's way, the stage number is the same as the variable part," Jess noticed.

"And the constant part is one more in Nancy's way than in Karena's way," Haley said.

"Oh, my gosh!" Nina blurted out in surprise. "The Total column on both charts is the same! You need seven blocks for Stage One on both charts!"

"And you need eight blocks for Stage Two on both charts!" Joanna said.

"I bet Stage Three for Karena's way will have a total of nine," Nina continued. "The constant is five and the tail is one more than the stage, so that's four. Five and four is nine. It is the same!" I added this information. The class was surprised and silenced by this revelation.

Karena's Way

Stage #	Body + Tail	Total # of Blocks
1	5 + 2	7
2	5 + 3	8
3	5 + 4	9

"Do you think it would still be the same total for Stage Ten?" I asked. Some shook their heads "no," some "yes," and a few still looked totally perplexed. "With your table group, see if you can figure this out." The room erupted into excited conversation. I had to remind a couple of groups to talk one at a time and give everyone a chance to speak.

After a few minutes of table group discussion, I settled the class again and asked for volunteers to share according to Karena's way of thinking. Hands flew into the air. I called on Avery.

"Our table thinks that if it's Karena's way, then the part that changes is eleven because that's one more than the stage number, which is ten. Add the eleven to the constant of five, and that makes a total of sixteen blocks."

"Me and Conner thought of it differently," Jess said. "There are seven blocks in Stage One, and Stage Ten is nine more stages, and one block gets added for each stage. We just added nine and seven and got sixteen."

"I noticed something about this," Karena said. "One way the stage number matches the variable part and the other way it doesn't. In Nancy's way, the stage number and the variable number are the same. In my way, the variable number is one more than the stage number."

"Someone already said that," Gary piped up.

"That's true," I said, "but sometimes we aren't quite ready to hear an idea or it doesn't quite make sense yet. Then, when we get more information, we have the opportunity to discover for ourselves what someone else discovered."

"I think the way where the stage matches the variable is right," Kasey said, moving the conversation in another direction. "In the other two patterns the stage number and variable number were the same."

"I think it depends on how you look at it," Karena said.

"What does that mean?" I asked.

"It means there is more than one way to look at it," Brad said. "Nancy's way includes part of the tail as the constant and Karena's way doesn't. Either way, they need the same number of blocks for the total."

"I think Karena's way is the right way," Alyssa said. "The body is constant. It's not growing. Only the tail is growing, so I think Karena's way shows the tail growing."

The class became quiet. "Which way is right?" Turner asked me.

I replied, "Both ways of thinking are fine. They've both produced the same answer for thinking about the number of blocks in different stages, so both work. It's just easier for some people to see the pattern Karena's way and for others to see it Nancy's way."

We had run out of time in the class, and this also seemed like a good stopping point in the investigation. I planned to give students other patterns to explore, with both pattern blocks and other materials, and I knew that they would encounter the same ideas in other investigations.

Extensions

Ask students to create their own patterns and explore how they might grow. For a first experience doing so, you might give the students specific guidelines that mirror the explorations they did with the first Iguana Pattern and the Caterpillar Pattern. For example:

> Create your own pattern using pattern blocks so that the constant part of the pattern is 4 and the variable part of the pattern and the stage number are the same. Record the first three stages.

Figures 6–9 through 6–13 show patterns that students created.

FIGURE 6-9 Joanna pointed out the constant and variable parts of her cat pattern.

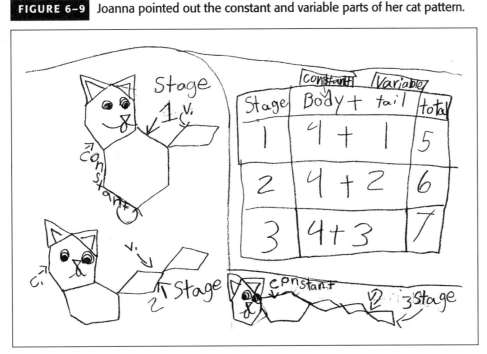

FIGURE 6-10 Allison drew and charted the first three stages of her butterfly pattern.

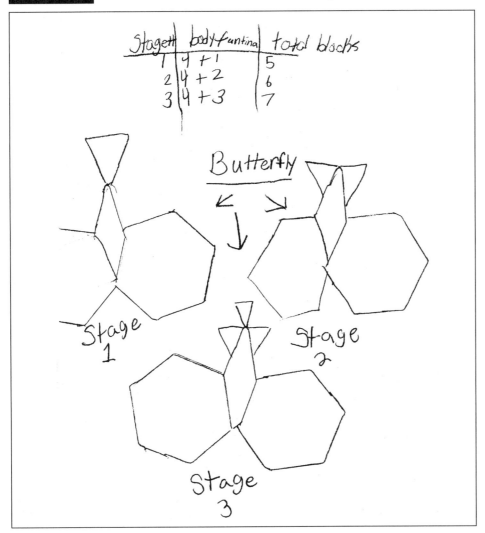

FIGURE 6–11   Turner drew and recorded the first five stages of his wasp pattern.

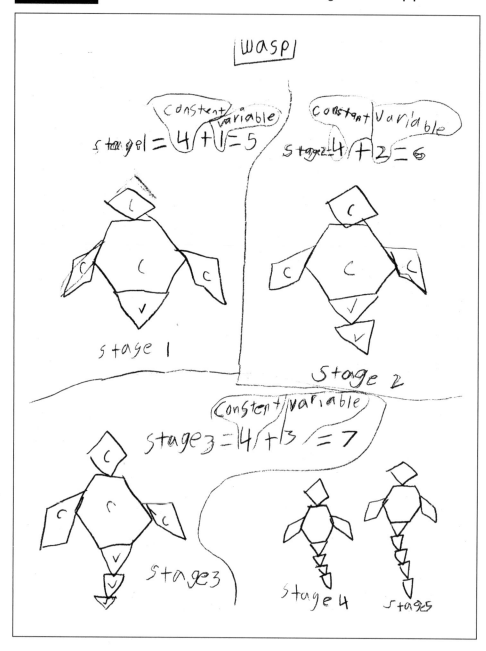

FIGURE 6–12 Karena labeled her pattern "Birds" and made a chart showing the total blocks in the upper left of her paper.

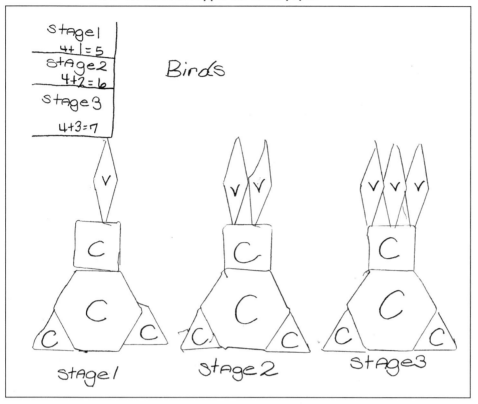

Stage1
4+1=5
Stage2
4+2=6
Stage3
4+3=7

Birds

stage1   stage2   stage3

FIGURE 6–13 Jasmine clearly showed the constant and variable parts of her pattern.

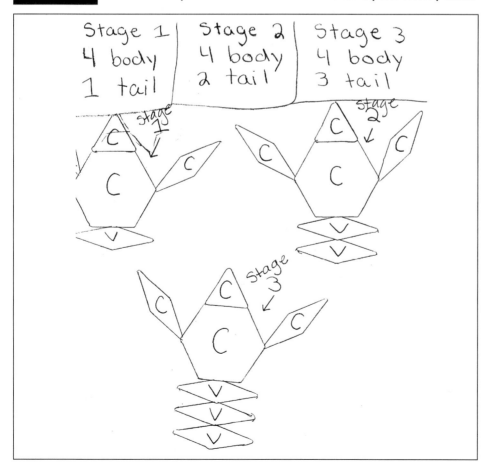

Stage 1	Stage 2	Stage 3
4 body	4 body	4 body
1 tail	2 tail	3 tail

## CHAPTER 7

Letter Patterns

Building with Color Tiles

OVERVIEW

In this lesson, students use the letters of the alphabet as the context for exploring growth patterns. After seeing how a letter T constructed from square tiles can grow into larger and larger Ts, students figure out and describe the pattern for how the T is growing. They count and record on a T-chart the number of tiles in each T, describe the rule for growth in words, and also represent the rule as an equation. The students then explore how other letters can grow, again recording each growth pattern on a T-chart and writing the rule with words and as an equation.

BACKGROUND

By building on students' familiarity with the letters of the alphabet and utilizing square tiles to make the exploration concrete, this lesson is effective for helping children investigate patterns that grow. The lesson is suitable as a first experience with growth patterns, or it can follow other experiences (see Chapters 1 and 6).

The lesson begins by presenting to students a "newborn" letter T, formed with five square tiles, and then showing them what the T looks like when it's one year old and two years old. Students predict and build what the T will look like when it's three and four years old. They count the tiles for each T, record the information on a T-chart, and describe how the T is growing. Then they figure out what a ten-year-old T looks like and the number of tiles it takes to construct it, which requires students to analyze the pattern of growth.

When the children record on the T-chart, the left column is labeled Number of Years and the right column is labeled Number of Tiles. Each number of years is paired with exactly one number of tiles; that is, a one-year-old T in this pattern has six tiles, a two-year-old T has seven tiles, and so on. The relationship between each pair of numbers is the same and is called, in mathematics, a *function*. The lesson doesn't, however, use the term *function*, but rather focuses on giving the children an introductory experience with this important mathematical idea.

Asking children to figure out what a ten-year-old T looks like and how many tiles are needed to build it requires them to make a prediction that's beyond the information they have at hand. Although the students will agree on the number of tiles in a ten-year-old T, it's typical for them to have different interpretations of how the Ts grow. Some focus on the numbers in the T-chart and notice that the number of tiles is always five more than the number of years. Some focus on the T-chart but pay attention to the pattern of the numbers going down in each column and use that information to predict for the ten-year-old and other "older" Ts. Some look at the Ts built with tiles and describe how the ten-year-old T will look, identifying the growth pattern geometrically. However, the numbers on the T-chart will be the same no matter how the children describe the pattern of growth.

Along with recording on a T-chart and describing the pattern in words, students are introduced to representing the relationship as an equation, using variables to represent the numbers of years and tiles. The samples of student work shown in this chapter draw from the efforts of younger students who were struggling to make sense of equations as well as from those of older students who were more comfortable with equations. When teaching this lesson, follow the lead of your students to decide how far and how fast to push the class. Keep in mind that this is an introductory experience and the goal is to lay a foundation of experience on which students' algebraic understanding can build.

VOCABULARY

constant, equation, pattern, prediction, T-chart, variable

MATERIALS

- color tiles, about 45–50 per pair of students
- centimeter graph paper, several sheets per student (see Blackline Masters)

TIME

- four class periods

Day 1

The Lesson

I began the lesson by writing *pattern* on the board and asking, "What do you know about patterns?"

Carlos answered, "It's something that goes on forever, like one, two, one, two, one, two."

Nadia added, "It doesn't have to be numbers."

Sean said, "You can go in either direction on a pattern."

Aaron raised his hand, but then when I called on him, he forgot what he was going to say.

Evie said, "You know what comes next because the pattern tells you." No one else had an idea to share.

I then wrote *prediction* on the board and asked, "Do you know what a prediction is? Can you think of times when you predict that something will happen?"

"It's when you think something might happen," Greg said.

"You don't know for sure," Eugenia added.

"They do it with the weather," Katie said.

I then said, "In our math lesson today, you'll have the chance to look for patterns that can help you make predictions. And we're going to do this by exploring letters in the alphabet." On the board, I drew the letter T formed with five squares:

"What letter is this?" I asked.

"T," they answered in unison. Next to the T, I drew another letter T, formed with six squares:

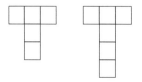

"It's a T, too," Sean said.

I said, "Yes, they're both Ts. The first one is a baby T, a T that's just been born. The second T is one year old. Next I'm going to draw a T that's two years old." I drew a third T on the board. Also, I wrote *1* below the one-year-old T and *2* below the two-year-old T.

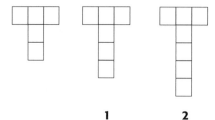

         1   **2**

"Each year, the T grows a little bit, and it grows each year in the same pattern," I said.

"It's getting longer," Lydia said.

"It's getting taller," Carla said.

I instructed the class, "In just a moment, you'll talk with your neighbor about how you see the T growing. While you're talking, I'll distribute color tiles. With your partner, use them to build Ts just like the ones I drew on the board. First build the newborn T, then a one-year-old T, and then a two-year-old T. Build them one next to the other." I pointed to the Ts on the board as I gave these instructions and then continued, "Next build what you think the T will look like when it's three years old. When you're done, you should have a row of four Ts built on your desk—a newborn T, a one-year-old T, a two-year-old T, and a three-year-old T."

As the children began to talk, I distributed a plastic bag of color tiles to each pair. Then I circulated, reminding some children to build the Ts in a row, reminding others to work with their neighbor and build just one set of Ts for the two of them. After a few minutes, all of the children had built the Ts as I had asked. I called the class to attention.

"Who would like to describe a three-year-old T so I can draw it on the board?" I asked. Many hands went up. I called on Miguel.

"You make three across the top, like the other ones. And then you put five more down," Miguel said.

I repeated Miguel's instructions as I drew on the board. "Let's see, we need three across," I said, and drew three squares in a row. "Then I need five squares down." I drew five squares underneath the middle one and turned to the class.

"That's right," Lydia said. Others agreed.

"That's exactly how I thought a three-year-old T would look," I confirmed, and I wrote *3* underneath my drawing.

"Can you build a four-year-old T?" I asked. The children nodded and reached for the tiles. In a moment, hands were raised to tell me how to draw it. I called on Eugenia, who gave clear directions. I drew the four-year-old T and labeled it. Now I had five Ts drawn in a row.

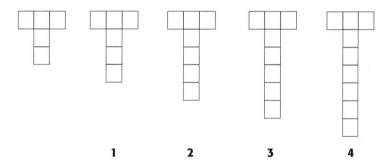

"Who can describe the pattern of how the Ts grow each year?" I asked. Only a few hands went up. Rather than call on a child to respond, I asked them to talk about my question with their neighbors. This gave more children the chance to share their thinking. "Talk about your ideas and then we'll discuss the pattern as a class."

After a few moments, I interrupted the children and asked who wanted to share.

"They get taller," Aaron said.

"Each time they get one more tile," Evie said.

No one volunteered to offer another idea and I didn't push for more specifics at this time. In a moment I planned to ask them to predict the number of tiles needed for a ten-year-old T, which I knew would push them to think more about the pattern. First, however, to establish the age of the first T, I said to the class, "Each of the Ts except for the newborn T has a number under it that tells how many years old it is. What number shall we use for the newborn's age?" Hands went up and I called on Katie.

"It should be zero," she said. Others agreed. I wrote a *0* underneath the first T.

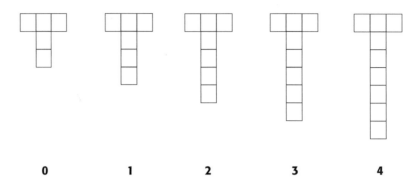

My next goal was to interpret the information about the growing Ts numerically. "How many tiles did it take to build a newborn T?" I asked. After most of the hands went up, I said, "Let's say the number together in a whisper voice." I heard almost all "fives" and a lone "six." I counted the tiles aloud to verify that there were five.

"And how many tiles did it take to build a one-year-old T?" I asked. Again the children responded together and I counted to verify that there were six. I continued in the same way for the other Ts on the board.

I then drew a T-chart on the board and labeled the columns *# of Years* and *# of Tiles*. This class hadn't seen T-charts before, but I've learned from past experience that children don't need much of an introduction to this way of recording information. Using a T-chart in the context of an activity is sufficient for introducing it.

# of Years	# of Tiles

"A chart like this is called a *T-chart* because it looks like a tall T. I'll record the information we know about our Ts on this chart. How many years old is the newborn T?" The children responded and I wrote *0* in the left column. "And how many tiles are there in the newborn T?" I asked. The children answered and I wrote *5* in the right column. I continued in this way until I had recorded the information for each of the Ts on the board.

# of Years	# of Tiles
0	5
1	6
2	7
3	8
4	9

"What patterns do you notice on the chart?" I asked. The children had several ideas.

"The numbers go in order," Carlos said.

"They go down in order, but they start with five on the right side," Lydia added.

"They're five apart," Nadia said.

I wasn't clear about what Nadia was describing and said to her, "I'm not sure what you mean. Can you tell me more about your idea?"

Nadia explained, "From zero to five is five, from one to six is five, from two to seven is five, like that."

"Now I see the pattern that you saw," I said. I paraphrased: "Whatever the age is, if you add the number five, you get the number of tiles." I pointed to several examples on the T-chart as I said this. Nadia agreed.

No other students had comments to make. I then focused the class on making a prediction. "Suppose I skipped down in the T-chart to a ten-year-old T," I said. I drew three dots vertically underneath the 4 and then wrote *10*. I left enough room between the 4 and the 10 so that later I could write in 5, 6, 7, 8, and 9. I explained to the class, "These dots mean that I've skipped some numbers."

# of Years	# of Tiles
0	5
1	6
2	7
3	8
4	9
.	
.	
.	
10	

"Can you predict the number of tiles it would take to build a ten-year-old T?" I asked. "Talk with your neighbor and raise your hand when you're ready to report." Conversation became animated. I was curious to hear how the children would approach thinking about this problem. I interrupted them when almost half had raised a hand. I called on Eugenia first.

"I think it would take fifteen tiles," she said.

"How did you figure that out?" I said.

Eugenia answered, "Well, like Nadia said, the numbers are five apart. You add five to the left number and get the right number. Ten plus five is fifteen, so it has to be fifteen."

"And what does the left number tell us?" I asked.

"It's how old the T is," Eugenia said.

"And what does the right number tell us?" I asked.

"The tiles," Eugenia answered.

"So you're saying that the number of tiles is equal to the number of years plus five?" I paraphrased. Eugenia nodded.

I then said, "I'm going to write Eugenia's explanation on the board. Watch as I do so. Eugenia, when I'm done, I want you to check that I've written what you were thinking." I wrote to model for the children how to write about a pattern, something I planned to have them do for other letters. For this first example, I didn't write a general rule, but focused on Eugenia's thinking about a ten-year-old T. I wrote on the board:

The number of tiles in a 10-year-old T is equal to 10 (the number of years) plus 5.

Carl had the same answer but a different idea. "I got fifteen, but I added twelve plus three."

I wasn't clear about what Carl was seeing, but I've learned to expect children to see patterns in ways that I hadn't predicted. I think it's important in a discussion not to let my preconceived notions of what I'm expecting or hoping to hear interfere with my goal of encouraging students to think in their own ways. I also think it's important to understand how students are thinking and to push them to clarify their ideas. I responded to Carl, "I agree that twelve plus three is fifteen, but I'm not sure why you added those two numbers."

Carl explained, "They all have three at the top. Then I saw that the zero T has two going down and the one-year-old T has three going down. It's always two more. So the ten-year-old has to have twelve going down. And twelve and the three more makes fifteen."

"Tell me a little more about what you mean by 'it's always two more going down,'" I said.

Carl said, "See, when it's one, there are three going down. And three is one plus two. It works like that for all of them, I think."

"Oh, I see," I said. "For the ten-year-old T, you took the three at the top, added ten for how old it is, and then added two more." Carl nodded. I wrote on the board:

To get the number of tiles in a 10-year-old T, you take the 3 at the top, add 10 for the number of years, and then add 2 more.

Lydia then explained her idea. "I counted down and followed the pattern. Five goes with ten, six goes with eleven, and I kept going and got ten goes with fifteen." I had expected a child to report this approach. It's typical for children to extend a T-chart pattern so that they can predict a number in a column from figuring out what the number before it is. While this method would be inconvenient if I had asked them to figure out the number of tiles in a hundred-year-old T (which I planned to do in a moment), it was a manageable strategy for figuring out the number of tiles in a ten-year-old T. I wrote on the board:

Fill in the numbers on the T-chart until you can see the number of tiles in a 10-year-old T.

"Let's fill in the T-chart and see how this works," I said.
"OK," Lydia said, and told me what numbers to write.

# of Years	# of Tiles
0	5
1	6
2	7
3	8
4	9
5	10
6	11
7	12
8	13
9	14
10	15

"Does anyone have a different way to describe the pattern?" I asked. No one did.

I then reviewed what Eugenia, Carl, and Lydia had reported to help the children relate the numerical representations on the T-chart with the Ts they were building with the tiles. I wanted to help them connect the arithmetic figuring they were doing with the geometric representations.

I returned to Eugenia's idea. "Eugenia added five to the age of ten to get fifteen. I know that five is the number of tiles in the baby T." I stopped and shaded in the five tiles in the newborn T on the board. "And these same five tiles appear in each of the other Ts," I continued, and shaded the newborn T's tiles in each of the others.

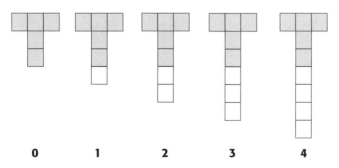

| 0 | 1 | 2 | 3 | 4 |

I added, "There's the same newborn T in every T, and this is the constant part of the pattern, the part that stays the same." I stopped to write *constant* on the board.

I continued, "What changes is how much to add to the five tiles of the newborn T for each older T. That amount is the variable part of the pattern." I wrote *variable* on the board.

"How many extra tiles are on the one-year-old T?" I asked. The children saw that there was one unshaded tile. "And how many extra tiles are on the two-year-old T?" I asked.

"Two," they replied, and I continued for the other Ts.

"Who thinks you know how many tiles Eugenia would predict are in a T that's twenty-five years old, or even one hundred years old?" I asked. As I wrote these numbers in the left-hand column of the T-chart, using dots as I had done before to indicate that I had omitted some numbers, I added, "Talk with your neighbor about this and see if you can use Eugenia's idea to figure the answers."

In a moment, I called the class to order. Most hands were raised, so I said, "Let's say the answers together in a whisper voice. How many tiles would there be in a twenty-five-year-old T?"

"Thirty," they answered.

"And in a hundred-year-old T?"

"One hundred five," they answered. I entered these numbers in the T-chart and looked to Eugenia for confirmation. She grinned and nodded.

# of Years	# of Tiles
0	5
1	6
2	7
3	8
4	9
5	10
6	11
7	12
8	13
9	14
10	15
.	.
.	.
.	.
25	30
.	.
.	.
.	.
100	105

"How did you get these answers?" I asked.

"I just added five," she said.

"Who can describe what a twenty-five-year-old or a hundred-year-old T will look like?" I asked.

"It will be tall, really tall," Miguel said.

"And very skinny," Katie added.

"But Carl saw the pattern differently," I said. "What he saw was that each T has the same three tiles on the top." I erased the shading from all but the top three tiles in each T. "So for Carl's idea, the constant is three tiles."

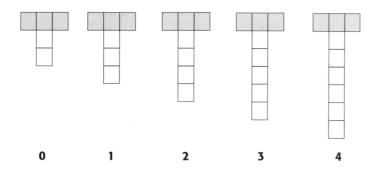

<table>
<tr><td>0</td><td>1</td><td>2</td><td>3</td><td>4</td></tr>
</table>

I continued, "Then Carl noticed that there were two extras for the zero-year-old T, three extras for the one-year-old T, and four extras for the two-year-old T." I pointed to the Ts as I explained. "So Carl saw that the number of tiles going down was always the age of the T plus two more. This was the variable part on Carl's pattern."

I then said, "I wonder if Carl would get the same answers for the twenty-five-year-old and hundred-year-old Ts."

"I know I do," Carl said. "I worked it out."

"Let's all think about this," I said. "Talk with your neighbor and see if you agree that Carl's answers will be the same as Eugenia's." In a moment, I called the class to attention. A few were confused about the part of adding two more than the age, but Carl did a nice job of explaining how he arrived at 30 and 105 using his method.

And for Lydia's idea, I pointed to the T-chart and said, "Lydia followed the pattern in the numbers and filled in the T-chart. Then she could see that a ten-year-old T needs fifteen tiles." While we had been discussing Eugenia's and Carl's ideas, Lydia had extended the chart on paper to 25. She showed the class her work.

"Do I have to go to one hundred?" she asked me.

"If you can use Eugenia's or Carl's ideas to figure out the number of tiles for a hundred-year-old T, then you don't have to write all of those numbers. Your method will work, but it seems that Eugenia's and Carl's ideas are a little easier to use for really old Ts."

"A *lot* easier," Lydia said.

It was the end of the class, so I asked the children to return the tiles to their plastic sandwich bags and be sure that the bags were zipped up securely.

Day 2: The I Pattern

To begin class, I told the children that we would explore the pattern of another letter. "We'll see what happens with a capital I," I said. On the board I drew a newborn I, a one-year-old I, and a two-year-old I.

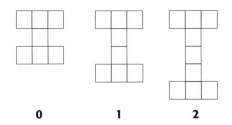

0   1   2

I then instructed, "With your neighbor, build these I's, and then build the three-year-old and four-year-old I's." The children got started easily, more familiar now with my instructions. They were animated and engaged. I interrupted them when I saw that most had completed the task. I asked for volunteers to tell me how to build the three- and four-year-old I's, and I drew them on the board. I then drew a T-chart to the right of the drawings and, with the children's help, labeled the columns and recorded the numerical information. Then I asked the students to figure out how many tiles we needed for a ten-year-old I.

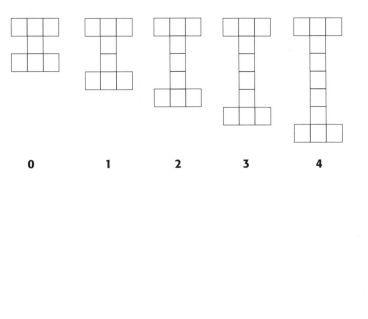

0   1   2   3   4

# of Years	# of Tiles
0	7
1	8
2	9
3	10
4	11
.	
.	
.	
.	
.	
10	

After giving the class time to work on this problem, I interrupted the students and asked who had ideas to share. I first called on Lydia, curious to see if she would use the same method she had used the day before, extending the T-chart. She didn't, but instead said, "It's seventeen. The top and bottom is the same for each, and that's six. Then you have the middle part, and that's always one more." I shaded in the top and bottom of each of the I's I had drawn:

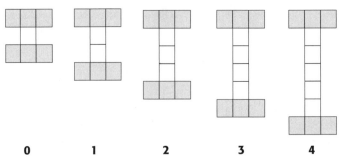

0   1   2   3   4

I explained Lydia's thinking, using the terms *constant* and *variable*, "I understand how you see the six as the constant. But what do you mean that the middle is always one more?"

Lydia answered, "See, for the one-year-old, the middle is two. That's one more."

"Oh, I see," I said. "The middle is one more than the letter's age. So how did you get seventeen?"

"I added six plus ten plus one more. Ten and six is sixteen, and one more is seventeen," Lydia explained. I wrote on the board, this time writing Lydia's idea as a generalization, not as a method that would work only for a ten-year-old I:

The top and the bottom six tiles are the same for each, so six is the constant. The middle part is the variable part and it is always one more than its age.

"Did I describe your idea?" I asked Lydia. She nodded.

Kailani had another way to look at the pattern. "The baby I is seven," she said. "Then you just add on the age."

"Did you get seventeen, too?" I asked.

"Yes," Kailani said. "You just go ten and seven is seventeen."

I paraphrased: "So for your idea, the constant part of the pattern is seven and the variable part of the pattern is the letter's age." Kailani agreed.

On the board, I shaded in the entire newborn I. Then I turned to Kailani and asked, pointing to the two tiles in the middle of the one-year-old I, "Which of these tiles was in the baby I and which is the one you added?"

"I added the top one," Kailani responded.

"So the tile at the bottom is from the baby tile?" I asked. Kailani nodded and I shaded in the bottom tile in the middle of each I.

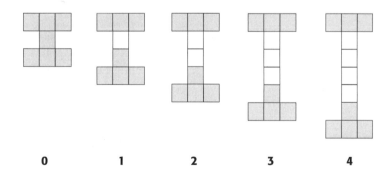

I recorded Kailani's idea:

The baby I has seven tiles, and that is the constant part of the pattern. For any other I, you add seven plus the age. The age is the variable part of the pattern.

No other student had a different idea for describing the pattern. I said to the class, "Let's use the method Lydia suggested yesterday of extending the T-chart to check that a ten-year-old I would have seventeen tiles." The children called out the numbers as I recorded, and cheered when the T-chart revealed that seventeen tiles were needed for a ten-year-old I. I then added *25* and *100* to the chart.

# of Years	# of Tiles
0	7
1	8
2	9
3	10
4	11
5	12
6	13
7	14
8	15
9	16
10	17
.	
.	
.	
25	
.	
.	
.	
100	

I said, "Talk at your tables about how many tiles you need for a twenty-five-year old I and a hundred-year-old I. Also talk about what you think these older I's will look like." After a few moments, I called for the students' attention and had them say the answers together as a class.

Sean described the letter I's as "very, very, very long."

An Independent Investigation   I then asked the children to investigate the letter U on their own. "You can work with your neighbor," I said, "but you each should record on your own paper." I drew on the board a newborn U, a one-year-old U, and a two-year-old U.

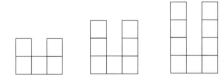

0   1   2

As I explained to the students what they were to do, I wrote the instructions on the board:

1. *Build U's up to at least four years.*
2. *Draw the U's on squared paper.*
3. *Make a T-chart.*
4. *Figure out the number of tiles for a 10-year-old U.*
5. *Write about the pattern.*
6. *If you can, figure out how many tiles for a 25-year-old U and a 100-year-old U.*

"Should we color them in?" Lydia wanted to know.

I answered, "That would be a good idea, but wait until after you draw all of them with pencil. Then you can color them to show how you're thinking about the pattern. Make the constant part, which stays the same, one color and use another color for the variable part, which changes."

All of the children were able to complete the first three steps of the instructions, building the U's, drawing them on centimeter graph paper, and recording on a T-chart. Some struggled to figure out the number of tiles for a ten-year-old U, but all recorded the correct answer. When children work together freely, as they were doing here, the correct answer often becomes public knowledge. Because of this, it's important to check with children to be sure that they know why their answer makes sense. For this problem, some of the children understood and others didn't. Their written explanations about the pattern showed differences in their understanding.

Carla, for example, wrote: *What did not change was the little baby u. What changed was it growed and growed it became a upercase U.*

Connor wrote: *The baby one didn't change. You just ceped* [kept] *add one, two, three and for, five, six. It got bigger and bigger it trind* [turned] *in to a big U.*

After talking with these two children, I knew that they understood only how to build the U's and record on the T-chart. Neither understood how to predict for older U's.

Miguel had carefully drawn the U's and colored in the newborn U blue and the rest orange on each of them. He wrote: *It's much eseyer if you use the same color for the base* [constant] *as the zero-year-old.* [He drew three U's to illustrate how he had colored.] *It grows upward slowly from a baby to a really old geezer.* When I talked with Miguel, even though he hadn't written much, he was able to predict the number of tiles for any age U I gave him. When assessing children, I find it's important not only to read their explanations but, whenever possible, to talk with them individually.

Nadia wrote a longer explanation in which she started with some specific examples and then tried to generalize. (See Figure 7–1 on page 132.) She wrote: *In the pattern I discoverd that it counts by twos and it allwase ends up in a odd number. In the # of years I found that you would add 10 + 10 = 20 + 5 = 25 then I would do 25 + 25 + 5 = 55 then I would go to the hundereds and 100 + 100 = 200 + 5 = 205. The 5 allwase stays the same it is the constant but the other numbers change. it is not allwase 25 It is other numbers like 200 and 30.* (**Note:** Nadia's mathematical notation—10 + 10 = 20 + 5 = 25—isn't correct. It incorrectly states that

FIGURE 7–1 Nadia used specific examples, then tried to generalize about the growth pattern of the letter U.

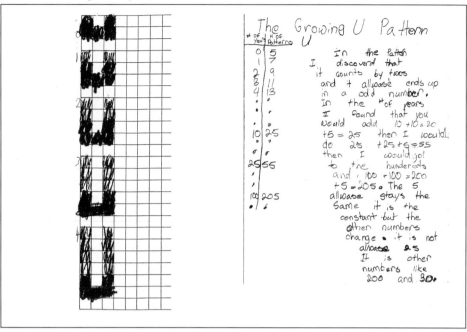

10 + 10 = 20 + 5, which isn't true. This is a common error, but I chose not to deal with it at this time.)

Evie wrote: *When I started to make my U chart, I figuard out that the new born U is always in the next bigger U. But I also found out that every time the U grows one year older it keeps adding on two. No matter what the number is it always adds on two.*

Lydia was able to generalize. (See Figure 7–2.) She wrote: *If I am figuring out a ten year old U, I know that there will be ten in each part going up. Ten plus ten is twenty. Three plus two is five and five plus twenty is 25.* # of

FIGURE 7–2 Lydia generalized about how to figure out the number of tiles for any age U.

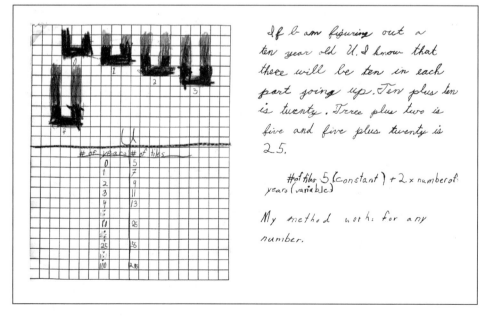

tiles = 5 (constant) + 2 × number of years (variable). My method works for any number.

An Additional Activity When I noticed some children completing the assignment, I interrupted the class to give them an additional activity. When I had their attention, I asked, "Do you think there are other letters of the alphabet that you can build with color tiles and show how they grow?" The room got noisy as children speculated. Some reached for tiles to try different letters. I quieted them and asked them to listen.

I said, "After you've finished the investigation of the letter U and I've checked your work, explore with the tiles which other letters you can build with color tiles. See how many you can find."

"Do we write about it?" Kailani wanted to know.

I didn't see the need to make this a formal writing assignment, but made it an option. "If you'd like, you can write down the letters you think would also work well for an investigation like the ones we did with the T, the I, and the U. Or use centimeter-squared paper and record what you build with the tiles." For the rest of the class, some students continued working on the U pattern while others began to explore which other letters were possible with color tiles. Most of the children recorded their findings by drawing on centimeter graph paper. Some also wrote about what they learned.

Greg, for example, recorded that thirteen letters were possible to grow: A, C, E, F, H, I, L, M, T, V, W, X, and Y. He wrote:

> *These letters have at least one line that gets bigger. But that is not why they grow. These letters do not look strange when they grow. They look the same but bigger. So for agsample P. You can grow it but it starts looking like a hammer. Of corse it will look weird when it gets huge but if it looks weird when it's two years old and it looks different, then it isn't right.*

Carl identified eleven letters that he felt could grow: A, C, E, F, H, I, L, T, V, X, and Y. Using color tiles, he built and traced a newborn and a one-year-old for each. He also wrote about the letters that he felt couldn't grow. (See Figure 7–3.)

FIGURE 7–3 Carl identified eleven letters that could grow.

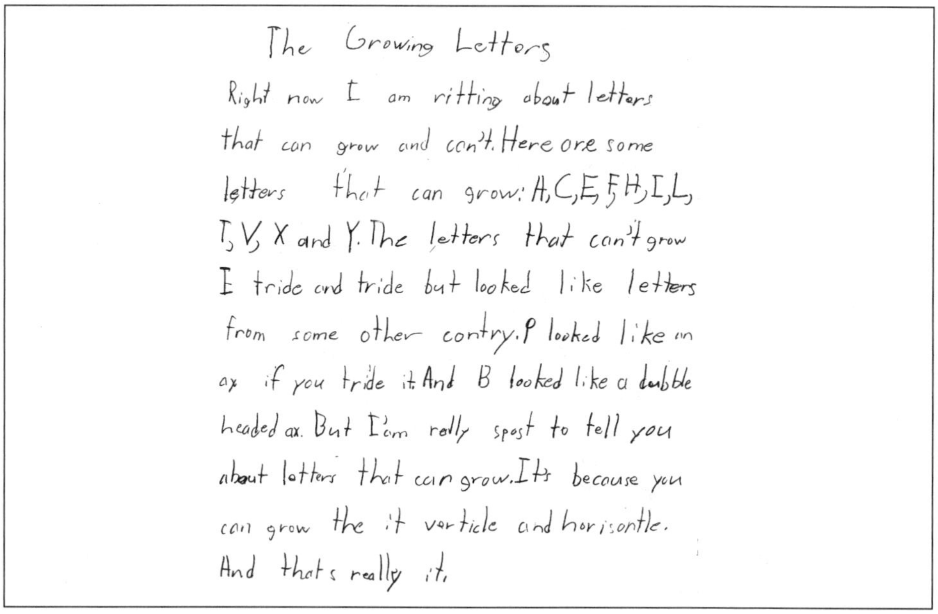

> The Growing Letters
> Right now I am ritting about letters that can grow and can't. Here ore some letters that can grow: A,C,E,F,H,I,L, T,V, X and Y. The letters that can't grow I tride and tride but looked like letters from some other contry. P looked like an ax if you tride it And B looked like a dubble headed ax. But I'om relly spost to tell you about letters that can grow. It because you can grow the it verticle and horisontle. And thats really it.

The children were eager to report their findings, both about the growing pattern for the U and about the other letters they could explore. I began by asking them what they had discovered about the U.

Carlos said, "I figured it out for a hundred years. I did one hundred plus one hundred plus five and I got two hundred five. The five is the baby U."

Aiden said, "What didn't change is the baby U. The change was that it gained more tiles, like twenty or thirty or one hundred."

Kailani said, "It seemed easier to use colors. I put blue for the baby U and green for the growing arms. The arms were always two times the age." She showed her paper with U's colored blue and green.

Sean said, "The U's got really, really, tall."

Katie had been thinking. She had recorded on her paper the same idea that Kailani had described, but now she had a different thought. She said excitedly, "Look! There are three on the bottom all the time, so that can be the constant. Then the part that goes up is the number of years plus one more. And you do that two times."

No one else had an idea to share about the letter U. The children were more interested in talking about the other letters that could work with the color tiles.

"The letters with loops are hard," Connor said. "They don't look right."

"Which letters are those?" I asked.

"Like B, D, O, P, Q, and R," Connor answered, referring to his paper.

"They have nothing to extend off," Lydia added.

Sean said, "I tried B and made the straight part grow, but it looked really funny."

"Can I tell which ones are good?" Evie asked. I nodded. She identified A, C, E, F, H, I, L, T, U, V, X, and Y. I had her read her list again while others checked their papers.

"How did you do A?" Cassie asked. Evie showed Cassie her paper. (See Figure 7–4.)

"I did H two ways," DeKoa said. DeKoa was a quiet child who didn't often participate in class discussions. This time she proudly showed her

FIGURE 7–4 Evie drew a newborn A, a one-year-old A, and a two-year-old A.

two ideas for how a newborn H might grow into a one-year-old H. (See Figure 7–5.)

FIGURE 7–5 DeKoa had two ideas for how a newborn H might grow into a one-year-old H.

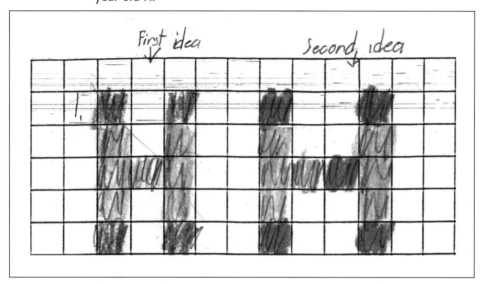

I then explained the next investigation they were going to do. I said, "You can choose any letter you'd like and investigate it the way you did for the letter U. But there's one more thing I want you to try to do." I then introduced the children to how they might use their written descriptions to represent rules as equations. I returned to the ideas that Kailani and Katie had expressed and recorded each on the board.

"Remember that there's more than one way to see a pattern. Watch as I write down Kailani's and Katie's ideas. I'll start with Kailani." I wrote on the board:

I used blue for the baby U and green for the growing arms. The arms were always two times the age.   Kailani

"How many tiles are in the baby U?" I asked Kailani.

"Five," she responded.

"And the same five are in every U?" I asked. Kailani nodded. I wrote some more on the board about Kailani's pattern.

I used blue for the baby U and green for the growing arms. The arms were always two times the age. There are five tiles in every U. The constant is 5. The variable part is the arms and that's two times the age. The number of tiles is equal to 5 plus two times the age.

Then I said, "Writing all the details takes a lot of words. Mathematicians have a shorter way to describe the rules for patterns. They write a mathematical sentence that's called an *equation*. Watch as I shorten the last sentence." I wrote on the board:

The number of tiles = 5 + 2 × the number of years

"I can shorten it even more," I said. "I'll use abbreviations for the number of tiles and the number of years. I'll use *t* for the number of tiles and *y* for the number of years. So I can write an equation like this." I wrote:

$$t = 5 + (2 \times y)$$

I said, "The parentheses keep the part about the arms of the U together." I didn't explain further about the parentheses.

"But Katie had another idea for a rule," I said. I wrote on the board:

The number of tiles is equal to three plus the part that goes up, which is the number of years plus one more, and you do this two times.   Katie

I then wrote this as an equation:

$$t = 3 + (y + 1) + (y + 1)$$

I didn't expect all of the children to understand what I had done, but I would be able to help them individually as they explored their own patterns.

I said, "Now you can choose any letter you'd like to explore. As you did with the U, follow the same steps. Also, try to write the rule as an equation. If you need help with this, raise your hand and I'll help you." Since the children had had experience with the U, getting started wasn't hard once they chose their letter. Whenever possible, students picked one of their own initials. The students worked on their investigations for the rest of the period and on the next day as well. Figures 7–6 through 7–9 show several students' investigations.

FIGURE 7-6 Katie investigated the growth pattern for the letter V.

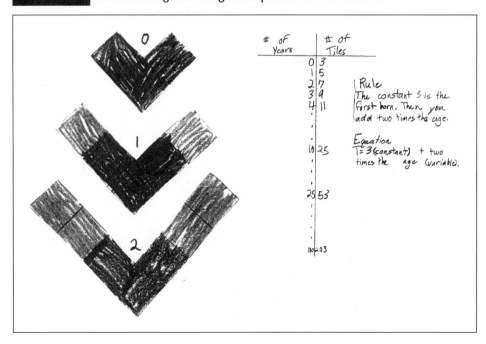

FIGURE 7-7 Evie investigated the growth pattern for the letter W.

Letter Patterns 137

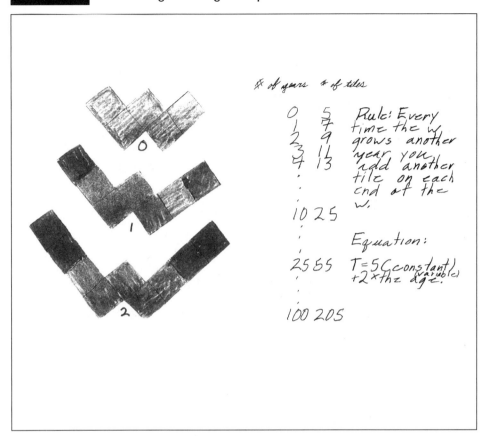

FIGURE 7-8 Miguel wrote two different equations to represent the growth pattern of the letter E.

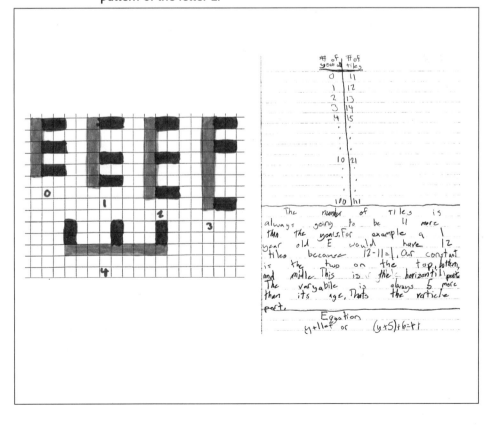

FIGURE 7-9 Carlos made a false start on an equation, then wrote one that worked.

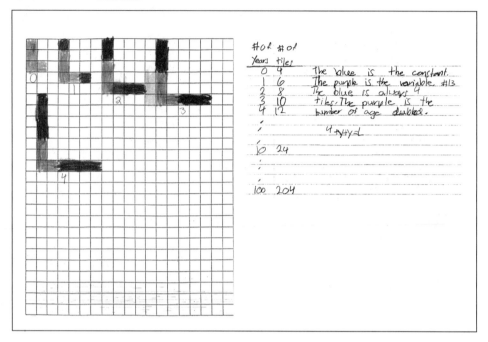

Extensions

Ask students to plot the points from their T-charts and compare the graphs. Typically, the points will all be in diagonal lines, indicating that the equations of the patterns are linear.

## CHAPTER 8

Pick a Number

Revisiting Open Sentences

OVERVIEW

This lesson gives students experience with solving equations. Students each pick a number between zero and twenty-five and use it with the following directions: Multiply the number by two and then add seven. Students present their result, and the others figure out what their starting number was and explain their strategies. Students later write open sentences to represent the problems. For extensions, they repeat the experience for other directions and then make up their own problems.

BACKGROUND

Before experiencing this lesson, students should have had experience exploring true, false, and open sentences. (See Chapter 2.) In this lesson, students first figure out answers to number problems presented only with words. Using problems that come from students' own results keeps interest high and encourages students to stay engaged.

When following the directions to multiply a number by two and then add seven, students arrive at different results depending on what number they started with. A result of fifty-seven, for example, means that the starting number was twenty-five. Two methods typically emerge from the students when they figure this out. One is to guess and check. For example, they might guess that the starting number is twenty and then check it by doing $(20 \times 2) + 7$. This results in forty-seven. Because forty-seven is less than fifty-seven, this guess is too small. The lesson explains how to use a number line to keep track of guesses that are too big or too small.

Another method that typically comes up in a class is the "undoing" method. It seems natural for students first to "undo" the addition. They either subtract by thinking, "Fifty-seven minus seven," or they add by thinking, "What number do I need to add to seven to get fifty-seven?" Then they figure out, either by multiplying or dividing, that the number that was multiplied by two to get fifty is twenty-five.

For this problem, all results are odd numbers. That's because no matter what number you start with, multiplying it by two will produce an even number. Then adding on seven will result in an odd number because the sum of an odd number and an even number is always odd. If a student comes up with an even result, and hasn't made a computation error, then the starting number involved a fraction. This situation occurred in the vignette that follows.

VOCABULARY

equation, open sentence

MATERIALS

- none

TIME

- one period to introduce, plus additional time for extensions

The Lesson

To begin the lesson, I said to the students, "Think of a number between zero and twenty-five. Don't tell me or anyone else what it is!" I paused for a moment and then asked, "Does everyone have a number?" The students nodded.

I continued, "Now listen carefully and follow my directions. Take your number and multiply it by two to get a new number." I paused to give the students time to think.

"Now add seven to your new number," I said. While the students were calculating in their heads, I wrote on the board:

Number multiplied by two, plus seven, results in _____

I wrote this on the board to help students realize that words, like numbers, can represent mathematical ideas. Also, it gave students a reference for what they were supposed to do. By the time I finished writing on the board, most of the students had a hand up, indicating they were ready to share. I called on Nick. "What result did you get?" I asked him.

"Fifty-seven," Nick replied.

"Did anyone else get fifty-seven?" I asked. No one else did. If other students had, I would have asked them to remain quiet for the following part of the discussion.

I then said, "Try to figure out what number Nick started with." I paused for a few moments to give students time to think. When about half of the students had raised a hand, I called on Joshua.

"Nick started out with twenty-five," Joshua said.

"That's right," Nick said.

"Let's check it and see how Nick could get fifty-seven if he picked the number twenty-five," I said. "What did I ask you to do first?"

"Pick a number," Tina said.

"Then what?" I continued.

"You multiply it by two," Jazmin replied.

"The last thing you said to do was to add seven," Cameron added.

As the students told me what we had done, I wrote the following on the board as a way to check Joshua's guess of twenty-five as Nick's starting number.

$(25 \times 2) + 7 = 57$
$50 + 7 = 57$

"It works!" I said. "How did you figure it out, Joshua?"

"I subtracted seven from fifty-seven to get fifty. Twenty-five is half of fifty," Joshua explained.

"Why did you subtract seven?" I asked Joshua. Joshua's method made sense to me, but I questioned him anyway for three reasons. One reason was to learn more about how Joshua was thinking; I've learned that correct answers sometimes mask misconceptions. Second, it's important in classroom discussions to question students not only when they're wrong but also when their thinking is solid; in this way, explaining your thinking becomes a regular part of class discussions. And third, I suspected that not all of the other students followed or understood how Joshua reasoned, and having him explain would slow down the discussion and, perhaps, help others catch up.

Joshua answered, "Well, you have something plus seven is fifty-seven, so the something must be fifty. Fifty-seven minus the seven is fifty."

"So you were going backward from the fifty-seven and undid the addition by subtracting?" I asked. Joshua nodded. "And how did you get to twenty-five?"

"Kind of the same way," Joshua responded. "Something times two was fifty, so the something had to be twenty-five."

I turned to the class. "Show thumbs up if you understand how Joshua reasoned." More than half of the students showed a thumb up. The others needed experience with more examples.

"So twenty-five is the number you started with, Nick," I confirmed. He nodded. On the board, I recorded Nick's result under the instructions I had written:

Number multiplied by two, plus seven, results in _____
Nick $(25 \times 2) + 7 = 57$

"Who came up with a different result?" I then asked. I called on Carmen.

"Forty-three," she said.

"Did anyone else get forty-three?" I asked the students. No one had.

"Figure out what number Carmen started with, and raise your hand when you think you know," I said to the class. I gave the students time to think and then called on Keith.

"I think that Carmen's starting number was eighteen," Keith said.

"Is that right, Carmen?" I asked. She said yes.

"How did you figure it out?" I asked Keith.

Keith explained, "I did it backwards, kind of like Joshua, but I divided at the end instead of multiplying. I started with forty-three and then I subtracted seven, and that got me to . . . oh yeah, that got me to thirty-six. Then I divided thirty-six by two to get eighteen."

"Did someone do it differently?" I asked.

Cameron said, "First I subtracted, forty-three minus seven. What I did was forty-three minus three gets to forty, and then I have to subtract four more and I get down to thirty-six. Actually, from there I did it the same way as Keith. Well, I didn't exactly. I didn't divide. I multiplied."

"What did you multiply?" I asked Cameron.

She explained, "When I had thirty-six, I asked myself, 'What number times two gives thirty-six?' Then I thought of eighteen."

"I think that your way is sort of different than Keith's strategy, but related because multiplication and division are related," I said to Cameron.

I recorded Carmen's result below Nick's.

Number multiplied by two, plus seven, results in _____
Nick (25 × 2) + 7 = 57
Carmen (18 × 2) + 7 = 43

"Can I share my result?" Steve asked. I nodded. He said, "I got eleven."

I said to the class, "Think about Steve's result and raise your hand when you know the number he started with," I said. I waited until about three-fourths of the students had their hands raised, then called on Kiko.

"Steve started with two," Kiko said.

"How did you figure it out?" I asked.

"First I did eleven minus seven, which equals four. Then I divided four by two, which equals two," Kiko explained.

"You used the same strategy as Joshua and Keith," I commented. Kiko nodded.

"Was two the number you started with, Steve?" I asked. Steve indicated it was.

"Did anyone use a different method to figure out Steve's number?" I asked.

Louise said, "I just guessed. First I guessed three and it was too big. Then I guessed one and it was too small. So it had to be two, and it worked."

"What happened when you guessed three?" I asked.

Louise said, "I did three times two is six, and six plus seven is thirteen." I wrote on the board:

(3 × 2) + 7 = 13

"How did you know that three was too big?" I asked.

"Steve's number was eleven, and I got thirteen," Louise answered.

I said, "When you guess, as Louise did, it helps some people to keep track of what happens on a number line." I drew a number line on the board to show the students what I meant:

"Would four be a good next guess for Louise?" I asked the class. Hands shot up. I called on Tina.

She said, "If three is too big, then four would be really too big."

I pointed to 4 on the number line and said, "Yes, it's definitely in the Too Big section." I turned back to Louise. "So then you guessed one?"

She said, "I went down from three to one, but I went too far. I did one times two is two plus seven is nine." I recorded on the board:

$(1 \times 2) + 7 = 9$

"Nine was too small," Louise concluded. "So I did two and it was just right. It's in the middle and it worked." I marked the number line to show that one was too small a guess.

I added Steve's result to the list on the board:

Number multiplied by two, plus seven, results in _____
Nick $(25 \times 2) + 7 = 57$
Carmen $(18 \times 2) + 7 = 43$
Steve $(2 \times 2) + 7 = 11$

Lucy shared her result next. "I got thirty-seven as my result," she said. Several students raised their hands, indicating that they also had gotten Lucy's result. I asked these students to listen as the others tried to figure out the starting number for thirty-seven.

I said to the class, "Let's try Louise's method to find out what number Lucy started with. Who would like to guess a number to test?"

"It has to be less than eighteen," Cameron said, looking at what I had recorded on the board. "I guess fifteen." I wrote on the board:

$(15 \times 2) + 7$

Terry did the figuring. He said, "Fifteen times two is thirty, and thirty plus seven is thirty-seven. It works!"

"You guessed right, Cameron," I said. "Who can figure it out using Joshua and Keith's strategy?"

Lisa said, "You do it backwards. They would take seven from thirty-seven, which gives thirty. Then you do thirty divided by two, which is the same as finding half. That's undoing the multiplying by two. You get fifteen."

I said to the class, "Show thumbs up if you understand how Lisa reasoned." More students showed a thumb up than when I had asked about how Joshua reasoned, but a few still weren't sure. I recorded Lucy's result:

Number multiplied by two, plus seven, results in _____
Nick $(25 \times 2) + 7 = 57$
Carmen $(18 \times 2) + 7 = 43$
Steve $(2 \times 2) + 7 = 11$
Lucy $(15 \times 2) + 7 = 37$

"Let's try one more different result," I said. Joshua looked at me hopefully. He had been raising his hand eagerly throughout the activity, and I now called on him.

"I got thirty-two," Joshua said. No one else did. The sly smile on Joshua's face gave me the clue to think for a moment about his result. All of the other results so far had been odd. That made sense because they all multiplied their initial number by two, which gives an even number, and then they added seven, an odd number. When you add an odd number to an even number, the answer will always be odd.

I asked the class, "Would a good guess for Joshua's starting number be twenty?"

"No," several students quickly replied.

"It's too big!" Rayno said. "Fifteen gave thirty-seven, so this has to be smaller." I drew a number line and indicated on it that all numbers from 20 on up were too big:

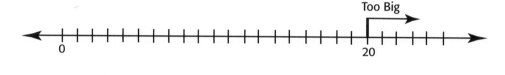

"How about five?" I asked.

"I think that would be too small," Cameron said.

"Are you sure?" I asked.

Cameron answered, "Well, five times two is ten, and plus seven is only seventeen. It's way too small." I indicated this on the number line:

"How about thirteen?" Jazmin suggested. I wrote on the board:

(13 × 2) + 7

Jazmin figured, "Thirteen times two is twenty-six, plus seven is . . . thirty-three. It's a little too big." I extended the Too Big arrow on the number line so it started from 13:

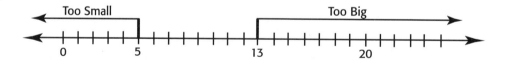

"What about twelve?" Jeremy suggested. I wrote on the board:

(12 × 2) + 7

Jeremy figured, "Twelve times two is twenty-four and seven is thirty-one. Hey, it's too small!" I adjusted the Too Small arrow on the number line:

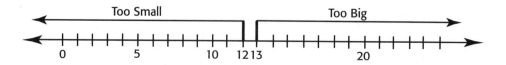

The students thought for a few moments and then hands began to go up. I called on Louise. "It's twelve and a half!" Louise said. "Twelve and a half times two is twenty-five, and twenty-five plus seven is thirty-two."

"I didn't know you could use fractions," Kenny said.

"I hadn't thought about using fractions myself," I said, "but Joshua did." Rayno's hand was up.

"What are you thinking, Rayno?" I asked.

"Louise is right. If you do thirty-two minus seven, you get twenty-five. You can't divide twenty-five by two without leftovers. Twenty-four divided by two is twelve, plus one-half would be twelve and a half. Twelve and a half plus twelve and a half equals twenty-five," Rayno explained. Joshua agreed that his starting number had been twelve and a half.

Jeremy said, "You could see from the number line how to guess. Twelve is too small and thirteen is too big. Twelve and a half is a half away from twelve and a half away from thirteen."

I added Joshua's equation to the list:

Number multiplied by two, plus seven, results in _____
Nick $(25 \times 2) + 7 = 57$
Carmen $(18 \times 2) + 7 = 43$
Steve $(2 \times 2) + 7 = 11$
Lucy $(15 \times 2) + 7 = 37$
Joshua $(12\frac{1}{2} \times 2) + 7 = 32$

Writing Open Sentences   I then asked the students to look at Nick's sentence on the board. I said, "Let's try to write it as an open sentence using mathematical symbols. Let's use a variable for the number Nick picked. Who has an idea about how to do this?"

Diego said, "You could draw a box for the number. Then you write a multiplication sign and then a two and then a plus sign and a seven. Next put equals and the number fifty-seven." I wrote on the board:

$\square \times 2 + 7 = 57$

"You should put in parentheses," Lisa added. I added them:

$(\square \times 2) + 7 = 57$

"How could we write an open sentence for Carmen's?" I then asked.

Steve said, "Write parentheses, then box times two, then parentheses, then plus seven, and then an equals sign and forty-three." I recorded:

$(\square \times 2) + 7 = 43$

We did the same for Steve's, Lucy's, and Joshua's equations.

An Individual Assignment   I then gave the class an assignment so that I could check their understanding. I wrote on the board:

Number multiplied by three, add eleven, results in fifty-six

I then gave directions, writing them on the board as I did so:

Write an open sentence using mathematical symbols.
Figure out the number that makes the open sentence true, and explain how you got it.

I circulated and observed the students. Few had any problem with this assignment. As I observed, I noticed that Jazmin had quickly written a correct open sentence and had started to figure out the answer. She subtracted eleven from fifty-six to get a difference of forty-five. Then she wrote a division problem—*45 ÷ 3*—but she didn't know how to proceed. I asked her what she thought she needed to do.

Jazmin explained, "I need to put forty-five things in three groups. I wonder if I could make three circles and then put tally marks in the circles one at a time until I have used up forty-five tallies."

"Try it and see what happens," I suggested. "I'll check back with you in a few minutes to see what you find out." When I checked back with Jazmin a little later, she had figured out that forty-five could be divided into three groups of fifteen. This information was enough for her to successfully complete the task. (See Figure 8–1.)

I noticed that Pablo seemed to be very intent on this assignment and I walked over to see what he was doing. He had figured out the answer using the "undoing" method, but then he wanted to also use the guess-and-check method. (See Figure 8–2.)

FIGURE 8–1 Jazmin drew three circles and used tally marks to figure out 45 ÷ 3.

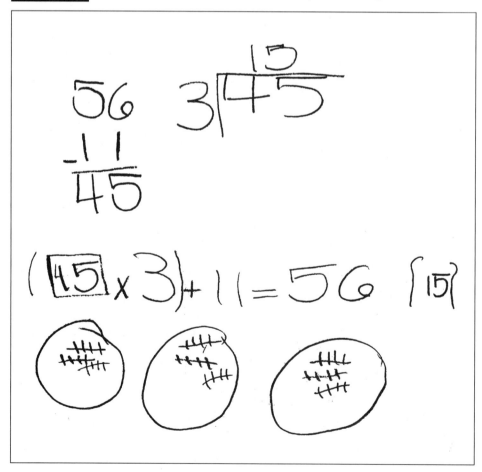

FIGURE 8–2 Pablo used the "undoing" method first, then the guess-and-check method.

Pick a Number 147

□ x 3 + 11 = 56

[15] x 3 + 11 = 56

First I got 56 and subtracted 11 and, it equaled 45 then I divided 45 by 3 and it equaled 15. The reason I did that was because it was like going back if you look back you can see insted of adding 11 I subtracted 11 and insted of multipling 3 I divided 3. Another reason I did that was because I wasn't adding up to fifty-six I was go down from fifty-six that why I subtracted and divided insted of adding and multipling.

I'm going to tell you another way to figure out an open problem. The way is first you guess a number under the number you have to get to then you multiply what you have to and add what you have to then you will probly not get the number you want so if it is to high of a number make the number you multipled and added, smaller if it is to small of a number make it higher. This could take a long time or a short time. Excample.

guess: 20

□ x 3 + 11 = 56
□ = 15

20 x 3 = 60 It is already high so I'm going to make it smaller.
19 x 3 = 57 It is already to high.
18 x 3 = 54
17 x 3   +11
       51 65 — It is to high.
16 x 3 = 48
   +11   +11 — It is to high.
   59   62
It is to high.
15 x 3 = 45
   +11
   56 It is the right answer.

As students finished, I checked over their work, sometimes making corrections or suggestions. Figures 8–3 through 8–5 show how some other students solved this problem.

FIGURE 8–3 Kenny's work is typical of how the students used the guess-and-check method to solve the problem.

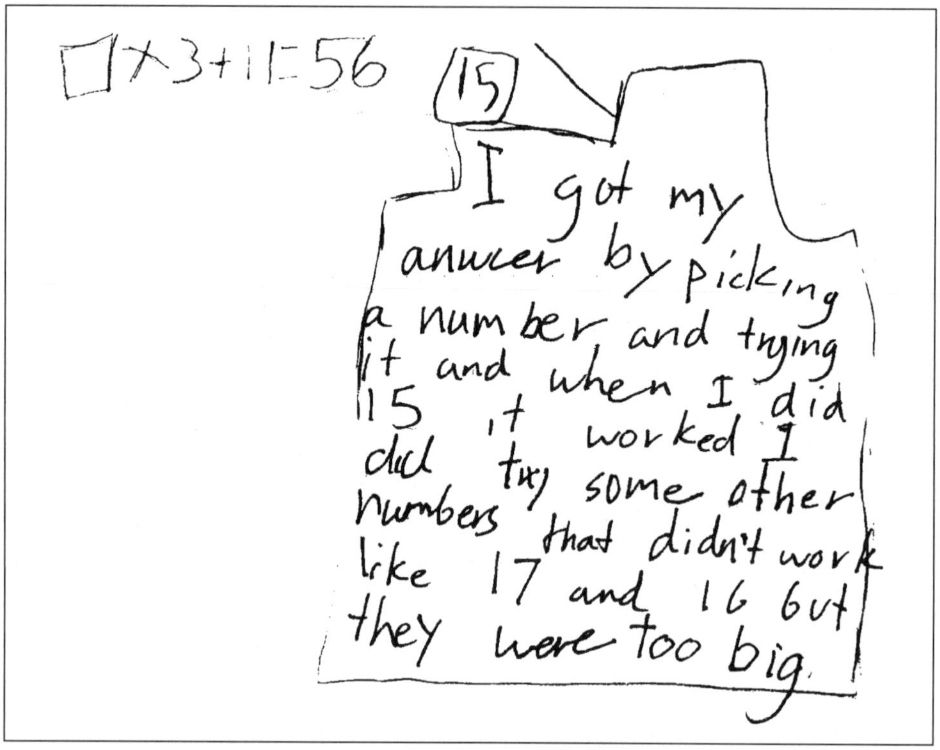

$$\square \times 3 + 11 = 56 \quad \boxed{15}$$

I got my anwcer by picking a number and trying it and when I did 15 it worked I did try some other numbers that didn't work like 17 and 16 but they were too big.

FIGURE 8–4 Rayno wrote equations to explain how she used the "undoing" method.

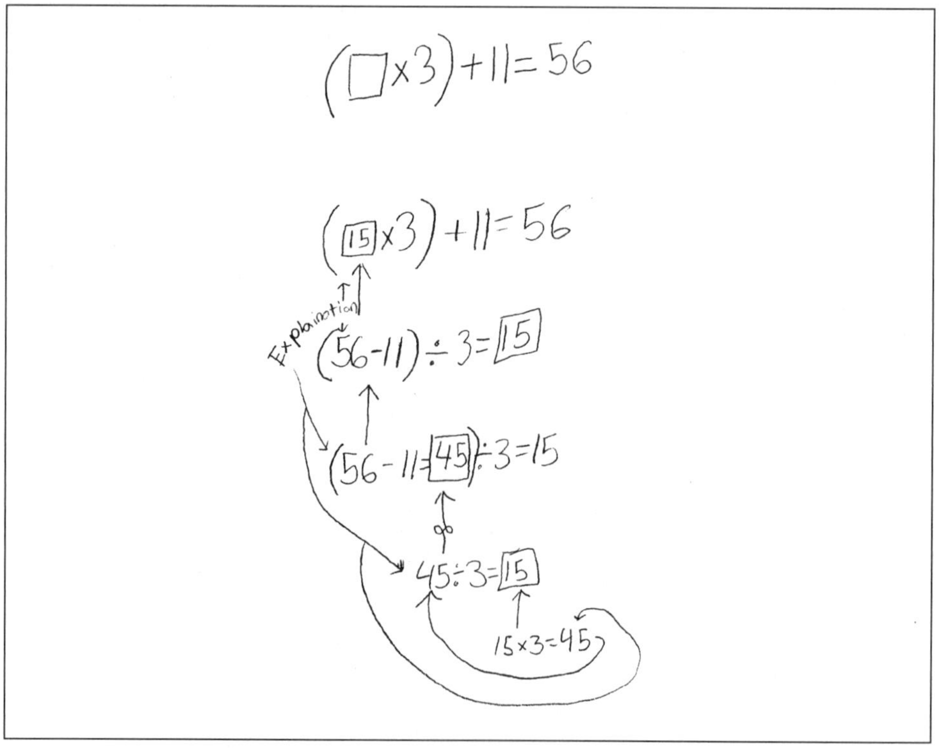

$$\left(\square \times 3\right) + 11 = 56$$

$$\left(\boxed{15} \times 3\right) + 11 = 56$$

Explanation

$$\left(56 - 11\right) \div 3 = \boxed{15}$$

$$(56 - 11 = \boxed{45}) \div 3 = 15$$

$$45 \div 3 = \boxed{15}$$

$$15 \times 3 = 45$$

FIGURE 8-5 Gabe showed his calculations and wrote an explanation.

Pick a Number **149**

$$3 \times \square = \triangle \quad \frac{\times \begin{array}{c} 15 \\ 3 \end{array}}{?} = \frac{\times \begin{array}{c} 15 \\ 3 \end{array}}{\begin{array}{c} 45 \\ +11 \\ \hline 56 \end{array}}$$

$$\frac{+11}{56}$$

$$3 \times \square = \frac{45}{\begin{array}{c} +11 \\ \hline 56 \end{array}}$$

$$\square = 15$$

$$\textcircled{3} \times \triangle = \frac{\square}{\begin{array}{c} +11 \\ \hline 56 \end{array}}$$

I found out you have 45 right before you add 11

So I did 3 × 15 which equals 45 because 2 × 15 equals 30 + 15 = 45 and 45 plus 11 = 56.

1. Repeat the activity on other days, presenting other directions that involve the students with different numbers and different operations. Also, if the challenge would be appropriate for your students, you could have them pick a number between zero and fifty. Following are directions for possible follow-up experiences:

Number multiplied by three, minus seven, results in _____ ($\square \times 3$) − 7
Number plus one, then multiplied by five, results in _____ ($\square$ + 1) × 5
Number plus ten, then divided by two, results in _____ ($\square$ + 10) ÷ 2

2. Have students make up their own examples. Give the following directions:

Think of an example with two operations and write it in words.
Write an open sentence to describe your example.

Then use the students' problems to provide the class with additional experiences. Either have a student read his or her example for others to write the equation, or have a student write the equation on the board and ask the others to give the words that go with it.

## CHAPTER 9

Four Points

Investigating Patterns in Coordinates

OVERVIEW

In this lesson, students investigate the coordinates of points in horizontal, vertical, and diagonal lines. The lesson not only gives students practice identifying the coordinates for points and using ordered pairs to locate points on a coordinate grid, but also engages students in looking for patterns in the coordinates of points in lines. The lesson is appropriate once students have had experience using ordered pairs of numbers to plot points.

BACKGROUND

The prerequisite skill necessary for this lesson is an ability to plot points and to identify the coordinates for points on a coordinate grid. This lesson is useful for preparing students for playing the game of *Tic-Tac-Toe* (see Chapter 4) and also an appropriate investigation after the children have learned to play *Tic-Tac-Toe*. For information about plotting points, see the "Background" section in Chapter 3, "Introduction to Coordinate Graphing."

VOCABULARY

axes, axis, coordinates, diagonal, horizontal, ordered pair, points, vertical

MATERIALS

- half-inch graph paper, at least 1 sheet per student (see Blackline Masters)

TIME

- one class period

I began class by projecting a transparency of half-inch squares with axes drawn. I marked the point (2, 5) and asked, "What are the coordinates of this point? Raise your hand when you've figured it out." About six hands went up immediately, then after a moment, a few more went up. I waited. I expected all of the students to figure out the coordinates of the point, so I gave another reminder, "When you know, raise your hand." I waited a bit more until everyone had a hand raised. I called on James.

"It's (two, five)," he said. The others showed thumbs up to indicate their agreement. I wrote *(2, 5)* on the board.

I then marked on the transparency three more points to the right of (2, 5) so that there were now four points in a row horizontally.

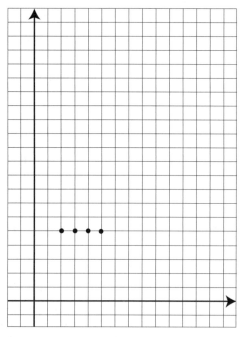

I said, "We know that the coordinates for the first point I marked are (two, five). Talk with your neighbor about what the pair of coordinates is for each of the three other points I marked." I gave the class a few moments to do this and then called them back to attention.

"Who would like to report?" I asked. I called on Nathan.

"They go in a pattern," Nathan said. "After (two, five) comes (three, five), then (four, five), and then (five, five)." On the board, I drew four dots horizontally and then underneath them wrote the coordinates Nathan reported:

• • • •
(2, 5)
(3, 5)
(4, 5)
(5, 5)

"What pattern do you notice in these ordered pairs?" I asked.

"The five is the same," Cami replied.

"These fives or these?" I asked, first pointing to the two 5s in the last pair of coordinates and then to the four 5s that were the second number in each pair.

"The five is the second number in them all," Cami clarified.

"And the others go up by one," Andrew said.

I paraphrased, "So for these points that go in a row horizontally, the first number in each ordered pair increases by one, but the second number in each ordered pair stays the same." The students nodded.

"Do you think that would be the same for the coordinates of any four points horizontally in a row?" I asked. Some students nodded "yes," others shook their heads "no," and others weren't sure. I then gave the students an assignment to do individually. I presented the assignment to the students in two parts. For the first part, students would investigate four points in a horizontal row. In the second part, they would do the same investigation for four vertical points, four points in a diagonal, and then four points in a diagonal going the other way. I planned the investigation in two parts so that the class could first compare and discuss their results about points arranged horizontally. The class discussion would help clarify the rest of the assignment for any students who were confused. Also, students could make conjectures about the coordinates for points arranged vertically and diagonally based on the patterns they noticed when points were arranged horizontally.

The Investigation, Part 1   I said, "In a moment, I'll give you each a sheet of graph paper. First draw axes, and then mark four points horizontally in a row, anywhere on the grid. After you've marked the four points, list the ordered pair for each. First write the pair for the point farthest on the left, and then for the others in order from left to right, as Nathan did. Above your list, draw four dots as I did to show that the list describes points that are in a horizontal row. Then see what pattern you notice in the pairs."

"Do we put the list of numbers on the graph paper?" Cami wanted to know.

"Yes, write your list on your graph paper, but write kind of small so that you'll have room a little later for another investigation on the same paper," I said. There were no other questions so I quickly distributed paper. The students were eager to work and began marking points on their grids.

In a moment, Michael called me over. "I don't get what to do," he said.

I looked at Michael's paper and said, "I see you've marked your four points and I see that they're in a horizontal row."

"But I'm still not sure how to figure the numbers," Michael explained. This had been a problem for Michael a few days before.

"When you figure out the coordinates for a point, where do you start?" I asked.

"Where the axes cross?" Michael responded with uncertainty. I nodded. Then Michael said, "I'm still not sure if I count where the lines cross as one or zero."

"Let's do it together," I suggested, sensing that Michael needed both practice and encouragement. "Put your pencil where you're going to begin." Michael placed his pencil on the origin. "Now what?" I asked.

"I move across," Michael said as he moved his pencil to the first line from the origin.

"How far did you move when your pencil was still at the origin?" I asked.

"Zero," Michael replied.

"Then you moved you pencil how far?" I asked.

"Oh, I see," Michael said. "It's zero until you move and then after you move, you count one. I really get it now. I move across first and then up next." Quietly, Michael began counting correctly to the right on the horizontal axis, "One, two, three, four. Now up. One, two, three, four, five, six, seven." He correctly figured out the ordered pair (4, 7) of the first point he had marked. I watched as he correctly figured the ordered pair of his second point, and then I left him to continue his work.

As I circulated through the class, I checked students' coordinates, helping those who made errors. (Errors are easy to spot by looking for a pattern; the first numbers in the ordered pairs should increase by one and the second should remain the same.) I noticed several students recording their ordered pairs next to the points they'd marked on their graphs. I reminded them to look at the example on the board and to list their ordered pairs as I'd shown them, rather than write them next to the points they had marked. I explained that this way of recording would help them to see patterns more easily. When I saw that most students were finishing, I gave a one-minute warning to those still working.

When I had the students' attention, I began the discussion by saying, "I'm interested in collecting and recording the ordered pairs for the points you've graphed. I'll list the ordered pairs you report on the board and we can all examine the information for patterns." Most students were eager to share and had raised a hand. I called on Annie and, as she reported, I recorded on the board below the list already there:

• • • •
(2, 5)
(3, 5)
(4, 5)
(5, 5)

Annie
(4, 12)
(5, 12)
(6, 12)
(7, 12)

"Hey!" Beatriz said. "It's like the other ordered pairs."

"Explain some more about that," I said.

"The first coordinate gets bigger by one and the second coordinate stays the same," Beatriz said. Most students nodded their agreement.

"That's what happened with my ordered pairs," Jaime commented.

"What were your ordered pairs, Jaime?" I asked.

"They were (six, seven), (seven, seven), (eight, seven), and (nine, seven)," Jaime reported. I recorded on the board below Annie's list:

• • • •
(2, 5)
(3, 5)
(4, 5)
(5, 5)

Annie
(4, 12)
(5, 12)
(6, 12)
(7, 12)

Jaime
(6, 7)
(7, 7)
(8, 7)
(9, 7)

"It's the same thing," Michael said.

"I think they'll all be that way for sure," Audrey added.

"Does anyone have ordered pairs that don't follow this pattern?" I asked. No one raised a hand. I didn't expect anyone to raise a hand, as I'd checked their papers while they were working.

The Investigation, Part 2   I then marked four points vertically on the over-head transparency.

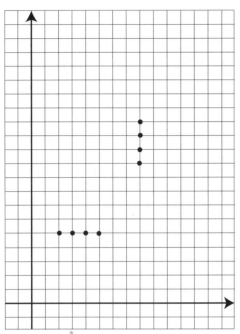

I asked, "If you mark four points vertically, do you think that the pattern in the ordered pairs will be the same as four horizontal points?" Some students nodded "yes," some shook their heads "no," and others weren't sure.

"We're going to find out. Do the same thing as you just did for four horizontal points; mark four vertical points, list their coordinates from the bottom point up, and look for patterns. Then you'll do the same for four points in a diagonal, and then four points in a diagonal the other way. List the co-ordinates for the diagonal points, starting with the point at the left each time." As I gave these last directions, I marked on the transparency four points diagonally one way and then four points diagonally the other way.

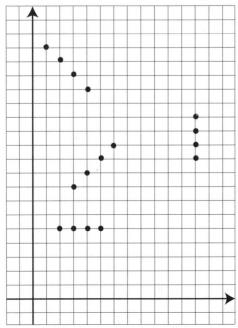

I then continued, "When you're done, we'll compare the patterns you found in the ordered pairs. Remember to use dots to indicate above each list the way that the points are going, vertically or diagonally. Are there questions?"

"Do we use the same paper for all of them?" Sam asked.

"Yes, you'll have room," I said.

"Does it matter which we do first?" Armando asked.

"No, you can do them in any order," I replied. There were no other questions. As the students returned to work I wrote the directions on the board. As I circulated, I checked the students' ordered pairs for accuracy and gave occasional reminders about indicating with dots above the list the way the points were arranged.

I noticed that while Jaime had marked all four of his horizontal points at the intersections of lines, when he marked the four vertical points, he placed them in spaces between the intersections. He was having difficulty determining the coordinates for the point he'd marked at $(3, 3\frac{1}{2})$.

"I know I start at the origin and count over three," Jaime explained as he put his pencil at the origin and then moved it three to the right on the horizontal axis. "Then I count up: one, two, three . . . the point comes after three and before four."

"Your point isn't on three or on four," I said. "How would you describe it?"

"It's about halfway," Jaime said.

I nodded my agreement and continued, "The coordinates for your point are three and three and a half. For today, let's stay with whole numbers. How could you move your point so that the numbers in its ordered pair would both be whole numbers?"

"Put it where the lines cross instead of in between," Jaime said as he erased his points and quickly marked new ones at the intersections of lines.

Kris and Sam were comparing the ordered pairs for their vertical points. "This is cool," Kris said. "It's like backward from the horizontal points."

"I don't get it," Sam said.

Kris explained, "The ordered pairs for the horizontal points had the first number get bigger by one and the second number stay the same. But with the vertical points, the first number stays the same and the second number gets bigger by one on both of our papers." Kris was quiet for a moment as Sam thought this over.

"I wonder why that's happening," Sam said after a few moments. Kris shrugged and the two boys returned to studying their papers.

"The diagonal pattern is really interesting," Brianna commented as I walked by. "The diagonal with the lowest point in the lower left has each number in the ordered pair getting bigger by one." Brianna's paper showed the coordinates (2, 5), (3, 6), (4, 7), and (5, 8). She said, "The first numbers go two, three, four, five, and the second ones go five, six, seven, eight."

"I see you haven't done the diagonal points going the other way," I said. "Do you think the pattern will be the same in the ordered pairs for those points?"

"The other ways haven't been the same, so these probably won't," Brianna said. "Maybe instead of both numbers in the ordered pair getting bigger by one, maybe the numbers will get smaller by one because the diagonal goes the other way." I left Brianna to continue. (See Figure 9–1.)

As students finished their work, I encouraged them to try additional groups of four points in a row and to talk with their neighbors to see what they found out. Soon most students were finished and I asked for their attention.

FIGURE 9–1 Brianna correctly wrote the ordered pairs for all four arrangements of points.

Four Points **157**

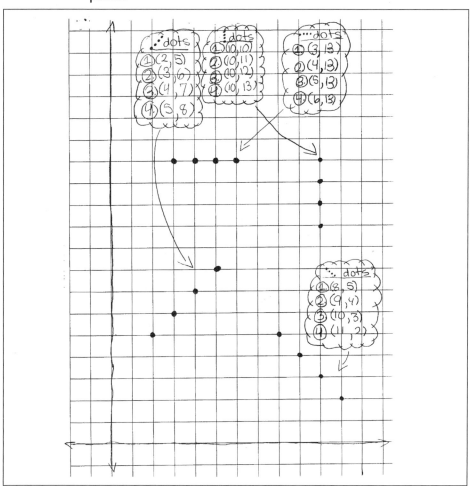

A Class Discussion As I had with the horizontal points, I asked several students to report the ordered pairs for their vertical points. I recorded on the board to the right of the lists of coordinates for points arranged horizontally so that students could compare the two sets.

	Kris
(2, 5)	(2, 5)
(3, 5)	(2, 6)
(4, 5)	(2, 7)
(5, 5)	(2, 8)

Annie	Karly
(4, 12)	(3, 12)
(5, 12)	(3, 13)
(6, 12)	(3, 14)
(7, 12)	(3, 15)

Jaime	Armando
(6, 7)	(9, 10)
(7, 7)	(9, 11)
(8, 7)	(9, 12)
(9, 7)	(9, 13)

"It's just like what happened with my points," Beatriz said. "I noticed that the first coordinate stayed the same and the second increased by one."

"That's backward from the horizontal points," Brianna added.

"Sam and I were thinking about that together," Kris said. "We think with the horizontal points, the second number stays the same because it tells how far up to go and it's always the same amount to make a horizontal line of points."

"Yeah," Sam added, "if you changed the up number, which is the second one, it wouldn't be a horizontal line."

To illustrate Sam and Kris's idea, I directed the students' attention to the four points marked horizontally on the overhead transparency and asked the students to watch as I counted from the horizontal axis up to each point. Several hands then went up.

"I have an idea," Rick said. "I think I know why with the vertical points the first number stays the same and the second one goes up by one. To be in a straight vertical line, you always have to go over the same amount. That's the first number, so that's why the first number is the same. What changes is how much you go up." Several students indicated their agreement and no one had anything else to add.

Students then shared ordered pairs for four points in a row in both diagonal directions, first for the diagonals that have their lowest point at the lower left and then for the diagonals with their lowest point at the lower right. I recorded on the board and the completed information looked as follows:

Class	Kris	Elisa	James
(2, 5)	(2, 5)	(2, 5)	(2, 17)
(3, 5)	(2, 6)	(3, 6)	(3, 16)
(4, 5)	(2, 7)	(4, 7)	(4, 15)
(5, 5)	(2, 8)	(5, 8)	(5, 14)

Annie	Karly	Gary	Nina
(4, 12)	(3, 12)	(3, 3)	(3, 5)
(5, 12)	(3, 13)	(4, 4)	(4, 6)
(6, 12)	(3, 14)	(5, 5)	(5, 7)
(7, 12)	(3, 15)	(6, 6)	(6, 8)

Jaime	Armando	Cami	Beatriz
(6, 7)	(9, 10)	(4, 4)	(11, 5)
(7, 7)	(9, 11)	(5, 5)	(10, 6)
(8, 7)	(9, 12)	(6, 6)	(9, 7)
(9, 7)	(9, 13)	(7, 7)	(8, 8)

"Hey," Cami noticed, "three of my ordered pairs are the same as Gary's and one is different. That's weird. Why did that happen?" I paused a moment to give the students time to consider Cami's question. I pointed to the ordered pairs that were the same in both Gary's and Cami's lists—(4, 4), (5, 5), and (6, 6)—and then pointed to the pairs that were different—(3, 3) and (7, 7). The students were perplexed. I erased the points on the overhead transparency and asked Cami to read aloud her list of ordered pairs. As she read her list I carefully marked each point. Then Gary read his list of ordered pairs. On the same transparency, I carefully marked each of Gary's points with an open dot, circling Cami's points where points overlapped.

Four Points   **159**

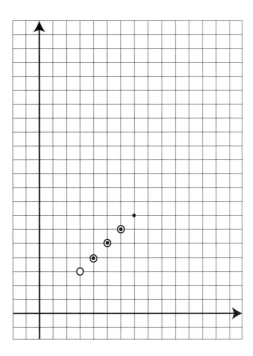

"Oh!" Cami said with surprise, "I see. Gary started a little lower on the graph, then we had the three points that were the same and then I went up one higher."

"We noticed a pattern," Audrey said, reporting what she and Elisa had discovered. "For the first list of diagonal points, both numbers in the ordered pairs go up by one."

"I noticed that, too," Brianna added. "It reminds me of going up stairs. You go across for each stair and up for each stair. I think that's why the numbers both go up."

"I don't think that works for the other diagonal," Armando said after a moment's thought. He was referring to the last list of ordered pairs. "The second diagonal has ordered pairs where the first number goes up one and the second number goes down one."

"Oh yeah," several students said.

I said, "I agree that James's ordered pairs have the pattern Armando described, one coordinate increases by one and the other decreases by one. Is this true for all ordered pairs on this list?" I asked, pointing to the fourth list. "Talk with your neighbor." I had just noticed that Nina's set of ordered pairs, on the fourth list, really belonged on the third list. Also, while both James's and Beatriz's ordered pairs were on the correct list, the pattern in the ordered pairs was different. This was the result of the order in which each student had recorded the coordinates for his or her points. James had started with the farthest point on the left, while Beatriz had done the opposite, starting with the uppermost point. The students became quite animated in their conversations as they thought about these three sets of ordered pairs. After several moments I asked for the students' attention. Several students were eager to share and had their hands up.

Michael explained, "We think something is weird with the last list. None of the groups of ordered pairs seems to have the same pattern. We don't know if the patterns Elisa, Audrey, and Armando just described work."

"We thought that at first, too," Brianna said. "Rick and I think that Nina's ordered pairs belong on the first diagonal list because they all have both coordinates go up one. James's and Beatriz's lists have one coordinate that goes up and one that goes down. It's just they're in different places."

"We think if you mark the points on the graph, then all the diagonals on the fourth list should look the same," Karly said. "At our table all our horizontal points go across the paper the same way, just in different places. Same with the vertical points."

"Let's mark the points and find out," Audrey suggested. If she hadn't suggested this, I would have done so.

I asked James to read the first four ordered pairs on the last list of diagonal points. Using a clean overhead transparency of grid paper, I drew axes and marked the points as their coordinates were read. The points on James's list formed a diagonal with the lowest point in the lower right, as it should have.

"Let's do Beatriz's list next," I suggested. I chose to do Beatriz's list next because I wanted to point out to the students that Beatriz and James had recorded their points in a different order, which made finding a pattern more challenging. Using the same transparency, I asked Beatriz to read her list, and I carefully marked the first point on her list as she read it. "Pay attention to the order in which I'm marking the points," I said to focus the class. "James's first point was the farthest on the left," I said, pointing to James's first point on the graph. "Here's Beatriz's first point, now let's see where her second point is." Beatriz read her second ordered pair and I marked the point.

"Beatriz's points are going up and to the left, and I think James's went down to the right," Karly said. There were several other "yeahs" and "uh-huhs," showing others agreed with Karly.

Beatriz read her third and fourth ordered pairs. I marked them on the graph, confirming for the students that both Beatriz and James had four diagonal points in a row going in the same direction, even though the pattern in the ordered pairs wasn't as obvious as it had been on the lists for the other three groups of points.

Kris said, "You could say that one number in the ordered pairs goes up one and the other goes down one instead of the first number goes up and the second one goes down." Several students nodded.

Brianna said, "I noticed a different thing. In the last group of diagonal points, if you add the numbers in the ordered pairs, they equal the same thing. Two plus seventeen is nineteen. Three plus sixteen is nineteen. Four plus fifteen is nineteen, and so is five plus fourteen."

"Hey, that works for James's list and my list!" Beatriz said with delight.

"Mine, too!" commented several other students as they checked their own lists.

"I think my ordered pairs are on the wrong list," Nina said.

"What makes you think that?" I asked, pleased that Nina had noticed her error.

"Well, both numbers in the ordered pairs go up one," Nina said. "I think it goes on the first list of diagonals because all of those have both numbers in the ordered pair going up one."

Annie offered, "You could use Brianna's idea of adding the numbers in the coordinate pairs to see if they equal the same thing and test Nina's list and see that way, too."

"I added them," Nina said. "They go eight, ten, twelve, fourteen. Three and five is eight and like that. They don't equal the same thing."

"Oh, wow!" Armando blurted out, then apologized for interrupting. "I added up the pairs of numbers on the first diagonal list and it increases by two, just like Nina said. Elisa's ordered pairs go seven, nine, eleven, thirteen if you add up the numbers. That's an increase of two. Gary's go six, eight, ten, twelve. That's two more each time."

"The vertical and horizontal points have sums that increase one each time," Beatriz said.

"I know why," Rick said. "It's because one number stays the same and the other increases by one, so the sum will increase by one."

"Cool!" Kris responded to Rick's explanation. There were no other comments.

To change the direction of the discussion, I said, "I'm going to list four ordered pairs on the board. See if you can figure out on which list of ordered pairs these new ones should be written. Will the points for these ordered pairs be in a row horizontally, vertically, or diagonally?" I indicated the points at the top of the lists as I spoke. "When you think you know, put your thumb up." I wrote on the board:

(4, 5)
(4, 6)
(4, 7)
(4, 8)

Students were eager to answer the question. "Using a whisper voice, tell me if the points will be horizontal, vertical, or on a diagonal," I said.

Most responded with "vertical" and a few students said "horizontal." No one said diagonal. "Who would like to share your thinking?" I asked.

Sam explained, "I think it should be the second list, with the vertical points. The first number is always the same, which means you always go across the same amount. It's how far up you go that changes, and that's the second number."

"Let's mark the points on the graph and see," Gary suggested. I would have done this if Gary or another student hadn't suggested it. Using a clean overhead transparency of grid paper, I drew the axes and marked the points, forming a vertical row.

I repeated this for a few more sets of ordered pairs on the board, asking the students to predict if the points would form a vertical, horizontal, or diagonal row. Then we plotted the points to verify their predictions.

A Writing Assignment   "You shared many interesting ideas during our class discussion," I said. "Now I'd like you to write about your ideas." I wrote on the board as the students watched:

Write about the patterns you notice in the ordered pairs.

"We use the lists on the board, right?" Annie asked.

"Yes," I clarified. "We talked about some patterns on these lists and you may write about those, or if you notice other patterns, you may write about those as well." There were no other questions. I handed each student a sheet of paper and they quietly went to work.

Almost all students wrote about the patterns we'd discussed. Since I hadn't written the students' ideas on the board, students had to use their own words to explain ideas they'd heard. As the students worked, I noticed that describing the two types of diagonals was creating difficulty for many. I interrupted the students and wrote *A* above the horizontal list, *B* above the vertical list, C above the first diagonal list, and *D* above the second diagonal list.

Cami's paper was like many in the class. She wrote: *I notice in colom A that the first numbers increase and the second numbers stay the same. I notice in colom B that the first numbers stay the same and the second numbers increase, it's the opisite of colom A. I notice in colum C that the first numbers increase and same with the second numbers. I notice that in colom D that the first numbers increase and the second numbers decrease.* (See Figure 9–2.)

Gary had difficulty expressing his thoughts in writing. He wrote: *I noticed in A it is (4, 12), and (5, 12), (6, 12), (7, 12) that's the problem. Your only adding 1 more in the first row. I notice in B that the first row is 2's. And the 2nd* row was 5, 6, 7, 8. Gary rewrote the ordered pairs. *I noticed in C that the 1st row is 2, 3, 4, 5 and the 2nd row is 5, 6, 7, 8.* Gary then rewrote the ordered pairs. (See Figure 9–3.)

Amy indicated an understanding about the last list of ordered pairs that was discussed but not included by most students. She wrote: *In the second diagonal patterns the first columm increases by one and the second columm decreases by one or the other way around. All that matters is where you start, the top or the bottom.* (See Figure 9–4.)

FIGURE 9–2 Cami's descriptions of the patterns were typical of what other students wrote.

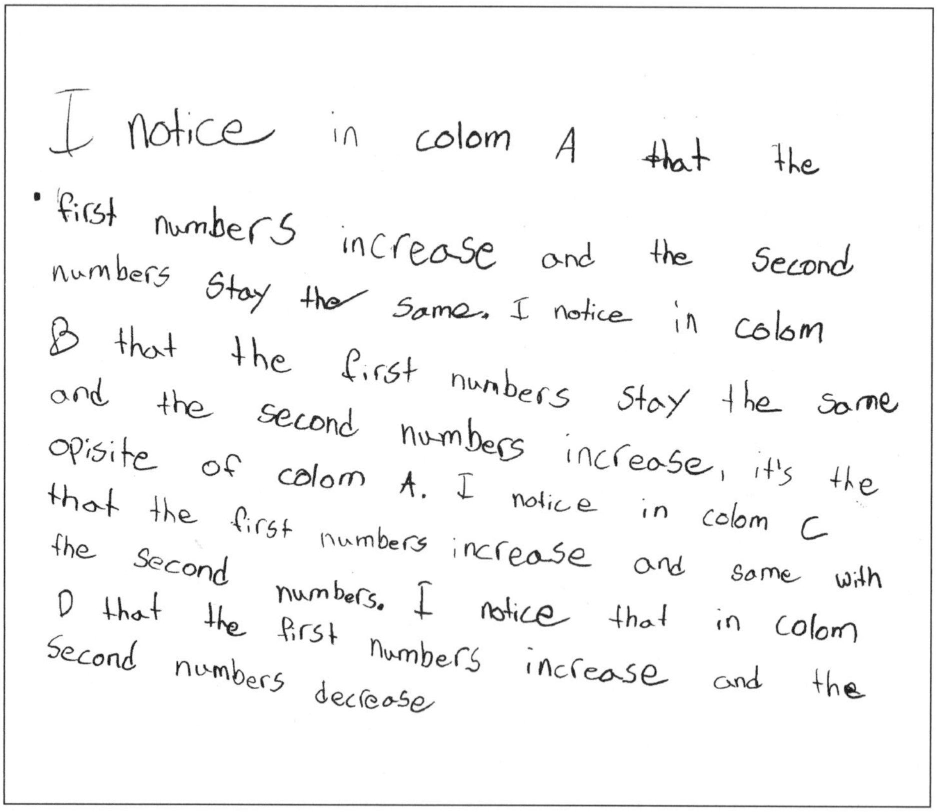
I notice in colom A that the first numbers increase and the Second numbers Stay the Same. I notice in colom B that the first numbers Stay the same and the second numbers increase, it's the opisite of colom A. I notice in colom C that the first numbers increase and same with the Second numbers. I notice that in colom D that the first numbers increase and the Second numbers decrease

FIGURE 9-3 Four Points 163

FIGURE 9-3 Gary had trouble expressing his thoughts, but was able to describe patterns for three of the four rows of points.

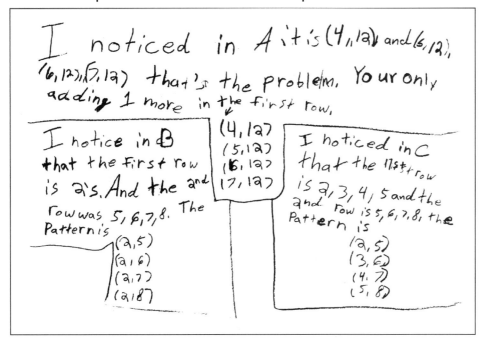

I noticed in A it is (4,12) and (6,12), (6,12),(7,12) that's the problem. Your only adding 1 more in the first row.

(4,12)
(5,12)
(6,12)
(7,12)

I notice in B that the first row is 2's. And the 2nd row was 5,6,7,8. The Pattern is
(2,5)
(2,6)
(2,7)
(2,8)

I noticed in C that the 1st row is 2,3,4,5 and the row is 5,6,7,8, the Pattern is
(2,5)
(3,6)
(4,7)
(5,8)

FIGURE 9-4 Amy understood that the order in which the ordered pairs were listed and their points charted did not affect the direction of the diagonal lines.

Writing About Patterns!

① In the horizontal patterns, I noticed that the first colums it increases by one and in the second colums it stays the same. ② In the vertical patterns, I noticed that the first columns stay the same and in the second columns it increases by one. ③ In the first diagonal patterns both of the columns increase by one. In the second diagonal patterns the first column increases by one and the second column decreases by one or the other way around. All that matters is where you start, the top or the bottom.

Several students were intrigued with the idea of adding the ordered pairs together and considering the patterns in the resulting sums. For example, Jaime showed on his paper the sums of one set of ordered pairs for each list. Then he summarized his thinking. He wrote: *A it goes 16, 17, 18, 19 so it add 1, add 1, adds 1, adds 1. B it goes 7, 8, 9, 10 so it adds everything totheger and goes up 1. C it goes 7, 9, 11, 13 so it adds 2 each time. D it goes, 19, 19, 19, 19 so they are all the same.* (See Figure 9–5.)

Karly was also intrigued with adding the ordered pairs to find the sum. She finished her writing with an "I wonder . . ." statement. She wrote: *In list D 2 + 17 = 19, 3 + 16 = 19, 4 + 15 = 19, and on the bottom 11 + 5 = 16, 10 + 6 = 16, 9 + 7 = 16, 9 + 7 = 16. I wonder why there is a differance between the numbers 19 and 16.*

Two students needed additional structure to be able to write. To help them, I wrote sentence starters on their papers. (See Figure 9–6.)

Brianna and Rick initially worked independently and then began quietly to discuss the pattern of the sums of the ordered pairs in the diagonal lists. I listened as they talked. Their writing was not as clear as their discussion had been, reminding me of how difficult written communication can be, especially when students are writing about new learning. (See Figure 9–7.)

FIGURE 9–5 Jaime focused on the sums of the numbers in the ordered pairs in each list.

FIGURE 9-6 I wrote sentence starters for each list to help Sam and another student write about the patterns.

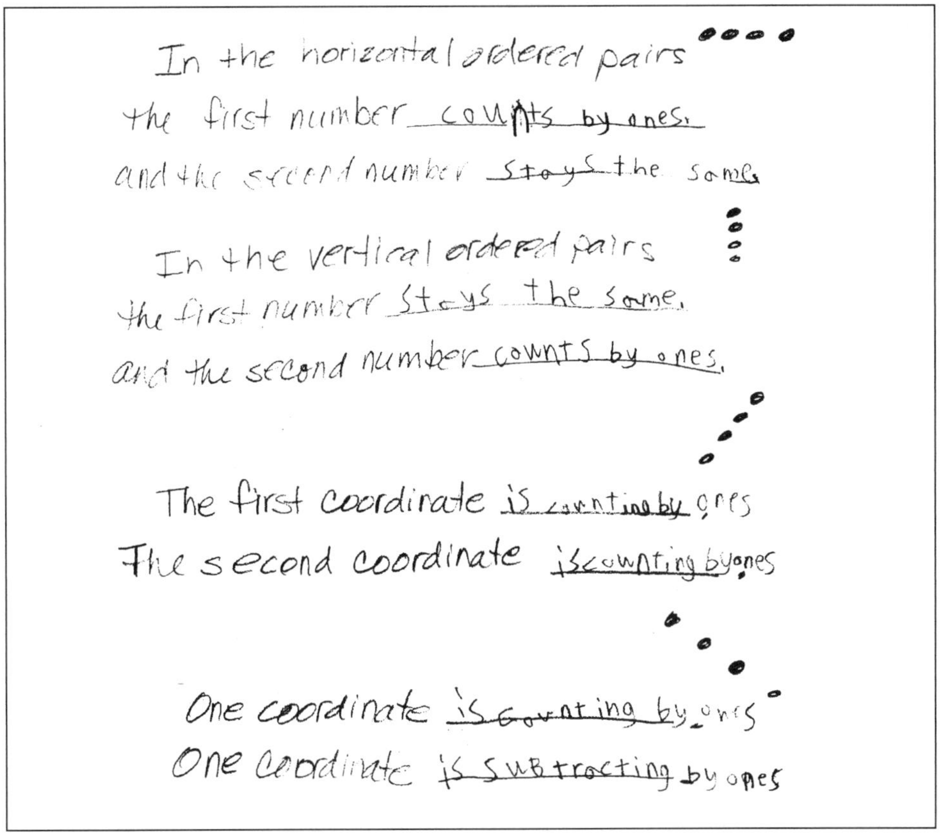

In the horizontal ordered pairs
the first number counts by ones.
and the second number stays the same.

In the vertical ordered pairs
the first number stays the same.
and the second number counts by ones.

The first coordinate is counting by ones
The second coordinate is counting by ones

One coordinate is counting by ones
One coordinate is subtracting by ones

FIGURE 9-7 In writing, Rick did not express what he discovered about the sums of the ordered pairs for points on a diagonal as clearly as he and Brianna did when they talked about their work.

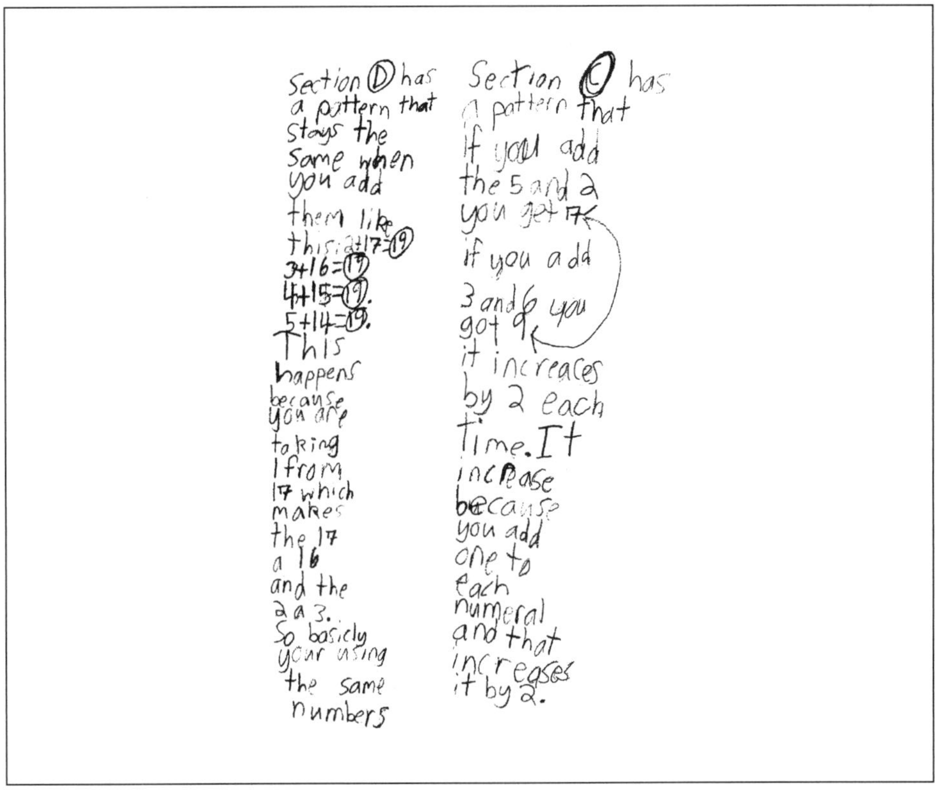

Section ① has a pattern that stays the same when you add them like this: 2+17=19 3+16=19 4+15=19 5+14=19. This happens because you are taking 1 from 17 which makes the 17 a 16 and the 2 a 3. So basicly your using the same numbers

Section ① has a pattern that if you add the 5 and 2 you get 7. If you add 3 and 6 you got 9 it increaces by 2 each time. It increase because you add one to each numeral and that increeses it by 2.

Michael's work showed that he had a clear understanding of adding ordered pairs and finding patterns. (See Figure 9–8.) Annie, another student, demonstrated her understanding in Figure 9–9.

FIGURE 9–8 Michael showed clear understanding and included examples to clarify his written explanation.

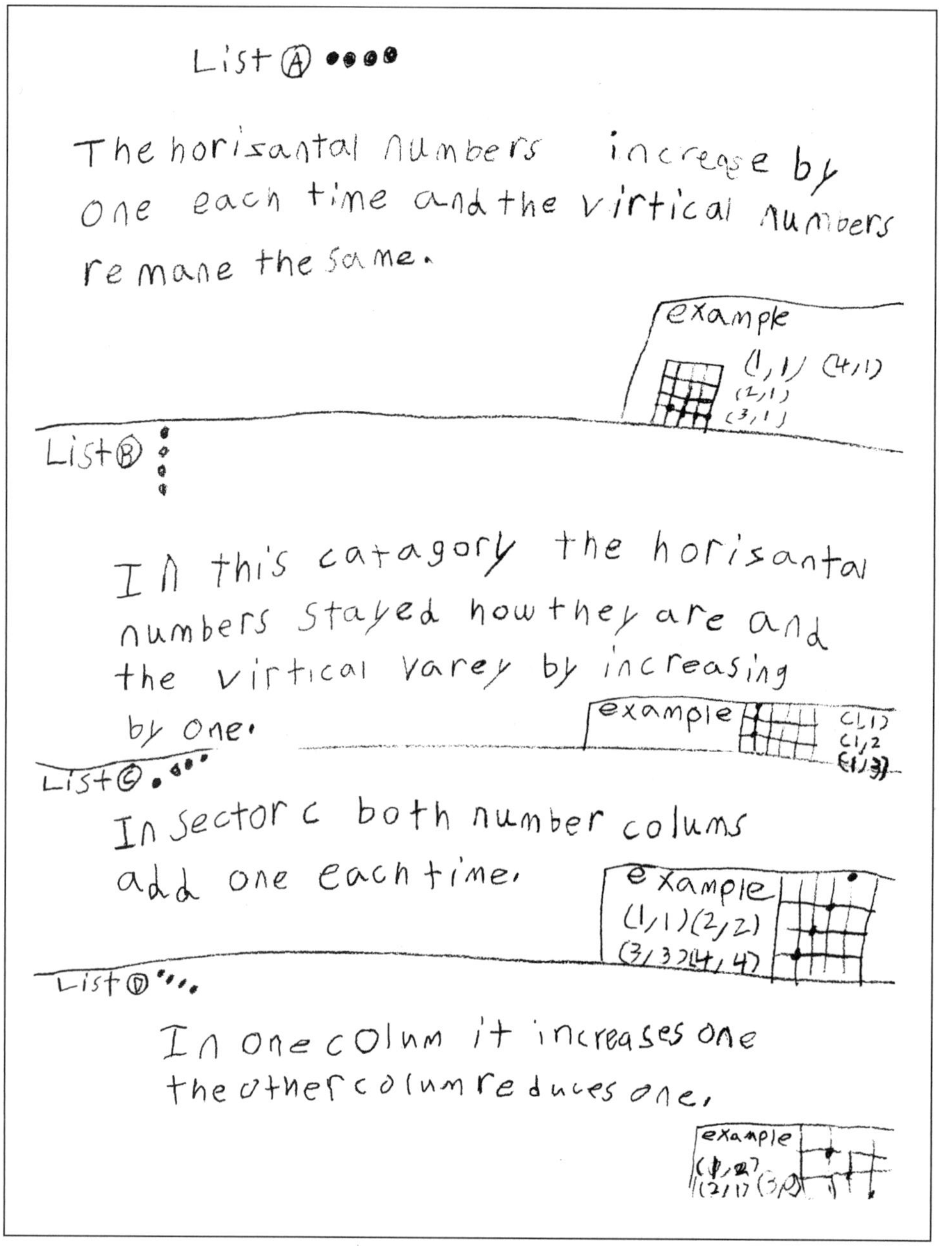

List Ⓐ ••••

The horisantal numbers increase by one each time and the virtical numbers remane the same.

example
(1,1) (4,1)
(2,1)
(3,1)

List Ⓑ

In this catagory the horisantal numbers stayed how they are and the virtical varey by increasing by one.

example
C(1)
C(1,2)
C(1,3)

List Ⓒ •••

In sector c both number colums add one each time.

example
(1,1)(2,2)
(3,3)(4,4)

List Ⓓ ••••

In one colum it increases one the other colum reduces one.

example
(1,2)
(2,1)(3,0)

FIGURE 9-9 Annie noticed an interesting pattern in column C but made an error in her writing about column D.

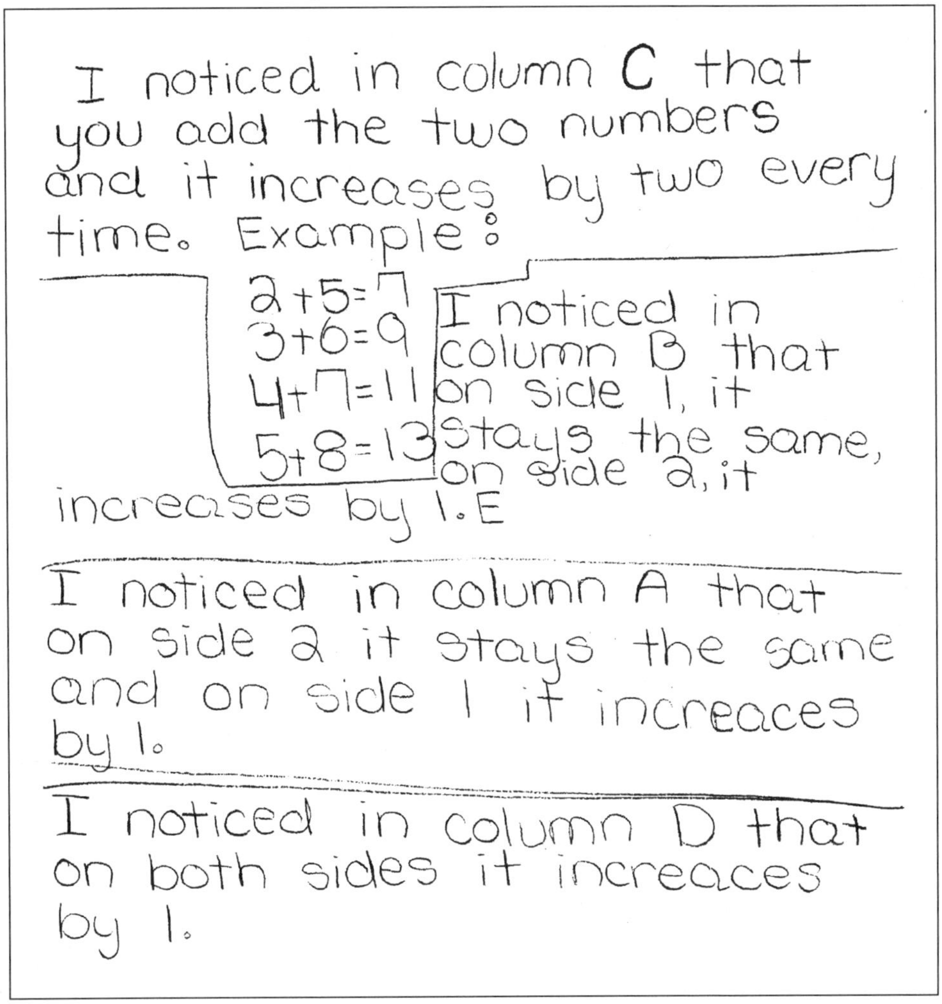

Four Points   **167**

I noticed in column C that you add the two numbers and it increases by two every time. Example:

2+5=7
3+6=9
4+7=11
5+8=13

I noticed in column B that on side 1, it stays the same, on side 2, it increases by 1. E

increases by 1.

I noticed in column A that on side 2 it stays the same and on side 1 it increases by 1.

I noticed in column D that on both sides it increases by 1.

## CHAPTER 10

Guess My Rule

A Variation on Two of Everything

OVERVIEW

The first chapter of the imaginative children's book *Anno's Math Games II*, by Mitsumasa Anno, initiates a lesson that provides students with experience with functions. The chapter describes a "magic machine" that follows a rule to change the items put into the machine into the items that come out. It's possible to change the controls on the machine to change the rule it follows, and the students try to figure out what the machine is doing each time. The lesson builds on the story and asks children to think about rules when numbers are the inputs and outputs. They use T-charts to represent the input and output numbers, guess the rules the machine is following, and describe the relationships using words and equations. Then students create rules of their own for others to guess. The lesson also describes how to connect the activity to graphing.

BACKGROUND

The first chapter in *Anno's Math Games II*, by Mitsumasa Anno, "The Magic Machine," opens by introducing Kriss and Kross and their wonderful magic machine. Their machine has two openings, and when Kriss and Kross put something into the opening on the left side of the machine, it comes out as something different from the opening on the right side. On each of the next six spreads of the book, Anno presents items on the left page—rabbits, ladybugs, shoes, pears, flowers, and so on—and shows on the right page how the machine changes them. Also, on each spread, Kriss and Kross change the controls of the machine so that it follows a different rule. The students try to figure out what the machine is doing each time.

In the Afterword of the book, Anno explains that the chapter uses the magic machine to symbolize the rules that govern relationships that exist between items, in this case between the items on the left and right sides of each spread. He writes: "It is the ability to engage in such relationship-seeking that enables imaginative problem solving to take place."

Anno's magic machine provides an ideal springboard for introducing students to the idea of functions. After considering the problems in the book, students think about relationships when numbers are the inputs and outputs. They learn that "setting the controls" of a machine establishes a rule that acts in the same way on each number put into the machine, and that for every input, there is exactly one output. They learn to record inputs and their resulting outputs on a T-chart and to describe the rule that the machine is following both in words and as an algebraic equation with variables representing the input and output values. By examining T-charts for other machines and figuring out the rules they follow, students get experience looking for numerical patterns, performing mental calculations, making conjectures and predictions, and using variables to express the relationships they find. To extend the lesson, students examine the graphs made from plotting on a coordinate grid the pairs of input and output numbers generated by the rules they create. If you're not familiar with this aspect of mathematics, read the background information in the Introduction for a more detailed explanation of the mathematics of functions.

This lesson is similar to the two lessons based on the children's book *Two of Everything* (see Chapters 1 and 5), providing a similar experience through a different context. However, while the lessons in these chapters are similar, there are variations in how they are presented and managed in the classroom.

When students invent their own rules in this lesson, they create T-charts with the input numbers from 0 to 20 in numerical order. However, even though ordering input values and then examining output values can reveal patterns that are useful for predicting rules, we don't impose this structure when students are engaged in guessing their classmates' rules. Rather, we encourage students to guess numbers and think about rules in any way they choose. Their guessing may seem disorganized and random, but it gives them control over how they choose to investigate and also gives them useful practice making conjectures and engaging in mental computation as they try to figure out the output values for input values using different rules.

VOCABULARY

coordinates, equation, equivalent equations, graph, input value, linear graph, output value, T-chart, variable

MATERIALS

- *Anno's Math Games II*, by Mitsumasa Anno (New York: Philomel Books, 1989)

- centimeter or half-inch graph paper, several sheets per student (see Blackline Masters)

TIME

- three class periods, then additional time for student presentations

I began the lesson with the students gathered on the rug. I showed them the cover of *Anno's Math Games II* and then opened the book to "The Magic Machine," the first chapter in the book.

I introduced the class to Kriss and Kross and their magic machine. "The machine changes what Kriss and Kross put into it, and it follows the same rule every time, unless Kriss and Kross change the controls. In a way, it's like a vending machine where you put money in and something comes out."

"You can get candy or chips," Blair said.

"Or drinks," Elyse added.

The students laughed when I showed them the first spread. All of the objects put into the machine—a glass, a change purse, a kettle, a sun, and a pair of glasses—come out with eyes.

"What would you call a machine that works this way?" I asked them.

"An eye-making machine," Tomas said.

"The eye and nose machine," George said, noticing that some of the objects also came out with a nose.

"But the glasses don't have a nose," Julie noticed.

The bottom of the next spread shows Kross getting into the machine and a baby Kross coming out. The children identified what else happens: the chicken becomes a chick, the butterfly becomes a caterpillar, and the frog becomes a tadpole.

"It makes things babies," Natalia said.

The third spread shows three rabbits turning into three dots, five ladybugs into five dots, six boxes into six dots, and four pairs of shoes into four dots. At the bottom, two cowboys riding on mules are about to get into the machine.

"What will come out?" I asked the class. Most thought that two dots would. Alan, however, thought that four dots would come out, two for the cowboys and two for the mules.

"Is there an answer book?" Amy wanted to know.

"No, there are no answers. We have to figure it out for ourselves," I responded. Alan said it could be either.

I pointed out to the class that the right handle of the machine was now down. "So you can't put dots into the machine from the right side," I said. "Why do you think they put that handle down?" No one had an idea.

"I've had this book for a long time," I told the class. "I've wondered about this and I think I've figured it out. No matter what you put into the left-hand side, you're sure what will come out: the same number of objects but just in dots. But if I put dots in the right side, I wouldn't know if those dots represented ladybugs or shoes or something else entirely." This seemed to make sense to the students.

I then turned to the next spread and hands flew up. "It's doubling," Kylie said. "The three gnomes become six and the two bugs become four and the five beans become ten." The page also shows Kross putting four glasses of juice into the machine.

"Eight glasses will come out," Ava said.

When I showed the following spread, several children immediately noticed that the machine was turning the objects into their shadows. "But look," I said, "the right handle is down again. Why do you think that's so?"

Teddy said, "You can't pick up your shadow. It's only there when you're in the sun, so you couldn't pick it up and put it in." No one else had an idea to offer.

I offered another possibility. "Even if we could pick up a shadow and put it in, if I put the car shadow into the right side, I couldn't be sure if I'd get a red car, a blue one, or some other color car."

I then showed the final spread to the class and asked the students to compare the left and right pages to decide what the machine was doing. It was obvious to them that the machine was adding one more each time—five gnomes changed to six gnomes, six pears to seven, and four flowers to five. Both levers of the machine were open, and the illustration at the bottom of the page shows Kriss putting six dragonflies into the right side. The students knew that five dragonflies would come out the other side.

Introducing Guess My Rule I then drew a picture of a machine on the board with both handles up, indicating how something went in and something came out.

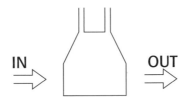

I said, "I'll set the controls for the machine, and your job is to try to figure out what my rule is. Here's how we'll play." I stopped and drew a T-chart on the board, labeling the columns *In* and *Out*.

I continued, "For my machine, I'm going to put a number in, then do something to it, and let you know what comes out. Until I change the controls, the machine will do the same thing to any number I put in. After I give you the first In and Out numbers, I'll write only an In number. If you want to guess what comes out, raise a hand. When I call on you, if you think you know what my machine is doing, don't tell the rule, but just tell what the output number is. After four students have correctly identified output numbers, then someone can tell the rule." I've taught this lesson many times over many years, and this is the best way I've found to manage the activity to keep the students involved and thinking, and to avoid someone blurting out the rule before others have had at least some time to think. I wrote the first pair of input and output numbers on the T-chart, *4* and *8*. I chose these numbers purposely because they initiate two conjectures, either that the machine is doubling the input or that the machine is adding four to the input. Typically, students' first guess is that the machine is doubling the input.

For that reason, I chose the rule of adding four to help students realize that more information is needed to guess a rule than merely one pair of numbers. I then wrote a *5* in the input column.

In	Out
4	8
5	

More than half the class wanted to respond. "Remember, don't tell what you think the machine is doing, just tell what number would come out if I put a five in," I reminded the class. I called on Lena.

"It's ten," she said confidently.

I responded, "That's a good guess, but it isn't what my machine is doing." Rather than have other students guess, I gave the correct answer for the input value of 5 by writing 9 in the output column. Giving the correct answer gives additional information that's useful for students to figure out the rule. Also, when I've tried having others make guesses for the same number, I find that their guessing sometimes becomes less thoughtful and more frantic as students try to get the answer right.

After I wrote the 9, some students said, "I get it!" Others weren't sure. I then wrote a *10* under the 5. Hands flew up. I called on Alex.

In	Out
4	8
5	9
10	

"I think it's fourteen," he said.

"Yes, that's right," I replied, writing *14* on the chart. I also made a tally mark next to the chart and said, "That's one correct guess. After three more correct guesses, someone can try to explain the rule." Then I wrote a *2* under the 10. After a moment, I called on Ally.

In	Out	
4	8	I
5	9	
10	14	
2		

"It's six, I'm sure of it," Ally said. I confirmed her answer, drew another tally mark, recorded the 6, and then wrote a 7 in the input column.

Now all but a few children wanted to respond. I called on Charlie, who correctly identified the output value as 11, making the third correct guess. I continued by writing *217* in the input column; Maria answered that the output would be 221. Now I had drawn four tally marks.

In	Out	
4	8	IIII
5	9	
10	14	
2	6	
7	11	
217	221	

"That makes four correct guesses," I said. "Before I ask someone to describe the rule, let me give you some instructions. Your rule should complete this sentence." I wrote on the board:

The value of the output number is

I called on Kylie to describe the rule. "It's plus four," she said.

"Can you say the rule using the sentence I began on the board?" I asked her.

Kylie said, "The value of the output number is plus four to the number that went in."

"Let me write your idea on the board," I said. I read the beginning of the sentence and then added Kylie's idea, paraphrasing to make it grammatical. Kylie nodded her agreement. I wrote:

The value of the output number is four plus the number that went in.

I then wrote *50* in the input column. "What would come out?" I asked. All hands went up and I had the students say the answer together. I recorded *54*, and then underneath it, in the output column, wrote *87*.

In	Out
4	8
5	9
10	14
2	6
7	11
217	221
50	54
	87

||||

"What number would I have to put in to get an output value of eighty-seven?" I asked. I asked this question to push the class to think flexibly. As well as figuring out output values for various input values, students should be able to figure out input values for given output values.

Frannie answered, "It's eighty-three." I recorded this on the chart.

"How do you know?" I asked.

"You just minus four," Frannie said. "You do the opposite."

"You seem to understand what the machine is doing," I said. "I'd like to do one more thing with the rule before I change the controls. I'd like to write it a shorter way." I wrote on the board:

Output number = 4 + Input number

"Who can explain what I wrote?" I asked.

"It's the same as what Kylie said," Teddy said. "You get the output by doing four plus the input."

"I can shorten the rule even more," I said. "Instead of writing 'output number' and 'input number,' I can use symbols to represent those numbers. Then we'll have an algebraic equation. For symbols we can use a shape, like a box or a triangle, or any letter of the alphabet. Who would like to try?" I called on Michael.

"I'll use v for the value of the output number and i for the input number," he said.

"What would the equation be?" I asked.

"It would be 'v equals four plus i,'" Michael said. I wrote on the board:

$v = 4 + i$

Later in the lesson, I planned to ask children to use the same variables for their rules, namely, a box for the input number and a triangle for the output number. While this consistency is useful for communicating about input and output values, it seemed better for this first experience for students to choose their own variables so that they would understand that the choice of symbols is arbitrary. Sometimes when teaching the lesson, however, I impose the convention of box and triangle at the outset. Either way is appropriate.

A Second Rule   "Now I'm going to change the controls on the machine," I said, erasing the numbers on the T-chart and the rules except for the sentence starter. I wrote 6 and 3 on the chart, then the input number of 7 under the 6. As I did with the first rule, I chose numbers for which students could make several initial conjectures about the rule.

In	Out
6	3
7	

I reminded the class about the need for four correct guesses before anyone could tell the rule and then called on Elyse.

"Four," she said, thinking that my rule was to subtract three.

"That's a good guess, but it doesn't follow my rule," I responded. "A little bit of information is never enough to be sure about something—that's important to remember when you're looking for a pattern or rule." I wrote $3\frac{1}{2}$ next to the 7. Hands flew up.

I said to the class, "It seems that some of you have an idea, but please wait until I write another number in the input column of the T-chart, and then raise a hand if you want to guess the output value." I wrote *10* on the T-chart, turned to the class, and called on Julie.

In	Out
6	3
7	$3\frac{1}{2}$
10	

"It's five," she said.

"You're right," I replied. "That's one right guess. Three more and someone can guess the rule." I recorded *5* on the T-chart and drew a tally mark. The next three students guessed correctly for inputs of 11, 4, and 1. I recorded the numbers and a tally mark for each correct answer.

In	Out	
6	3	IIII
7	$3\frac{1}{2}$	
10	5	
11	$5\frac{1}{2}$	
4	2	
1	$\frac{1}{2}$	

George stated the rule clearly, "The value of the output number is half the value that went in."

"Would you like to try the rule as an equation?" I asked him. George nodded and came up to the board.

George said, "I'll use *o* and *i* for out and in."

"That's fine, but write a cursive *o* so it doesn't look like a zero," I said.

George continued, writing on the board as he said, "O equals . . . ." Then he paused, not sure how to proceed.

"Can I use *h* for half?" he asked.

"How would you figure out the output number if twenty went into the machine?" I said.

George said, "I'd divide by two. Oh, I get it." He wrote:

$$o = i \div 2$$

"That works," I said. It wasn't a conventional algebraic representation, but I didn't want to discourage George's thinking, which was correct. I said, "Watch as I write the same rule a few other ways." I wrote on the board:

$$o = \frac{i}{2}$$

$$o = \frac{1}{2}i$$

I pointed to each and read, " 'O equals *i* divided by 2' or 'O equals one-half of *i*.' "

A Third Rule   "How about a rule that's a little more complicated?" I said. The class was eager.

"This might stump you for a little bit, but remember that you're just learning about how to figure out rules like these." As I had before, I erased the numbers from the T-chart and all but the sentence starter. I wrote on the T-chart:

In	Out
5	11

For this rule, I gave directions that were slightly different from what we had been doing. I said, "This time, instead of my choosing the input numbers, when I call on you, you can decide on the input number I should write on the T-chart. I'll record your number. Then, after a moment for the other students to think, you can tell what you think the output number is." I made this change to prepare the students for how they would work independently later. About half of the students had a hand raised.

"What input number would you like, Elyse?" I asked.

"Six," Elyse said. I wrote 6 in the In column.

"Let's give the others a chance to think for a moment," I said. Then I said to Elyse, "So what number do you think is the output value for six?"

"Twelve," Elyse guessed and then added, "That's probably not right. It would be too easy."

I responded, "No, twelve isn't right, but it was a reasonable guess. And remember that a wrong answer is often a good opportunity to think about what the rule might be." I wrote *13* next to the 6.

In	Out
5	11
6	13

I called on Maria next. "What number would you like to put in?" I asked her.

"Ten," she replied. I recorded *10* on the T-chart, waited a moment, and then asked Maria to guess. "Thirty?" she said, tentatively. I shook my head and wrote *21* next to the 10.

Nick went next. "I'll put three in," he said and, in a moment he added, "I think seven comes out."

"Yes, you're right," I said, recording *7* next to the 3 and making a tally mark for the correct guess.

In	Out	
5	11	|
6	13	
10	21	
3	7	

"I got it! I got it!" Nick exclaimed.

"I don't get it," Paul complained.

"You haven't figured it out yet," I said to Paul. "Keep thinking and looking at the clues."

Nick's hand was up again, but I told him that since he had already had a turn, I would call on other students. I called on Julie.

"I want to put a four in," she said. I recorded the *4*.

"Is it nine?" Julie asked.

"Yes, it is," I said.

Julie grinned happily. "I know it now," she said. I recorded the *9* and made another tally mark.

In	Out	
5	11			
6	13	
10	21	
3	7	
4	9	

"I still don't get it," Paul said.

"That rule is too hard," Charlie said.

"No, it isn't," Nick said.

"Nothing is hard when you know it," I said. "Keep looking for patterns in the Out numbers for clues. Try out ideas. Remember, this is still a new activity and you haven't had much experience with it." I chatted to buy some time for others to think. I called on Ally.

"One hundred," she said for the input value. "I think the out number is two hundred one." I nodded, recorded the *100*, then next to it recorded *201*. I made a third tally mark.

Frannie came to life and I called on her. "I think if you put in two hundred, then four hundred one comes out," she said.

"You're right," I said, recording the information and making the fourth tally mark. Then about half a dozen other students had breakthroughs and were waving their hands.

In	Out	
5	11					
6	13	
10	21	
3	7	
4	9	
100	201	
200	401	

"We have four correct guesses now. Who wants to describe the rule?" I asked. A few hands went down and a few others went up. I called on Alan and recorded on the board what he said:

The value of the output number is double the number that goes in and then you add one more.

Conversation broke out in the class as students talked among themselves about Alan's rule. For some, the rule clarified what the machine was doing. Others were still confused. After a moment, I called the class back to attention.

"Who would like to tell me how to write the rule as an equation?" I asked. About half the class was willing.

I added, "Before I call on someone, I'd like you to use specific symbols for the variables: a triangle for the output values and a box for the input values." On the T-chart, I drew a box above In and a triangle above Out. I made this request to introduce some consistency to the rules. Also, using a box and a triangle would allow me to more easily show the students how to test the rule using the values on the T-chart. It's sometimes easier for students to see how numbers can be put in for variables when they see numbers written in boxes and triangles. I called on Elyse and recorded as she reported:

$$\triangle = \square \times 2 + 1$$

I then said, "We can test the rule using some of the values on the T-chart. Suppose we put the first input value, five, in the box." I did this and continued, "Then the equation says, 'Triangle equals five times two plus one.' How much is five times two plus one? Raise a hand when you've figured this out." I waited until everyone had raised a hand.

"Let's say the answer together," I said.

"Eleven," they chorused.

"Is eleven the output value for five?" I asked, pointing at the T-chart. They agreed. We tested several other values the same way.

Maria had a question. "Can you write the equation with the triangle at the end?"

"Tell me what to write," I said. I recorded what Maria suggested:

$$\square \times 2 + 1 = \triangle$$

"This is fine," I said and added, "Even when we use the same variable, we can write the equation in several ways." I listed the following on the board, validating Maria's idea by also writing each with the triangle at the end:

$$\triangle = (\square \times 2) + 1 \qquad (\square \times 2) + 1 = \triangle$$
$$\triangle = \square \cdot 2 + 1 \qquad \square \cdot 2 + 1 = \triangle$$
$$\triangle = 2 \cdot \square + 1 \qquad 2 \cdot \square + 1 = \triangle$$

I explained, "The parentheses tell you to be sure to do what's inside first, so we know to multiply before we add the one. If there were no parentheses, the rule in math is that the correct order is always to multiply first before adding or subtracting." Students would study the order of operations at other times, but it seemed to make sense to mention it here.

"Who knows what this dot means?" I asked, pointing to the dots I had used in two of the equations. Some students were familiar with using the raised dot to mean multiplication. "If we use a dot for the multiplication sign, then we don't confuse the times sign with an *x* we might be using for a variable," I said.

"I know another way to write the equations," Charlie said. I recorded his suggestion:

$$v = 2 \cdot i + 1$$

"Charlie used *v* and *i* for variables instead of the triangle and the box, and that's fine," I commented.

Day 2

To begin the class, I engaged the children in guessing another rule. I started by entering *0* and *2* in the In and Out columns of a T-chart. I like to take opportunities to use zero and reinforce for students that zero is a number. (Some students erroneously think of zero only as a placeholder.) Also, while it's obvious to students that zero plus two is two, this isn't the rule I was using, again reinforcing for students that more information is necessary to determine a pattern. The rule I had chosen was to multiply the input number by five and then to add two. For the input value of 0, five times zero gives zero, and two more brings the output value to 2. Using five as a multiplier produces patterns in the output column that are noticeable and interesting to students.

As I had before, I called on students to choose input numbers and then guess their output numbers, keeping track of their correct guesses until I had made four tally marks. It took eight guesses after the initial clue for four students to guess correctly. The students were amazed that all of the numbers in the output column ended in either 2 or 7.

□ In	△ Out	
0	2	IIII
5	27	
10	52	
2	12	
4	22	
1	7	
3	17	
100	502	
6	32	

I then called on Michael to verbalize the rule. "The value of the output number is five times the input plus two," he said. I recorded this on the board and then, as Ally reported, I recorded the equation. Ally directed me to use a dot to represent multiplication.

$$\triangle = 5 \cdot \square + 2$$

I then gave the students instructions for an assignment they would work on in pairs. "You'll now invent your own rules and then have a chance to present them, as I did mine, for others to guess." The students were excited about this idea and some began to reach for paper. I interrupted them and said, "Listen carefully to all of my directions first."

I then explained. "For your rule, so that you're sure when you come up to the board to give the correct output number for whatever input number someone gives you, you should make a T-chart for all of the numbers from zero to twenty. Then you won't have to figure an answer each time someone chooses a number. I didn't make a T-chart for the rule I just presented, but it would have been easier if I had done so. Then I would have had a T-chart cheat sheet that I could have used."

I then drew another T-chart on the board to model for the class, using the rule they had just guessed, what I meant by constructing a T-chart cheat sheet. I listed the numbers from *0* to *20* in order in the input column of the chart. With the students' help, I entered the output values.

□	△
In	**Out**
0	2
1	7
2	12
3	17
4	22
5	27
6	32
7	37
8	42
9	47
10	52
11	57
12	62
13	67
14	72
15	77
16	82
17	87
18	92
19	97
20	102

"What patterns do you notice?" I asked.

"All of the output numbers end in two or seven," Lena said.

"They go even, odd, even, odd, like that," Charlie said.

"They go up by fives," Teddy added. No one else had an observation to make.

None of the students noticed a connection between Teddy's observation on the T-chart and the multiplier in the equation. I didn't expect students to do so yet, but knew that they would have many more opportunities to look at T-charts and equations and possibly make this discovery.

I then gave the students instructions about their assignment, writing on the board as I explained:

1. *Think of a rule.*
2. *Make a T-chart cheat sheet for the input numbers 0–20.*
3. *Write your rule in words.*
4. *Write your rule as an equation.*

I concluded, "After you all finish your work, you'll take turns coming to the front of the room and the rest of the class will try to guess your rule." The room became noisy as the students got to work. Some pairs were able to think of a rule quickly, and others took more time. As I circulated, I answered questions, guessed the rules for some of their T-charts, and gave feedback on their equations. Common throughout the room was that students were trying to think of rules that would be hard for others to guess. In some cases, they made rules that were too hard for themselves!

For example, Charlie and Kylie were having a problem. "How much is three divided by four?" Charlie asked me in a stage whisper.

"Is it one-fourth?" Kylie asked, also whispering.

I sorted out that their rule was to divide the input number by four. They had figured out the outputs for some of the numbers—4, 8, 12, 16, and 20. Now they were working on the output value for an input of 3. I asked them, "How did you figure out that the output value for eight is two?"

"Easy," Kylie said. "Eight divided by four is two."

I drew eight small circles on their paper and said, "Suppose these are eight cookies and you're going to share them among four people. How many will each person get?"

"Two," they both answered.

"Show me how you would share them," I said. Kylie drew circles around pairs of cookies and said, "See, they each get two."

"So this is a picture of the math problem 'eight divided by four equals two,' " I said. They nodded.

"What if you had only one cookie to share among four people?" I asked, drawing another circle on their paper.

"It's one-fourth," Kylie said excitedly. "See, I knew it was one-fourth."

"What does one-fourth tell you?" I asked.

"It's how much each person gets," Charlie answered.

"Yes, it's how much each person gets if I divide one cookie among four people," I said, and I wrote the following as I did so:

$1 \div 4 = \frac{1}{4}$

I added, "But the problem you're trying to figure out is three divided by four, not one divided by four. How would you share three cookies among four people? That will give you the answer to three divided by four." After posing that question, I drew three circles on their paper and left them to work on the problem. (When I returned to them later, I learned that Charlie and Kylie had decided to change their rule to $\triangle = 3 \cdot \square + 4$. They had successfully completed their T-chart. [See Figure 10–1.])

Tomas and Elyse were also having a problem. They were excited about their rule of dividing the input number by two and then subtracting one and one-half to get the output number. "But three is the smallest number we can put in," Tomas said.

"If you put three in, you get zero out," Elyse said.

"What would the output value be if you put two in?" I asked.

"You can't do that one," Tomas said.

"I think that your machine will work for any number," I said.

"Wait," Elyse said, "we can do it." She started to figure out loud, "Two divided by two is one. Then you minus one and a half. Hey, it must be zero again," she said.

As Elyse figured, Tomas was thinking. "I know what to do," he said. "It has to be a negative number. You take away one and get to zero, then you go down one-half more. Can you have a negative one-half?" Tomas looked at me. They both looked confused.

"It's right!" Tomas realized. "Look, Elyse, I can prove it." I left them to continue their work. (See Figure 10–2.)

FIGURE 10–1 Using the rule $\triangle = (3 \cdot \square) + 4$, Charlie and Kylie predicted output values for 1–20 and 100.

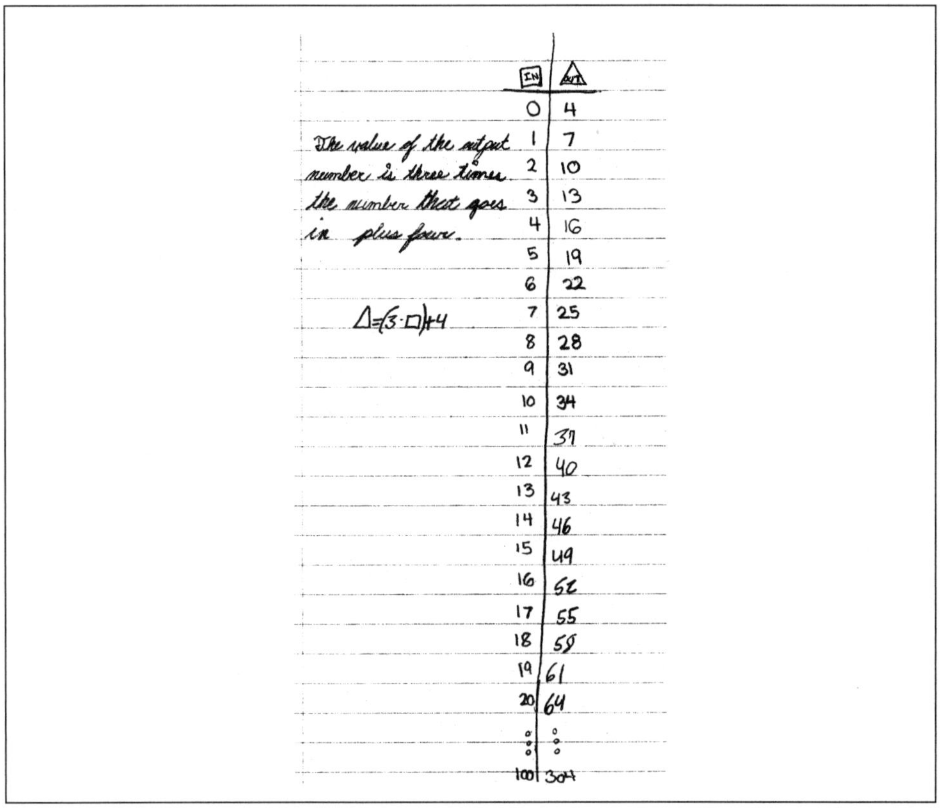

IN	△
0	4
1	7
2	10
3	13
4	16
5	19
6	22
7	25
8	28
9	31
10	34
11	37
12	40
13	43
14	46
15	49
16	52
17	55
18	58
19	61
20	64
⋮	⋮
100	304

The value of the output number is three times the number that goes in plus four.

$\triangle = (3 \cdot \square) + 4$

FIGURE 10–2 Tomas and Elyse learned that their output values could be negative numbers.

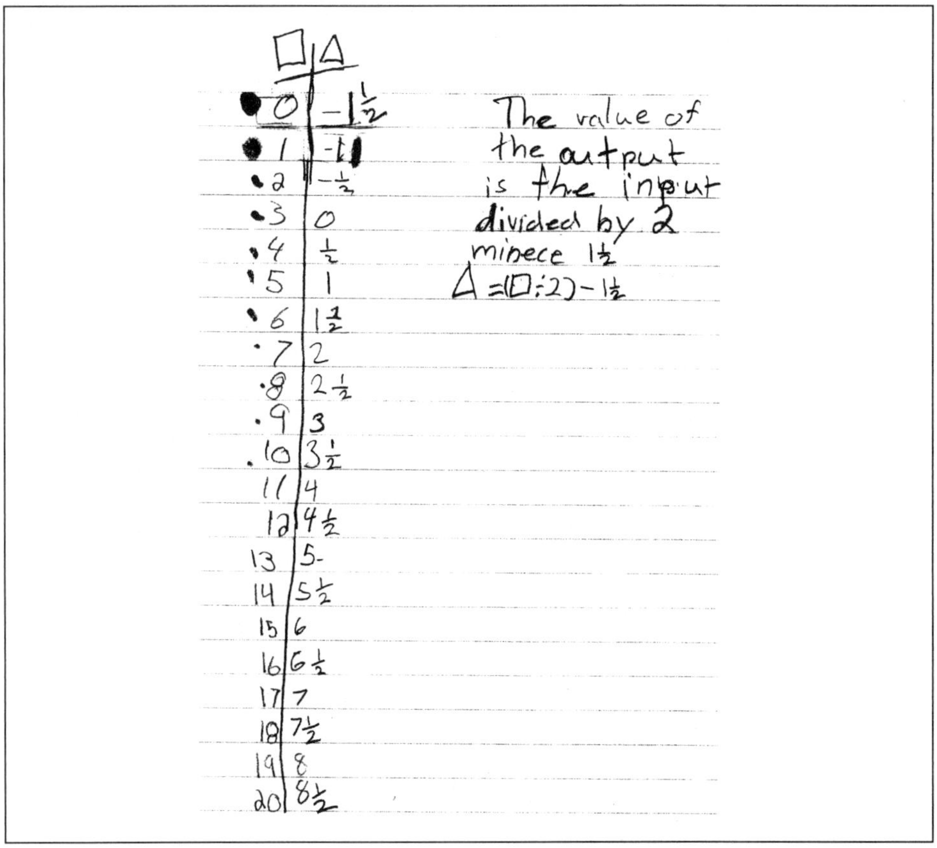

□	△
0	$-1\frac{1}{2}$
1	-1
2	$-\frac{1}{2}$
3	0
4	$\frac{1}{2}$
5	1
6	$1\frac{1}{2}$
7	2
8	$2\frac{1}{2}$
9	3
10	$3\frac{1}{2}$
11	4
12	$4\frac{1}{2}$
13	5
14	$5\frac{1}{2}$
15	6
16	$6\frac{1}{2}$
17	7
18	$7\frac{1}{2}$
19	8
20	$8\frac{1}{2}$

The value of the output is the input divided by 2 minece $1\frac{1}{2}$

$\triangle = (\square \div 2) - 1\frac{1}{2}$

Julie and Ingrid were pleased with their work. "I thought of the rule, but Julie is doing the figuring," Ingrid said.

"What's your rule?" I asked.

"You take the number and divide it by two and then you add itself on," Ingrid said.

"Did I write it right?" Julie asked. She had written:

$$\triangle = \square \div 2 + \square$$

"Which do you do first, divide by two or add?" I asked. Julie quickly inserted parentheses.

$$\triangle = (\square \div 2) + \square$$

"That makes it clear," I said. (See Figure 10–3.)

As students finished their papers, I collected them for the next day, when I planned to have pairs of students present their rules for the rest of the class to guess.

FIGURE 10-3 Julie and Ingrid clarified their rule by adding parentheses:
$\triangle = (\square \div 2) + \square$.

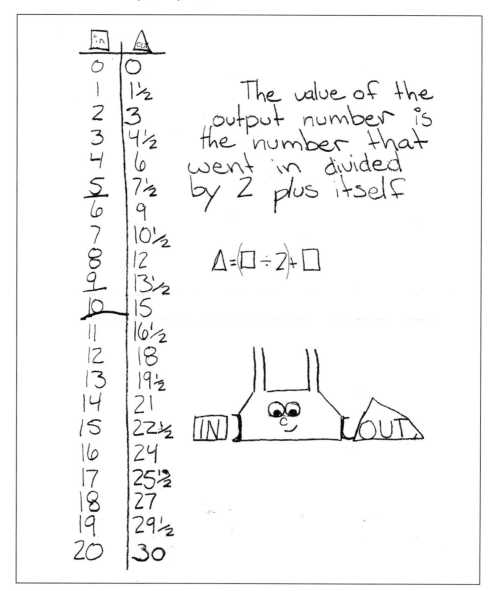

The students were eager to have others guess their rules. I reviewed the procedure for the students to follow. I said, "Decide how you will call on students; who will record the guesses on a T-chart; and who will check the answers against your T-chart cheat sheet. When four students have guessed output numbers correctly, then you should call on someone to describe the rule."

I called on Teddy and Blair. I chose them because their rule was similar to the ones I had presented and I thought that the class would have success figuring it out. Also, while some students had rules that involved negative numbers or fractions, Teddy and Blair's rule involved only whole numbers. Their rule was to multiply the input number by two and then add six. (See Figure 10–4.)

The boys decided that Teddy would hold their T-chart, Blair would record on the board, and they would take turns calling on students to guess. Blair carefully drew a T-chart, turned to the class, and called on Marco. I interrupted, "Don't forget that you have to give the class a first clue. You and Teddy should agree on a pair of numbers to write on your T-chart on

FIGURE 10–4 Blair and Teddy's T-chart cheat sheet for the rule
$(\square \times 2) + 6 = \triangle$.

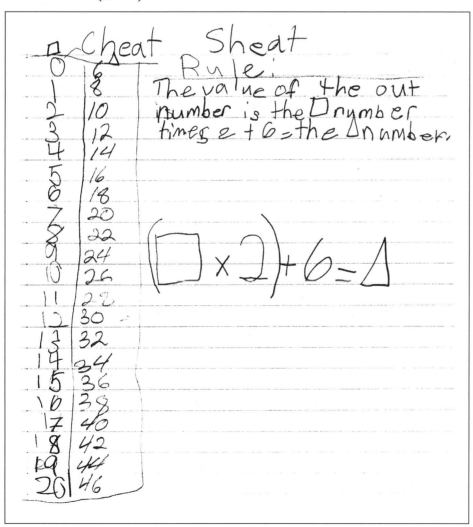

the board." The boys conferred and Blair entered *4* and *14* on the chart. Then Blair called on Marco again.

"Five," Marco said. Blair recorded the *5*. Teddy began to give the output number, but I stopped him before he did so.

"Remember to give Marco a chance to guess," I said. The first time students engage in an activity, there typically are rough spots that I know will smooth out with some practice. I motioned to Marco to guess.

"Seventeen?" he said tentatively.

"No, it's sixteen," Teddy said. Blair recorded *16* next to the *5*, and Teddy called on Kylie.

"Three," she said, and then, after Blair recorded it, "Twelve."

"That's right," Teddy said. Blair recorded *12* and made a tally mark. About ten students had their hands up, eager to guess next. Blair called on Michael.

"Ten," he said, and then said for the output value, "Twenty-six."

"That's right," Teddy said.

"They're guessing it too quick," Blair said as he entered the *26* and made another tally mark. Now more hands were raised. The boys called on George and then Lena, and they both made correct guesses.

| □ | △ | |
In	Out	
4	14	IIII
5	16	
3	12	
10	26	
0	6	
8	22	

"There were four correct guesses," I said, "so you can call on someone to describe the rule." Teddy called on Tomas.

"It's times two plus six," Tomas said. Others agreed. I wrote on the board:

The value of the output number is

"Can you state the rule again beginning with what I wrote on the board?" I asked Tomas.

Tomas nodded and said, "The value of the output number is times two plus six." I recorded this on the board.

"What are you multiplying by two?" I asked Tomas.

"The In number," he said.

"Can you insert something about the input number in your rule?" I asked. Tomas restated the rule and I added to what I had written on the board:

The value of the output number is the input number times two plus six.

"Are we done?" Blair asked.

"Not until we have the equation," I said. Blair turned to the class and called on Ingrid. She dictated and I recorded:

$$\triangle = (\square \times 2) + 6$$

After we tried three of the numbers on the T-chart to be sure that the equation worked, Blair and Teddy sat down.

Next I called on Ally and Julien. Their rule was $\triangle = (6 \cdot \square) - 9$, and it was more challenging for the class. Not only were 6 and 9 larger than the numbers others were using in their rules, but the input numbers 0 and 1 had negative output numbers. (See Figure 10–5.) However, Ally and Julien followed the procedure correctly and the class was able to guess their rule in eight guesses after the initial clue.

$\square$ In	$\triangle$ Out	
6	27	||||
1	−3	
5	21	
3	9	
0	−9	
10	51	
2	3	
4	15	
9	45	

FIGURE 10–5 As their cheat sheet shows, Ally and Julien's rule produced negative output numbers for the input numbers 0 and 1.

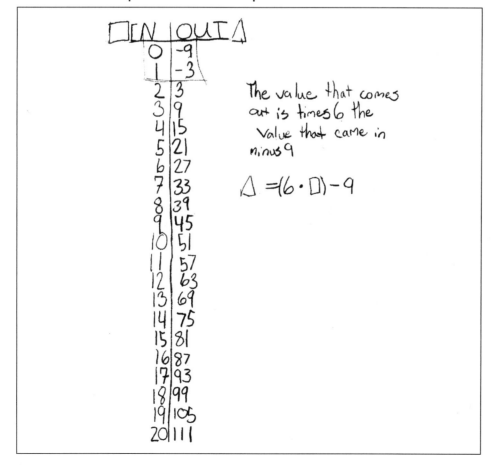

"All of the output numbers are odd," Elyse noticed.

I called on Ava and Alan next. Their rule was $\triangle = \square \cdot \square$ (see Figure 10–6), and guessing it took the class six guesses after the initial clue. Students guessed incorrectly for the input numbers of 0 and 1, but the output of 144 for 12 was the telling clue.

$\square$ In	$\triangle$ Out	
16	256	‖‖
0	0	
1	1	
2	4	
12	144	
4	16	
3	9	

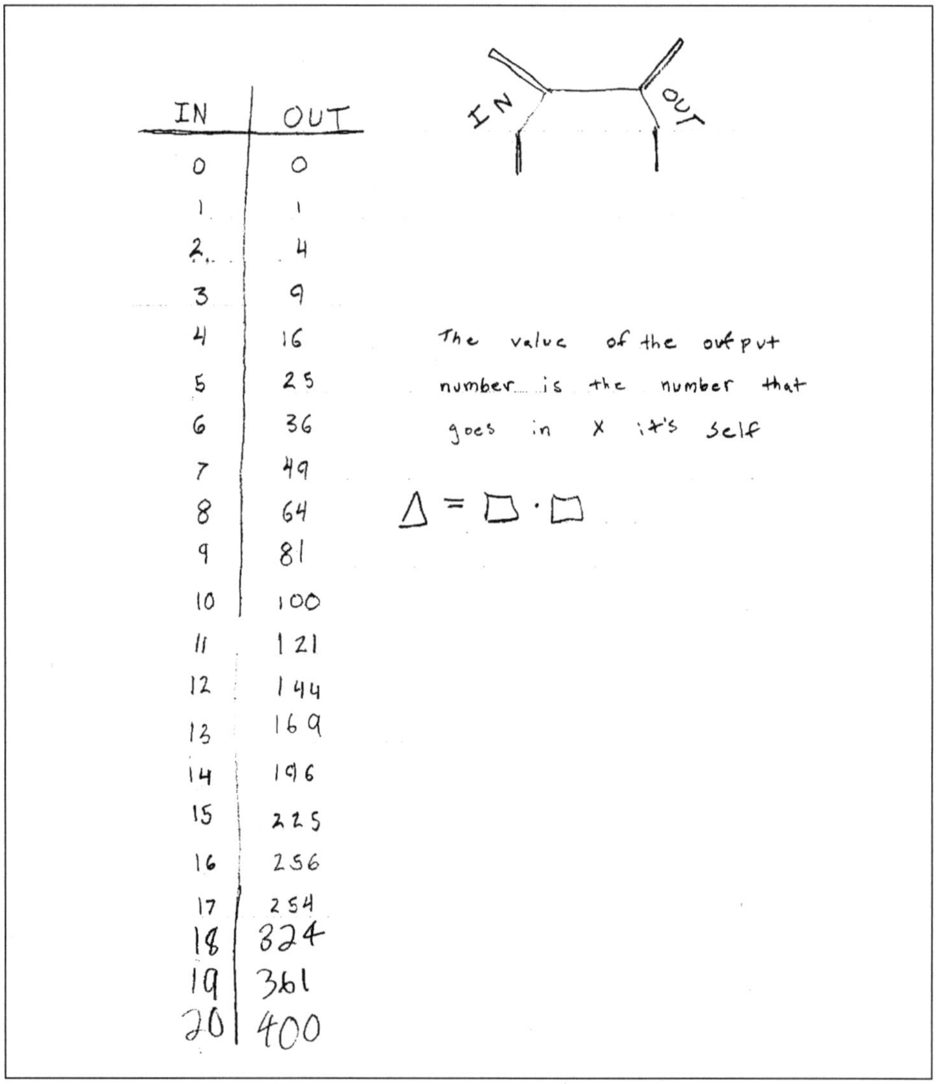

FIGURE 10-6 Ava and Alan's cheat sheet for the rule $\triangle = \square \cdot \square$.

IN	OUT
0	0
1	1
2	4
3	9
4	16
5	25
6	36
7	49
8	64
9	81
10	100
11	121
12	144
13	169
14	196
15	225
16	256
17	254
18	324
19	361
20	400

The value of the output number is the number that goes in X it's self

$\triangle = \square \cdot \square$

After these three presentations, I told the children that they would have the chance on other days to try guessing more of each other's rules.

Continuing with Student Presentations Over the next week, one or two pairs of students presented their rules each day until everyone had had a chance to do so. Julie and Ingrid's rule led to a rich discussion. Their rule was $\triangle = (\square \div 2) + \square$ (refer back to Figure 10–3). The class had four correct answers after six guesses.

$\square$ In	$\triangle$ Out
6	9
0	0
10	15
5	$7\frac{1}{2}$
4	6
3	$4\frac{1}{2}$
2	3

Julie called on Socoro for the rule. Socoro said, "The value of the output is the input divided by two times three." I recorded what Socoro said on the board.

"That's not right," Julie said. I suggested that Socoro tell the equation for her rule so that we could look at it more carefully. I recorded on the board as Socoro dictated and then checked with her to be sure she agreed with where I put the parentheses.

$$\triangle = (\square \div 2) \times 3$$

"Before we discard Socoro's rule, let's try using it with the input and output values on the T-chart," I said. We did so and found that Socoro's rule worked. Julie and Ingrid were surprised and confused, but most of the students said that they saw the rule the same way that Socoro had.

Ally, however, had a different rule. She said, "The output value is the number that goes in times two minus half of the number that goes in." I recorded Ally's idea and then her equation:

$$\triangle = (\square \times 2) - (\square \div 2)$$

We tried Ally's rule and it worked for all of the values on the T-chart. "But that's not what we wrote," Ingrid said.

I responded, "Write on the board the equation that you and Julie came up with." Ingrid wrote the equation and we then tested it with the values on the T-chart.

$$\triangle = (\square \div 2) + \square$$

"So what do you think?" I asked the class. "Try a few input and output values to check Julie and Ingrid's rule." I gave the class a few moments to do so and then called them back to order.

"They're all right," Teddy said.

"They have to be; they all work," Michael added.

I told the class, "I'm glad this happened because it shows you that different equations can represent the same rule. These are called *equivalent equations* and all of them are correct. Only one is the exact equation that Julie and Ingrid came up with, but you could represent their T-chart correctly with the other two equations as well."

The opportunity to talk about equivalent equations usually comes up in classes when I do this activity. In this class, it also came up with Lena and Amy's rule. When they came to the front of the room, Amy drew a T-chart and entered the numbers for their first clue, 5 and 92.

"This is going to be a hard one," Paul said.

"We hope so," Lena responded. Amy called on Frannie. She gave the input number of 0 and then guessed 0 for its output.

"No," Lena said. "It's ninety-two again." For the first time in this activity, no hands were raised. Then, after a moment, Ally raised a hand.

"One," she said. Then, after Amy had recorded *1* in the input column, Ally said, "Ninety-two."

"That's right," Lena confirmed, and Amy recorded 92 and made a tally mark to indicate the correct response.

□ In	△ Out	
5	92	I
0	92	
1	92	

Now hands were waving and the next three students, Marco, Alex, and Natalia, made correct guesses of 92 for their input values.

□ In	△ Out	
5	92	IIII
0	92	
1	92	
10	92	
3	92	
4	92	

"That can't be right," Charlie said. The class was again quiet.

"Ooh, I think I've got it," Ally said.

"What's your idea?" I asked.

Ally said, "The value of the output number is the input number times zero plus ninety-two. So it's 'triangle equals box times zero plus ninety-two.'" I recorded on the board:

$$\triangle = (\square \times 0) + 92$$

"That's it," Amy said. (See Figure 10–7.)

"I don't get it," George said.

Ally said, "To get to ninety-two all the time, you have to get to zero first and then add on ninety-two." Ally's explanation seemed to help George. Also, we tried the equation for each of the input numbers on the T-chart and saw that it produced ninety-two for each of them.

FIGURE 10–7 As Lena and Amy's cheat sheet shows, 92 was the output value for all input values.

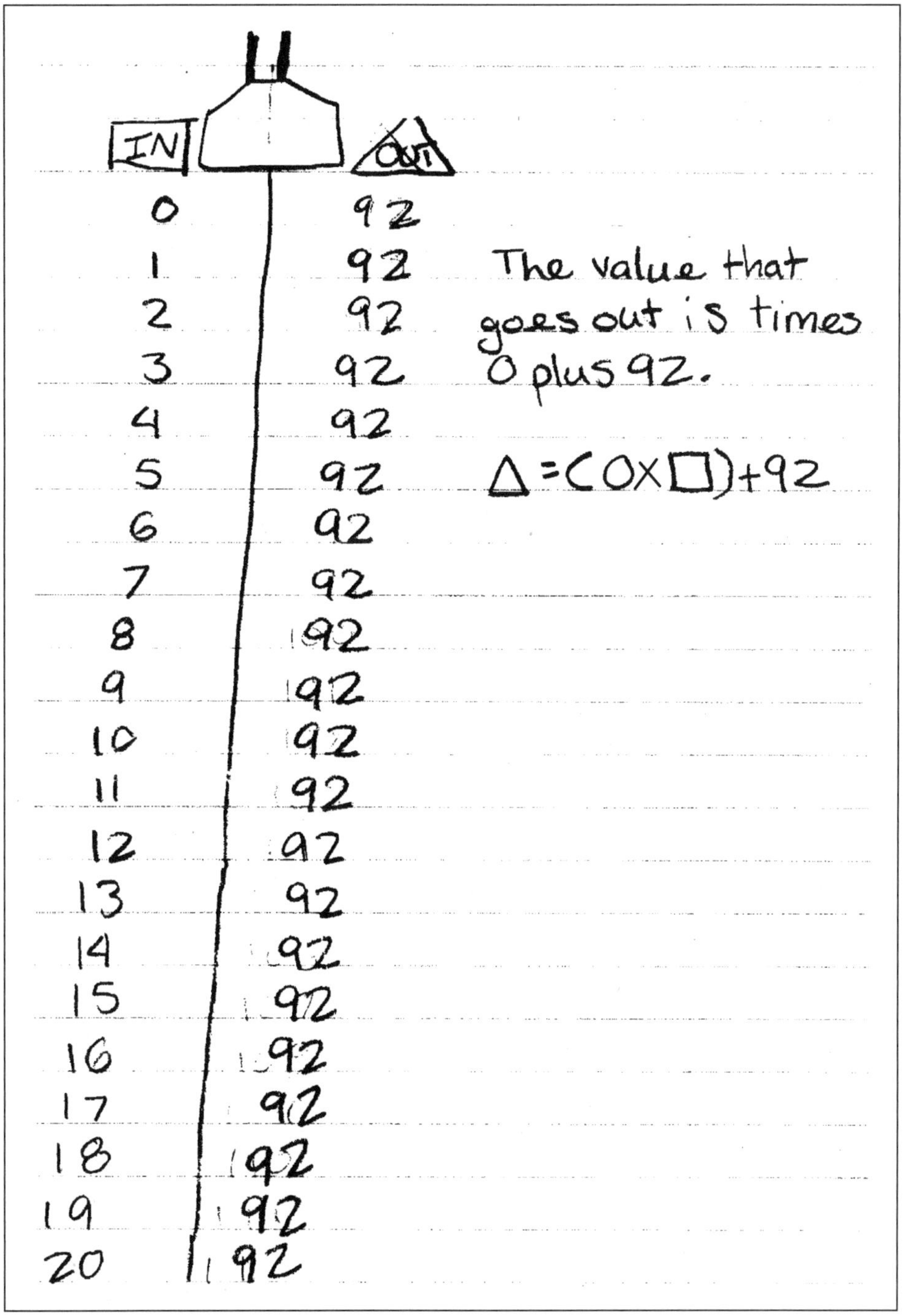

Michael had another idea. He said, "I think you can do the input number minus itself and then plus ninety-two."

"How would you write that as an equation?" I asked. I recorded on the board as Michael gave the equation:

$$\triangle = \square - \square + 92$$

We tried it for several input values and it worked.

Extensions

To introduce the students to graphing their rules, I began class one day by having them guess my rule, using the same procedure we had been following and a rule I had presented to them before. I wrote in the initial clue of *0* for the input and *3* for the output and the students quickly made four correct guesses.

□ In	△ Out	
0	3	IIII
1	5	
2	7	
8	19	
6	15	
5	13	

They successfully identified the equation:

$$\triangle = 2 \cdot \square + 3$$

On a chart-size sheet of one-inch graph paper, I drew two axes. "Let's mark a point for each pair of numbers on the T-chart," I said. I had a student come up and mark each point.

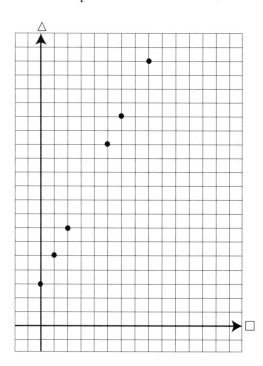

"What do you notice?" I asked.

"The points are going up," George said.

"And they seem to be going in a line," Socoro said.

I took a yardstick and drew a line through the points to illustrate Socoro's observation. We identified the coordinates for several other points on the line and verified that they belonged on the T-chart. The students were fascinated that the points went in a line.

I then gave the class directions. "For the rules you invented, graph each of the pairs of numbers on your T-chart cheat sheet and see what pattern you get." The students eagerly got to work, curious about what they would learn. Everyone's graph made a line except for Ava and Alan's. Their rule was that the output number was equal to the input number times itself, or $\triangle = \square \times \square$. The graph of this equation, using only positive numbers for inputs, is a curve that is the right half of a parabola. (See Figure 10–8.)

FIGURE 10–8 Ava and Alan produced the right half of a parabola when they graphed the pairs of numbers on their T-chart cheat sheet. They had to tape two sheets of graph paper together to plot just six points.

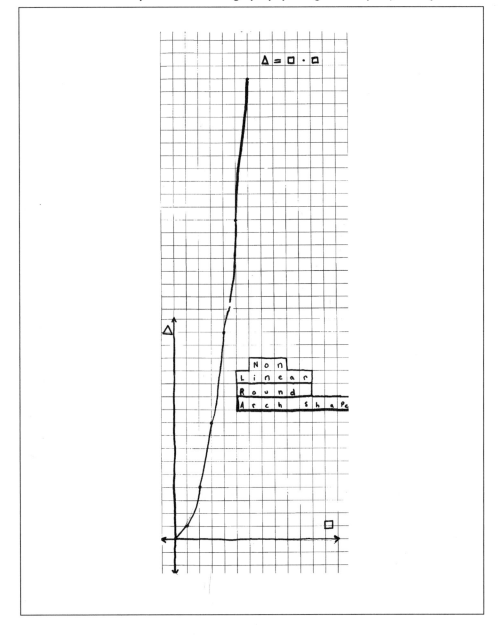

"If your points go in a line, then your graph is linear," I said. I wrote *linear graph* on the board and underlined *line* in *linear* to show the children why this word made sense. I asked students to post their graphs so that they could see one another's. (See Figures 10–9 through 10–11 for examples.) I didn't talk more about them, as I knew that we'd have a chance at other times during the year to discuss relationships between graphs and equations.

FIGURE 10–9 Lena and Amy's graph of their rule produced a horizontal row of points.

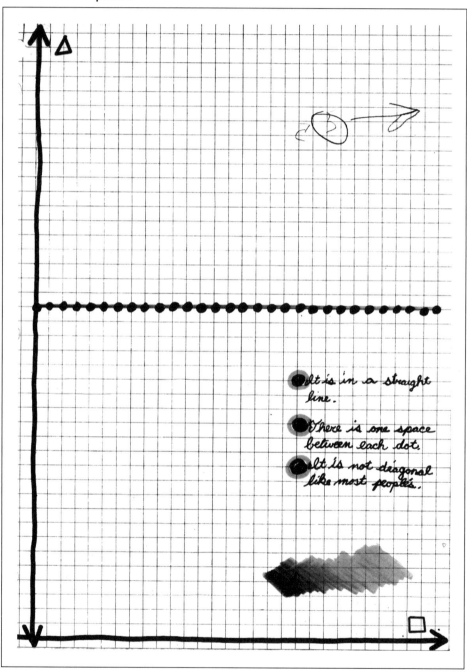

It is in a straight line.

There is one space between each dot.

It is not diagonal like most people's.

FIGURE 10–10 Julie and Ingrid's rule, $\triangle = (\square \div 2) + 2$, produced a linear graph, with the line slanting up to the right.

Guess My Rule   **195**

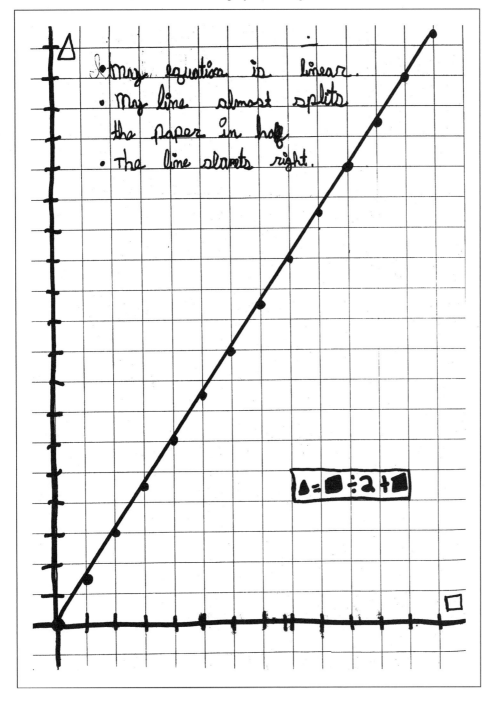

Caption from figure:
- My equation is linear.
- My line almost splits the paper in half.
- The line slants right.

$\triangle = \blacksquare \div 2 + \blacksquare$

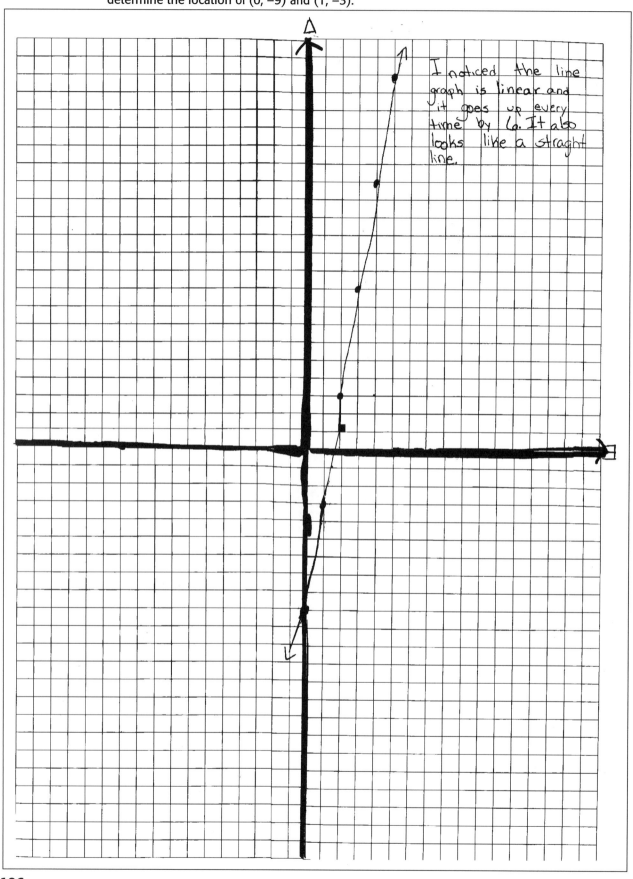

I noticed the line graph is linear and it goes up every time by 6. It also looks like a straight line.

## CHAPTER 11

Piles of Tiles

Investigating Patterns with Color Tiles

OVERVIEW

In this lesson, students use square tiles to make and check predictions about geometric patterns. After seeing the first three piles of tiles in a pattern, the students predict what the fourth and fifth piles look like. They record on T-charts, write about the patterns they discover, and represent the patterns with equations and graphs. The arrangements of tiles chosen for this lesson typically evoke several geometric interpretations from students, but the numerical patterns are the same for each interpretation.

BACKGROUND

Using square tiles gives students a concrete way to interact with patterns that grow. Also, investigating the growing shapes gives students experience connecting geometry, number, and algebra.

Students first see the following three piles of tiles:

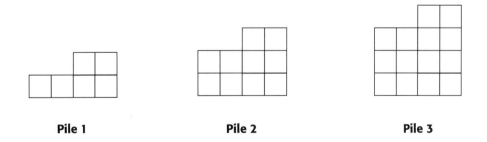

Pile 1   **Pile 2**   **Pile 3**

When they think about extending the pattern beyond the first three piles, they typically offer several interpretations, as occurred in this class. Several ways are valid. Some students focus on the rows of four and then add the two extra tiles on the top. In this interpretation, they notice that the number of rows is the same as the pile number.

197

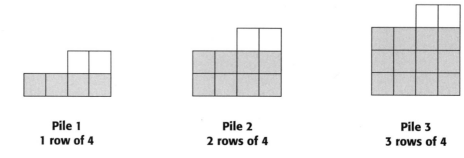

Pile 1
1 row of 4

Pile 2
2 rows of 4

Pile 3
3 rows of 4

Other students focus on the columns and see two shorter columns on the left and two longer columns on the right. They notice that the number of tiles in the shorter columns is the same as the pile number, and the number of tiles in the longer columns is one more than the pile number.

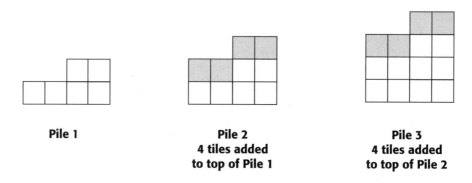

Pile 1
2 columns of 1
2 columns of 2

Pile 2
2 columns of 2
2 columns of 3

Pile 3
2 columns of 3
2 columns of 4

Some students see that the next pile in the pattern can be constructed by adding a tile to the top of each column in the previous pile. Some think of this as adding two rows of two.

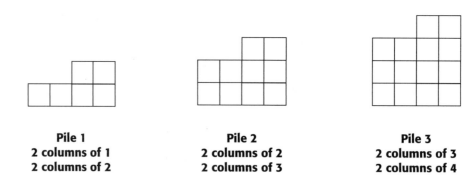

Pile 1

Pile 2
4 tiles added
to top of Pile 1

Pile 3
4 tiles added
to top of Pile 2

Other students also look to the previous pile but think of adding four tiles to the bottom of it to get the next one.

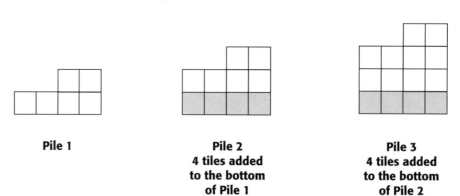

Pile 1

Pile 2
4 tiles added
to the bottom
of Pile 1

Pile 3
4 tiles added
to the bottom
of Pile 2

In the lesson, students use the patterns they discover to predict how the tenth and hundredth piles will look. They also write equations to represent the patterns and use the ordered pairs on the T-chart to plot points to make a coordinate graph. While the students can explore the tile patterns with no prerequisite preparation, they should have had experience writing equations and plotting points before being asked to do so for this lesson. The class in the vignette had previous experience with both.

Extending the pattern backward in the T-chart presents the opportunity to talk with the students about the distinction between looking at the patterns mathematically by focusing only on the numerical data and looking for patterns in the numbers, or looking at the pattern in relation to the concrete situation of building with tiles. For example, it's possible to extend the pattern back and see that the ordered pair (–1, –2) fits the pattern of the other pairs of numbers on the T-chart. However, it's not possible to build a pile with a negative number of tiles. While we can talk about the numbers and plot the points on a graph, there's a "loss of reality" when relating those numbers to the problem-solving situation.

During the course of the lesson, students use variables when representing the patterns with equations. The lesson is useful for reinforcing for students that variables represent numbers and that various symbols, such as letters or shapes like boxes or triangles, can be used.

Students may suggest different equations to represent the same mathematical idea. For example, one student might describe the pattern as $(4 \times \square) + 2 = \triangle$, while another might describe it as $(2 \times \square) + [2 \times (\square + 1)] = \triangle$. Recognizing that there are many ways of representing one idea algebraically helps students learn about equivalent equations.

If you haven't had a good deal of experience with patterns like these, try investigating the problems in the "Extensions" section. Following are equations for each of them. Keep in mind that there is more than one way to represent these patterns with equations and you may see the pattern geometrically in a way that leads to a different algebraic representation. Also, don't provide these answers to your students. Let them work at their own level now. They will encounter these ideas many times as they continue their study of algebra.

A. $(4 \times \square) + 1 = \triangle$

B. $(2 \times \square) + 1 = \triangle$

C. $(4 \times \square) + 1 = \triangle$

D. $\square + 2 = \triangle$

E. $(2 \times \square) - 1 = \triangle$

F. $4 + (\square - 1) = \triangle$

G. $(\square \times \square) + 1 = \triangle$

VOCABULARY

axes, axis, column, coordinate graph, equation, equivalent equations, linear, ordered pair, pattern, plot, point, row, T-chart, variable

MATERIALS

- color tiles, about 50 per pair of students

- centimeter graph paper, several sheets per student (see Blackline Masters)

- 1 chart-size sheet of one-inch graph paper or 1 overhead transparency of centimeter graph paper

- Optional: *Piles of Tiles* activity sheet, 1 per pair of students (see Blackline Masters)

TIME

- at least three class periods

The Lesson

Day 1

Before class, I distributed a small plastic bag of approximately fifty color tiles to each pair of students. I said to the students, "Please leave the tiles in the bags for now. We'll use them soon."

I then built three piles of tiles on the overhead projector and numbered them 1, 2, and 3. I used regular tiles rather than overhead tiles to keep the students focused on the arrangements rather than on the colors used.

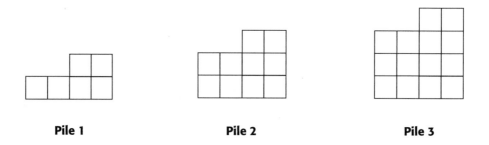

Pile 1   **Pile 2**   **Pile 3**

I explained, "I built these three piles of tiles following a particular pattern. Please talk with your partner about how the fourth pile will look and then build your idea using tiles from your bag." The discussion was lively.

I circulated and listened to students explain their thinking, challenging those who finished more quickly to find a second way to think of the pattern. After a few minutes, I glanced around the room and noticed that most students had completed the fourth pile correctly. I asked for the students' attention and began a discussion.

A Class Discussion   "Who would like to explain how to build the fourth pile?" I asked. About half the children had a hand raised. I called on Kurt.

Kurt explained, "You make four rows of four tiles and add two on top." He described what I had observed Tomo and Tim build. I wrote on the board:

"Oh, wait," Kurt said after reading what I wrote. "The two tiles on top should be in the right corner." I revised what I had written:

Kurt *Four rows of four and two on top in the right corner*

"That's it," Kurt said.

"Who else thought of building Pile Four the same way as Kurt?" I asked. Several hands went up.

"Let me draw your idea on the board," I said. I sketched Kurt's idea, drawing a row of four tiles, then another row of four tiles above the first, then two more rows, and finally two tiles on top on the right. Kurt confirmed that was what he had done.

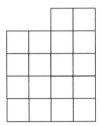

"Did anyone think about building the fourth pile a different way?" I asked.

Bradley explained, "You could do rows—no, I mean columns. You can do columns. You need two columns of four and two columns with five." Bradley's mistake of using the word *row* when he meant *column* is a common one. During the year the students participated in several lessons that involved the use of the words *row* and *column*. I was pleased Bradley caught his error. If he hadn't, I would have corrected him by restating his thought using the correct word.

I wrote Bradley's idea on the board under Kurt's:

Bradley *Two columns of four and two columns of five*

"Who would like to build the fourth pile on the overhead according to Bradley's idea?" I asked. "First I'll draw Piles One, Two, and Three on the board to make room on the overhead." I drew and labeled Piles 1, 2, and 3 to the left of Pile 4 so they were all in a row.

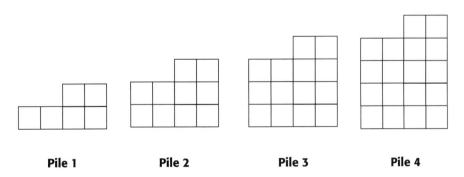

Pile 1   **Pile 2**   **Pile 3**   **Pile 4**

Many students were eager for the opportunity. I asked Bradley to call on someone and he called on Carmen. As Bradley read his directions, Carmen built two columns with four tiles in each and then two columns with five in each. Bradley nodded his approval.

"It's still the same as Kurt's," Bradley commented.

"Yes, it's the same shape," I said and then asked, "Who has another way?"

Joanna explained, "You just add two rows of two on top."

I wasn't sure what Joanna meant, so I asked, "Can you come up to the overhead and show how you built it?" As Joanna was coming up, I cleared the tiles from the overhead projector and said, "The rest of you should build with your tiles as Joanna builds on the overhead. Joanna, please explain as you build so that the rest of the students can follow your directions with their tiles."

Joanna said, "First you build Pile Three." She stopped explaining to do this and I reminded the others also to build the third pile. "Then you add a row of two on top of these," Joanna said, placing a tile on the top of each of the two shorter columns. "And then you put two on top of these," she concluded, placing a tile on top of each of the two taller columns. The others did the same.

Joanna explained further, "See, these two columns are the same size, and so it's like adding a row of two. Then columns three and four both have one more tile than the first two, so I added one more to each of them and that was like another row of two because they were higher and the first two columns were lower."

"Joanna's way comes out the same," Alana commented. Several others nodded. There were no other comments. I wrote Joanna's idea on the board under the first two:

Joanna   Add two rows of two to the top

"Does someone have another way?" I asked. Only a few hands went up. I called on Jerry.

"You could do one row of two and four rows of four," Jerry suggested. Jerry's idea was essentially the same as Kurt's, but he started building at the top, not the bottom. I recorded Jerry's idea under the others.

Jerry   One row of two and four rows of four

"Is Jerry's like Kurt's, just turned around?" Rebecca asked hesitantly. Had Rebecca or one of the other students not raised this question, I would have addressed it with the class.

I said, "Yes, they're similar. They both looked at the rows and the two on top, but Jerry built from the top down and Kurt built from the bottom up." I left both ideas on the board to reinforce that there is more than one way to express the same idea. Also, I put a check next to each of their ideas and said, "I put these checks to show that they're similar."

Karena had another idea. She said, "I think my idea is like Joanna's, but I'm not sure. You could add a row of four to the bottom. Joanna added to the top, and I'm just thinking of adding it to the bottom instead. Either way, it's adding a row."

I wrote Karena's idea on the board under the others:

Karena   Add a row of four on the bottom

"Talk with your partner about whether you think Karena and Joanna have the same idea." I said. The room came alive with conversation. In a moment, hands began to go up as students made their decisions. When I called for the students' attention, almost all hands were in the air.

"Adam and I think they're the same," Geraldo said. "Like Karena said, you're adding a row of four either way."

"Penny and I think it's different because Joanna's way is two rows of two on top and Karena's way is one row of four on the bottom," Callie explained.

"But adding two rows of two like Joanna showed us is the same as adding one row of four," Rebecca argued.

"I think that adding four on the top or four on the bottom is the same thing," Jon said. He had no explanation.

I said, "I see how you can look at it both ways." I left Karena's idea on the board. There were no other ideas for building the fourth pile.

Building Pile 5 I then said, "Some people saw the pattern of rows of four, as Kurt and Jerry did. Others looked at the columns, as Bradley did. And others saw the pattern as adding tiles on top or the bottom, as Joanna and Karena did. Now I'd like you to use these ways to build Pile Five. Take turns with your partner. First one of you chooses a way from the board and uses it to build Pile Five as your partner watches. Then your partner guesses which way you used. Then switch roles so the builder becomes the observer and the observer becomes the builder." The students were excited and got to work immediately. After a few minutes, I called the students to order.

"Raise your hand if you built Pile Five using Kurt and Jerry's idea about the rows," I said. About half the students raised a hand. I called on Tim and asked him to describe what he did. I followed his directions and built Pile 5 on the overhead projector. Tim and the other students agreed with what I did.

"Raise your hand if you used Bradley's column method to build Pile Five," I continued. About a fourth of the students raised a hand. I cleared the overhead and built Pile 5 as Rebecca gave directions. Again, the class agreed that I built Pile 5 correctly according to the column method.

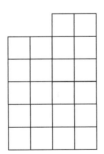

The rest of the children indicated that they used Joanna's idea of adding one row to the previous structure. I again cleared the overhead and Penny explained how I should build Pile 5 using Joanna's idea.

Extending the Pattern "What about the tenth pile?" I said. "What would the tenth pile look like if I built it according to Kurt and Jerry's row method?" Hands went up immediately. I paused to give others time to think and then called on Tomo.

Tomo said, "You'd have ten rows of four and two more on top on the right." I built the tenth pile on the overhead projector.

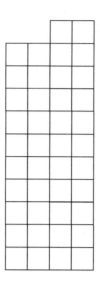

"Thumbs up if you agree, thumbs down if you disagree, thumbs sideways if you're not sure," I said. Thumbs were up. "How do you know there should be ten rows?"

"That's easy," Tomo said. "In Pile One there was one row of four; in Pile Two, two rows; in Pile Three, three rows; and it goes on like that. So for Pile Ten there should be ten rows of four." Many students nodded in agreement. There were no other comments.

"How would I build the tenth pile according to Bradley's column method?" I asked.

Cara explained, "You'd have two rows of ten . . . no, I mean two columns of ten, and then two columns of eleven."

"Can I tell where the two columns of eleven come from?" Callie asked. I nodded. "The eleventh tile is from the extras at the top."

"I think the adding-on way is harder," Rebecca mused aloud.

"Why do you think that?" I asked her.

Rebecca explained, "Well, with the first two ways, you just know what to do and you can build the tenth pile with rows or columns. With the adding-on way, you have to build all the piles in between, Pile Five, Pile Six, like that, and add one row of four each time." Rebecca sighed and then added, "That seems like a lot of work to me!"

"I think I get what Rebecca's saying," Tim said. "You have to have the old pile before you can add a row of four to make the new pile. The first two ways are like a shortcut." Several students nodded and there were no more comments.

"What about the hundredth pile?" I asked. Eyes got big as the students thought about this for a moment. Then hands shot into the air as the students grasped how to describe the hundredth pile.

Penny explained, "You need to make one hundred rows of four and then add two on top. It's easy and it works!"

"Penny used the row method. What about the column method?" I asked.

Tim explained, "You'd need two columns of ten and two columns of eleven." I reminded Tim that I was asking about the hundredth structure. He looked confused.

"This is what the tenth pile looks like," I said, pointing to what I had built on the overhead projector. "The tenth pile has two columns of ten and two columns of eleven. I want to know about the hundredth pile." Tim's eyes began to light up.

"Oh, I see now," Tim said. "It's two columns of a hundred and two columns of one hundred one!"

"Use your thumb to show if you agree or disagree with Tim," I said. All thumbs were up in agreement with Tim.

"What about the adding-a-row-of-four way?" I asked. Several students moaned. "Why are you moaning?" I asked.

"That would take forever because you'd have to build all the piles before it!" Callie said.

"Well, if you had the tenth pile, like we have right now, couldn't you just keep adding rows of four to it until there were one hundred?" Geraldo asked.

"How would you know about many rows to add?" I asked Geraldo.

"Well, you'd have to know that the pile number tells how many rows of four should be in the pile, so I guess in a way that would be like the row method." Several students nodded.

Making a T-Chart I drew a T-chart on the board and labeled the columns *# of Piles* and *# of Tiles*.

# of Piles	# of Tiles

I pointed to the sketches on the board of the first four piles and asked, "How many tiles do we need to build Pile One?"

"Six," the students chorused. On the T-chart, I wrote *1* in the left column and *6* in the right column. I didn't write these numbers at the top of the chart but left room so that later I could write numbers above them.

"How many tiles are needed to build Pile Two?" I continued.

"Ten," the class responded. I recorded *2* and *10*.

# of Piles	# of Tiles
1	6
2	10

"You can figure it out by multiplication," Rebecca shared. "Two times four is eight and the two on top make ten."

"So for the first pile, would it be one times four plus two?" Callie asked. I nodded. She smiled, pleased with her insight.

"How many tiles for Pile Three?" I asked.

"Fourteen," the class replied.

"Who can explain?" I asked. Almost all hands were up.

Chase explained, "There are three rows of four in Pile Three. I know because the pile number and the number of rows are the same. So three times four is twelve. Then you have to add the two on top, and that makes fourteen."

"Hey, I just noticed something," Adam said with surprise. "All the numbers in the tiles column are even. I bet they'll all be even."

"So you'd be suspicious if I wrote thirty-nine or forty-three on the right side of the chart?" I asked. He nodded.

"I think I know why what Adam says is true," Karena said. "You're always adding four. The first pile had six tiles and that's an even number, and four is an even number, so no matter what, you'll always get an even number because an even number added to an even number is an even number."

I wrote Adam's and Karena's ideas on the board near the T-chart:

Adam   All the numbers in the # of Tiles column are even.
Karena   The # of Tiles numbers will always be even because four is always being added to another even number.

I added *3* and *14* to the T-chart, then asked the students how many tiles would be needed for Pile 4. Carmen said, "Eighteen, because you need two columns of four and two columns of five. Two times four is eight and two times five is ten. Ten and eight equal eighteen."

"Carmen figured it out using my way of columns," Bradley commented.

The class agreed with Carmen and I recorded *4* and *18* on the T-chart. After I asked about the fifth pile and recorded *5* and *22* on the chart, I drew three dots under the *5* and wrote *10* and three dots under the *22* and wrote a question mark.

# of Piles	# of Tiles
1	6
2	10
3	14
4	18
5	22
.	.
.	.
.	.
10	?

I explained, "The dots mean I've intentionally skipped some numbers. In the Number of Piles column, I skipped six, seven, eight, and nine. In the

Number of Tiles column, I also made some dots, which means I skipped some numbers. Then I made a question mark. Why do you suppose I did this?"

"We're skipping some piles so we're also skipping some numbers of tiles, and the question mark means you want to know how many tiles for the tenth pile," Sadako said.

"That's just what I was thinking," I responded. "How many tiles are needed for the tenth pile, and how do you know? Talk with your partner. Try to think of more than one way to figure it out." The students talked eagerly and with confidence about their ideas. Most looked at the board and used the ideas I had recorded to help make their case. After a few moments, I called the students to order.

Tomo began the discussion. "Tim and I think forty-two is the number of tiles. All you have to do is use Kurt and Jerry's idea about rows, and then it's really easy to figure out."

Tim continued the explanation. "For Pile Ten there would be ten rows of four. Multiplying by ten is easy: four times ten is forty. Then there are the two on top, so you add two to forty and that's forty-two." Most students indicated their agreement by putting their thumbs up.

"Did anyone figure it out a different way?" I asked.

Alana explained, "Me and Karena knew there were twenty-two tiles in Pile Five, so for Pile Ten, we added twenty-two plus twenty-two, and that's forty-four."

"Hey," Karena noticed. "That's not right. It should be forty-two."

The girls looked at each other surprised, then started whispering. Alana exclaimed, "I know why! The twenty-two from Pile Five already has the two on top. We added the two at the top twice. That's why!"

"It's forty-two," Karena confirmed. There were no other comments. I erased the question mark and wrote *42*. Then I added some more dots at the bottom of both columns, wrote *100* in the # of Piles column, and wrote a question mark next to it in the # of Tiles column.

# of Piles	# of Tiles
1	6
2	10
3	14
4	18
5	22
.	.
.	.
.	.
10	42
.	.
.	.
.	.
100	?

"How many tiles are needed for the hundredth pile?" I asked. Hands flew into the air as students were eager to share. "When I call on you, tell us how many tiles you think are needed for the hundredth pile and how you thought about it. The rest of us will listen carefully and think about which method you're using to figure."

Tim shared first. He said, "You need two columns of one hundred and two more columns of one hundred plus two extras for the top. That makes four hundred two tiles." I wrote an equation on the board to represent Tim's thinking:

Tim $(2 \times 100) + (2 \times 100) + 2 = 402$

Sadako said, "That's Bradley's way. Another way of saying what Tim said is two columns of one hundred and two columns of one hundred one." I recorded:

Sadako $(2 \times 100) + (2 \times 101) = 402$

"I see another way!" Bradley blurted in excitement. He continued after apologizing, "This is really cool! Take Tim's way. If you put the two times one hundreds together, you get four times one hundred. Then there's the two on top. Four times one hundred is like the row way that Kurt and Jerry thought of. "

"Hey!" Dana said, "I did the row way. Four times one hundred plus two, and Bradley's right. They're the same!" I added Dana and Bradley's idea to the list:

Dana and Bradley $(4 \times 100) + 2 = 402$

"How many tiles would be needed for the thirty-fifth pile?" I asked.

Jon quickly replied, "Thirty-five. You'd have seven rows of five." Hands went up. I called on Alana.

"I disagree," Alana began. "Jon figured out how to make a rectangle with thirty-five. But in the pattern you have to have thirty-five rows of four and two on top."

"Oh yeah!" Jon said and hit his forehead with his hand. "Or you could have two columns with thirty-six and two columns with thirty-five."

"I agree," I said. "How many tiles would that be?" Jon shrugged. "Can I call on someone?" I nodded. Jon called on Tim.

"It's thirty-five times four," Tim said. "I know that thirty-five and thirty-five makes seventy. Seventy and seventy is one hundred forty, and then add two more for the top, and it's one hundred forty-two."

I wrote on the board:

Tim
$(4 \times 35) + 2$
$35 + 35 = 70$
$70 + 70 = 140$
$140 + 2 = 142$

I added *35* and *142* to the T-chart. I ended class and left the T-chart on the board for the next day.

# of Piles	# of Tiles
1	6
2	10
3	14
4	18
5	22
.	.
.	.
.	.
10	42
.	.
.	.
.	.
35	142
.	.
.	.
.	.
100	402

Day 2

To begin the lesson, I drew the students' attention to the T-chart from the day before and explained, "Work with your partner. You need to draw the T-chart and fill in the numbers for Piles One, Two, Three, all the way to Ten. Don't skip any of the numbers as I did yesterday. Record the number of tiles for each. Then write about the patterns you notice in the T-chart. The last thing for you to do is figure the number of tiles needed for Pile Twenty-Seven and explain how you figured it out."

"Do we go past Pile Ten?" Chase asked.

"You may if you wish, but you can stop at Pile Ten," I said.

"Do we each write on our own paper?" Dana asked.

I replied. "Yes. Talk with your partner and share your ideas, but I'd like each of you to show your work on your own sheet of paper." There were no other questions and the students got to work. I quickly wrote the following directions on the board as a reminder to the students:

1. *Fill in the T-chart to the tenth pile.*
2. *Write about the patterns you see in the numbers on the T-chart.*
3. *Figure the number of tiles needed for Pile 27. Show how you know.*

As I circulated through the class, I reminded a few students to label the columns on their T-charts, answered a few questions, and stopped to talk with some students about their thinking. The students had little trouble with the task. As students finished, I checked their work and, when needed, asked them to make either corrections or clarifications. (See Figure 11–1.) I gave some students an additional challenge of figuring out the number of tiles for another pile number. I soon gave a one-minute warning to the students and then asked for their attention.

FIGURE 11–1   Lizzie illustrated the twenty-seventh pile correctly but made an addition error and didn't get the right answer.

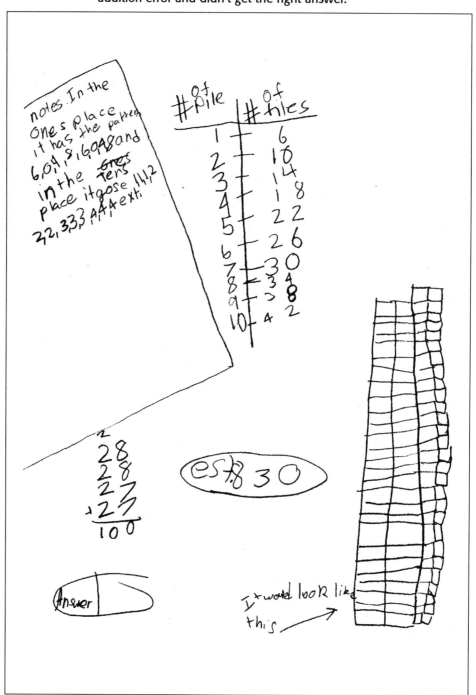

# of Piles	# of Tiles
1	6
2	10
3	14
4	18
5	22
6	26
7	30
8	34
9	38
10	42

Then I asked, "Who would like to share a pattern?" Almost all hands were up.

Callie shared, "I noticed all the numbers are even."

I paused for a moment, then pointed to the 3 in the # of Pile column. "Is three an odd number or an even number?" I asked. Although I knew that Callie was referring to the numbers in the # of Tiles column, I wanted her to be precise.

"It's odd," Callie replied. "I mean all the numbers on the other side are even."

"I see," I replied. I wrote on the board next to the T-chart:

Callie   All the numbers in the # of Tiles column are even.

"Is this what you mean?" I asked. She nodded.

Tim shared next. "The number of tiles always increases by four." I added Tim's pattern to the list:

Tim   The number of tiles always increases by four.

"What you wrote is right," Tim acknowledged.

Cassie shared next. She said, "In the Number of Tiles column, all the numbers in the ones place go six, zero, four, eight, two, six, and so on. They go in that order." I added Cassie's idea to the list and asked if what I wrote was correct. She nodded.

Cassie   In the # of Tiles column, the numbers in the ones place go 6, 0, 4, 8, 2, 6, . . .

"I know another pattern," Dana said. "The left column, where it says Number of Piles, well, it goes up by one." I wrote Dana's idea on the list:

Dana   The # of Piles column increases by one.

"Is this what you mean?" I asked to be sure that my paraphrasing accurately represented her idea. Dana nodded.

Karena reported the last idea. "If you look in the Number of Tiles column, and then look in the tens place of all the numbers, there's a pattern. It goes three ones in the tens place, then two twos, and then three threes, and I think it would be two fours in the tens place, forty-two and forty-six. Then if we kept going the pattern would go on like that." I recorded Karena's idea:

Karena   In the Number of Tiles column, the tens place has 3 ones, then 2 twos, then 3 threes, and 2 fours, and so on.

I said, "I noticed as you worked that most of you wrote about how the number of tiles increases by four as we move down the T-chart." I used my finger to point this out on the chart. Stopping at 42 I said, "If we go back up the chart, what happens?"

"You're subtracting four," the students said. Starting with 42, we tested this idea by going up the chart and subtracting four each time. When we got to Pile One, with six tiles, I said, "The next pile up would be Pile Zero. If we subtract four from the six tiles for Pile One, how many tiles will that leave for Pile Zero?"

There was a flurry of conversation. "A zero pile is too weird."

"What's a zero pile?"

"You can't do that!"

"Yes, you can," Kurt said. "There are zero rows of four, and that's zero, and the two is the two left on the top." Again there was a flurry of conversation.

I settled the class and asked, "What do you think about Kurt's idea?"

Rebecca said, "I think he's right. The number of rows is always the same as the number of the pile, so the zero pile would have zero rows of four and just the two on top."

"I don't think so," Tomo said. "It doesn't make sense to have a zero pile. We have the first pile, the second, the third, like that, but there's no such thing as a 'zeroth' pile." The others giggled.

"Who's right?" Cara asked.

"In a way, they're both right. Kurt figured out a mathematical way to extend the chart that fits the pattern, so it's mathematically correct. But Tomo has a point, too. As he said, we don't think of a 'zeroth' pile." He was thinking in ordinal numbers.

"So is it OK to write zero and two on the chart?" Alana wanted to know.

"If you're thinking about the pattern mathematically, yes, as long as you know that you're not thinking about the situation of building with the tiles. What if we followed the chart up further and I wrote negative one above the zero? Then I have to subtract four from two to figure out the number to write next to negative one."

"Now that's really weird," Bradley said. "It's negative two, and you can't have negative two tiles."

"I bet if you could have negative two piles then you'd have negative six tiles," Penny conjectured. Many students nodded their agreement. I added this information to the T-chart and also drew a wavy line just below the zero and two:

# of Piles	# of Tiles
−2	−6
−1	−2
0	2
1	6
2	10
3	14
4	18
5	22
6	26
7	30
8	34
9	38
10	42

I then said, "Remember, these numbers are mathematically correct, but there's a loss of reality above the wavy line. Keep in mind that some of the numbers we can write on the T-chart don't relate to the actual tiles."

Number of Tiles for Pile 27   To change the direction of the conversation, I said, "I asked you to find the number of tiles needed for Pile Twenty-Seven. How many are needed?"

Matthew said, "I think one hundred eight."

"I think that's wrong," Dana said. "Twenty-seven times four is one hundred eight, but there are the two tiles on top. You can't just ignore them. The answer should be one hundred ten." Others agreed. I wrote on the board:

$(27 \times 4) + 2 = 110$

"I did it differently," Tim said. "There's forty-two tiles in the tenth pile, so I added forty-two and forty-two to get the tiles in the twentieth pile. That's eighty-four. There's seven from twenty to twenty-seven, so I looked at the T-chart for Pile Seven and it says thirty tiles. I added eighty-four and thirty and got one hundred fourteen. What happened?" (See Figure 11–2 on the following page.)

"Oh, I know," Adam volunteered. "It's like what Karena and Alana did. You added the top two tiles twice and you should've only added them once."

Some students looked confused, so I tried to explain with smaller numbers so that the students could visualize the tiles. I said, "Suppose we think about smaller numbers, say Piles One and Two. Pile One needs six tiles." I drew Pile 1 on the board. "If we figure out the number of tiles for Pile Two by doubling the six tiles in Pile One, we get twelve." I drew Pile 2 on the board, then asked, "How many tiles do I really need for Pile Two?"

FIGURE 11–2 Tim got an incorrect number of tiles for Pile 27 by adding the number of tiles in Pile 10 to itself and then adding on the number of tiles in Pile 7.

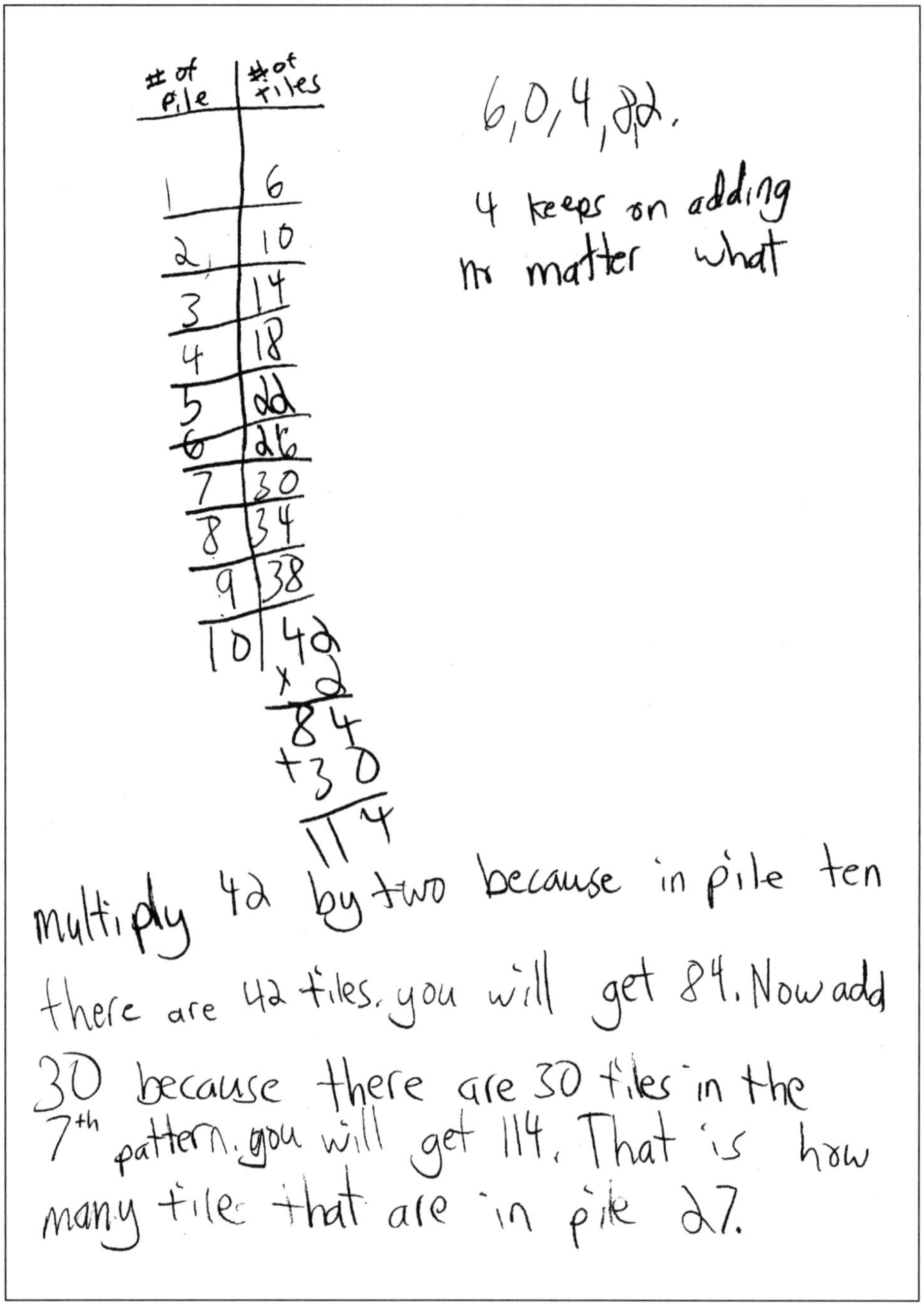

# of Pile	# of tiles
1	6
2	10
3	14
4	18
5	22
6	26
7	30
8	34
9	38
10	42

6,0,4,22.

4 keeps on adding no matter what

$$42 \times 2 = 84$$
$$84 + 30 = 114$$

multiply 42 by two because in pile ten there are 42 tiles, you will get 84. Now add 30 because there are 30 tiles in the 7th pattern, you will get 114. That is how many tiles that are in pile 27.

"Ten," the class replied.

"Oh," Tim said. "If I just multiplied Pile One by three to get the number of tiles for Pile Three, that wouldn't work. It would be eighteen tiles and Pile Three needs fourteen."

Chase then returned to the twenty-seventh pile. He said, "I added twenty-seven and twenty-seven and twenty-eight and twenty-eight and it was one hundred ten."

I wrote Chase's idea on the board:

27 + 27 + 28 + 28 = 110

No one had anything else to share. I added 27 and 110 to the T-chart. Figures 11–3 through 11–5 show how three students worked on this activity.

FIGURE 11–3 Bradley correctly figured the number of tiles in twenty-seven rows of four.

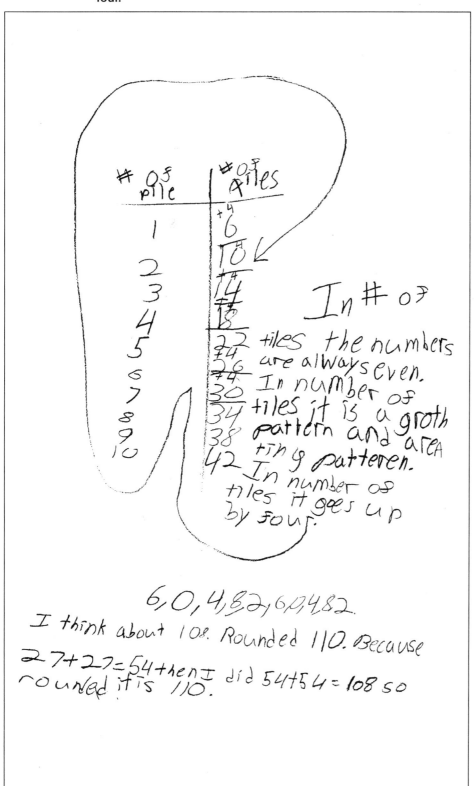

FIGURE 11–4   Tomo extended the T-chart to figure the number of tiles in the twenty-seventh pile. He also verified the answer with an equation.

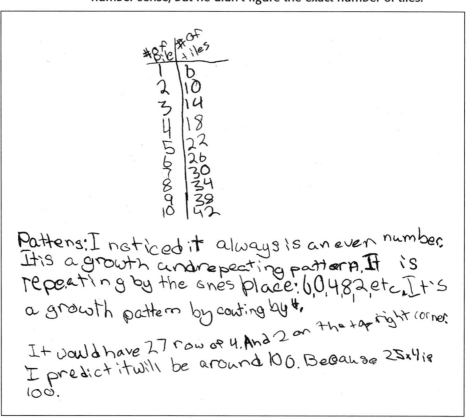

My prediction is
# of tiles 27 and 110.

(27×4)+2=110

I noticed that the # of tiles goes by 4

It also goes by 0, 8 and 2. This is because it goes by 4.

All of the numbers are even 'cause you add an even number to an even #

# of piles	# of tiles
1	6
2	10
3	14
4	18
5	22
6	26
7	30
8	34
9	38
10	42
11	46
12	50
13	54
14	58
15	62
16	66
17	70
18	74
19	78
20	82

# of piles	# of tiles
21	86
22	90
23	94
24	98
25	102
26	106
27	?
28	114

FIGURE 11–5   Chase's prediction for the number of tiles for Pile 27 shows good number sense, but he didn't figure the exact number of tiles.

# of Pile	# of tiles
1	6
2	10
3	14
4	18
5	22
6	26
7	30
8	34
9	38
10	42

Patterns: I noticed it always is an even number. It is a growth and repeating pattern. It is repeating by the ones place: 6,0,4,8,2, etc. It's a growth pattern by counting by 4.

It would have 27 row of 4. And 2 on the top right corner. I predict it will be around 100. Because 25×4 is 100.

Writing Equations   Next I asked, "What if I wanted to know how to figure the number of tiles for any pile number? What would I do?" I paused to give the students a few moments to think. About half of the students had a hand up.

Jon said, "Well, for any pile number, multiply it by four, and add two to the product, and that equals the number of tiles."

"Why would you multiply by four and add two?" I pushed.

"The four is because there are four tiles in each row and the two is for the two tiles on the top," he explained. I wrote on the board:

Jon   For any pile number, multiply it by 4, add 2 to the product, and that equals the number of tiles.

"I know another way," Bradley said. "Take the pile number, multiply it by two. Then take the pile number plus one and multiply that by two. Add the two numbers up. It's the column way and will give you the number of tiles."

I wrote on the board:

Bradley   Take the pile number and multiply it by 2. Take the pile number, add 1, and multiply that by 2. Add the products and it equals the number of tiles needed for the pile.

There were no other comments. "It took me a long time to write Bradley's and Jon's ideas on the board," I said. "It would be much quicker if we wrote equations." I drew a box above the left column of the T-chart and a triangle above the right column.

□ # of Piles	△ # of Tiles
−2	−6
−1	−2
0	2
1	6
2	10
3	14
4	18
5	22
6	26
7	30
8	34
9	38
10	42

I explained, "We'll let the box stand for the pile number and the triangle stand for the number of tiles. Let's look at Jon's idea." I pointed to Jon's idea. I read it aloud and wrote an equation, then put in parentheses for clarity:

$$(\square \times 4) + 2 = \triangle$$

"Sometimes mathematicians use letters for the variables instead of symbols," I said. "How could we write an equation with letters to describe Jon's idea?" Most hands were up.

Penny said, "You could use p for piles and t for tiles. Then it would be 'p times four plus two is equal to t.' " I wrote p and t at the top of the T-chart above the box and triangle and then wrote on the board:

$$(p \times 4) + 2 = t$$

"These are two ways to write equations using variables for Jon's idea," I said. "Let's look at Bradley's idea and see if we can write an equation for it." I pointed to Bradley's idea and paused to give the students time to think. Hands went up quickly.

Dana said, "It's box times two, then box plus one times two, add those, then an equals sign and a triangle." I recorded:

$$\square \times 2 + \square + 1 \times 2 = \triangle$$

I said, "Dana's almost correct. Watch as I add some punctuation." I recorded:

$$(\square \times 2) + [(\square + 1) \times 2] = \triangle$$

I explained, "We do what's in the parentheses first, and then the brackets."

Making a Graph I posted a large sheet of one-inch squared paper. An overhead transparency of centimeter graph paper can be used instead "We get to graph!" Joanna said.

"You're right," I replied. "First I'll draw the axes, and then let's look at the T-chart." I drew the axes.

"Let's start with the ordered pair (one, six). Who would like to mark the point for (one, six)?" The students were eager and their hands danced in the air. Cara came up, put the marker at the origin, counted over one and up six, and marked a point. Other students came up and plotted the next three ordered pairs. Some students commented about the pattern of the points going in a straight line.

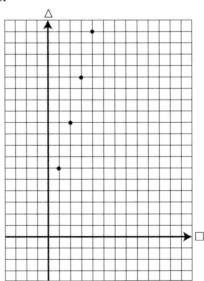

Then I said, "What about the ordered pair (zero, two)? Will it fit the pattern?" Most thought it would. Sadako came up and marked it.

"Who's feeling brave and would like to mark the point for the ordered pair (negative one, negative two)?" Not as many hands were up; the students were less experienced with the other quadrants of the graph and how to graph negative numbers. I called on Javier. He came to the front and marked the point for (–1, 2) instead of (–1, –2). Several students disagreed.

Javier stepped back and shrugged. "It doesn't look right," he said.

I said, "Let's check. Starting at the origin, you counted to the left one for negative one. But then you went up. That would work for two, but not for negative two."

"Go down two," Kurt suggested.

"Oh, I see now," Javier said as he correctly marked the point.

Penny said, "Now that Javier moved his point, they all line up."

"That's correct," I said as I held a straight-edge along the points to show the line they made. "This is called a linear graph because the points make a line." I wrote *linear* on the board.

"I notice something else," Alana said. "If you go up the points like stairs, to go from one point to the next is four just like to go from one pile to the next is four."

"Oh yeah!" "Cool!" mumbled the students.

"I know what the four means!" Jon said with great excitement. "It's the number in each row of tiles! Wow! On the T-chart, the number of tiles goes up by four, and on the graph it goes up four!" There were no other comments and I ended the lesson.

Extensions

Students can work in pairs and explore patterns on their own. (See the *Piles of Tiles* activity sheet in the Blackline Masters.) For each, have the students follow these directions:

1. Build Piles 4 and 5 with tiles, then draw them on graph paper.

2. Make a T-chart and fill it in to the tenth pile.

3. Write about the patterns you notice in the tiles and on the T-chart.

4. Write an equation.

5. Make a graph.

Even though students work in pairs, you might want them to record individually so that they each get practice doing so.

You may want to assign the same pattern to everyone, or post the patterns and let students choose one that interests them (see the example at the top of page 220).

Lead class discussions for students to share their ideas and compare their T-charts and graphs. Figures 11–6 through 11–8 show how three students worked on this extension activity.

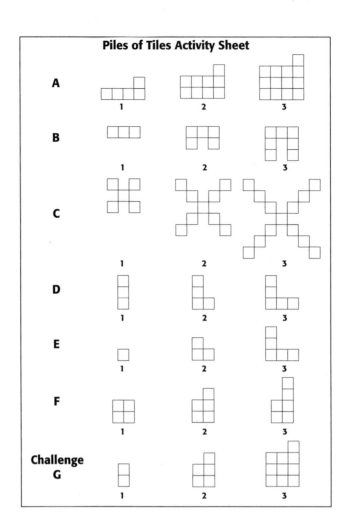

Piles of Tiles Activity Sheet

FIGURE 11–6 Cara successfully completed all parts of the investigation for Pattern B.

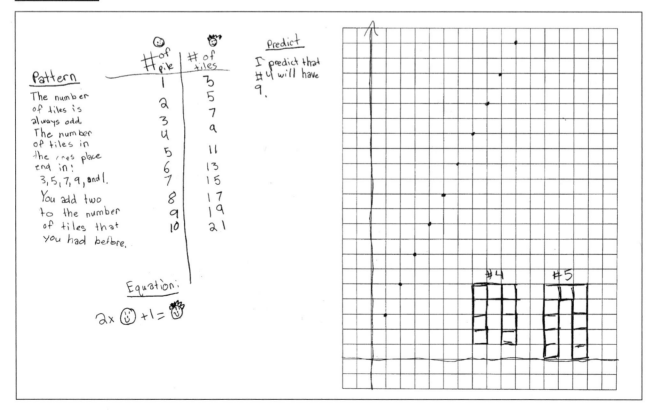

FIGURE 11-7 Jon investigated Pattern A, explaining how the pattern grew and graphing the point.

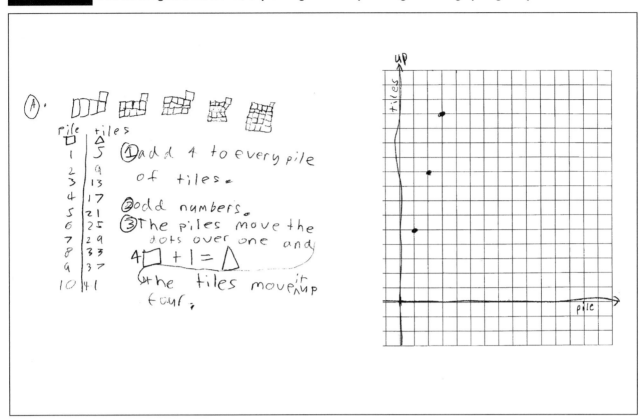

FIGURE 11-8 Dana discovered that the number of tiles in Pattern F is equal to the pile number plus 3.

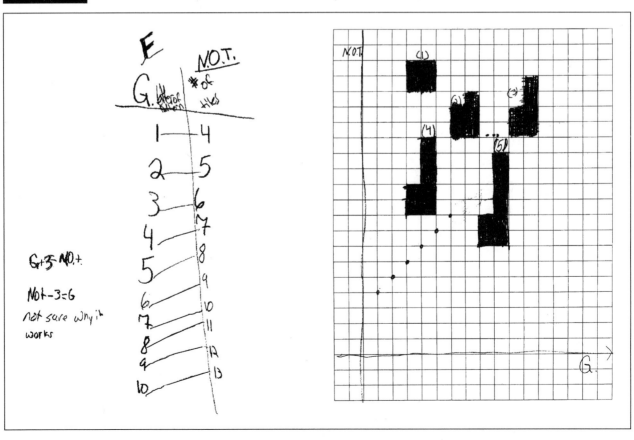

## CHAPTER 12

Table Patterns

Investigating Seating Arrangements

OVERVIEW

This lesson uses the context of seating people at tables in restaurants to investigate growth patterns. The students are first introduced to a restaurant where four people sit at each square table. After figuring out the number of people that can be seated at one, two, three, and so on tables up to ten, they figure out the number of people that can be seated when the tables are pushed together in a row for banquet-style seating. The students then repeat the investigation for tables that seat three, five, and six people each. They collect information about the patterns on T-charts, describe the rules, and write equations.

BACKGROUND

The McSquares, A Restaurant Tale of Tables and Algebra, a story by Marilyn Burns, provides the context for the investigations in this lesson. In the story, Mr. and Mrs. McSquare decide to open up a burger restaurant in their town. Everything in their restaurant is square—the sign, the tables, the plates, the bottoms of the cups, and even the burgers and buns. They start small, with three square tables seating four people each, but soon grow to ten tables. Also, they accommodate private parties, where they arrange the tables banquet style—one long row of tables pushed together. The McSquares are so successful that others are inspired to open their own restaurants. Mr. and Mrs. McTriangle specialize in grilled cheese sandwiches that they cut on the diagonal into triangles. The tables in their restaurant are triangles that seat three people each. Mr. and Mrs. McTrapezoid open a restaurant with trapezoidal tables that seat five people each, and Mr. and Mrs. McHexagon open a restaurant with hexagonal tables that seat six people each.

For each restaurant, students investigate the number of people that can be seated at from one to ten tables set individually, restaurant style. Then they investigate the number of people that can be seated at from one to ten tables when the tables are pushed together into a long row, banquet style.

For each arrangement, the students compile information in a T-chart, describe the pattern, and, if they can, write an equation to represent the rule.

Students use pattern blocks to construct the various table arrangements. In this way, they can concretely verify information about how many people are seated at various arrangements. It's generally obvious to the students that the green triangle seats three people, the orange square seats four, and the yellow hexagon seats six. However, it's important to be sure that the students see how the red trapezoid, even thought it only has four sides, actually can seat five people since one of its sides is twice as long as the other sides. In this lesson, the trapezoid substitutes for a pentagon, a shape that isn't included in the pattern blocks.

As students discover numerical patterns in the T-charts, it's important to help them relate the patterns to the arrangements of tables. For example, for the banquet tables made from squares, students notice that the number of people that can be seated increases by two each time another table is added to the row. As you'll see in the student work included, some students figure out the pattern that multiplying the number of tables by two, then adding two, produces the number of people that can be seated.

t # of Tables	p # of People	
1	4	
2	6	
3	8	
4	10	$p = (2 \times t) + 2$
5	12	
6	14	
7	16	
8	18	
9	20	
10	22	

Students come up with different explanations for this pattern. Some notice that when you add a square table to the end of a banquet arrangement, you're only adding three sides, since one touches the existing table and can't be used, and you're removing one of the sides previously used. Adding three sides and losing one is the same as adding two sides, which explains why adding one table increases the seating by two each time.

Another way to visualize this is to imagine adding tables not at the ends, but instead squeezed into the middle of an existing banquet table arrangement. That way, you don't disturb any of the existing place settings, but merely cause the addition of two more place settings. Looking at the tables this way, each square table in the long row has two place settings, one on each long side of the banquet table, but the end tables each have an extra place setting. So, for a row of any number of square tables, you have two place settings for each table, plus two extra place settings at the ends. This is a way to explain the equation $p = (2 \times t) + 2$.

Expect students to see patterns in different ways. Some may notice one or both of the geometric explanations just mentioned. Others may be more comfortable looking at the numbers on the T-charts and focusing only on the numerical patterns. Also, some may be able to write equations, while others may not yet be algebraically proficient.

The students in the vignette that follows had had several weeks of experience with the activities in several other chapters in this book prior to this lesson. They were accustomed to examining T-charts and describing patterns, and were becoming proficient at writing equations. Also, they knew how to plot points on a coordinate plane and had graphed other patterns. However, this prior experience isn't necessarily a prerequisite. The concrete aspect of this investigation makes it accessible to students who haven't yet had much experience looking at patterns, and it can be a good initial lesson. For these students, you'll have to explain the use of a T-chart more explicitly than is done in the vignette, but using T-charts is typically easy for students to understand.

As an extension to the lesson, older students can plot the points from their T-charts and look at the graphs that result.

VOCABULARY

equation, equivalent equations, hexagon, square, T-chart, trapezoid, triangle

MATERIALS

- pattern blocks, 1 bucket per pair of students
- *The McSquares*, by Marilyn Burns (see Appendix)
- optional: centimeter graph paper, 1 sheet per student (See Blackline Masters)

TIME

- at least three class periods

The Lesson

Day 1

"Who likes to eat burgers?" I asked the class. Most students raised a hand.

I then said, "I'm going to read you a story about two people, Mr. and Mrs. McSquare, who loved burgers." I began to read. When I got to the part about the McSquares adding another table, the students knew that the sign in the window would change to say: "We can serve 16 people at a time!" Later in the story, when the McSquares expanded the restaurant to ten tables, Tomas said, "Now forty people can sit."

I read about how, after the Tuckers inquired about rearranging the tables into a banquet arrangement, Mrs. McSquare got paper and pencil to sketch two tables pushed together and see how many people could be seated. I stopped to draw on the board two square tables pushed together.

"How many people can be seated?" I asked. I called on Michael.

"Six," he said.

"Can you come up and show where the six people would sit?" I asked. Michael came to the board and marked six Xs.

"Can't more people squeeze in?" Elyse asked.

"It would get too crowded," Lena said.

"These tables can only accommodate one person on a side," I clarified, and then asked, "How many people would two tables seat if they were separate?"

"Eight," Teddy answered.

"Come up and show us," I said, and drew two separate square tables. Teddy came up and marked eight Xs.

I continued reading to the end of the first part of the story. The last paragraph tells about how Mr. and Mrs. McSquare investigated the number of people who could be seated, banquet style, with two tables pushed together, then three tables, four, five, and so on up to ten tables.

I then said, "You'll now investigate these banquet arrangements to see what Mr. and Mrs. McSquare discovered. In a moment I'll give each group a bucket of pattern blocks. You can fish out the orange squares for the tables. Here's what you'll do." As I explained, I wrote the directions on the board for the students' reference:

Take 10 squares.
Make arrangements of 2, 3, 4, . . . , 10 tables in a row and figure out how many people can be seated at each.
Record on a T-chart.
Write about the patterns you notice.

I also drew on the board a T-chart, labeled the columns *# of Tables* and *# of People*, and wrote the numbers from *2* to *10* in the left column. I didn't start with 1 because one table isn't enough to begin a banquet arrangement. However, I left a space at the top of the left column so we could insert a 1 later when we were looking for patterns.

# of Tables	# of People
2	
3	
4	
5	
6	
7	
8	
9	
10	

"Do the tables have to go just in a row?" Ingrid wanted to know.

"Yes," I said, "for a banquet arrangement, the tables are placed in a row."

"Do we work with partners?" Paul asked.

"Yes, work with the person next to you," I responded.

There were no other questions. I said, "Let's see if you can complete this in ten minutes. Then we'll discuss what you found out." The students got to work. As with any new assignment, there was some confusion and I circulated to answer questions.

"Do we have to draw the tables?" Amy asked.

I answered, "You can sketch them if you want, but please don't spend a lot of time making drawings. I'm more interested in what you record on the T-chart and the patterns you notice."

"How far does the T-chart have to go?" Charlie asked.

"Up to a banquet arrangement made with ten tables," I said.

"What do we write?" Tomas asked after he and Elyse had recorded on the T-chart.

"What did you notice?" I asked.

"It goes up by two," Elyse said.

"What goes up by two?" I asked.

"The number of people," she said. "Oh, I know what to write."

"Be sure to talk with Tomas about your ideas," I said.

I gave the students a one-minute warning when I noticed that most were almost finished. Then, when I called time, I initiated a discussion.

A Class Discussion   "First let's enter the numbers on the T-chart on the board so we can look at the information together," I said. Frannie told me the numbers and I recorded them.

# of Tables	# of People
2	6
3	8
4	10
5	12
6	14
7	16
8	18
9	20
10	22

Ally shared an observation first. "The number of people goes up by two each time you add a table," she said. All of the students had come to this same conclusion. I wrote on the board:

The number of people goes up by two each time you add a table.

Then Ingrid said, "When you add one table, you lose one space and you gain three spaces, so you really only gain two spaces." Several others had made this same interpretation. I wrote on the board:

When you add one table, you lose one space and gain three spaces, so you really only gain two spaces.

Julie said, "You take the tables plus itself plus two and that equals the number of people." I wrote on the board:

The # of tables plus itself plus 2 = the # of people.

"I have a different rule," Teddy said. "It's times two plus two."
"What is times two plus two?" I asked.
Teddy answered, "It's the number of tables times two and then you plus two. Can I come up and write the equation?" I agreed, and Teddy came up and wrote:

$p = t \times 2 + 2$

"I used p for the people and t for the tables," he explained. On the T-chart, I wrote p above # of People and t above # of Tables.
"Hey, does that work?" Marco asked.
"Let's try it," I said. We tried several of the numbers and saw that Teddy's equation worked.
"How would you write your rule as an equation?" I asked Julie. She came up and wrote:

$p = t + t + 2$

"What if there were twenty-five tables arranged banquet style?" I asked. "How many people would be seated according to Teddy's equation? Raise your hand when you think you know." I waited for all of the students to raise a hand and then called on Ally.

"Fifty-two," she said. The others showed their agreement with thumbs up.

"It's the same for Julie's," Maria said.

Julie raised her hand. "I noticed something else," she said. "If you add the numbers from left to right, they go up by one."

"I'm not sure I understand what you see," I said.

"Can I come up and show?" Julie asked. I agreed and she came up and wrote *+ 4* next to the 2 in the left column, then *+ 5* next to the 3, *+ 6* next to the 4, and continued down to *+ 12* next to the 10.

t **# of Tables**	*p* **# of People**
2 + 4	6
3 + 5	8
4 + 6	10
5 + 7	12
6 + 8	14
7 + 9	16
8 + 10	18
9 + 11	20
10 + 12	22

"See, you add across by one more each time," Julie explained.

I asked, "What if you had only one table? Would your pattern hold?" Julie added a *1* above the 2 and showed that you would add three to get the 4 in the right column.

t **# of Tables**	*p* **# of People**
1 + 3	4
2 + 4	6
3 + 5	8
4 + 6	10
5 + 7	12
6 + 8	14
7 + 9	16
8 + 10	18
9 + 11	20
10 + 12	22

"I think I know why Teddy did plus two," Ally said. "I think it has to do with doing what Ingrid said before about losing one side but adding three sides, so you add two sides. I think that's why you add two."

"And why did Teddy multiply by two?" I asked.

"I haven't figured that part out yet," she said.

Ally's thinking wasn't accurate, but she was trying to connect the equation and the tables, and I didn't want to discourage her. Instead, I tried to suggest some other ways for the class to look at the pattern and see how it related to the seating at the tables. I drew on the board four tables in a row and marked the ten seats.

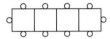

"If I add one more table, how many more seats do I add?" I asked.

"Two," the students responded.

"Instead of putting the table at the end, suppose I squeeze it in the middle. Then I don't lose any of the place settings already there." As I said this, I erased the two tables on the right and redrew them apart to leave room for another table.

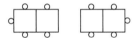

"Now I'll squeeze in the new table," I said.

"Oh, look," Maria said, "you're adding two more seats."

"You need two more place settings," Ava added.

"You don't lose any if you do it that way," Nick said.

"And how many seats did I add?" I asked.

"Two," they responded.

"So every table has room for two seats?" I asked.

"Except the ends," Michael said. "They have three seats." He then got very excited and said, "Look! If you count the tables in the middle, without the tables on the ends, they each have two seats, so you multiply by two. Then you add six on for the three and three at the ends." I wrote on the board:

The number of people is equal to the tables in the middle times two plus six for the tables at the ends.

"Do you think you could write that as an equation?" I asked. Michael came up to try, but he got stuck about what to write for the tables in the middle.

"If there were ten tables, how many would be in the middle?" I asked.

"Eight," Michael said.

"And if there were nine tables, how many would be in the middle?" I asked. "Seven," Michael said. "Oh, I get it. It's always two less, so you do t minus two for the tables in the middle." He then wrote on the board:

$p = t - 2 \times 2 + 6$

"What are you multiplying by the two?" I asked. "I think you need parentheses." Michael corrected his equation:

$p = (t - 2) \times 2 + 6$

Not all of the students followed Michael's reasoning, so I shifted to looking at the pattern for the tables arranged restaurant style. I drew another T-chart to the left of the one on the board and labeled the columns # *of Tables* and # *of People*. Also, I titled the T-chart *Restaurant* and titled the other T-chart *Banquet*. On the Banquet T-chart, I erased the numbers Julie had written to show her idea about adding across the columns. The students helped me quickly fill in the Restaurant T-chart.

Restaurant		**Banquet**	
t _# of_ _Tables_	p _# of_ _People_	t _# of_ _Tables_	p _# of_ _People_
1	4	1	4
2	8	2	6
3	12	3	8
4	16	4	10
5	20	5	12
6	24	6	14
7	28	7	16
8	32	8	18
9	36	9	20
10	40	10	22

"Who knows the rule?" I asked.

All hands went up. I called on George. He came up and wrote:

$p = t \times 4$

"That one is easy," Amy said.

It was then the end of the period and I collected the students' papers. Figures 12–1 and 12–2 show how two pairs interpreted this problem.

Day 2

I began class by reading aloud the next part of the story, about the McTriangles and their restaurant.

"What do you think I'll ask you to investigate now?" I asked.

"How their tables work," Nick said.

"How the people sit in the Triangles restaurant and what happens for banquets," Maria added.

"We'll make T-charts like we did yesterday and try to figure out the equations," Kylie said.

I said, "Yes, now you'll investigate how many people Mr. and Mrs. Mc-Triangle could seat if their triangular tables were arranged restaurant style

FIGURE 12–1 Ingrid and Julien explained and illustrated that the number of people increases by two each time a table is added because one seat is lost and three are gained.

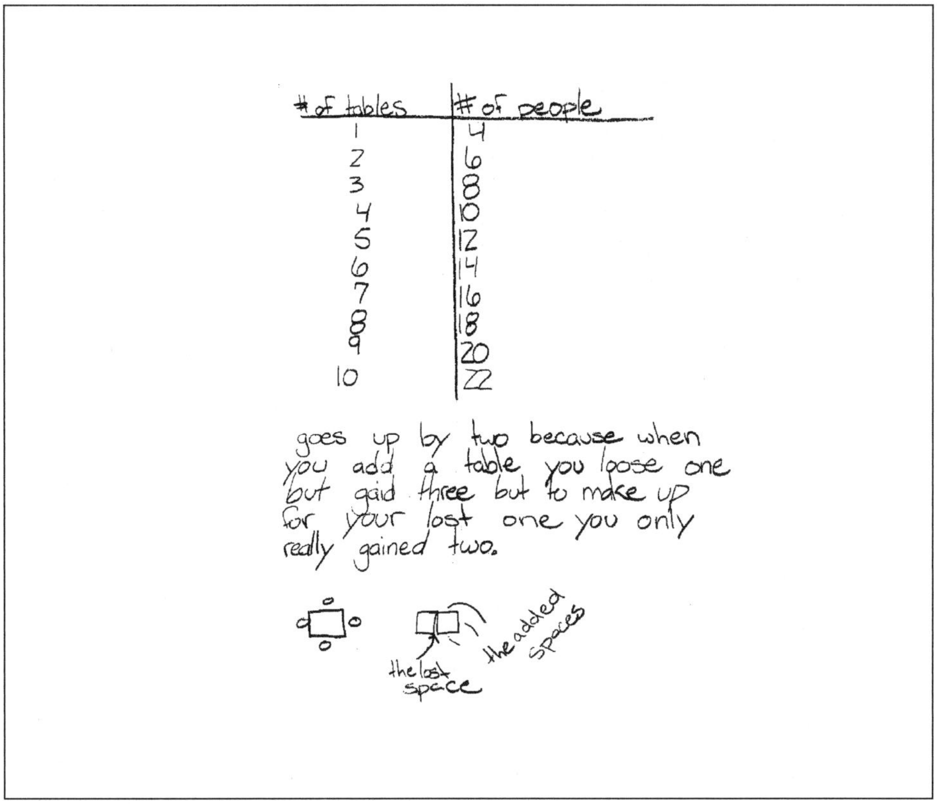

# of tables	# of people
1	4
2	6
3	8
4	10
5	12
6	14
7	16
8	18
9	20
10	22

goes up by two because when you add a table you loose one but gaid three but to make up for your lost one you only really gained two.

the lost space   the added spaces

FIGURE 12–2 Nick and Socoro reasoned that the end tables each seat three people and the other tables each seat two people.

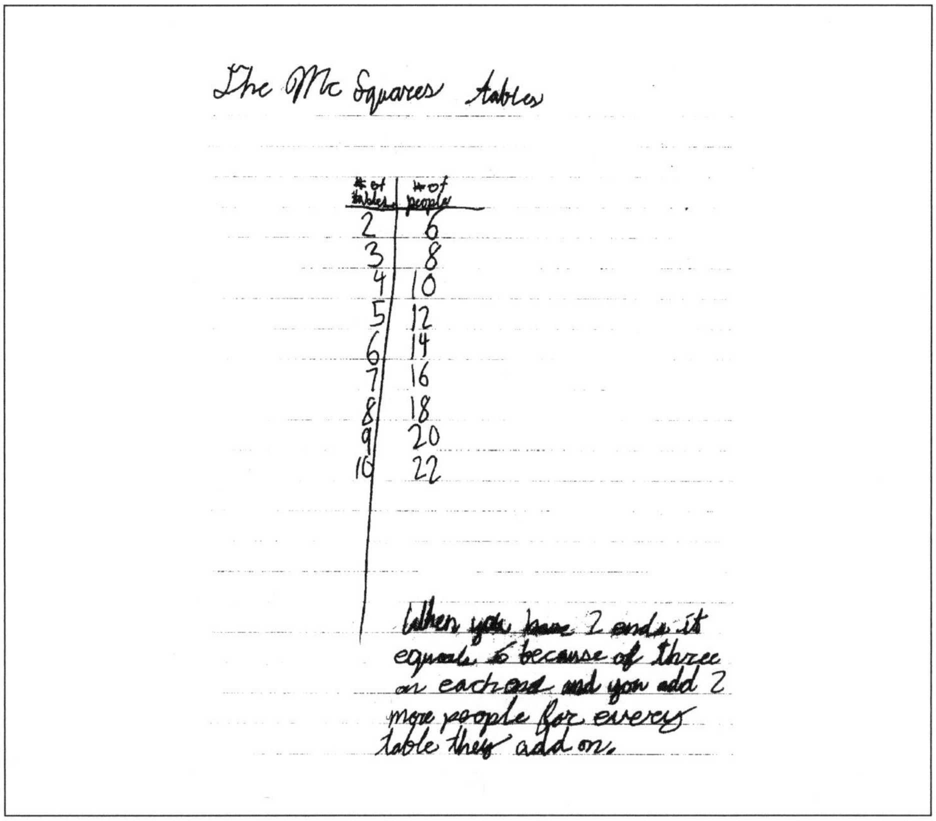

The Mc Squares tables

# of tables	# of people
2	6
3	8
4	10
5	12
6	14
7	16
8	18
9	20
10	22

When you have 2 ends it equals 6 because of three on each end and you add 2 more people for every table they add on.

and banquet style. On your paper today, you'll do a T-chart for each arrangement." I wrote the directions on the board:

1. *Figure out the # of people that can sit at 1, 2, 3, . . . 10 tables in restaurant seating. Make a T-chart and write about the patterns.*
2. *Figure out the # of people that can sit at 1, 2, 3, . . . 10 tables in banquet seating. Make a T-chart and write about the patterns.*
3. *If you can, write equations for each.*

Then I sketched on the board how they should set up their papers, saying as I did so, "So that you can compare the two T-charts, do the restaurant arrangement on the left side of your paper and the banquet arrangement on the right side. Also, label the two T-charts."

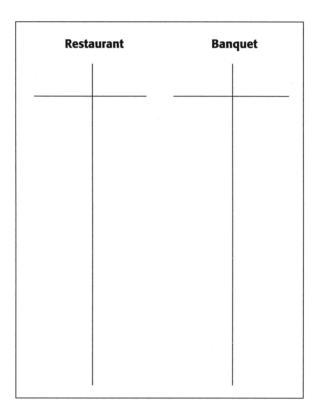

I then gave a few last directions. "For the tables, use the triangles from the pattern blocks," I said. "When you arrange them in banquets, you'll have to turn every other one upside down." To explain what I meant by this, I drew on the board an illustration of a banquet table made from six individual triangular tables.

I then said, "Title your paper so that we can distinguish it from your paper about the tables in the McSquares' restaurant." I wrote on the board:

McTriangles' Restaurant

The students got to work. Because of their experience the day before, the students were much clearer about what they were to do and didn't need very much assistance as I circulated.

I noticed that Lena and Michael were each writing on a separate paper. Lena was recording for the restaurant style and Michael for the banquet style. "It was easier to divide up the writing this way," Lena explained to me.

"It's important that you each understand what the other person wrote," I said. They assured me that they did. They wrote the equation in several ways for the restaurant-style pattern, but couldn't find an equation for the banquet arrangement. To describe the banquet pattern, Michael wrote: *It only goes up one person per new table because the table only have three sides to begin with and when you add on a table it gets rid of one side and only adds on two table setting so there is only one left over after making up for the one you got rid of.*

"What's the equation?" Michael asked me. The thinking he had done the day before about the banquet arrangement with square tiles didn't transfer to this situation. This didn't surprise me. When learning something new, students' understanding typically is fragile. I decided not to respond to Michael's question, but to see if the class discussion could help him. (See Figure 12–3 for Lena's and Michael's writing.)

I then said to the class, "Five more minutes and then we'll gather for a discussion."

I asked the students who worked more quickly to figure out how many people would be seated in both arrangements if there were one hundred tables. Ingrid and Julien did so quickly, so I asked them to record their T-charts on the board for our class discussion.

"Do we write our equations?" Ingrid asked.

"No, just the T-charts," I said.

FIGURE 12–3 Lena described the pattern for restaurant seating at the McTriangles' and wrote the equation in three different ways. Michael explained why banquet seating increases by one each time a table is added.

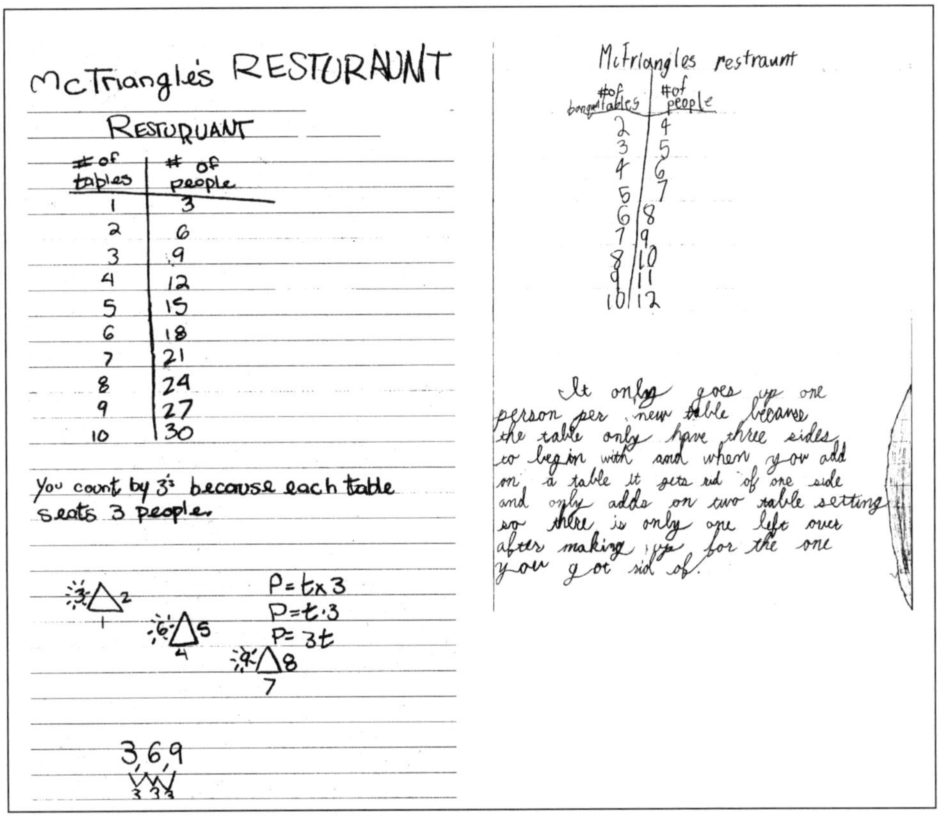

After Paul and Ally figured out that one hundred tables would seat 300 people restaurant style and 102 people banquet style, Paul made an observation. He said, "Look, if you add one hundred to each of these, you get the answers for one hundred tables in the McSquares' restaurant."

I suggested that he and Ally record this discovery. "How about trying to figure out the equations, too?" I asked. They went back to work. (See Figure 12–4.)

"Did we do enough?" Amy asked me as I walked by her and Natalia. They typically were a bit unsure of their work and often had difficulty. They hadn't attempted to write equations, but their paper showed that they had done the T-charts correctly. "Your paper is fine," I said, "and the drawings help me understand how you were thinking." (See Figure 12–5.)

I then gave the class a one-minute warning. "Look your paper over once more and see if there is anything you want to change on it," I said.

FIGURE 12–4 Ally and Paul described the patterns they noticed, but their equation for banquet seating, among other things, was incorrect.

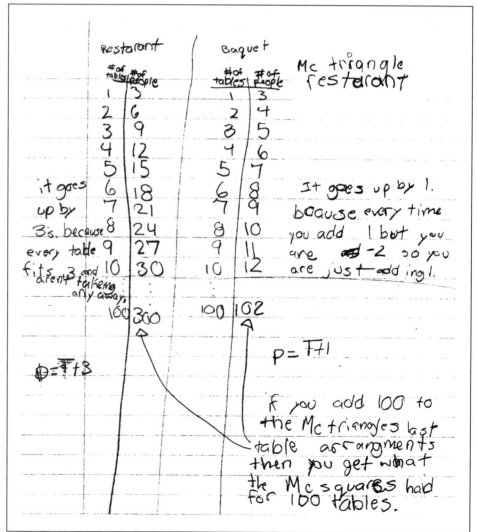

FIGURE 12–5 Amy and Natalia's T-charts were correct, but they did not attempt to write equations.

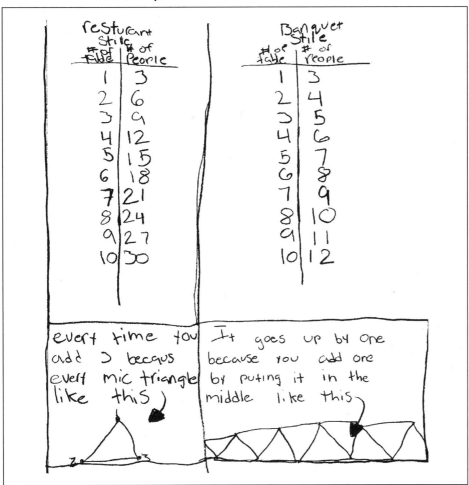

A Class Discussion I began a class discussion by asking the students to check their T-charts against what Ingrid and Julien had recorded on the board.

McTriangles

Restaurant		Banquet	
t **# of Tables**	p **# of People**	t **# of Tables**	p **# of People**
1	3	1	3
2	6	2	4
3	9	3	5
4	12	4	6
5	15	5	7
6	18	6	8
7	21	7	9
8	24	8	10
9	27	9	11
10	30	10	12

"Let's talk first about the restaurant-style seating," I said.

George said, "The pattern counts by threes." Everyone agreed.

"What counts by threes?" I pushed.

"The number of people goes up by threes," George clarified.

Frannie, George's partner, added, "That's because when you add a table, you add three table settings." Again, everyone agreed.

I wrote on the board:

The number of people goes up by threes.
When you add a table you add three table settings.

"Who would like to come up and write the equation?" I asked. More than half the class volunteered. I called on Kylie first. After she recorded, hands were still up. Three other students came up to write their versions of the equation:

$p = t \times 3$
$p = t \cdot 3$
$p = 3 \cdot t$
$p = 3 \times t$

I said, "All of these ways are fine for writing the equation, and I'll add one more to the list. In algebra, when you have a number times a letter, it's OK to omit the times sign or the dot, as long as you put the number first." I wrote on the board:

$p = 3t$

I then asked the class to focus on the T-chart for the banquet seating. "Who would like to share an idea about this pattern?" I asked. Ally went first and I recorded verbatim what she said:

The # of people goes up by 1s. When you add a table, you lose 1 seat, but you gain 2, so you gain 1.

Julie went next. "I'm not exactly sure about my idea, but it seems to work," she said.

"Try it. I'll write down what you say, and then we can all take a look," I said. I wrote as she spoke:

Any table in the middle only contributes 1 seat, but the end ones contribute 2 seats each.

Conversation broke out as students talked about Julie's idea. I called the class back to attention and asked if someone else could state Julie's idea in his or her own words.

Nick said, "Well, suppose you had forty-eight tables. Then there are forty-six in the middle, and there's only one seat at them. But the ends have two seats, and that's four more. So I think you would do forty-six plus four." Some students understood Nick's idea, but others weren't so sure. I pointed to the drawing I had made earlier on the board of a banquet table made with six triangular tables. I shaded in the two end tables.

"Who can come up and show what Julie and Nick meant by the middle tables having one seat each?" I asked. Socoro came up and showed. I drew a little circle to indicate a place setting on each of the middle tables, and then drew Xs to show the two place settings on each of the end tables.

"How many middle tables are there in this banquet table?" I asked.

"Four," Ava answered.

"It's six minus the two ends," Elyse said.

"So how many middle tables would there be if there were seven tables altogether?" I asked.

"Five," the class answered together.

"And eight?" I asked. Again, the class answered correctly: "Six." I asked again, for nine and ten tables.

"And how many middle tables are there in a long banquet table with one hundred small tables?" I asked.

"Ninety-eight," they answered with certainty.

Alex almost jumped out of his seat. He said, "I know the equation. Can I try?" I motioned to him to come up, but he said, "I'll say it and you can write it." I agreed and recorded, putting in parentheses as Alex directed:

$$p = (t - 2) + 4$$

"Can you explain what you wrote?" I asked.

He said, "The middle tables are always all the tables minus the two ends, and there's one seat for them. Then you have to add on the four seats from the end tables."

"Hey, that's like Michael's equation from yesterday for the square tables," Alex commented excitedly.

"It is?" Michael asked, not sure of the connection.

"That's right, it is," Socoro added.

"Does it work?" Blair asked.

"Let's try it," I answered. We tried it for four of the numbers on the T-chart and the class was satisfied.

Michael then blurted out, "Oh, I remember now about the squares. This one can be done the same way!" While Michael seemed to make the connection to the thinking he had done the day before, I sensed that his understanding was still fragile.

Elyse's idea moved the discussion in a different direction. "Couldn't you just say 'p equals t plus 2'?" she asked. I recorded underneath Alex's equation:

$$p = t + 2$$

"What gave you this idea?" I asked Elyse.

"Well, I got it from the T-chart," she said. "You just add two to any number in the first column and you get the number in the second column."

"That's what we got," George said. We tried Elyse's equation for several numbers.

"Both equations work," Tomas said.

"Yes, they're equivalent equations, and both are perfectly fine," I said. "Are there any other thoughts about these patterns before we end our discussion?" Paul reported the idea he told me before, about how the McTriangles' numbers related to the McSquares' numbers.

"It's always good to look for connections between different problems," I said.

No one had another idea. About five minutes were left in the period. I said to the class, "Look over your papers and see if there is anything you'd like to add to your work as a result of our discussion." A few students added the equations; others chose not to change their work. Ingrid and Julien wrote: *I learned: I don't want to start a restaurant* and *Julie's was cool. I never thought of it that way.*

FIGURE 12–6   After the class discussion, Ingrid and Julien added both equations and comments to their paper.

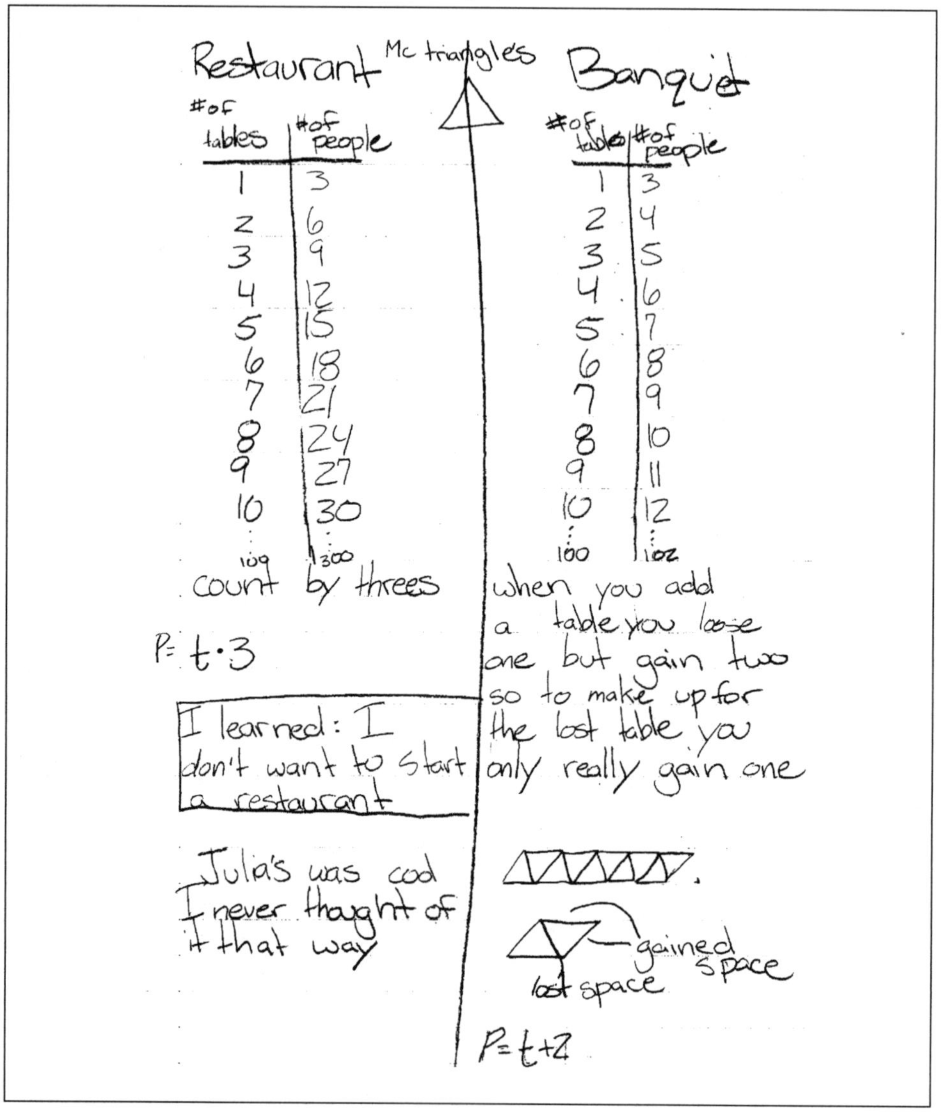

I began class by reading the last part of the story to the students, and I asked them to investigate the same patterns for the McTrapezoids' and McHexagons' restaurants. The students were familiar with the pattern block shapes, but I wanted to clarify the seating around the trapezoids. I drew a single trapezoid on the board and marked where five people would sit. I also drew a four-trapezoid banquet table to show them how the trapezoids had to be placed to make banquet tables:

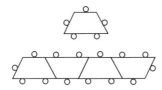

I explained, "Five people can sit around a trapezoid, two on the long side and one on each of the short sides. And when you use the trapezoids to make banquet tables, you need to turn every other one upside down, as you did with the triangles."

"Do you have to do that for the hexagons, too?" Julien asked. I sketched a single hexagon and then a banquet table made from four hexagons.

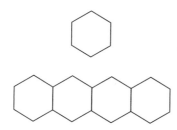

"Does this help?" I asked Julien.

"I see now," he said.

I then said, "Organize your papers as you did for the McTriangles investigation."

"Do we do them on separate papers?" Elyse asked.

"Yes, and title each one with *McTrapezoids* or *McHexagons*," I answered.

"Does it matter which we do first?" Alex asked.

"No, you can do the investigations in either order," I answered.

There were no further questions. "We'll have a class discussion later in the period after you've had a chance to do your investigation," I said. The students got to work.

As I circulated, I noticed that students had different ways to think about the information they collected on T-charts. Some students looked only at the patterns in the numbers on the T-charts. For example, for the restaurant-style tables in the McHexagons' restaurant, Maria and Alex wrote: *Count by six's. The value that comes out is times six that came in!!* For the banquet-style tables, they wrote: *Count by four's. The value of the output # is times four of the input # plus two!!* (See Figure 12–7.)

FIGURE 12-7 Maria and Alex described the numerical patterns in the T-charts and used that information to write correct equations.

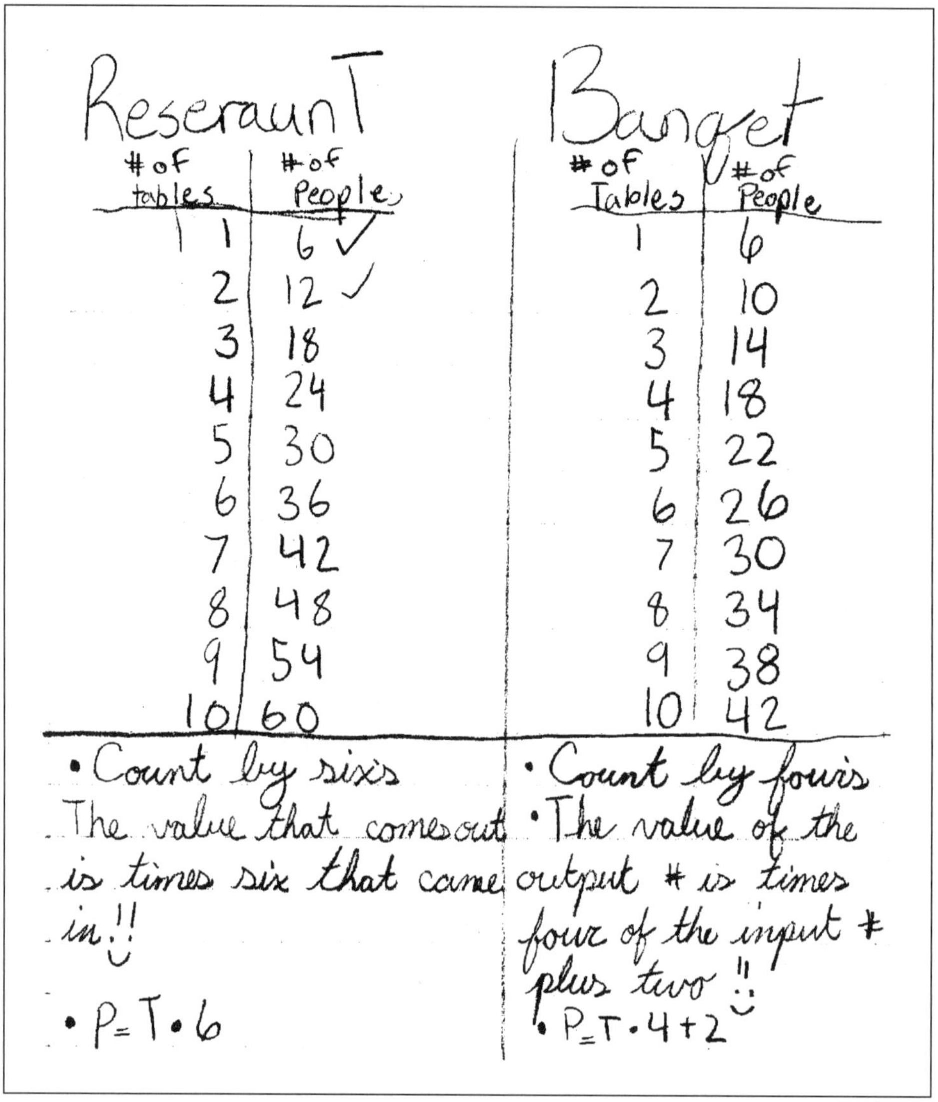

Reseraunt

# of tables	# of People
1	6 ✓
2	12 ✓
3	18
4	24
5	30
6	36
7	42
8	48
9	54
10	60

- Count by sixs
The value that comes out is times six that came in!!
- $P = T \cdot 6$

Banqet

# of Tables	# of People
1	6
2	10
3	14
4	18
5	22
6	26
7	30
8	34
9	38
10	42

- Count by fours
- The value of the output # is times four of the input # plus two!!
- $P = T \cdot 4 + 2$

Other students tried to relate the pattern to the hexagon tables. For example, for the restaurant-style tables in the McHexagons' restaurant, Frannie and George wrote: *The patern is that it goes up by sixes because each hexagon has 6 sides.* For the banquet-style tables, they wrote: *The patern is that you count by 4's. It's like that because whenever you add 6 table settings you minus 2 table settings.* (See Figure 12–8.)

Charlie and Kylie had a method of figuring out the number of people seated banquet style at McTrapezoids' that depended on the previous size table. They wrote: *All you have to do to find the # of the people is add 3 to your previous # of people at a table.*

For the same tables, Alan and Ava wrote: *The pattern is that the number of people goes up every time by 4 but you lose 2 because of where you connet the two tables. Also the number that comes out is always three more than the one before it.*

FIGURE 12-8 For the hexagon patterns, Frannie and George explained how the numerical patterns on the T-charts relate to the hexagons.

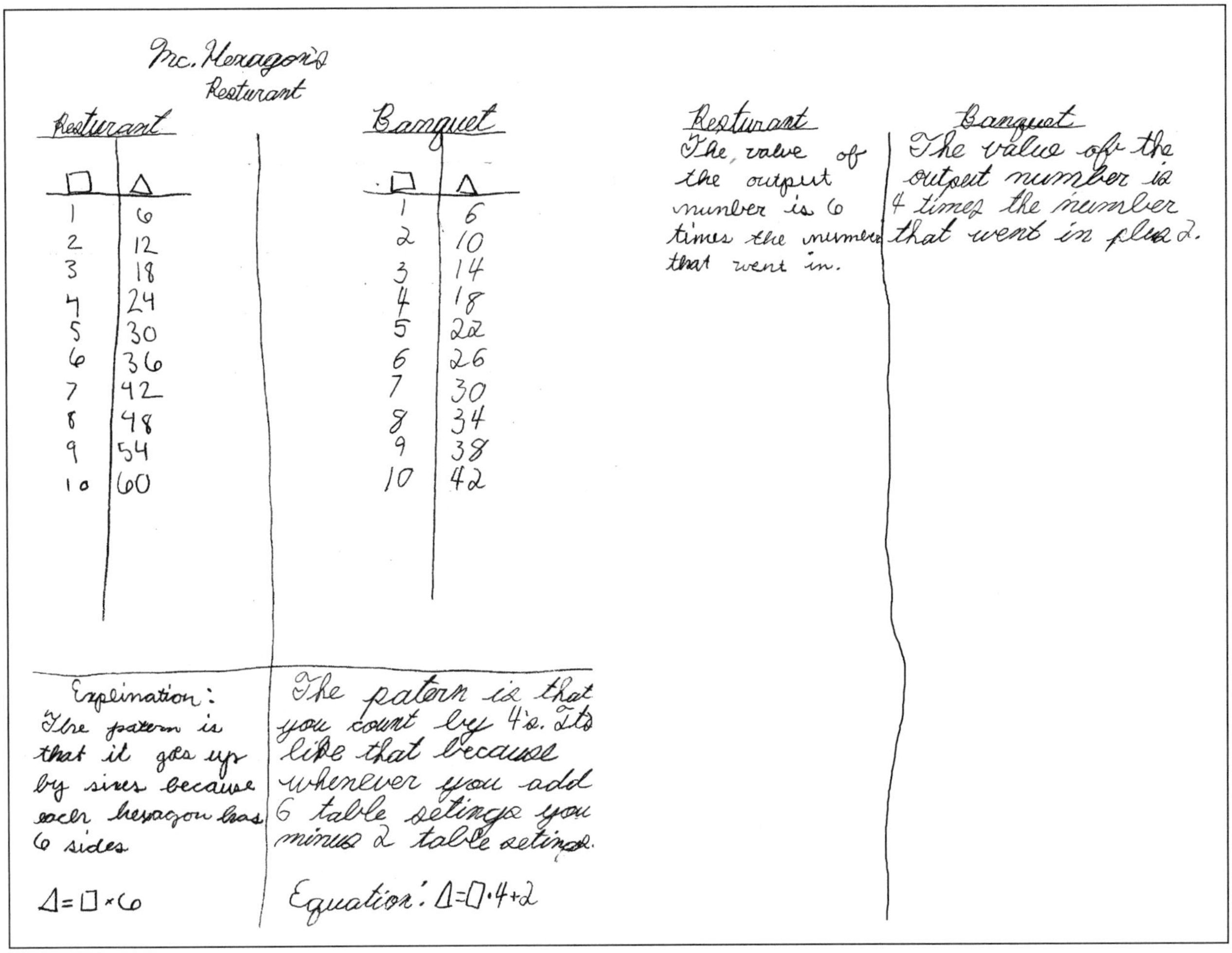

Mc. Hexagon's
Restaurant

Restaurant

□	△
1	6
2	12
3	18
4	24
5	30
6	36
7	42
8	48
9	54
10	60

Banquet

□	△
1	6
2	10
3	14
4	18
5	22
6	26
7	30
8	34
9	38
10	42

Restaurant
The value of the output number is 6 times the number that went in.

Banquet
The value of the output number is 4 times the number that went in plus 2.

Explination: The patern is that it goes up by sixs because each hexagon has 6 sides

$\triangle = \square \times 6$

The patern is that you count by 4's. Its like that because whenever you add 6 table settings you minus 2 table settings.

Equation: $\triangle = \square \cdot 4 + 2$

Lena and Michael made a unique observation about the pattern of banquet tables at the McHexagons' restaurant. They wrote: *Number of people goes up by four after each new table because each time a table is added two table settings go away and four new table settings come. The value of of the output # is the input number plus three more than than what was added to the input number before it or in 1's case 5.* They had difficulty, however, figuring out how to write an equation. Michael still wasn't able to draw on his discovery from two days earlier about seating at the square banquet table. (See Figure 12–9 at the top of page 242.)

A Class Discussion When most of the students were getting close to completing the assignment, I gave a five-minute warning. As the students finished, I organized the board for our class discussion, drawing two T-charts for each of the shapes and labeling them *Restaurant* and *Banquet*. I asked students who had completed their papers more quickly to enter the numbers on the T-charts. When I called the class to order for a class discussion, all of the information was posted (see page 242).

RESTURAUNT STYLE

t	P
1	6
2	12
3	18
4	24
5	30
6	36
7	42
8	48
9	54
10	60

The value of the output number is the input number times 6.

$$A = \square \times 6$$

Mc Hexagon's banquet tables

# of tables	# of people
1	6
2	10
3	14
4	18
5	22
6	26
7	30
8	34
9	38
10	42

Number of people goes up by four each new table because each time a table is added two table settings go away and four new table settings come. The value of of the output # is the input number plus three more than than what was added to the input number before it or in 1's case 5

McTriangles				McSquares				McTrapezoids				McHexagons			
Restaurant		Banquet		Restaurant		Banquet		Restaurant		Banquet		Restaurant		Banquet	
# of Tables	# of People	# of Tables	# of People	# of Tables	# of People	# of Tables	# of People	# of Tables	# of People	# of Tables	# of People	# of Tables	# of People	# of Tables	# of People
1	3	1	3	1	4	1	4	1	5	1	5	1	6	1	6
2	6	2	4	2	8	2	6	2	10	2	8	2	12	2	10
3	9	3	5	3	12	3	8	3	15	3	11	3	18	3	14
4	12	4	6	4	16	4	10	4	20	4	14	4	24	4	18
5	15	5	7	5	20	5	12	5	25	5	17	5	30	5	22
6	18	6	8	6	24	6	14	6	30	6	20	6	36	6	26
7	21	7	9	7	28	7	16	7	35	7	23	7	42	7	30
8	24	8	10	8	32	8	18	8	40	8	26	8	48	8	34
9	27	9	11	9	36	9	20	9	45	9	29	9	54	9	38
10	30	10	12	10	40	10	22	10	50	10	32	10	60	10	42

"Look at all of the charts and see what you notice," I said to the class. Some hands went up immediately, but I waited until practically everyone had a hand raised. I called on Socoro first.

She said, "The first numbers on the lists are the same for triangles and for squares and for trapezoids and hexagons, too." Others weren't sure what Socoro was seeing, so she added, "See, it's one, three and one, three for the McTriangles, then one, four and one, four for McSquares, like that." Now the others saw what Socoro was referring to.

"Who can explain why this makes sense?" I asked.

Teddy said, "Well, one table is the same if it's by itself or if it's for a banquet."

Ally then said, "My idea is about the restaurant tables only. For McTriangles, they go up by threes; for McSquares, they go up by fours; for McTrapezoids, they go up by fives; and for McHexagons, they go up by sixes. It's a pattern—three, four, five, six." Everyone seemed to understand Ally's idea.

"Why does it make sense?" I asked.

"It has to do with how many people sit at one table," Ally said. "That's the number it goes up by."

Marco had a different way to explain. He said, "You could say it's because of the number of sides of the tables, but the trapezoid has four sides and it goes up by fives. That's because it has room for five people to sit."

Nick then said, "There's a pattern for the banquet tables, too. For the triangles, they go up by one; for the squares, by two; for the trapezoid, by three; for the hexagon, by four."

"And why does that happen?" I asked. No one was sure. I waited until I was sure no one had an idea and added, "It has to do with the idea we discussed yesterday about the seats in the middle tables."

Paul came to life and said, "The middle one is always minus two seats from when the table is by itself."

Others seemed confused so I said, "Can you tell us a little more about that?"

Paul said, "The ones in the middle lose two seats where they touch the ones next to them, so it's minus two." This seemed to help others.

"Can I tell an equation?" Lena asked. I nodded.

She said, "Well, there's a pattern in the equations for the restaurant ones. It's 'three times t', then 'four times t', then 'five times t', then 'six times t.'"

"Would you like to come up and write these equations?" I asked. Lena came and wrote the four equations—$p = 3 \times t$, $p = 4 \times t$, $p = 5 \times t$, $p = 6 \times t$—under their matching T-charts.

"That's really cool," Charlie said.

It was the end of class, so I ended the discussion and collected the students' papers. There was a good deal more mathematics that we could discuss, but my goal wasn't for students to understand the mathematics completely. Rather, I wanted to give them an introduction that could serve as a foundation for their later learning. Figure 12–10 shows one more pair's work on this activity.

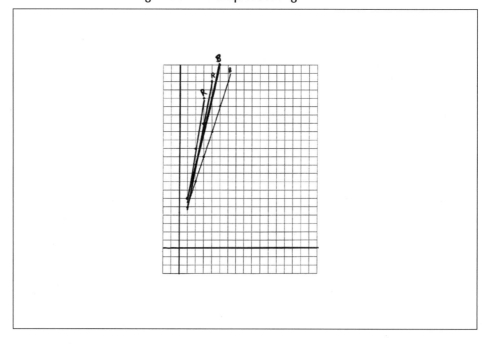

Restaurant Style

# of tables	# people
1	5
2	10
3	15
4	20
5	25
6	30
7	35
8	40
9	45
10	50

It goes up by 5. You x the # of tables by 5. △ □+5

The value of the output number is 5 × # of tables
$$\square = \triangle \times 5$$

# of tables	# of people
1	6
2	12
3	18
4	24
5	30
6	36
7	42
8	48
9	54
10	60

It goes up by 6. You x the # of tables by 6. Plus 6.

The value of the output number is # of tables × 6.
$$\square = \triangle \times 6$$

Banquet Style

# of tables	# of people
1	5
2	8
3	11
4	14
5	17
6	20
7	23
8	26
9	29
10	32

× 3 +2 # of tables It goes up by 3. I goes up by 3.

The value of the output number is the # of tables × 3 +2.
$$\square = (\triangle \times 3) + 2$$

# of tables	# of people
1	6
2	10
3	14
4	18
5	22
6	26
7	30
8	34
9	38
10	42

It goes up by four. # of tables × 4 +2.

The value of the output number is the # of tables × 4 +2
$$\square = (\triangle \times 4) + 2$$

Extensions

This class had learned to graph ordered pairs, so I asked the children to plot the points for the McTrapezoid and McHexagon T-charts for homework. "You won't have room on the graph paper to plot all of them. Just plot

FIGURE 12–11 On their graph of the points for the McTrapezoid and McHexagon T-charts, Ava and Andrew labeled their lines *R* for restaurant seating and *B* for banquet seating.

enough so that you can see the paths the points take." (See Figure 12–11 for one pair's graph.)

The next day, we talked about their graphs. The students noticed that the points for each equation were in a straight line. They also noticed that the steepest line represented the restaurant arrangement of hexagon tables. I pointed out, "I knew that because the number of people increases by six, and that's the biggest jump."

I also talked with the students about why connecting the points to make a line wasn't correct when we talked about tables. I said, "When you connect the points, it means that you can interpret any point on the line.

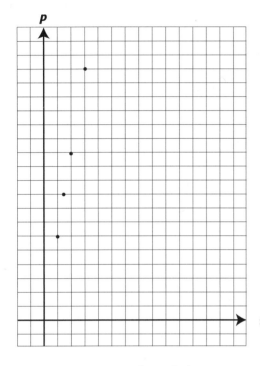

t # of Tables	p # of People
1	6
$1\frac{1}{2}$	9
2	12
3	18

But you can't." I plotted three points for the hexagon restaurant seating pattern and marked another point at $(1\frac{1}{2}, 9)$.

I said, "This point fits the pattern on the graph, but it would mean that at one and a half tables, nine people were sitting. That doesn't make any sense. For this particular situation, your graph should just show points, not the line that connects them."

I wasn't sure that the students understood why they shouldn't join the points, but I felt it was important to explain the correct mathematics in this situation.

A Note about Third Grade

When I did this lesson in a third-grade class, the children were able to construct T-charts and notice patterns. Some were even able to write equations, because, I think, this class had had a good deal of experience playing *Guess My Rule* (see Chapter 10) and making up problems based on the book *Two of Everything* (see Chapter 1). Third graders did the papers shown in Figures 12–12 through 12–14.

FIGURE 12-12   For the McSquares' banquet seating, third graders DeKoa and Colton charted the number of seats for 1–10 tables, then determined how many people would be seated at a 100-table banquet.

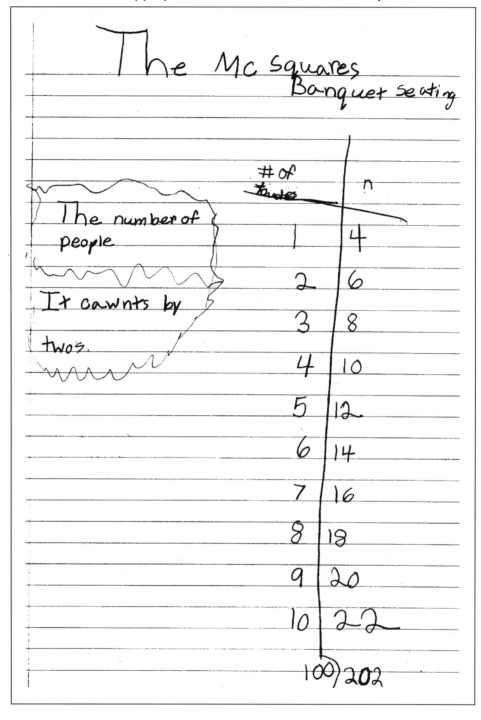

The Mc Squares
Banquet seating

The number of people

It cawnts by twos.

# of tables	n
1	4
2	6
3	8
4	10
5	12
6	14
7	16
8	18
9	20
10	22
100	202

FIGURE 12-13 Carla and Aaron completed the T-charts for the McTriangles' restaurant correctly and described the patterns, but they didn't write equations.

Table Patterns **247**

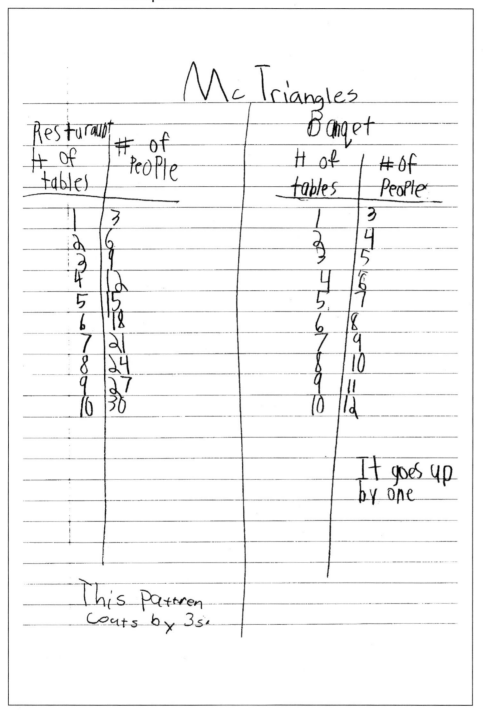

McTriangles

Resturaunt	
# of tables	# of People
1	3
2	6
3	9
4	12
5	15
6	18
7	21
8	24
9	27
10	30

This Pattren Couts by 3s.

Banqet	
# of tables	# 0f People
1	3
2	4
3	5
4	6
5	7
6	8
7	9
8	10
9	11
10	12

It goes up by one

FIGURE 12–14 For the McSquares' banquet tables, Evie and Christopher completed the T-chart, described the pattern, and wrote the equation.

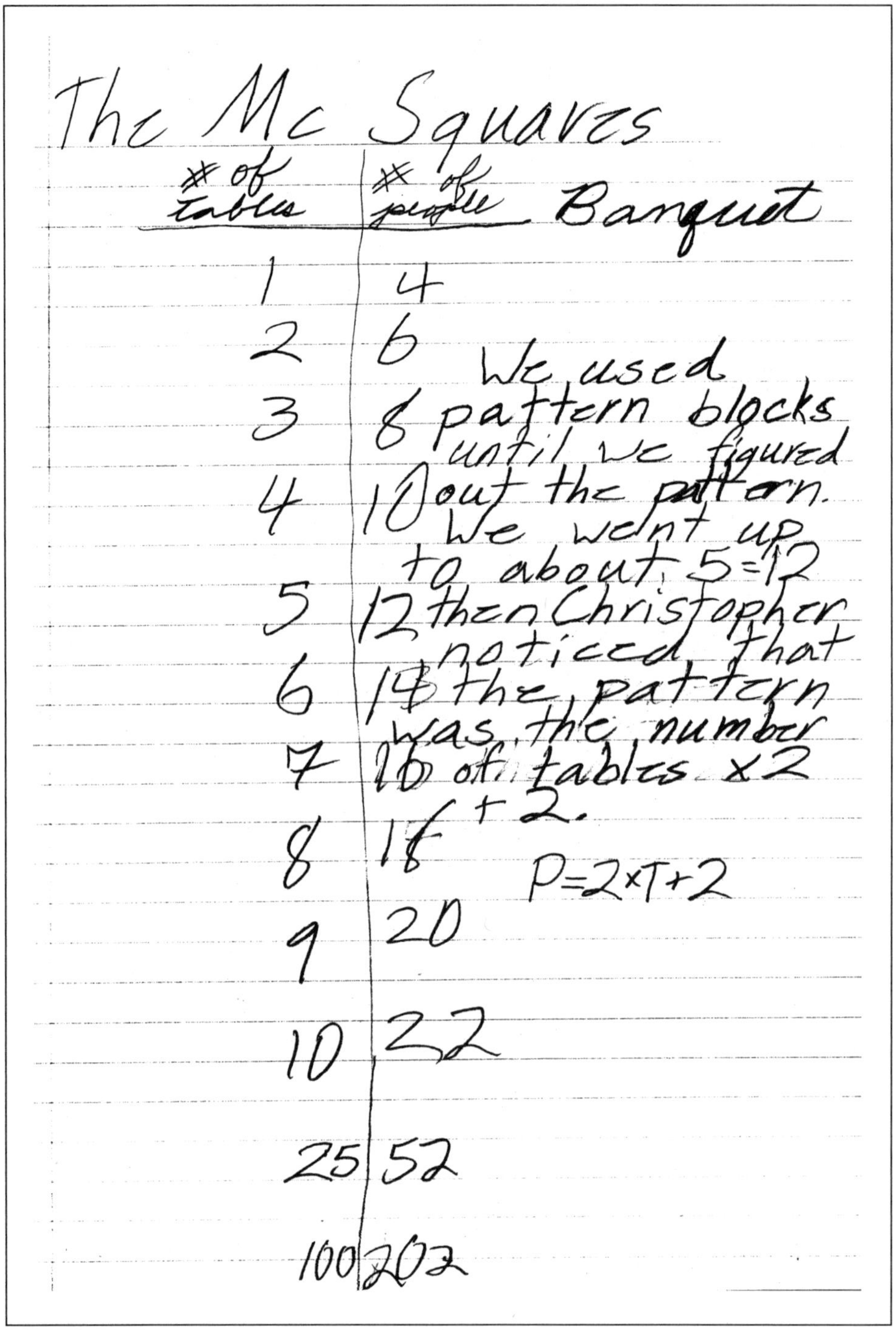

The Mc Squares

# of tables	# of people	Banquet
1	4	
2	6	
3	8	We used pattern blocks until we figured out the pattern.
4	10	
5	12	We went up to about 5=12 then Christopher noticed that
6	14	the pattern was the number
7	16	of tables x2 + 2.
8	18	
9	20	$P = 2 \times T + 2$
10	22	
25	52	
100	202	

## CHAPTER 13

Amanda Bean

Linking Multiplication and Algebra

OVERVIEW

The children's book *Amanda Bean's Amazing Dream*, by Cindy Neuschwander, provides a context for connecting multiplication and algebra. This lesson gives students experience connecting multiplication and rectangular arrays, organizing information on T-charts, and creating a coordinate graph. Using one-inch square tiles to represent windowpanes, the students build all the possible rectangular windows for eighteen panes. They record the dimensions of the arrays on a T-chart and graph the information. Students then repeat the activity for other size windows. This investigation gives students experience with nonlinear graphs.

BACKGROUND

Amanda Bean's Amazing Dream, by Cindy Neuschwander, tells the story of Amanda Bean, who loves to count. She counts anything and everything, from sheep as she tries to fall asleep (6,727 sheep, to be exact) to tiles on the countertop in her kitchen. Sometimes Amanda Bean can't count fast enough. Her teacher has tried to convince her that multiplication is a way for her to count faster, but Amanda isn't so sure. One night Amanda Bean has a wild dream about sheep on bicycles. While trying to count the wheels on the bicycles and the legs on the sheep, she chases them into a barn to find knitting grannies, knitting needles, balls of yarn, and arms of sweaters, all of which she tries to count and can't! "Multiply!" suggest the sheep and grannies. Upon awakening, Amanda Bean announces to her mother that she will learn the multiplication facts—she has decided that they are useful when she wants to know "how many" and she wants to know it fast.

The illustrations on the first two pages of the book show various size windows, each a rectangular array of square windowpanes, providing a geometric representation of multiplication. Multiplying the number of windowpanes on one side of a window by the number of windowpanes on an adjacent side produces a product that represents the total number of windowpanes in the entire window. The lesson builds on this idea. Using one-inch square tiles to represent windowpanes, students find all possible ways to arrange eighteen tiles into rectangular windows, following four rules:

- Tiles must be arranged in rectangles (which includes squares).

- Tiles must lie flat in a single layer.

- Complete sides of tiles must match.

- The window must not have space inside; that is, it should be a filled-in rectangle.

Using grid paper, the students record and cut out the rectangular arrays. On the second day of the lesson, on a chart-size piece of grid paper, the students plot the points for each pair of dimensions, creating a coordinate graph. Students use the horizontal axis to represent the number of columns in a window and the vertical axis to represent the number of rows. Each window produces two different points on the graph. One point results from orienting the window vertically, and the other from orienting the window horizontally. For example, the coordinates of a 6-by-3 window held vertically are (3, 6); the coordinates of the same window held horizontally are (6, 3).

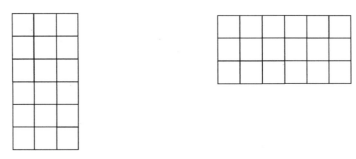

Because the students use their cutout rectangles to verify the points they plot, it's important that the chart-size grid paper have the same size squares as the grid paper the students used to cut out the arrays. One-inch grid paper works well because it can be seen from a distance for a whole-class discussion.

When they record the dimensions of the rectangular windows on a T-chart, students are recording the factor pairs for the product of eighteen. When they graph the pairs on the T-chart, the series of points lies on a curve, not on a straight line as in many other investigations. When the points on a graph are in a straight line, the graph is said to be *linear*. The curve produced in this particular *nonlinear* graph is called a *hyperbola*. Actually, it's only half of a hyperbola, because the students are working only with positive integers; using negative numbers would produce the mirror image of the curve, something students will encounter in their later studies of algebra.

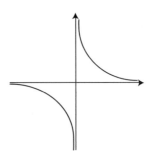

Hyperbola

After the whole-class activity, students repeat the investigation for other size windows, choosing from windows with twelve, sixteen, twenty, twenty-four, thirty, or thirty-six windowpanes. Sixteen and thirty-six are included in these choices to give students experience with square numbers, for which one window for each—the 4-by-4 and the 6-by-6—is represented by only one point on the graph. For this part of the lesson, students use centimeter-squared paper.

It may be appropriate to push fifth graders and capable fourth graders to describe the graph with equations; for example, $x \cdot y = 18$ or $\square \times \triangle = 18$. Use your judgment to decide if your students are ready for this algebraic representation.

VOCABULARY

array, axes, axis, column, coordinates, curve, factor, graph, horizontal, ordered pair, origin, plotting points, point, rectangle, row, square, T-chart, vertical

MATERIALS

- *Amanda Bean's Amazing Dream*, by Cindy Neuschwander (New York: Scholastic Press, 1998)
- color tiles, about 20 per student
- one-inch graph paper, 1–2 sheets per student (see Blackline Masters)
- centimeter graph paper, several sheets per student (see Blackline Masters)
- 1 chart-size sheet of one-inch squared paper
- letter-size envelopes, 1 per pair of students

TIME

- at least three class periods

Day 1 | **The Lesson**

"Today, I'm going to read aloud *Amanda Bean's Amazing Dream*," I said, holding up the book for the class to see.

"Hey, that's a funny book," Suzanna said.

"How many of you have heard the story before?" I asked. Three or four students raised their hands. This didn't concern me, as children enjoy hearing stories more than once. Also, the story was not the main objective of the lesson; rather, it provided a context for thinking about multiplication, T-charts, and nonlinear graphing.

"Did you enjoy the book?" I asked. They nodded.

I read aloud the first four pages of the story, showing the students the illustrations and asking them to figure out the answers to such questions as How many cakes are in the case? and How many cookies are on the tray?

"What in the illustrations can help you more easily answer these questions?" I asked as I focused the students' attention on the page with the cakes and cookies. I wanted students to notice that things were arranged in equal groups and in arrays, and to talk with them about how the information about the arrays was useful.

"They're all lined up," Tomas said. "All the lines have the same amount. So with the cakes, I just count three, six, nine, and I know how many cakes."

"Same thing with the cookies," Nathaniel added. "There are four rows of cookies and each row has seven cookies."

"If there are four rows with seven cookies, do I count by fours or sevens?" Ginny wondered.

"I think you could count by fours," Wayne said. "You can see where all the fours are in the picture. There are seven of them. You can go four, eight, twelve, sixteen, twenty, twenty-four, twenty-eight."

"You could go the other way, too," Lisa added. "I can see four groups of seven. The trouble with that is it's harder to count by sevens." Lisa paused a moment, then began counting. "Seven, fourteen, twenty-one, twenty-eight." She used her fingers to help her count and keep track of how many sevens she counted.

Annie continued, "I think it can work either way. It depends on how you look at the picture. But either way you look at it, you still get twenty-eight cookies." Several students nodded their agreement. No one had anything to add.

When I showed the students the fourth and fifth pages, they immediately noticed the sidewalk.

"Hey look," Andrew said. "The sidewalk is three groups of something. I don't know what—there's too many to count—but it's three groups."

"Maybe it could be something groups of three," Elise commented.

"I agree with both of you," I said. "Let's see what happens next." I continued reading and discussing the story.

Presenting the Investigation   After I finished reading the book, I opened it to the first two pages and held it up so that the students could see the illustrations.

"Lots of windows on that page!" Tomas observed. Had Tomas or some other student not made this observation, I would have directed the students' attention to the illustrations of the windows.

"I agree with Tomas," I replied. "There are lots of windows on these pages. What do you notice about them?"

"They're different sizes," Lisa said.

"Tell me more," I encouraged.

"They have different numbers of squares in them," Lisa clarified.

"Some are tall and skinny," Ginny noticed.

"Some have many squares and some are just one big piece," Chris said.

"Does anyone know another name for the squares in the windows?" I asked.

"They're called windowpanes," Wayne answered.

"Yes, they're windowpanes," I said. I drew a 6-by-3 window on the board to be sure all students could easily see it.

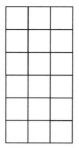

"How many windowpanes are in the window I drew?" I asked.

"Eighteen," Tammy responded.

"Hey, that's what I got," Nathan added.

"Me, too," Ginny said.

"How did you get eighteen, Tammy?" I asked.

"I counted by ones," Tammy said.

I recorded Tammy's explanation on the board:

1, 2, 3, 4, . . . , 18　*Tammy*

"The dots I put between the four and the eighteen tell us I've left some numbers out," I explained. "Did anyone figure it a different way?"

"I did it by counting by threes," Tomas said. "Three, six, nine, twelve, fifteen, eighteen, like that."

I recorded on the board:

3, 6, 9, 12, 15, 18　*Tomas*

"You could do it by counting by sevens," Nathaniel said. I wasn't sure how Nathaniel was thinking about this, so I asked him to come to the board to show me where he saw the groups of seven.

"The sevens are right here," Nathaniel said as he counted the long side of the window. "Uh oh! It's not seven, it's six," Nathaniel realized. "You could count by sixes, not sevens."

"How would you count by sixes, Nathaniel?" I pushed.

"Six, twelve," Nathaniel said quickly and then paused to count by ones from twelve. "Eighteen," he concluded.

I recorded Nathaniel's idea on the board:

6, 12, 18　*Nathaniel*

"How could we use multiplication?" I asked.

"You could do six times three," Nathaniel responded.

"Why does that work?" I asked.

"There are three in each row," he explained. "You can count the top row—one, two, three. Then if you count down, you can see that there are six rows and all six rows have three." I recorded on the board:

6 × 3 = 18　*Nathaniel*

"There's also three times six," Suzanna said after thinking for a moment.

"Why do you think three times six would work, Suzanna?" I asked.

"Well, because there are six going down and there are three groups like that," Suzanna replied. I recorded:

3 × 6 = 18   Suzanna

There were no further ideas, so I asked, "What if I rotated my window so it was turned sideways?" I drew a window oriented as I described.

"It's like the first one, only going sideways," Chris said.

"Yeah," said several students, while others nodded their agreement with Chris.

"Why do you believe it's like the first one?" I asked.

Warren explained, "It's because both ways have sides that are three windowpanes and sides that are six windowpanes. If you tipped over the first window, it would be the same as the second one you drew."

I replied, "I agree that they both have sides with six and three windowpanes. In that way they're the same. I could say that the first window I drew has three columns and six rows." I wrote *row* and *column* on the board.

I asked, "Who can explain what are rows and what are columns?" Several hands went up. I called on Tonya.

"A row goes across," Tonya said. "It's like you're standing on a stage in a theater and you look at the seats. The rows go across in front of you."

"I have a different way of remembering," Nathan said. "I like buildings with columns and columns go up and down to hold up buildings. Columns go up and down, so rows must go across."

"Rows are horizontal," Lisa added. "Columns are vertical."

I wrote the following on the board based on the students' ideas:

column—vertical, goes up and down
row—horizontal, goes across

I also drew a vertical line next to *column* and a horizontal line next to *row*. I find it useful to include an illustration whenever possible to support students with reading difficulties and those just learning English.

I then pointed to the window I had drawn oriented horizontally. "Who knows how many rows and columns there are in the window shown this way?" I asked.

"It has three rows across and six columns," responded Tomas. The students showed their agreement with thumbs up.

Although the windows I drew on the board were oriented differently, they had the same dimensions, were the same size and shape, and had the same number of windowpanes. Both were 3-by-6 arrays of windowpanes. Or we could say that they both were 6-by-3 arrays. There's no correct order or agreed-upon convention for whether the vertical or horizontal dimension is named first when describing a rectangular array. However, when plotting points on a graph, the order of the coordinates does matter; for example, the ordered pairs (6, 3) and (3, 6) determine different points. Thinking about the rows and columns in the two orientations of windows becomes important later in the lesson when students create a graph and the factor pairs locate different points, depending on their order.

I then said, "Your task now is to use color tiles to find as many ways as possible to arrange eighteen separate windowpanes into one larger window. There are four rules you must follow when doing this. Rule one, you must use eighteen tiles and arrange them into a rectangle. Remember that a square is a rectangle, too. Rule two, the tiles must lay flat in a single layer. Rule three, complete sides of tiles must touch." I stopped to sketch on the board what this rule meant.

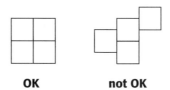

OK   not OK

I continued with the directions, "Rule four is that the window can't have space inside that would let in rain or bugs; it must be all glass." As I explained the rules, I wrote each on the board as a reminder for the students as they worked.

Arrange 18 tiles into rectangles (which includes squares).
Tiles must lie flat in a single layer.
Complete sides of tiles must match.
The rectangle must be filled in—no holes allowed.

I gave a final rule, "When you find an arrangement of eighteen windowpanes that follows the rules, trace it onto the squared paper and cut it out." I added to the board:

Trace your window on squared paper and cut it out.

"Do we work by ourselves?" Andrew asked.

"No, you'll work in pairs," I said. Before class I had put one-inch square tiles in baskets, figuring about twenty tiles per student and one basket for each table group. I had put the baskets on the counter in the back of the room along with one-inch squared paper. There were no more questions and the students were eager to get to work.

"You'll need to choose one person from your table to get the tiles and squared paper from the back counter," I said. "Also, be sure to cut out a rectangle for the windows we already talked about. Your job is cut out all the possible windows you can make with eighteen windowpanes."

Observing the Students   The table groups quickly delegated someone to get the materials and then got to work. I circulated through the class, observing, answering occasional questions, and asking a few as well.

As I walked by Becky's table, she said, "We have two windows. We think there are more, but we aren't sure."

"What's your plan for making sure you have all the windows for eighteen windowpanes?" I asked.

"We aren't too sure about that either," said Catriena, one of Becky's table partners. "We think it has to do with pairs like the pair of windows you have on the board."

"That's an interesting idea," I said. "Why don't you explore it a little more and let me know what you find out."

I walked across the room to check on Nathaniel's table. I noticed one of their windows was four down and five across. "I see you've been working hard," I said. "Did you count to be sure you have eighteen panes in each window?"

"Yeah," Nathaniel said. He started recounting the tiles in the 3-by-6 window. "This one has eighteen," he said.

"Uh oh!" Andrew said after counting the panes in the 4-by-5 window. "This one has twenty. We made a boo-boo." Andrew and Nathaniel began talking and moving tiles to correct the error.

I also noticed that Wayne had cut a 1-by-12 strip. "Wayne, how many panes are in your window?" I asked, pointing to the 1-by-12 strip. He paused a moment and counted.

"Twelve," he replied.

"How many panes should there be?" I asked.

"Eighteen, " Wayne replied.

"How many more do you need?" I asked.

"Six," Wayne said. "What should I do?"

"I know," said Annie, who was sitting nearby and listening. "Just cut out six more and tape them on the end of the first ones."

"Oh yeah," Wayne said, giggling at himself.

"Look what I made," Tammy said.

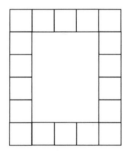

"I see you used eighteen tiles and they're arranged in a rectangle," I said. "But I think rain and bugs might get in your window."

"Oh, you're right," Tammy said, a bit disappointed. Tammy worked with her tiles for a few moments, finally rearranging them into an array that was three down and six across. "What about this?" she asked.

"Let's check that it follows the rules on the board," I said. I wanted Tammy to learn to use available information to evaluate her own work. "Did you arrange eighteen tiles into a rectangle or square?" She nodded. "Are your tiles laying flat and are they in a single layer?" She nodded again. "Do the sides of the tiles match? And is the window filled in with no holes?" She smiled and nodded.

"It's OK then?" Tammy asked. I nodded.

"What do you do next?" I asked.

"Draw it on squared paper and cut it out," Tammy responded as she reached for the paper and a pencil.

I continued to circulate and observe as the students worked, reminding them to record their windows on squared paper. I checked back with Becky and Catriena to see if their strategy of using pairs to find all the windows for eighteen windowpanes worked. The girls were excited and both talked at the same time.

"We've got them all," Becky began. "There are three of them."

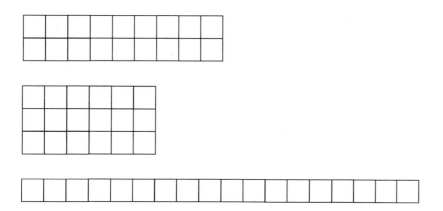

"How are you sure you have all the windows now?"

Becky explained, "We can make a window with one on a side, two on a side, three on a side, but not four or five. That brings us to six. Six goes with three, and we already have that one. There's no window with seven or eight on a side. Nine goes with two. You can't do it with ten, eleven, twelve, thirteen, fourteen, fifteen, sixteen, or seventeen. Eighteen goes with one." I was impressed with their thinking and the clarity of Becky's explanation.

When I noticed that other pairs of students had found the three ways to arrange eighteen tiles into rectangles, as Becky and Catriena had done, I asked them to explain how they knew they had all the ways. When most groups were finished, I asked for the students' attention.

A Class Discussion "Let's see what ways you found to arrange eighteen windowpanes," I said to begin a discussion. "Who would like to share one way?" Almost all hands were up. I called on Chris. "Hold up one window that you'd like to share, Chris." He held up the 2-by-9. "How would you describe your rectangle?"

"It's two on one side and nine on the other and there are eighteen panes altogether," Chris explained.

"If you have the same rectangle as Chris, hold it up. If not, you'll have time in a moment to make one," I instructed the class.

I then asked, "Who has a different rectangle to share?" I called on Lisa.

Lisa held up a 1-by-18 rectangle. "We have one that's got one row and eighteen columns if you hold it this way," she explained, holding the rectangle horizontally, "or one column and eighteen rows if you turn it like this." She rotated the rectangle so it was now vertical. The other students found their rectangle like the one Lisa was holding.

"That leaves just the three-by-six, which we already know about," commented Warren. I nodded my agreement with Warren. I glanced around and could see easily that all the students had the rectangles they should.

Investigating Other Windows There was still time left in the math period, so I continued with the next part of the investigation. For this part of the lesson, students explore making windows that have twelve, sixteen, twenty, twenty-four, thirty, and thirty-six windowpanes. I listed these numbers on the board.

(**Note:** In some classes, more often with younger children, I didn't begin this extension until the next day, and to end this first class briefly introduced the children to the idea of investigating windows for other numbers of windowpanes. Also, students who explore the numbers twenty-four, thirty, and thirty-six will have to tape together squared paper to cut them out, while students exploring twelve, sixteen, and twenty will not. And when students later create graphs, twelve, sixteen, and twenty require a single sheet of graph paper, while twenty-four, thirty, and thirty-six require several sheets taped together. If you think that taping the paper will be a problem or distraction for your students, then limit their choice to windows with twelve, sixteen, or twenty panes.)

I focused the students' attention on the six numbers on the board and said, "You and your partner will choose one of these numbers for your next investigation. The number you choose is the number of windowpanes you use. You'll take that number of tiles and find all the ways to arrange them into rectangular arrays, just as you did with eighteen tiles. When you find a way, draw it onto grid paper and cut it out. Also, write the number of windowpanes on the back of your cutout rectangle." I suggested that the students label their rectangles as a way of keeping them organized should they have time to investigate additional numbers.

The students were eager to begin, but I wanted to be sure that all of the numbers on the board would be investigated by at least one pair of students. I explained this to the class. "It's OK for some of you to investigate the same number, but I want to be sure that each of the numbers is chosen. Then we can compare results about the different-size windows. Talk with your partner about which number you'd like to investigate. Also, have a second choice in mind in case too many people choose the same number. One of you raise a hand when you've decided on your first and second choices." I gave the pairs a moment to decide and then called on students, writing their names next to the number they chose.

I gave another direction. I said, "Also, rather than use the one-inch squared paper as we used for eighteen, use this paper with centimeter squares." I pointed out the pile of centimeter graph paper on the back counter.

"So we do the same thing we just did, only with our new number and using centimeter paper, right?" Annie asked. I nodded. There were no other questions and the students were eager to return to work.

The students had little difficulty with this part of the lesson. They worked well together and cooperated, especially when things needed to be taped together. As the students finished making the windows for their first number, they were given the opportunity to choose a second number to explore. Toward the end of the work period, I gave the students paper clips and letter-size envelopes. "Put your names on your envelope. Clip all the rectangles together for one number and then put the clipped rectangles into your envelope. You will need at least two clips, one for your windows for eighteen, and one for the windows for the number you drew." The students put away their tiles and put their rectangles into their envelopes. I collected the envelopes for safekeeping.

Day 2

Before class, I ruled vertical and horizontal axes on a chart-size sheet of one-inch grid paper. If you don't have chart-size one-inch grid paper, rule a large sheet of paper into a one-inch grid, or tape together several smaller sheets to create a sheet that's at least 20-by-20 squares. I posted the grid on the board for use later in the lesson. Also, I distributed the envelopes with the cutout rectangles.

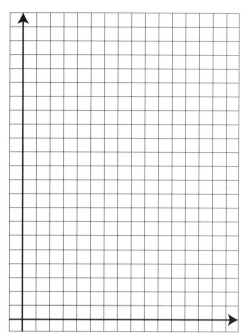

To begin the lesson, I asked the students to place their cutout windows for eighteen in front of them on their table and to return all others to their envelopes. I then said, "In a little bit, we're going to organize the information about these windows on a T-chart, but first we're going to check that every group has a set of three windows. If you're missing a window, please quietly get a sheet of one-inch graph paper from the back counter and make one." The students had checked this during the class discussion on Day 1, and I had checked at the end of the work session to be sure all of the sets were complete, but sometimes things get lost. "Each group should have three windows—one-by-eighteen, two-by-nine, and three-by-six," I said.

I drew a T-chart on the board and labeled the left column *# of Columns* and the right column *# of Rows*.

# of Columns	# of Rows

I showed the class a cutout 1-by-18 window, holding it up vertically. "How many columns in this window if I hold it this way?" I asked.

"One," the students responded. On the T-chart under the first column, labeled # of Columns, I wrote *1*.

"How many rows?" I asked.

"Eighteen," the class responded. In the second column, across from the 1 I'd just written, I wrote *18*.

# of Columns	# of Rows
1	18

"You could turn that window for the horizontal partner," Andrew suggested.

"Let's do it," I said. I rotated the vertical window to become a horizontal window. "What should I put on the chart?" I waited until most students had their hands up, then called on Nathaniel.

"Under the first column you should put eighteen," Nathaniel said.

"Why?" I asked.

"Because there are eighteen columns," Nathaniel said. Several students nodded their agreement. I wrote *18* in the first column, under the 1.

"I wrote eighteen for the number of columns in my window," I continued. "What should I put in the Number of Rows column on the T-chart?"

Ginny said, "There's only one horizontal row, so you have to put one on the T-chart under Number of Rows." I did as Ginny suggested.

# of Columns	# of Rows
1	18
18	1

"Let's record for another window. Who has an idea?" All hands flew into the air. I called on Carter.

"This window has two columns and nine rows," Carter said as he held up a 2-by-9 window vertically.

"What should I write on the T-chart?" I asked.

"You should put a two under Number of Columns and a nine under Number of Rows," Carter explained.

"Who would like to record on the T-chart the information that Carter gave us?" I asked. I called on Tonya, who came to the board and wrote *2* and *9* on the T-chart.

"You can turn Carter's vertical window to be a horizontal window," Lisa said. "On the T-chart you'd write the nine in the first column and two next to it in the right column."

"Lisa, would you please come to the board and do what you just explained?" I requested. Lisa did so. We continued in the same way and added to the T-chart the information about the 6-by-3 window.

# of Columns	# of Rows
1	18
18	1
2	9
9	2
3	6
6	3

I said to the class, "Sometimes it's helpful to arrange numbers in a T-chart in order so that we can look for patterns and be sure that we've included all the information we have." It wasn't essential to do this for this lesson, but the students were familiar from other activities with organizing the information in T-charts in order, so I presented this option for examining T-charts for patterns. Next to the first T-chart, I drew another T-chart and labeled the columns the same way. Also, I wrote the first pair of numbers as I did before.

"If I wanted the numbers in order, what would I write next?" I asked.

"The two and the nine," Catriena said. I recorded these.

"Next comes three and six," Tammy said. I recorded these and continued until I had reordered all six pairs.

# of Columns	# of Rows	# of Columns	# of Rows
1	18	1	18
18	1	2	9
2	9	3	6
9	2	6	3
3	6	9	2
6	3	18	1

"What patterns do you notice?" I asked.

Wayne said, "The numbers go up in the Columns column and down in the Rows column." Some students giggled when Wayne said "Columns column."

Becky said, "There's sort of a pattern. The numbers go one, two, three, but then they skip. You can't do four and five."

"Yeah, it didn't work with the tiles," Nathaniel added, remembering what he had erroneously built.

"So the T-chart this way can help us check that we've included all of the information," I commented.

"You can't do seven or eight," Suzanna said.

"And you can't do any of the numbers after nine until you get to eighteen," Tomas added.

"Hey!" Bethany piped up. "What I notice on both T-charts is that if you multiply each number with the number next to it, you always get the same answer." I pointed to the pairs on the charts to show the students what Bethany meant. Had she or some other student not noticed this, I would have pointed it out to the class.

"It's always eighteen," Nathaniel said.

"The windows all have eighteen windowpanes," Carter said.

Creating a Graph   I directed the students' attention to the chart-size grid posted on the board. This class had had previous experience plotting points on a coordinate graph. (If your class hasn't had this experience, see Chapters 3 and 4 for how to introduce students to this skill.) "In the past, we've plotted points using ordered pairs from a T-chart. Who would like to come and point to where the ordered pair (three, six) goes on the graph?" I asked as I pointed to the 3 and 6 on the T-chart. I called on Chris. When Chris got to the graph, he seemed to go blank. I prompted him, "Where do you start?"

"Where the heavy lines cross," Chris said, pointing to the origin, where the axes crossed.

"I think I go across three," Chris continued hesitantly. I nodded. Chris correctly counted three to the right on the horizontal axis, paused a moment, then counted up six and put his finger on the point (3, 6).

"If you agree with Chris please put your thumb up, if you disagree put your thumb down, and if you're not sure put your thumb sideways," I said. The students gave Chris thumbs up and he returned to his seat smiling while I marked the point (3, 6) on the graph.

"Where is the point (three, six) represented on the T-chart?" I asked to give the students as many opportunities as possible to make the connection between the points on the graph and the numbers on the T-chart. "Let's look at the T-chart with the numbers in order." Tomas came to the T-chart and pointed to the correct ordered pair. I put a check where Tomas had pointed to indicate that we had located that ordered pair on the graph.

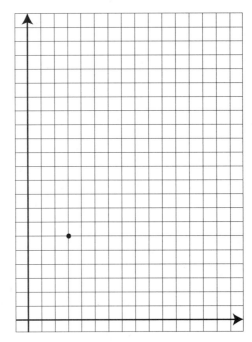

"Look at the windows on your tables and hold up the one that represents the ordered pair (three, six) that I checked on the T-chart and marked on the graph." The room came alive with animated discussion and all groups quickly identified the 3-by-6 window. I asked Catriena to bring the window she was holding to the front of the room. I took the window from Catriena and said to her and the rest of the class, "Watch what I do." Holding the window vertically, I placed the lower left corner of the window at the origin of the graph, matching the bottom side of the window with the horizontal axis of the graph and the left side of the window with the vertical axis.

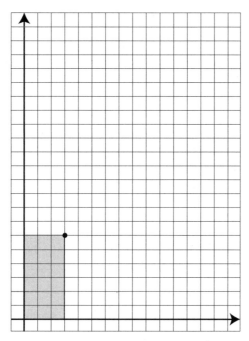

I heard "oohs" and "aahs" as the students saw that the upper right corner of the window touched the point Chris had indicated for the ordered pair (3, 6). I handed the window back to Catriena and she returned to her seat.

"Talk with your table group and pick a different window for us to graph," I said. I called on Warren's group. Warren held up the 2-by-9 array horizontally.

"Which ordered pair of numbers on the T-chart represents your window?" I asked. Warren came to the T-chart and indicated the correct ordered pair, and I marked it with a check.

"Can you place your window on the graph the way I placed Catriena's?" I asked Warren. He nodded and laid his window on the graph, careful to match the lower left corner of the window with the origin.

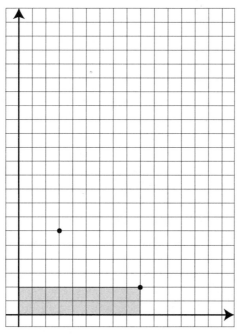

"Should I put a mark where the upper right corner touches the graph?" Warren asked. I nodded and handed him a marker. Warren marked the point (9, 2), took his window, and returned to his seat.

"Let's check what Warren did another way," I suggested. "When we graph an ordered pair and we don't have a window to help us, where do we start?"

"Where the axes cross," the class responded together.

"Yes, at the origin," I said, reinforcing the correct terminology.

"Go across nine and up two," Ginny said. I did as Ginny suggested and landed on the point Warren had marked.

We continued in this way for the other pairs on the T-chart. Each time, a different table group chose a window and indicated the ordered pair on the T-chart it represented. Then they placed the window at the origin and marked the point where the upper right corner of the window touched the graph. We then checked the coordinates of the point they marked by counting over and up from the origin. When all the points were graphed, I copied the T-chart onto the upper right corner of the graph. The completed graph looked as follows:

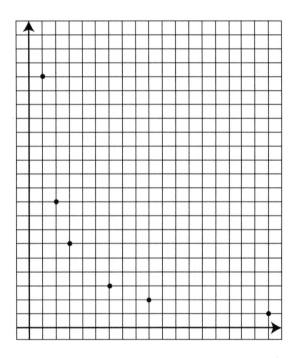

# of columns	# of rows
1	18
2	9
3	6
6	3
9	2
18	1

A Class Discussion I said to the class, "Talk with your table group about what you notice about the graph. Also, see if you have any new ideas about the information on the T-chart." As the students talked, I circulated through the class, listening to conversations. At some tables, to stimulate conversation, I asked, "How is this graph different from the other graphs we've done?" Or, "Is there anything about the graph or T-chart that surprised you?" After five minutes or so I asked for the students' attention. "Who would like to share?" I asked. I called on Nathaniel.

"We noticed that you can just turn the number pairs around," Nathaniel explained. "Near the top is a two and nine and then near the bottom is nine and two. They're just turned around."

"Does that work for all of the pairs?" I asked.

"Yes," the students responded together.

I recorded Nathaniel's idea on the board:

The pairs of numbers on the T-chart switch around.   Nathaniel

"They all use eighteen panes," Suzanna shared. I added Suzanna's idea to the list:

They all use eighteen panes.   Suzanna

"There are six factors of eighteen," Elise said.
"Where are they on the T-chart?" I asked.
"There are six pairs of numbers," Elise said. "Also, there are six points on the graph."
"But the numbers are on the T-chart twice," Andrew said. "Does that count?"
"Well, they're on the T-chart twice, but they're in different columns," Elise explained. "There are six numbers in the first column and the same six in the second column, but they're in a different order."
I recorded Elise's idea on the board:

There are six factors of eighteen.   Elise

After a pause, Lisa added a final thought. "If you connected the points on the graph, I think they'd go in a curve and usually they go in a straight line." I heard a few "yeahs," and some heads nodded in agreement with Lisa. To verify Lisa's observation, I motioned with my finger how the points would connect.
"I wonder why that happened?" Chris said.
No one had any other comments. Time was up, so I ended the class. (In other classes, time still remained, so I began the investigation presented in the following section for Day 3.)

Day 3

For the next part of the lesson, the students worked again with their partners and created a T-chart and graph using the rectangles for the number they had investigated. I reviewed with the students what they were to do, using as a model the graph and T-chart we made for windows with eighteen windowpanes. "Using the windows you made for the number you chose, make a T-chart, and then graph the points. Finally, write about the patterns you notice on the T-chart and on the graph. Bring your paper to me when you're finished and I'll post it for our class discussion later. If you have time, you can investigate another number." I wrote the directions on the board:

Use the windows for the number you chose yesterday.
Make a T-chart.
Make a graph.
Write about the patterns you notice in the T-chart and on the graph.
Bring your paper to me when you're finished.
If you have time, investigate another number in the same way.

"One last thing," I added. "Those of you who have larger numbers will need to tape together several sheets of squared paper to make a graph that is large enough. I've put several rolls of tape here on the back counter, along with a supply of centimeter paper for you to use. Something that's helpful when many people need to share tape is to take a long strip from the tape dispenser and leave the dispenser on the back counter so others don't have to look for it. Then tape the end of your long strip to your desk and let it hang down. When you need tape, tear off a piece."

"Do we work with our same partners?" Tammy asked. I nodded.

"Do we have to do the first number we did, or can we just do one of the other numbers if we did extra numbers yesterday?" Nathaniel wanted to know.

"Please use the number you investigated first," I explained. "Then if you have time, you may do one of the other numbers."

"Where do we write the T-chart?" Elise asked.

"I think you'll have room in the upper right corner of the graph paper, as I did on the chart," I said and pointed to the T-chart on my graph. Elise nodded. There were no more questions. The students took out their cutout windows and began.

Suzanna and Ginny were working together, making their graph for windows with twenty panes. As I walked by, they were disagreeing about where to place the 4-by-5 rectangle on the graph. "Look," Ginny said with exasperation, "if we do it your way, the point will be marked at (five, six) and it's supposed to be at (four, five). You have to put the corner at the origin, not one space away." Suzanna thought about this a moment, then carefully counted across the horizontal axis four and up five. Next she laid the 4-by-5 window with the corner at the origin. Finally, she nodded her head in agreement with Ginny.

"Let me do the next one," Suzanna said. She laid the 2-by-10 window with its corner at the origin and correctly marked where its upper right corner touched the graph at (2, 10). Then she checked herself by counting across the horizontal axis two and up ten.

"Are we supposed to make two T-charts, like you did?" Ginny wanted to know.

"No, one is enough," I replied. "I rewrote the T-chart with the numbers in order to be sure no information was missing and to help you look for patterns."

"OK," Ginny said and nodded. "It's not hard, so I'll put it in order." I left Ginny and Suzanna to work. (See Figure 13–1.)

Before long, Nathaniel and Tomas brought their work to show me. They had made a T-chart and had plotted the points for the T-chart on their graph. "Tell me about your work," I said.

"Our number was twelve," Tomas began. "We looked at our rectangles. We counted the columns and rows for a window and put that information on the T-chart. Then we turned the window and counted the columns and rows again and put that on the T-chart."

"Yeah," Nathaniel interrupted. "We did that for all the windows. Then we made the graph with the windows by putting them on the graph and marking the point."

"Did you check to be sure you marked the point correctly?" I asked. Both boys nodded.

"We started at the origin, then counted across and up," Tomas added.

"Yep, that's what we did," Nathaniel agreed.

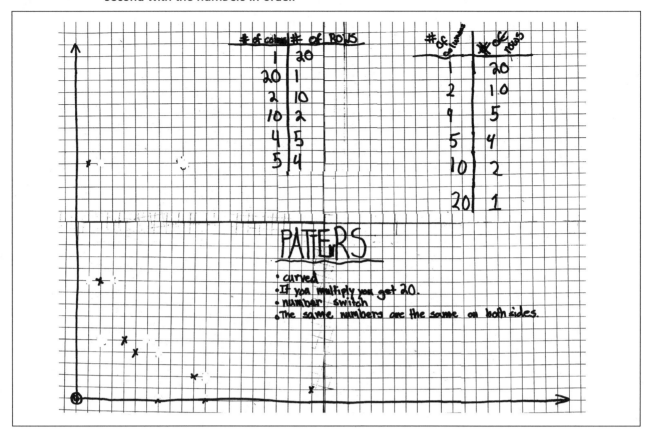

"You have a good start on your work, but I don't see that you've written about the patterns on the graph and in the T-chart," I said. Both boys moaned. They had a difficult time with putting their thoughts into words. To help them I asked, "What patterns do you see on the T-chart?"

"The numbers switch," Nathaniel said, pointing to the first two pairs of numbers.

"The points on the graph look like a quarter pipe at the skate park," Tomas commented.

"What's the shape of a quarter pipe?" I asked.

"It goes like this," Tomas said, using his hand to draw a curve in the air.

"Oh," I said. "It's a curve." Tomas nodded. "You each have one good idea you need to write on your paper. Then you need to talk together to see what other patterns you can find." (See Figure 13–2.)

"Look!" Erik said with excitement. "I just switch the windows and the numbers on the T-chart switch." Using a 4-by-3 window, he continued, "When it's horizontal, then there are four columns and three rows. Switch the window to a vertical window and there are three columns and four rows. Switch the window, and the numbers switch!" (See Figure 13–3.)

"I see why we had to put the number on the back of our windows," Nathaniel commented as I walked by. "It helps me find the windows for a certain number in a hurry." Nathaniel had made windows for several numbers.

Catriena and Elise ignored the labels of the columns on their T-chart and instead listed pairs of coordinates in each column. After I spent some time helping them understand how to record on a T-chart, they were able to complete the chart correctly. (See Figure 13–4.)

267

FIGURE 13-2 Tomas and Nathaniel graphed the ordered pairs for windows with 12 windowpanes. Tomas wrote that the points curved like a quarter pipe at the skate park.

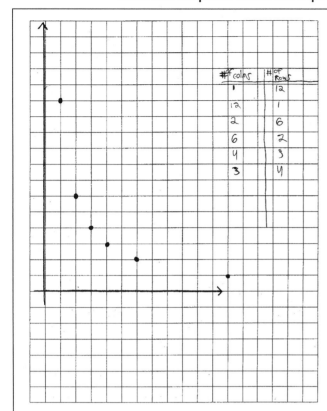

the t chart on both sides their are the same numbers on each side. And they are swiching sides.
The graph has a quarter pitpe.

#† colns	#Of Rows
1	12
12	1
2	6
6	2
4	3
3	4

FIGURE 13-3 Erik's second T-chart showed how the numbers in the ordered pairs switch when a window's orientation is changed from horizontal to vertical.

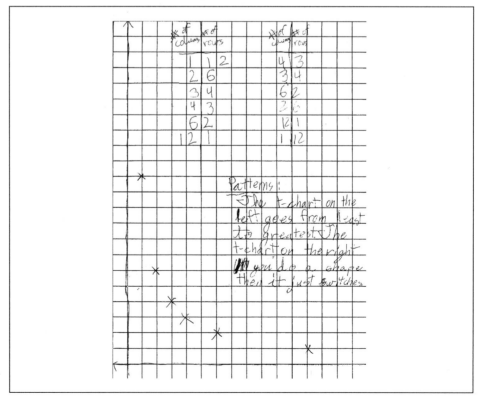

# of columns	# of rows		# of columns	# of rows
1	2		4	3
2	6		3	4
3	4		6	2
4	3		2	6
6	2		12	1
12	1		1	12

Patterns:
The t-chart on the left goes from least to greatest. The t-chart on the right if you do a shape then it just switches.

FIGURE 13–4 At first, Catriena and Elise didn't understand how to record correctly on a T-chart.

Amanda Bean   269

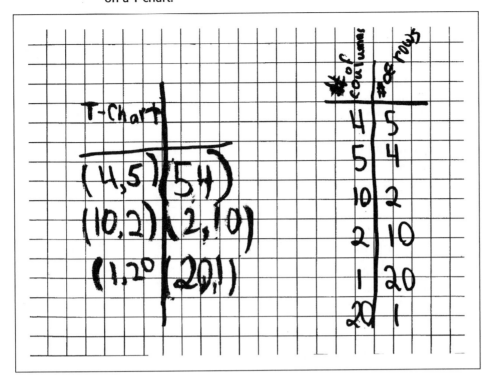

The students worked well together. I helped a few tape their sheets together, but most students worked with their partner with no help from me. However, I found that many of the students had difficulty writing about the patterns they noticed. Also, most students noticed the same patterns.

As pairs finished and discussed their work with me, I posted their graphs on the board where all could see them. Then I instructed the students to repeat the investigation for another number from the list. When all of the students had finished the T-chart, graph, and writing about patterns for at least one number, I gathered the class in front of the board, where they could see the posted graphs and T-charts.

A Class Discussion   "Take a few moments to study the graphs and T-charts posted on the board," I began. The children studied their classmates' work quietly for a few moments, then began to talk quietly with each other. After several minutes, I asked for their attention.

I said, "I heard some interesting comments as you were talking with each other. Who would like to share?" Hands were up, as students were eager to share. I called on Catriena.

"Me and Elise think all the graphs go in an unstraight line," Catriena explained.

"Raise your hand if you know another way to describe 'an unstraight line,'" I said as I pointed to one of the graphs.

"It looks like a skateboard ramp," Chris commented.

"Or it looks like a wave," Warren added. Warren was just learning to surf.

"Is it a crooked line?" Nathaniel ventured.

"Oh, I know," Annie said. "It's a curve. I remember now."

I continued, "A skateboard ramp and a wave both are curves, like the paths of the points on your graphs."

"I bet you chose those numbers for windows just because they make curves," Lisa said.

"What do the rest of you think about that?" I replied.

"Well, they're all even numbers," Tammy noticed. "Maybe even numbers of windowpanes make a curve and windows with odd numbers don't."

"That's an interesting idea," I commented. "How could we test Tammy's idea to find out if her idea is true?"

"Try an odd number and see," Nathaniel suggested.

"Explain what we should do," I said.

"Take fifteen as an example," Nathaniel explained. "Find all the windows for fifteen and then put them on the graph. Mark where the corner is, and then turn them and mark again. Then see how all the points go." I decided that this would be a good extension for students who were interested. I wrote on the board:

Will odd numbers create a curve?

I read aloud what I wrote: " 'Will odd number create a curve?' I think something's missing from the question. What is it that we are actually plotting on the graph?" I wanted the students to recognize that we were plotting the factors of even numbers or odd numbers.

"Oh, I know," Tomas said. "The numbers on the T-chart and on the sides of the windows are factors. We've been plotting factors of certain numbers."

Several of his classmates said, "Oh yeah!" or nodded their agreement.

"How should I change my question?" I asked. I paused and waited until most students had their hands up. I called on Becky.

"The question could be 'Will the factors of an odd number cause a curve?'" Becky said. I nodded and changed the question on the board to:

Will points plotted for the factor pairs of an odd number create a curve?

I then said, "If you're interested, you can investigate this later. For now, let's look again at all the graphs posted and see what else you notice."

"Some graphs have more dots on them," Wayne said.

"Which graphs have more points?" I said, using the correct terminology.

"Ours did," Tammy said. "We did the number thirty and we have eight points."

"Ours does, too," Maria said.

"What number did you investigate?" I asked.

"Twenty-four," Maria answered.

"I thought ours should have the most points," Becky said. "We did thirty-six, and that was the biggest number." (See Figure 13–5.)

"How many points did you plot?" I asked.

"Nine," she said.

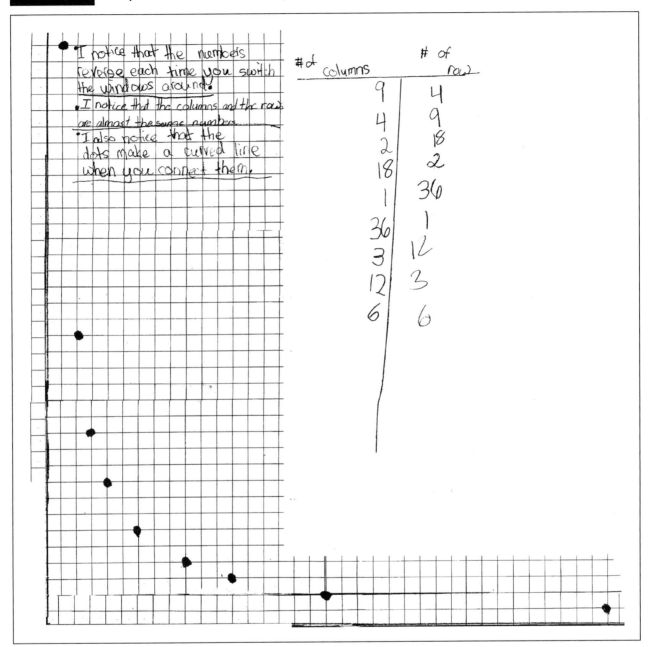

FIGURE 13–5 Becky found nine factors for thirty-six.

I notice that the numbers reverse each time you switch the windows around.

I notice that the columns and the rows are almost the same numbers.

I also notice that the dots make a curved line when you connect them.

# of columns	# of rows
9	4
4	9
2	18
18	2
1	36
36	1
3	12
12	3
6	6

Extensions

With third-grade classes and some fourth-grade classes, I wouldn't continue the discussion further. But I felt that I could push these students a bit more, and I had several choices about where to lead the discussion. One direction could be to talk about which graphs had an odd number of points plotted and which had an even number of points. Most numbers have an even number of points because each window, representing a pair of factors, can be rotated to locate two different points. However, numbers that are square numbers all have a factor pair that is a number times itself—$4 \times 4 = 16$ and $6 \times 6 = 36$, for example. When you rotate either of these square windows, you don't locate a different point. (See Figure 13–6.)

FIGURE 13-6 The graph of a window with 16 windowpanes has an odd number of points because the coordinates for a 4-by-4 window are the same no matter which way the window is rotated.

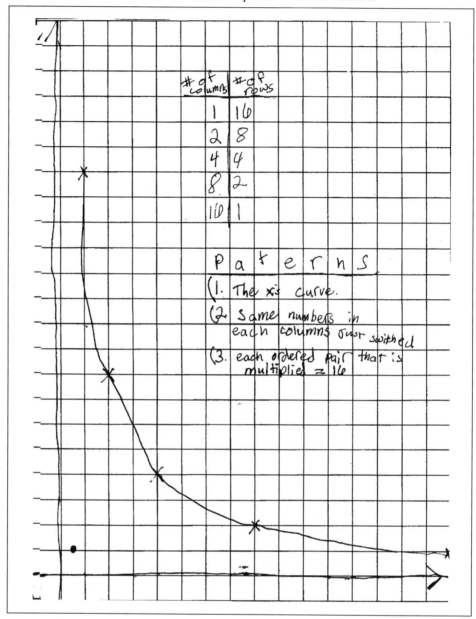

With this class, however, I chose a different direction to extend the discussion. I focused the students again on the chart-size graph we had made for windows with eighteen windowpanes. I said, "When we made this graph, we marked two points for each cutout window. But I could have made other windows as well. Watch as I use the three-by-six window to make another." As the students watched, I took one of the cutout 3-by-6 windows and carefully cut it in half lengthwise so that I had two pieces, each six squares long and one and a half squares wide. Using clear tape, I taped the two pieces into one long window that was 12 panes by $1\frac{1}{2}$ panes.

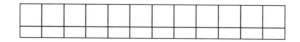

"Does this window still have eighteen windowpanes?" I asked.

"Some of the houses in my neighborhood have half windows," Suzanna said. "They look cool." Several other students made comments similar to Suzanna's.

I repeated my question. "Does this window that's one and a half by twelve still have a total of eighteen windowpanes?"

"I think so," Annie said. "I watched you cut it, so I know all eighteen panes are there. You just put them in a different way."

Wayne added, "I think there are eighteen, because you have one row of twelve, and the other row is one-half plus one-half twelve times, and that's six. Twelve and six make eighteen."

Bethany added, "It's the same window. It has to have eighteen panes."

"So I can write these numbers on the T-chart," I said. I added $(12, 1\frac{1}{2})$ and $(1\frac{1}{2}, 12)$ to the T-chart.

"Who would like to come up and plot points for this window?" I asked. I chose Chris and Nathaniel to come up and do it together. They placed the window and marked one point, then rotated it and marked another point.

"Who would like to come up and check the coordinates of these points?" I asked. Annie and Elise came up and verified that the points were located at $(1\frac{1}{2}, 12)$ and $(12, 1\frac{1}{2})$.

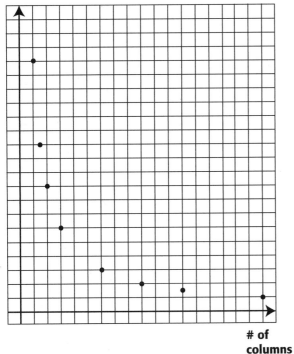

# of columns	# of rows
1	18
2	9
3	6
6	3
9	2
18	1
$1\frac{1}{2}$	12
12	$1\frac{1}{2}$

"Cool, they fit," Nathaniel said.

"They're right on the curve," Catriena added.

"Can we do that for ours?" Bethany wanted to know.

"We're out of time now," I said, "but if you're interested, you can do it later. Or you can investigate what might happen for an odd number of windowpanes."

In several classes, sometime during this lesson a student has made the comment that the points for prime numbers wouldn't go in a curve. For example, in this class, the next day, Bethany shared an idea. She had been thinking about our question from the day before about whether the points plotted for the factor pairs of an odd number always create a curve. She said, "Prime numbers only have two factors. That would make a straight diagonal line." Bethany knew that a prime number has exactly two factors, itself and one; therefore, she assumed that the factors would locate just two points, which could be connected by a straight line.

To respond to Bethany's idea, I posted a sheet of one-inch graph paper on the board. "Bethany, can you give me an example of a prime number less than ten?" I asked.

"Seven," Bethany suggested. "The factors are one and seven and there would be only one window, a one-by-seven. You'd mark (one, seven) and (seven, one) on the graph." I made a T-chart and wrote on it the pairs of numbers that Bethany had mentioned.

# of Columns	# of Rows
1	7
7	1

"Would you please come up and mark these two points?" I asked. Bethany came up and marked the points correctly. While Bethany marked the points, I quickly cut a 1-by-7 rectangle from one-inch grid paper. I placed the rectangle on the graph with a corner at the origin, first oriented one way and then the other. Each time, the upper right corner matched a point that Bethany had marked.

I said to the class, "Bethany is right that the number seven has only two factors, itself and one. That's why it's a prime number. But what if I cut the rectangle in half and taped together the two halves so it becomes a window that's two windowpanes by three and a half windowpanes?" I did this as the students watched.

I asked, "Would a window that's two windowpanes by three and a half windowpanes still have a total of seven windowpanes?" Some students raised a hand immediately and others didn't. I paused and waited a few moments to give the students time to think. When more than half the students had a hand up, I called on Annie.

Annie said, "I think there are still seven, because three plus three is six and one-half plus one-half is one. Six and one is seven."
I recorded Annie's idea on the board:

$3 + 3 = 6$
$\frac{1}{2} + \frac{1}{2} = 1$
$6 + 1 = 7$

Ginny said, "You can use multiplication instead of addition. Two times three is six and two times one-half is one. Six and one is seven."
I recorded Ginny's thinking on the board:

$2 \times 3 = 6$
$2 \times \frac{1}{2} = 1$
$6 + 1 = 7$

"You could just count them," Tammy suggested. She came up and counted, pointing to the squares in the window, "One, two, three, four, five, six, six and a half, seven." I added Tammy's idea to the list.

I then said, "When we think only about whole numbers, seven has only two factors. But if we use fractions, too, then we can add two and three and one-half to the T-chart as numbers that also give an answer of seven when you multiply them." I added the information to the T-chart.

"Now let's graph the points for these pairs and see what happens. Who would like to mark the points on the same coordinate grid that Bethany used to mark (one, seven) and (seven, one)?" I called on Wayne. He came up and correctly located points for $(2, 3\frac{1}{2})$ and $(3\frac{1}{2}, 2)$ on the graph.

Several students responded. "Hey!" "Wow." "Cool."

"It does make a curve," Bethany said.

The discussion had gone in an unexpected direction and the students had remained engaged throughout.

Identities

Investigating Properties of Numbers

OVERVIEW

In this lesson, students think about equations, called *identities*, that become true no matter what numbers are used for the variables. The lesson begins by introducing students to three examples of open sentences—one with only one solution, one with no solution, and one that is true for all numbers. Students then work in pairs and write equations like the third example, all of which are identities. Pairs report their identities for a class list. They then choose one of their equations and write a convincing argument explaining why it is an identity.

BACKGROUND

Before experiencing this lesson, students should have had experience with true, false, and open sentences. (See Chapter 2.) It's especially important that students understand that when the same variable appears more than once in an equation, it must represent the same number.

When asked to create identities, students typically make false starts and suggest open sentences that aren't identities. When a student makes a suggestion, follow the same procedure each time of recording the equation on the board and asking the students to test whether it becomes true for several numbers. If it seems to be an identity, then ask students to explain why it would be true for any number. Handling students' suggestions in this way gives them the opportunity to decide on their own whether the equation is an identity. Also, it's important to encourage students to take risks in class and offer ideas even if they're not well formed or correct. Therefore, when a suggestion is incorrect, acknowledge the contribution and encourage the student to try again. Often a student's suggestion can be turned into an identity with a minor change. Take care not to make students feel foolish or deficient for making an error; rather, applaud their willingness to take risks and share their thinking.

In every class in which I've taught this lesson, students come up with one or both of these two ideas for an identity:

$$\square \div 0 = \square$$
$$\square \div 0 = 0$$

This typically occurs after we've already discussed one or more identities like the following and students have looked to them for other ideas:

To help students think about why it's not possible to divide by zero, I write on the board a sequence of three division problems, asking the students for the answers as I do so:

$6 \div 3 = 2$
$6 \div 2 = 3$
$6 \div 1 = 6$

"What problem do you think I'll write next?" I ask. The students see the pattern of decreasing divisors, identify the next problem in the sequence as $6 \div 0$, and give six for the answer. I record this on the board under the other problems, even though the answer isn't correct:

$6 \div 0 = 6$

Next I talk with the students about how we use multiplication to check answers to division problems. "For the first problem," I say, "we multiply two times three and check that the answer is six." I point out that the answer to the multiplication is the same as the starting number for the division problem, the *dividend*. The students repeat this procedure to check the others and I record on the board:

$6 \div 3 = 2 \quad 2 \times 3 = 6$
$6 \div 2 = 3 \quad 3 \times 2 = 6$
$6 \div 1 = 6 \quad 6 \times 1 = 6$
$6 \div 0 = 6 \quad 6 \times 0 = 0$

If no student notices, I point out that the last problem doesn't check. "The answer to six times zero is zero, not six, as it would have to be if six were the correct answer," I tell them.

A student may suggest that the correct answer to $6 \div 0$ should be zero, not six, so the identity should be $\square \div 0 = 0$. I rewrite the answer and then test by multiplying to show that this doesn't check either:

$6 \div 0 = 0 \quad 0 \times 0 = 0$

"There's no answer that checks when you divide by zero. We just can't divide by zero," I tell them.

Often a student notices that dividing zero by zero, $0 \div 0$, gives an answer of zero that checks:

$0 \div 0 = 0 \quad 0 \times 0 = 0$

I point out a problem. "Yes, zero checks. But suppose I thought that the answer was ten. Or twenty. Or even a hundred. These answers check, too." And I record:

$$0 \div 0 = 0 \qquad 0 \times 0 = 0$$
$$0 \div 0 = 10 \qquad 10 \times 0 = 0$$
$$0 \div 0 = 20 \qquad 20 \times 0 = 0$$
$$0 \div 0 = 100 \qquad 100 \times 0 = 0$$

"In this example, any number seems to check. Division by zero just doesn't make sense. For zero divided by zero, any answer is possible, and for any other number divided by zero, no answer is possible. Not even a calculator can divide by zero—it will show an error message with an E or some other symbol. Mathematicians have agreed that we just can't divide by zero."

While I don't expect children to grasp this concept from this one explanation, I think it's important not to ignore the issue when it comes up, but to give the explanation a try. Students will encounter this idea about dividing by zero again as they continue their study of mathematics.

VOCABULARY

equation, identity, open sentence, variable

MATERIALS

■ chart paper, at least 1 sheet

TIME

■ three class periods

The Lesson

Day 1

I began the lesson by writing on the board three open sentences:

$$5 + \boxed{} = 8$$
$$\boxed{} + 1 = \boxed{}$$
$$\boxed{} + 0 = \boxed{}$$

I chose these equations deliberately. The first equation can be changed into a true sentence in exactly one way; by writing a 3 in the box. However, it's not possible to make the second equation true no matter what number is placed in the boxes. The third equation is true for all numbers put into the boxes and is, therefore, an identity.

I pointed to the equations on the board and asked, "Are all of these open sentences?" There had been confusion when the students first saw equations with a variable appearing more than once, and I wanted to find out what they now thought.

"The first one is for sure," Monty said, "but I'm not sure about the others."

"Does someone have an idea about the others?" I asked.

"I think they are," Julie said. "We had other ones that had two boxes."

"And we had some with triangles and *x*s, too," Louise added.

"So they all are?" Monty asked.

"Yes," I said. "They're all open sentences, equations that are neither true nor false because they have at least one variable in them. It's OK for the variable to appear more than once, or for there to be more than one kind of variable in an equation."

"But you have to put the same number in the boxes," Teddy said. I was pleased Teddy brought this up, because I wanted to be sure the students remembered this important mathematical convention.

"Say a little more about that," I said to Teddy.

"If you write a number in a box, then you have to write the same number in the other box, too," Teddy explained.

"Do you have to use the same number in all three sentences?" Amy asked.

I turned to Teddy. "Um, I hadn't thought about that," Teddy said, unsure for a moment. I gave him time to think and he then said, with confidence, "No, no, you just have to write the same number in the boxes in the same equation."

"Teddy is right," I said. "Whatever number you write in one box in an equation has to go in all the boxes in the same equation. If you have a box and a triangle in the same equation, then the numbers you write in them can be different. They could be the same, but they don't have to be."

"Oh, I remember," Tonya said. Others also nodded.

"What can we write in the box in the first equation to make it true?" I asked the class. Practically everyone raised a hand, so I said, "Let's say the number together in a whisper voice."

"Three," they said. I wrote a *3* in the box and we read the sentence together, "Five plus three equals eight." Everyone agreed that it was true.

"What about the next equation?" I asked. "What can we write in the box to make it true?" Fewer hands were up.

"Zero?" Elyse said tentatively.

"Let's try it," I said. Even though I knew Elyse's answer wasn't right, I wrote *0* in each box to test whether it made the equation true:

$$\boxed{0} + 1 = \boxed{0}$$

Elyse read, "Zero plus one equals zero. Oh, no, that's not right."

"It would be right if you put a one in the second box," Louise said. "Then it would be zero plus one equals one, and that works."

"Like this?" I said. I erased the second 0 and replaced it with a 1.

$$\boxed{0} + 1 = \boxed{1}$$

"Hey, you can't do that!" Pablo said. "You have to write the same number in both boxes."

"Oh yeah," Louise said.

"How about negative one in both boxes?" Ingrid suggested. I erased the 0 and 1 and wrote –1 in both boxes.

$$\boxed{-1} + 1 = \boxed{-1}$$

As I finished writing, Julie blurted out, "Nothing works!"

"Hold that thought for a moment, Julie, while we talk about Ingrid's idea," I responded.

"Sorry," Julie said, apologizing for blurting. In the meantime, students put up their hands to talk about Ingrid's suggestion. I called on Marvin.

Marvin said, "I don't think it works. If you add negative one and positive one, you get zero, and you can't write a zero in the second box if you wrote negative one in the first box. This is hard."

"It would work if the first box could be one and the second box could be two because one plus one is two," Amy shared and then added, "but I know that can't be right." Julie was waiting patiently to explain her idea.

"It doesn't work for any number," Julie said. "I tried a lot of them, and then I figured out why. If you add one to a number, the answer is one bigger. So whatever you write in the first box, you need to write a number that's one bigger in the second box, and you can't. So you can't do it." I waited a few minutes for the others to think about Julie's idea.

"Maybe fractions would work," Tony said. "Try two and a half. " I wrote $2\frac{1}{2}$ in both boxes:

$$\boxed{2\tfrac{1}{2}} + 1 = \boxed{2\tfrac{1}{2}}$$

"Nope, it doesn't work," Tony said, withdrawing his suggestion.

Scott then said, "Kylie and I discovered something, and we agree with Julie. We discovered that no matter what you put in the box, 'box plus one equals box' would never be true. If the number has to be the same in both boxes, it won't work because the things you're adding are always smaller than the sum, so what you're adding and the sum can't be the same number, unless everything is zero, but it's not." He gave a heavy sigh.

Kylie said, "Yep, that's what we think. You can't add one to a number and still have it equal itself. It's impossible." Scott's explanation confused some of the students, but Kylie's seemed easier for them to follow.

"So you can write an open sentence like that, that you can't make true?" Nick asked.

I replied, "Yes, you can."

"I think I know another one," Frannie said. "Box times five equals box." I wrote on the board:

$$\square \times 5 = \square$$

I gave the class a moment to think and soon hands were in the air. I called on Jeremy.

"Zero works," he said. I wrote 0s in both boxes.

"Oh yeah," Frannie said. "I was wrong."

"Thanks for trying, Frannie," I said.

I moved the lesson forward and asked the students about the third equation on the board. Some had already been thinking about this one.

Monty shared first. He said, "Well, first I thought it was like the second one and nothing would work. But then to check I tried zero, and it worked. And then I noticed that one would work, and so would two, and any other number."

"Let's try your first idea about writing a zero in both boxes," I said. I wrote on the board:

$$\boxed{0} + 0 = \boxed{0}$$

"Let's read it together quietly," I said, and we read, "Zero plus zero equals zero." Everyone agreed that this was a true sentence.

"What number did you try next?" I asked Monty.

"One," he answered.

"It works," several students said. I erased the 0s I had written and wrote *1* in both boxes:

$$\boxed{1} + 0 = \boxed{1}$$

Again, I had the students read the sentence aloud. They agreed it was true. We repeated this for the number two.

"Monty's right, it works for anything," Kylie said.

"Even for a thousand," George said. "A thousand plus zero is still a thousand."

"This is cool!" Tony commented.

"Can anyone find a number to put in the boxes to make the sentence false?" I asked. The students talked with their partners for a moment. I called them back to attention.

"I think all numbers work, even fractions," Pablo said. "One-half plus zero is still one-half." Most students nodded, indicating their agreement with Pablo.

"Did anyone find a number that didn't work?" I asked. No one had.

"Who would like to make a convincing argument about why this open sentence will be true no matter what number we write in both boxes?" I asked. A few hands went up immediately. I waited a moment, but no one else raised a hand. To encourage the students to think about my request, I said, "Talk with your neighbor about how to explain why any number in both boxes in this equation makes it true. Take turns, first one talking for thirty seconds and then switching. Remember just to listen when your partner is talking. I'll time you."

After a minute, many more hands were raised. I called on Frannie.

"The open sentence says to add zero to the number in the box," she said. "And if you add zero, you're not really adding anything, so the number in the box stays the same."

"Zero plus a number is always the number," Alex added.

Introducing Identities I then summarized, "Some equations, like the ones you wrote for homework the other day, have exactly one solution. Some equations have no solution. And then there are equations like this one, that are true no matter what numbers you use for the variables. Mathematicians have a name for open sentences that are always true; they call them *identities*. 'Box plus zero equals box' is called an identity." I wrote *identity* on the board.

Julie said, "I think I have a way to fix 'box plus one equals box' so you can make it work."

"Tell us more about what you're thinking," I encouraged.

"I think it could be made true if the plus sign was a times sign," Julie explained. "It would be 'box *times* one equals box.' I tried it with four in the boxes, and four times one is four." Julie hesitated and then added, "Hey, it will work for anything!" I wrote on the board:

Julie $\quad \square \times 1 = \square$

I gave the class a few moments to think about Julie's idea. Then I called on Nick.

"I tried a bunch of numbers, like forty-five, thirteen, and even one hundred," he said. "They all make the problem true." Other students were nodding in agreement.

"I tried some fractions, too," Teddy said. "They all worked because any number times one equals itself."

"This is another identifying," Louise said.

"I think you mean identity," Amy corrected her.

I said, "When we're trying to decide if an open sentence is an identity, it makes sense to try some numbers. But an identity has to be true for *all* numbers, and it isn't possible to try every number there is. So we have to rely on a convincing argument. Teddy just gave a good argument for why Julie's open sentence is an identity. He knows that any number times one equals itself."

"What about zero?" Jeremy asked.

"Let's try it," I said. "If we find even just one number that makes the open sentence false, then it's not an identity." I wrote 0 in both boxes.

"It works," Jeremy conceded.

"Teddy's explanation was good enough for me," I said. I wrote Teddy's explanation on the board next to Julie's open sentence:

Julie $\square \times 1 = \square$ *Any number times one equals itself.*

I then returned to the first identity I had written on the board and said, "Frannie and Alex gave arguments for why 'box plus zero equals box' is an identity. Who remembers what they said?" Several students were interested in sharing.

"When you add zero, nothing happens. The number stays the same," George said.

"If you don't add anything on, then you get the same number in the answer," Louise said.

"Anything plus zero equals the number you started with," Blair said.

"All of your ideas make sense," I said. I wrote an explanation on the board, drawing from each of the students' ideas:

$\square + 0 = \square$ *When you add zero to any number, the sum is the same as the number.*

I wrote both of these explanations to model for the students what I planned to have them do later. "Can I give one?" Ingrid then asked. I nodded and wrote on the board as she dictated:

Ingrid $\square \times 0 = 0$

I gave the class a few moments to think and then said, "Thumbs up if you agree that this is an identity, thumbs down if you disagree, thumbs sideways if you're not sure." All thumbs were up.

"Let's test a few numbers," I said. We first tested Ingrid's equation for six, then ten, and then seventeen. It was true for each number.

I then said, "Remember, we can't test every number, so we have to rely on a convincing argument to explain why it's an identity. Who would like to give one?" Ingrid's hand was up, and since it was her suggestion, I called on her.

"Anything times zero is always zero," Ingrid said with confidence. I recorded on the board, changing "anything" to "any number" to be more mathematically precise:

"Does anyone have another idea for an identity?" I asked. No one raised a hand immediately. I've learned when teaching this lesson to wait and give students time to think. I find that if I wait, someone will offer an idea. And even if a student's idea isn't correct, it often sparks other ideas. After some students had raised a hand, I called on Kylie.

"Box minus box equals zero," she said. I wrote on the board:

Kylie   □ − □ = 0

"With your partner, try some numbers and see what you find out," I said. A buzz broke out in the room as students tested numbers for Kylie's open sentence. I let the conversation continue for a moment and then called the class to attention.

"It works," George said. "If you minus something from itself, you get zero."

"Anything minus anything equals nothing," Amy said.

"It's an identity," Ally said. I wrote on the board next to Kylie's identity:

Kylie   □ − □ = 0   *Any number minus itself equals zero.*

I called on Blair next. "Box times five equals box," he said. I recorded on the board:

Blair   □ × 5 = □

Some students protested, but I quieted them and said to Blair, "What numbers did you try?"

"It's zero," Blair said. "Zero times five is zero." I wrote a *0* in each box to verify Blair's idea.

I then said, "I agree that zero makes the equation true. What if we tried another number, Blair? How about one?" I erased the 0s and wrote *1* in both boxes.

Blair read aloud, " 'One times five equals one.' Hey, that doesn't work."

"Remember that an identity has to work for all numbers," I said. "The open sentence that you wrote is like the first one I had on the board when the class began. It has one solution. Keep trying to think of open sentences that are true for all numbers." I erased Blair's idea.

I called on Nick next. "I have a really cool one," Nick said. I recorded on the board as he dictated:

Nick   □ + 0 = □ − 0

"Let's test it," I said. "What number should we try first?"

"Seven," Nick said. As I wrote *7* in both boxes, Nick added, "Both sides will be seven."

I said to the class, "With your partner, test Nick's equation for some other numbers and see if it's true each time." I gave a few moments for the students to do this. They all agreed that the equation was true for all of the numbers they put in the boxes.

"What about a convincing argument?" I asked.

Nick responded, "A number doesn't change if you add zero to it or subtract zero." I recorded his idea.

It was about the end of class, so I said, "I'm going to write the identities we created so far on chart paper." I titled a sheet of chart paper *Identities* and had students dictate the identities I had recorded on the board:

$$\square + 0 = \square$$

Julie $\square \times 1 = \square$

Ingrid $\square \times 0 = 0$

Kylie $\square - \square = 0$

Nick $\square + 0 = \square - 0$

To end the class, I said, "We'll think about more identities tomorrow, so if you have ideas for other open sentences that you think are identities, write them down." I didn't make this a formal homework assignment. I knew that while some students would be able to come up with identities, others needed more experience before being able to do so. I didn't want to frustrate students before they had further support for learning.

Day 2

I began class by asking, "To review quickly, who can explain what an identity is?"

"It's an open sentence that's always true," Teddy said.

"It's an open sentence that's true no matter what you put in the boxes. You can't make it false," Maria added.

" 'Box times one equals box' is an identity," Tony said. I pointed to this identity on the chart paper list.

$$\square \times 1 = \square$$

"We don't have to use boxes," Alex said. "We could use *n* instead, and we could use a dot to means times." I wrote Alex's idea on the board:

$$n \cdot 1 = n$$

"Yes, this is another way to write the same identity," I said, and then asked, "Who remembers the rule about writing numbers in boxes when they appear more than once in the same equation?"

"You have to use the same number," Louise said.

"You have to write the same number in the same shape, but not in different shapes," Ally added.

I summarized, "Yes, you must use the same numbers for the same variable in an equation. Also, to be an identity, the mathematical sentence must be true no matter what number you use for the variable."

"I thought of some others," Julie said, eager to share.

I replied, "I'm interested in your ideas, but first I'd like everyone to talk with your partner about identities. If you wrote some last night, then share them. If you didn't write any, that's OK; the two of you should think together and write some now. It's sometimes easier to think of identities when you talk with someone else. Then we'll talk about your ideas."

"Can we write on one paper?" Amy wanted to know.

I responded, "Yes, that would be fine. You can write on one paper, or you can each record on a sheet of paper."

A few pairs of students had difficulty thinking up identities. Blair and Jeremy spent a good amount of time exploring $\square \times 10 = \square$. They both understood that when multiplying by ten you can add a zero to the other factor to get the product; for example, $22 \times 10 = 220$. They were confusing the idea of a pattern or rule with an identity. Finally they gave up trying to write an equation about their rule. "Look at the identities on the board and see if they give you ideas about others," I suggested to them.

Natalia and Amy wrote $6 \div 1 = 6$ and concluded that it was an identity. Then they wrote $20 \div 1 = 20$, which they thought was another identity. I told them that they had written true mathematical sentences, but that identities required the use of variables. "Like a box or a triangle?" Amy asked. I nodded.

The girls thought for a moment and Natalia then said, "Let's use boxes instead of the sixes."

Julie and Ally were very excited about the identity they thought of—$\square + \square = 2 \times \square$. Their excitement spread throughout the class and other students came up with a variety of related identities, such as $3 \times \square = \square + \square + \square$. After fifteen minutes or so I asked for the students' attention. Figures 14–1 through 14–4 show how some pairs worked on this activity.

FIGURE 14–1   All of Blair and Jeremy's open sentences were true for all values of the box, so all were identities.

$$\text{``Identities''}$$

1. $\square \times 0 = 0 + 0$
2. $\square + \square - \square - \square = 0$
3. $\square + 2 - 2 = \square$
4. $\square + 2 - 2 + 10 - 10 = \square$
5. $10 + 10 + \square - \square = 20$
6. $\square + 10 - 10 = \square$
7.
8.

FIGURE 14–2   Two of Kylie and Marco's open sentences showed the misconception that dividing a number by zero results in an answer of zero. (See the "Background" section in this chapter for an explanation of why it's not possible to divide by zero.)

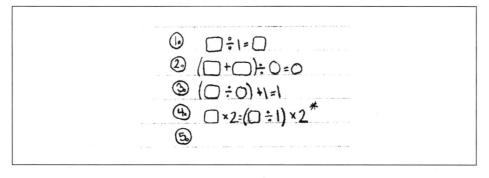

1. $\square \div 1 = \square$
2. $(\square + \square) \div 0 = 0$
3. $(\square \div 0) + 1 = 1$
4. $\square \times 2 = (\square \div 1) \times 2$ *
5.

FIGURE 14-3 Julie and Ally used trial and error to come up with open sentences. They learned later that their third and seventh equations weren't identities.

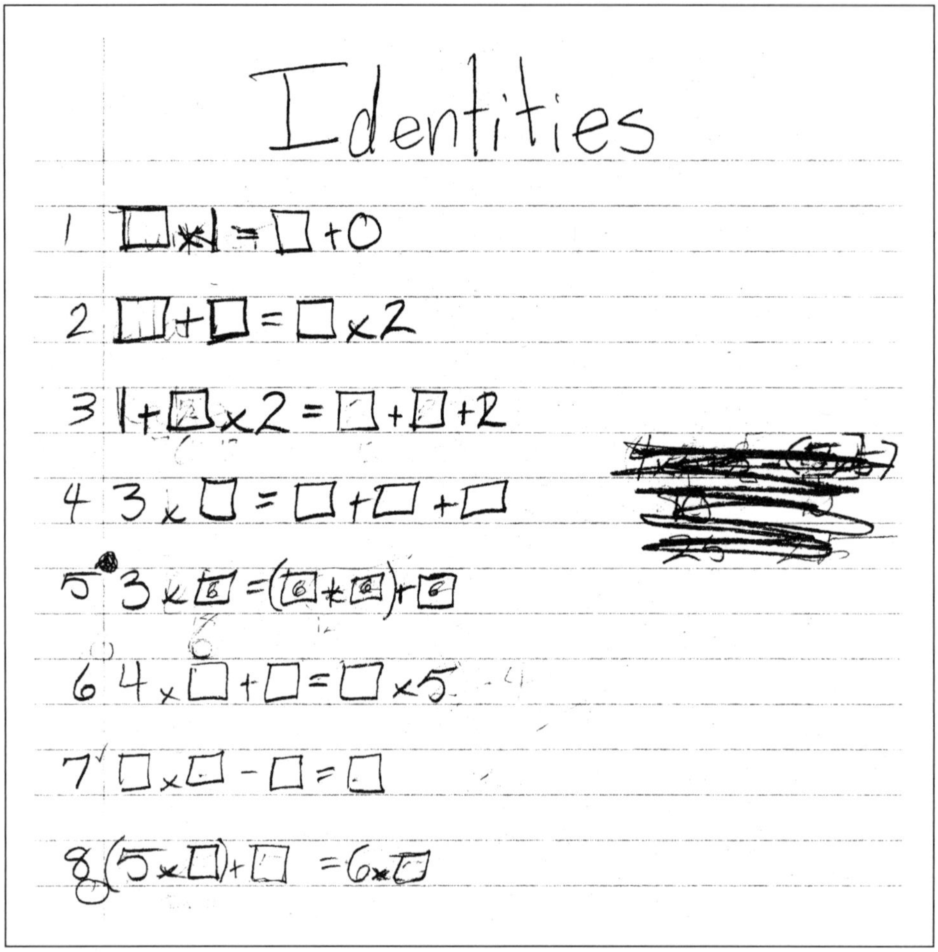

FIGURE 14-4 Tony and Elyse correctly decided that their sixth open sentence wasn't an identity. In their last equation, they used parentheses incorrectly. It should read $(\square \times 5 - \square) \times 5 = \square \times 5 \times 4$.

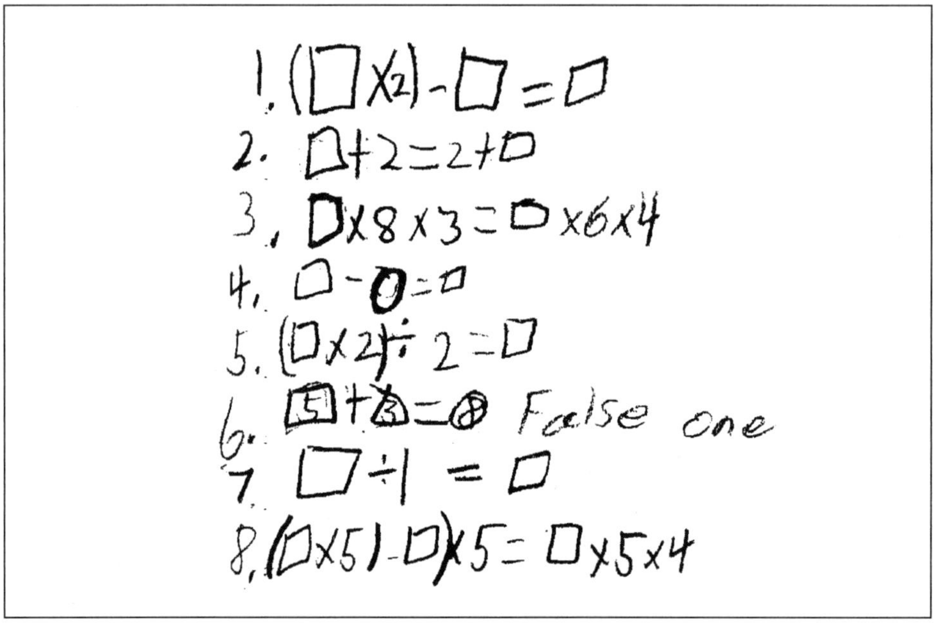

A Class Discussion "Who would like to share an identity?" I asked. About half the students raised their hands. I called on Tony and Elyse.

"Box minus zero equals box," Elyse said. I recorded on the board:

$$\square - 0 = \square$$

"Let's test it for a few numbers," I said. "What number should we try first?"

"One hundred," Tony said. I wrote *100* in both boxes and Tony read aloud, "One hundred minus zero equals one hundred. It's true."

"Let's try sixty-three," I said. I erased the 100s and wrote *63* in both boxes. This time we read aloud as a class, "Sixty-three minus zero equals sixty-three."

"Can I explain why it's an identity?" Elyse asked. I agreed.

Elyse explained, "When you minus zero from a number, it's the same as adding zero—nothing happens. You're not taking anything away, so you wind up with the same number." I wrote quickly, trying to capture Elyse's words:

$\square - 0 = \square$ *When you subtract zero, it's the same as adding zero. You're not taking anything away, so you wind up with the same number.*

I recorded Tony and Elyse's identity on the class chart I had begun the day before and asked, "Who else would like to share an open sentence that you think is an identity?" I called on Amy and Natalia.

"Natalia and I had this idea," Amy began. "We discovered that six divided by one is six. We thought it was an identity."

Natalia continued, "We tried twenty and it worked; twenty divided by one equals twenty. But we didn't have any boxes. So we put boxes where the six and twenty were and it worked."

"What shall I write?" I asked the girls.

"A box, then a divided by sign, then a one, then equals, and then a box," Amy said, referring to their paper. I recorded on the board:

$$\square \div 1 = \square$$

I said, "Someone give me a number and let's try their idea."

"Nineteen," Tony suggested. I wrote *19* in both boxes. I called on Scott to read the equation and the class agreed it was true. We repeated this for two other numbers.

"Who would like to make a convincing argument to explain why Amy and Natalia's equation is an identity?" I asked. I called on Marvin.

"If you divide a number by one, it doesn't change at all, and the answer is the same number you started with," Marvin said. I recorded on the board, next to their equation:

If you divide a number by one, the answer is the same number you started with.

I then added Amy and Natalia's identity to the class chart.

We continued in this way, with students sharing an open sentence, the class testing several numbers, and then someone offering an explanation that I'd record. Some students suggested open sentences that weren't identities. For example, Pablo and Ally suggested the following:

$$\triangle \times 1 = 1 \div \triangle$$

When we tested it for the number six, Pablo said, "Oh no, it doesn't work."

"Right. All we need is one number to make the open sentence false, and it's not an identity. Does anyone have an idea about how to change Pablo and Ally's open sentence so that it is an identity?" I asked.

"It would be if you turned the second part around," Maria suggested.

"Tell us your idea," I said to Maria. I recorded as Maria reported:

$$\triangle \times 1 = \triangle \div 1$$

We tested this open sentence for several numbers and then Alex gave an explanation. He said, "Multiplying by one and dividing by one are kind of the same thing. They don't change the answer from what you started with."

Whenever a student gave an open sentence that wasn't an identity, I followed the same procedure: tested it, then asked for a suggestion about how to alter it, tested the new version, and then asked for a convincing argument to prove it was an identity.

When students share identities, they often spark others' ideas. For example, Frannie and George's suggestion for an identity was:

$$\square \times 1 = 1 \times \square$$

We tested it for several numbers and then Kylie offered an explanation. She said, "If you multiply a number by one, you get the same answer if you turn the numbers around and do one times the number."

Teddy added, "If it's six in the box, you either have six groups of one or one group of six, and it's the same thing." I wrote the identity on the class chart.

Marvin, Jeremy, and Louise suggested the next three identities and I recorded them:

$$\square \times 2 = 2 \times \square$$
$$n \times 0 = 0 \times n$$
$$\square \times 10 = 10 \times \square$$

We tested each and students gave explanations similar to Kylie's explanation for $\square \times 1 = 1 \times \square$. After writing the last identity on the class chart, I said over the students' giggles, "We could go on like this for quite a while. Talk with your partner about these and raise your hand when you think you can describe what's the same about them." I gave the students a few minutes to talk and then called them to attention. Several were interested in reporting.

Ally said, "They all just switched the number and the box. And that's OK because box times any number equals that number times box." I wrote on the board:

$\square$ *times any number equals that number times* $\square$.

Monty reported next and I recorded his idea on the board underneath Ally's:

Any first number times any second number is the same as the second number times the first number.

Then Jeremy reported and I recorded his idea:

They all say that you can multiply two numbers in either order and you get the same answer.

I then said, "Listen to my next question and think by yourself for a moment. Then I'll give you a chance to talk with your partner. My question is, How can we use Ally's, Monty's, and Jeremy's ideas to write one identity that describes these four?" I pointed to the identity that Frannie and George had suggested and the three look-alikes that followed. I gave the students a minute to think by themselves and then told them to talk with their partners. Then I had all who wanted to report an identity do so. I didn't stop to discuss them but recorded them all on the board:

Alex $\square \times \square = \square \times \square$
Kylie $\square \times \triangle = \triangle \times \square$
Nick $\square \times n = n \times \square$

I then said, "Talk with your partner about which of these you think works the best and why. Then we'll share our ideas." In a few moments, several hands were up. I called on Alex.

"I think the second one is better than mine," Alex said.

"Why do you think that?" I asked.

Alex answered, "Well, in mine if you put one in the boxes, you get 'one times one equals one times one.' But in the second one, you can put one in the box and some other number in the triangle. There are more choices, like the others on the board. I think you shouldn't use all boxes."

"I agree, Alex," I said. "You had a good idea, but you need to use two variables to express the ideas that Ally, Monty, and Jeremy gave." I then said to the whole class, "Which of the other two identities do you think is better?"

Ingrid said, "I like Kylie's better, but Jeremy likes Nick's better."

"But we think they're pretty much the same," Jeremy added.

"Do you agree that they're pretty much the same?" I asked the class. Most students held a thumb up. "Who can explain why they're the same?" I asked.

Scott said, "You can have any number be either a box, or an n, or an x, or anything for a variable."

George added, "But whatever you use on the left side, you should use the same ones on the right side, just backwards."

"So either is fine. Which one should I add to the class chart?" I asked. The class voted to use $\square \times \triangle = \triangle \times \square$. I wrote this generalized version on the chart and said, "If we wanted to shorten our list, then we could use this identity to replace the other four."

"I have a different one," Monty then said. I recorded his idea:

$\square - 1 = 1 - \square$

Students protested and Monty realized that his open sentence wasn't an identity. He offered an edited version:

☐ – *1* = ☐ – *1*

We tested it for several numbers, and then Louise said, "That works, but it seems too obvious. It has to work because both sides are exactly the same."

"So it is an identity?" I asked Louise. She nodded, and I added Monty's identity to the chart.

Elyse then suggested another identity and I recorded it on the board.

☐ ÷ *0* = ☐

Elyse's idea about dividing by zero typically comes up when students are thinking of identities. When it does, I explain to the class why division by zero isn't possible. (See the "Background" section of this chapter for this explanation.) No one had a suggestion about how to fix Elyse's suggestion. However, a few minutes later, after we had added several other identities to the growing list, Pablo returned to Elyse's identity with a new idea.

"I think I've found a way to fix it," he said. I recorded his idea on the board:

☐ ÷ *0* = *0*

I returned to the explanation I had given for Elyse's suggestion and extended it for Pablo's idea. I concluded my explanation by saying, "Mathematicians have decided that dividing by zero just doesn't make sense, so we simply won't do it. We say that division by zero is *undefined*. That means forget about it. It will only get you in mathematical hot water." I'm not sure that all of the students understood the dilemma, but it was the best I could do at the time.

By the end of class, our list of identities included the following:

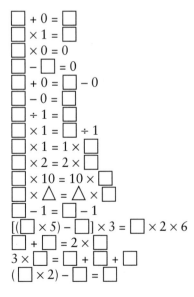

Over the next few weeks, I returned to the topic of identities from time to time and encouraged students to think about the identities on the chart and see if they could come up with others. Sometimes I'd spend part of a class taking a few students' suggestions, testing them, asking for convincing arguments, and then adding them to the chart. Other times I initiated a discussion about a particular identity. Lists from different classes, of course, differ, but there are usually many similarities, which reflects the students' knowledge of how our number system works.

With third graders and some fourth graders, I don't extend the lesson beyond this. However, for some fourth graders and for fifth graders, I teach the extensions that follow.

Extensions

1. If students don't suggest identities such as the ones that led to $\square \times \triangle = \triangle \times \square$, but involving addition, you might do so to give the students another opportunity to generalize and to introduce the term *commutative property*. Record four identities on the board, writing them so that the numbers are in order:

$$\square + 1 = 1 + \square$$
$$\square + 2 = 2 + \square$$
$$\square + 3 = 3 + \square$$
$$\square + 4 = 4 + \square$$

Ask the students to extend the list in both directions:

$$\square + 0 = 0 + \square$$
$$\square + 1 = 1 + \square$$
$$\square + 2 = 2 + \square$$
$$\square + 3 = 3 + \square$$
$$\square + 4 = 4 + \square$$
$$\square + 5 = 5 + \square$$
$$\square + 6 = 6 + \square$$

You might want to ask students for sentences to write above $\square + 0 = 0 + \square$ to include negative numbers, such as $\square + -1 = -1 + \square$. Or you may ask for open sentences that you could write between two others so that students will realize that fractions are possible, such as $\square + \frac{1}{2} = \frac{1}{2} + \square$, $\square + \frac{1}{3} = \frac{1}{3} + \square$, and so on.

Finally, a class discussion should lead to the generalization of the list to $\square + \triangle = \triangle + \square$. Introduce the correct term *commutative property for addition* to describe this identity. Return to the class chart and ask students to find the identity that illustrates the commutative property for multiplication.

2. Ask students to work in pairs and choose one identity from the class list or their own list, or a new one they just thought of. Then have them write a convincing argument to explain why it's an identity. You may want to introduce this assignment by writing on the board one from the class list. Frannie and George were pleased that I had chosen one from their paper.

$(\boxed{} \times 0) + \boxed{} = \boxed{}$

"What do you do first to help you decide if an open sentence is an identity?" I asked.

"You test it," Louise said.

"What number shall we try first for Frannie and George's open sentence?" I asked.

"Six," Teddy chose. I wrote 6 in each box and Teddy did the math. He said, "Six times zero is zero, plus six is six. It works."

"Let's try another number. Testing one number isn't enough," I said. We tested the equation with seven and then ten.

"The first part of our explanation should tell about what we tested," I said, and wrote on the board:

First we tested the equation for 6, 7, and 10, and they all worked.

I then said, "Once you're convinced that it's an identity, then you have to think about how to explain why. Does anyone have an idea?"

Ally said, "Well, we know that box times zero will be zero for anything, because anything times zero is zero. Then you add on a box to zero and you get six."

"I'll record on the board what you said so that we can all take a look at it," I said. I wrote:

Box times zero is zero because any number times zero is zero. Then if you add on a box to zero you get six.

"Would you read this aloud, Ally, and see if it's what you meant?" I asked. I like to give the student who gave the idea a chance to reflect on what I recorded before others comment. Ally read it aloud and nodded her approval. I then asked the class for comments, hoping that a student would raise a concern about the last part of Ally's explanation. If not, I would. I called on Alex.

"I don't think that the six at the end is right, because we're supposed to explain why it works for everything, not just one number," he said. I turned to Ally.

"Do I have to change it?" she asked.

"If you're not sure, ask someone in the class for help," I said. Ally looked around the room and called on Julie.

Julie said, "I think that if you add on a box to zero . . . I mean, if you add on a zero to a box, no matter what's in the box, you'll always get the box number."

"Does that make sense to you?" I asked Ally. She nodded.

"Julie, do you have an idea about how to change what I wrote on the board?" I asked. I made a change as Julie directed. Then the following was written on the board:

$(\boxed{} \times 0) + \boxed{} = \boxed{}$
First we tested the equation for 6, 7, and 10, and they all worked.
Box times zero is zero because any number times zero is zero. Then if you add on a box to zero you get the same number that's in the box because $0 + \boxed{} = \boxed{}$.

"Does anyone have anything to add to this explanation?" I asked. There weren't any suggestions, so I said, "Choose one of your identities and do what we did here: test it and then write an explanation that you think shows why it's an identity."

I gave one final direction: "You may find it easier for one person to talk and the other to record, as I did for Ally. But you should both agree on the explanation." (See Figures 14–5 through 14–9.)

FIGURE 14–5 Michael and Lena tested their equation for 5 and 10 and explained why they thought it was an identity.

$$\Box \div 1 \times 2 \times 18 = \Box \times 1 \times 6 \times 6$$

It works because ÷1 the same number you started with. And $2 \times 18 = 36$ the same as $6 \times 6 = 36$. I tested it with 5 and 10 and it worked because its always going to be the number you put in the box times 36.

FIGURE 14–6 Kylie and Marco didn't test numbers, but their explanation of why their equation is an identity is clear and convincing.

$$\Box \times 2 = (\Box \div 1) \times 2$$

Our equation works because on the right side were we wrote $(\Box \div 1) \times 2$ and when you do the equation $\Box \div 1$ that we'll leave the number the same because when you divide by 1 it the number don't cange so it's just like saying $\Box \times 2 = \Box \times 2$ wich is like saying $\Box = \Box$.

FIGURE 14–7 Elyse and Tony tested their equation for three numbers and explained why it would be true for all numbers.

$$(\Box \times 2) \div 2 = \Box$$

First we tryed 2, 4 and 6 and they worked because it's just $\Box \times 2$ dubbles the number and then $\div 2$ makes it go back to the origanl number because your just undoing what you already did.

FIGURE 14–8 Frannie and George tested their equation with the number 2 and explained why it would work with any number.

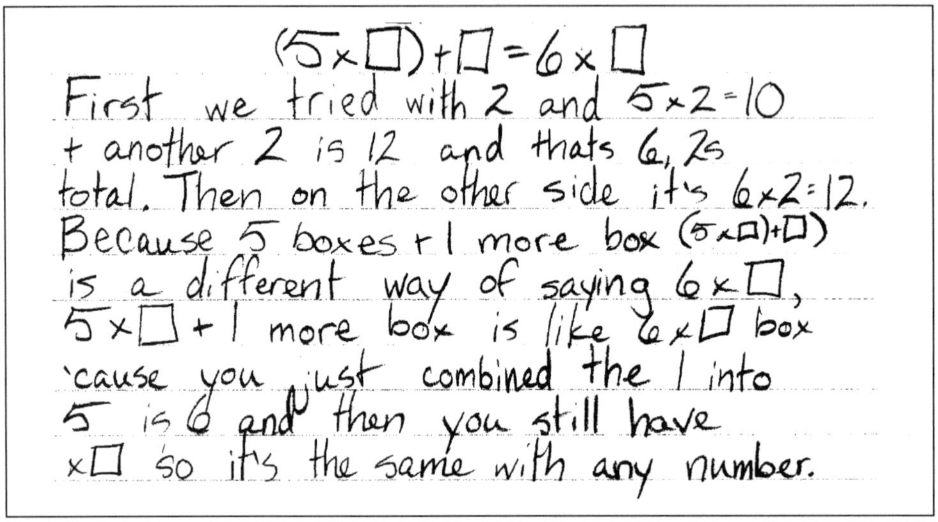

$$(5 \times \square) + \square = 6 \times \square$$

First we tried with 2 and 5×2=10 + another 2 is 12 and thats 6, 2s total. Then on the other side it's 6×2=12. Because 5 boxes + 1 more box (5×□)+□) is a different way of saying 6×□, 5×□ + 1 more box is like 6×□ box 'cause you just combined the 1 into 5 is 6 and then you still have ×□ so it's the same with any number.

FIGURE 14–9 Nick wrote a complicated identity; however, his explanation is not correct. The equation he included in the explanation isn't equivalent to his original identity, nor is it an identity.

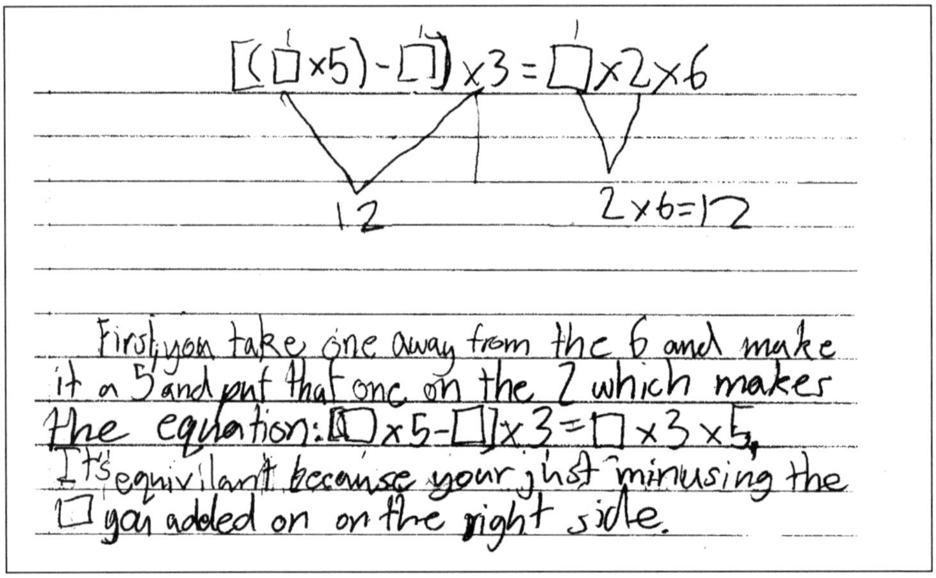

$$[(\square \times 5) - \square] \times 3 = \square \times 2 \times 6$$

12   2×6=12

First, you take one away from the 6 and make it a 5 and put that one on the 2 which makes the equation: □×5-□×3=□×3×5, It's equivilant because your just minusing the □ you added on on the right side.

The McSquares:
A Restaurant Tale of Tables and Algebra

by Marilyn Burns

Mr. and Mrs. McSquare loved burgers. They loved to eat burgers and they loved to cook burgers.

When friends and family came to visit, the McSquares always served burgers for dinner, and that made everyone happy. "The McSquares' burgers are delicious," said Aunt Sadie.

"They're the best," said Cousin Larry.

"They're better here than at any restaurant," added their friend, Ben. Everyone agreed.

One July, Mr. and Mrs. McSquare went on vacation and drove to visit other towns in other states. When they went out to eat, they both ordered the exact same dinner—burgers. They never got tired of burgers.

After they had a terrific burger dinner one night, Mr. and Mrs. McSquare also had what they thought was a terrific idea. "What our town needs is a good burger restaurant," said Mrs. McSquare.

"Yes, I agree," said Mr. McSquare.

They were both silent for a moment. Then, at the same time, they both came up with the same idea. "Why don't we open a burger restaurant?" They got very excited.

"Our friends love our burgers," said Mr. McSquare.

"And there's no burger restaurant in our town," said Mrs. McSquare.

They left the restaurant, went back to the motel, and talked and talked about ideas for their own restaurant until they were so sleepy that they had to go to bed.

Mr. and Mrs. McSquare woke up the next morning still excited about the idea. "Let's do it," they agreed. And they did. As soon as they arrived home, they got busy with their plans. The name for the restaurant was easy—McSquares. Everything in the restaurant would be square—the restaurant sign, the tables, even the burgers and buns. "We decided on our own theme," Mrs. McSquare explained when the local newspaper reporter came for an interview.

They also decided to start small and see if they were successful. "Being small will give us a chance to practice and learn," said Mrs. McSquare.

"Then we can grow the restaurant," said Mr. McSquare.

Finally the kitchen was ready for the grand opening. The McSquares set up three tables (square tables, of course), set four chairs at each, and put out silverware and plates (square plates, of course). They posted a sign in the window:

Grand Opening!
Welcome!
We can serve 12 people at a time!

In no time, the restaurant was full and the McSquares were very, very busy. And while people were eating, a line was forming outside. People didn't mind waiting, especially since Mr. McSquare served complimentary lemonade (in cups with square bottoms, of course).

At the end of their first day of business, when Mr. and Mrs. McSquare were cleaning the restaurant to get ready for the next day, Mr. McSquare said, "How about we add another table so people won't have to wait so long?" "That's a fine idea," said Mrs. McSquare, "but we'll have to change the number in the sign in the window.

"No problem," said Mr. McSquare. With a marker, he crossed out the 12 and wrote a 16. They both smiled, tired, but very, very happy.

McSquares was a huge success. They kept adding and adding tables, and pretty soon had expanded their restaurant so that they had ten tables. The sign in the window no longer said Grand Opening. It now read:

Welcome!
We can serve 40 people at a time!

Life was good for the McSquares.

One day, after Mr. and Mrs. Tucker had eaten dinner at McSquares, they asked Mr. and Mrs. McSquare if they could arrange to have a private banquet in the restaurant.

"Of course," Mr. and Mrs. McSquare said. They were flattered to be asked.

But Mr. and Mrs. Tucker had a special request. "Instead of having the tables arranged separately so that people sit in fours, we'd like to have everyone sit at one long banquet table. Can you rearrange the tables for our party?"

"No problem," said Mr. McSquare.

"How many people will be coming to your party?" asked Mrs. McSquare. Mr. and Mrs. Tucker weren't sure yet and said they would go home and think about it.

"And we'll think about how many people we can accommodate in a banquet style," said Mr. McSquare. They agreed to meet the next day.

That night, Mr. and Mrs. McSquare thought about Mr. and Mrs. Tucker's request for rearranging tables. "It won't be any problem to push the square tables together," said Mr. McSquare.

As they thought about how a banquet arrangement might look, Mrs. McSquare got paper and pencil and began to sketch. After drawing two tables pushed together and marking the places for chairs, she was very, very surprised. "Look at my drawing," she said to Mr. McSquare. "If we push two tables together, there are places only for six people to sit, not eight people as we usually have at two tables."

Mr. McSquare looked at Mrs. McSquare's drawing. "Well, look at that!" he said, also surprised. "We'd better do some thinking here."

So Mr. and Mrs. McSquare cut out ten small squares from a large piece of cardboard and began to investigate. They made arrangements of two tables in a row, three tables in a row, four tables in a row, and so on up to ten tables in a row. For each size banquet table, they figured out how many guests they could seat. Finally, they drew pictures and recorded the information on a chart so that they could explain clearly to the Tuckers what they learned.

What did Mr. and Mrs. McSquare learn from their investigation?

Mr. and Mrs. Triangle were so impressed with the success of the McSquares' restaurant that they decided to open up their own restaurant. Their specialty was grilled cheese sandwiches. They made all kinds of grilled cheese sandwiches—with tomato, with bacon, with peppers, with tomato and bacon, with tomato and peppers, and on and on. They were busy figuring out for their menu all of the possible combinations of grilled cheese sandwiches. (But that's a math problem for another day.) And they always cut their sandwiches on the diagonal and served customers two grilled cheese triangles. Also, the tables in their restaurant were all triangles. (And so were the plates and the bottoms of the cups, of course.)

They called their restaurant McTriangles.

How many people could Mr. and Mrs. Triangle serve at one time with one table? With two tables? With three, four, and so on up to ten tables?

How many people could Mr. and Mrs. Triangle serve by rearranging the tables into banquet style?

Two more restaurants eventually opened in town. One was McTrapezoids and the other was McHexagons. Investigate the table seatings for these two restaurants, both for restaurant style and for banquet style.

Blackline Masters

Centimeter Graph Paper
Half-Inch Graph Paper
One-Inch Graph Paper
Tic-Tac-Toe Grids
Tic-Tac-Toe Gameboard
Piles of Tiles Activity Sheet

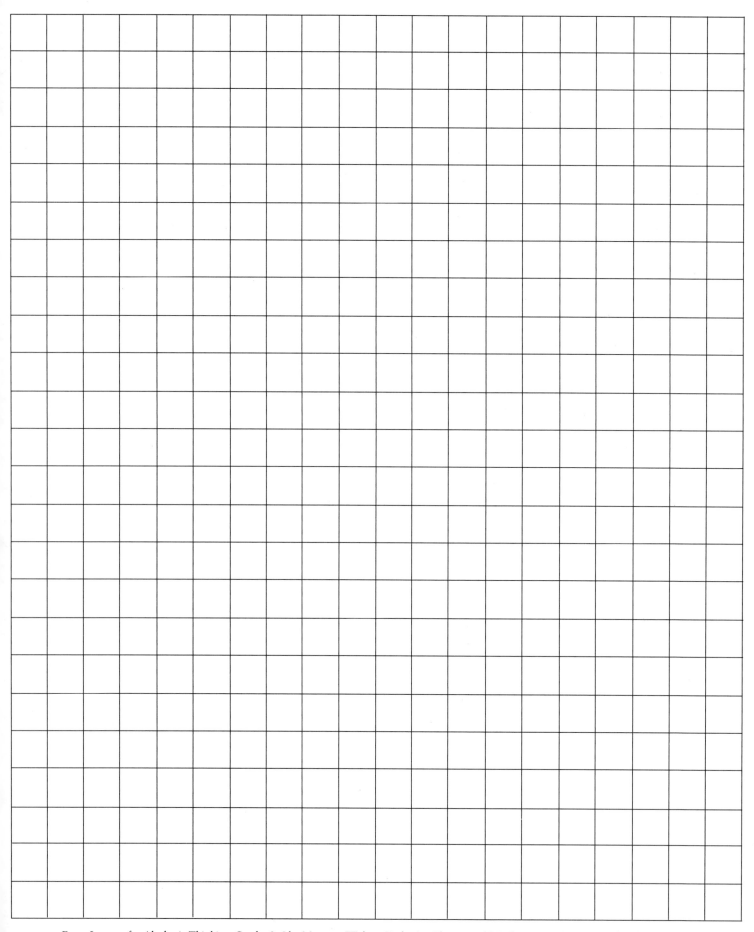

From *Lessons for Algebraic Thinking, Grades 3–5* by Maryann Wickett, Katharine Kharas, and Marilyn Burns. © 2002 Math Solutions Publications.

From *Lessons for Algebraic Thinking, Grades 3–5* by Maryann Wickett, Katharine Kharas, and Marilyn Burns. © 2002 Math Solutions Publications.

From *Lessons for Algebraic Thinking, Grades 3–5* by Maryann Wickett, Katharine Kharas, and Marilyn Burns. © 2002 Math Solutions Publications.

Tic-Tac-Toe Grids

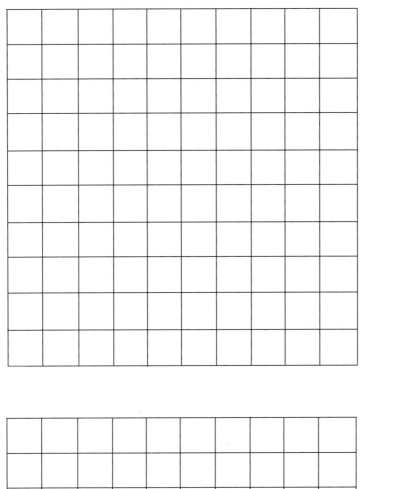

X | O

X | O

Tic-Tac-Toe Gameboard

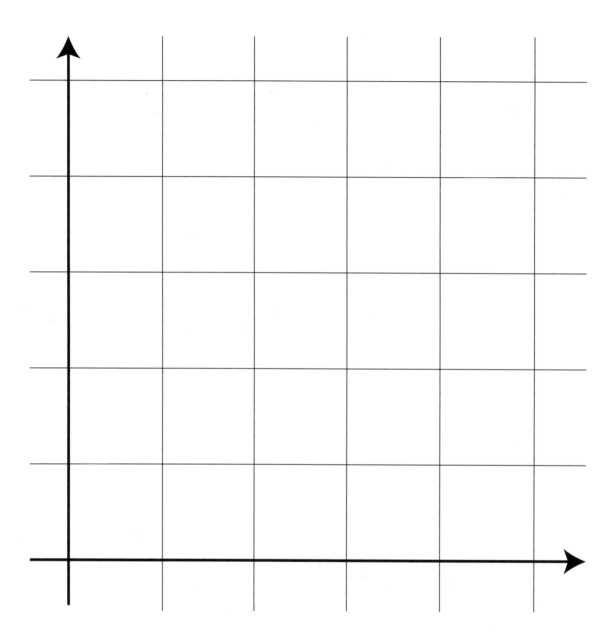

Piles of Tiles Activity Sheet

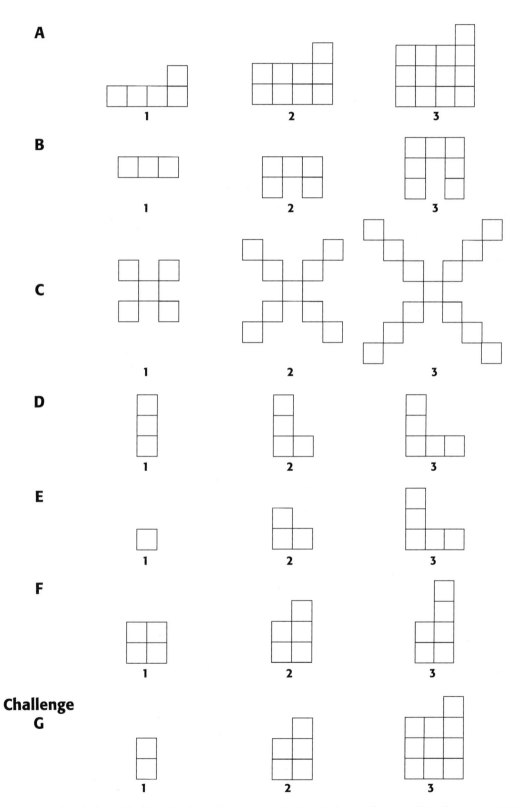

From *Lessons for Algebraic Thinking, Grades 3–5* by Maryann Wickett, Katharine Kharas, and Marilyn Burns. © 2002 Math Solutions Publications.

Glossary

We've included in this glossary mathematical terms, phrases, and expressions that appear in the book and relate to algebraic thinking. We've also included some that we didn't use in the lessons but that students will encounter in middle school. We wrote the definitions to be both mathematically accurate and useful to students who are struggling to make sense of these ideas. We tried to use language that is accessible to elementary students, and we have provided examples and illustrations when we felt they were needed.

We hope that you use the definitions in this glossary as guidelines and give your students as many opportunities as possible to express ideas in their own words and listen to how their classmates express those ideas. We don't expect our students always to use the language that we choose and we don't require them to learn our definitions. A reasonable goal is that students recognize the terms, phrases, and expressions and can use them in the context of the learning activities they experience.

axis (*plural: axes*)—a reference line on a graph used for locating points. On a coordinate graph, the horizontal reference line is often called the *x*-axis and the vertical reference line is often called the *y*-axis.

Cartesian coordinates—see *coordinates*. Named after René Descartes, a French mathematician (1596–1650) who worked on linking algebra and geometry, making it possible to visually represent an equation as a set of points on a graph.

Cartesian plane—see *coordinate plane*

coefficient—the numerical factor of a term; for example, $4x$ means "4 times x" and 4 is the coefficient of x. By convention, the coefficient precedes the variable and no multiplication sign is needed.

constant—a quantity whose value does not change. In a function rule, the constant term doesn't have a variable and, therefore, stays the same for every stage.

constant function—a function for which every ordered pair has the same second number. The graph of a constant function is a horizontal line.

coordinate graph—a visual representation of a set of ordered pairs seen as points on a grid (called a *coordinate plane*); each point is graphed using the axes to locate the position indicated by an ordered pair of numbers.

coordinate grid—see *coordinate plane*

coordinate plane—a grid formed by intersecting horizontal and vertical number lines used for plotting points identified by ordered pairs; often referred to as *Cartesian plane* or *coordinate grid*.

coordinates—the numbers in an ordered pair used to locate a point on a coordinate plane; the first number in the pair is often called the *x*-coordinate and the second number, the *y*-coordinate.

dependent variable—in a function with two variables, the variable that represents the output value in each ordered pair; the values are determined by applying a rule to the input values. See also *independent variable*.

domain of a function—the set of the first numbers (the input values) in the ordered pairs that make up the function.

equation—a mathematical sentence that contains an equals sign.

equivalent equations—rules or equations that may not look alike but that produce the same result for every input value; for example, $y = 2x$, $y = x + x$, and $2y = 4x$ are equivalent because they produce the same value of y for each value of x.

equivalent expressions—expressions that may not look alike but that produce the same result for every input. For example, $(x + 1) + 4$ and $x + 5$ are equivalent expressions because they produce the same result for every value of x.

function—a relationship between two variables in which the value of one variable (often called the *output*) depends on the value of the other variable (often called the *input*); if the variable y is a function of the variable x, then there is exactly one y value for every x value.

function rule—a description of a function that uses words and/or symbols to pair every input number with exactly one output.

graph—see *coordinate graph*

horizontal axis—the number line on a coordinate grid that goes left and right, usually called the *x*-axis.

identity—an open sentence that becomes true for all numerical values of the variables; for example, $\square \times 1 = \square$ and $\square + 0 = \square$ are identities.

independent variable—in a function with two variables, the variable that represents the input value in each ordered pair. The output values are determined by applying a rule to each input value. See also *dependent variable*.

inequality—a mathematical sentence that contains an inequality sign such as ≠ (not equal to), > (greater than), < (less than), ≥ (greater than or equal to), or ≤ (less than or equal to).

intercept (y-intercept)—when graphing a function, the point on the vertical axis (the *y*-axis); for example, the point $(0, 4)$ is the *y*-intercept for the function $y = x + 4$. The input value of the ordered pair for the *y*-intercept is zero. The term is also used for the output value of a function when the input value is zero; for example, 4 is the *y*-intercept for the function $y = x + 4$.

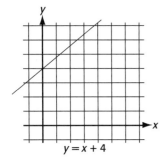

$y = x + 4$

linear function—a function whose ordered pairs, when graphed on a coordinate plane, form a straight line.

multiple representations—different forms for presenting information about a set of data; for example, diagrams, words, tables, graphs, and symbols.

open sentence—a mathematical sentence that contains at least one variable; it can be an equation and contain an equals sign (=), or it can be an inequality and contain an inequality sign (≠, >, <, ≥, or ≤). It is neither true nor false, but can be made true or false by replacing the variables with numbers.

order of operations—the agreed-upon order to follow when performing mathematical operations: (1) simplify inside grouping symbols, (2) evaluate all powers,

(3) do all multiplication and division from left to right, and (4) do all addition and subtraction from left to right.

ordered pair—a pair of numbers in a specific order; an ordered pair can be used to plot a point on a coordinate plane.

origin—the point where the horizontal and vertical axes intersect on a coordinate plane; the point on a coordinate plane located by the ordered pair (0, 0).

plot—to use an ordered pair to mark a point on a coordinate plane.

quadrant—one of the four regions of a coordinate plane formed by the two axes. The quadrants are numbered counterclockwise, starting with the upper right region. Points on the axes are not in a quadrant.

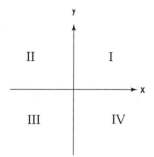

range of a function—the set of the second numbers (the output values) in the ordered pairs that make up the function.

slope—the steepness or slant of a line on a graph, measured by how much it rises or falls for each unit the line moves to the right. For the line represented by $y = x$, some points are (0, 0), (1, 1), (2, 2), (3, 3) and so on; as points move one unit to the right, they move one unit up and, therefore, the slope is 1. For the line represented by $y = 2x$, some points are (0, 0), (1, 2), (2, 4), (3, 6), and so on; as points move one unit to the right, they move two units up and, therefore, the slope is 2.

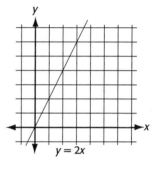

stage number—term, step, or figure number in a pattern; also, a member of the domain of a sequence or function.

T-chart—a table for recording ordered pairs of functions with two variables. For each row, the first column contains the stage or input number and the second column contains the value or output number.

term—a member of a sequence of numbers arranged according to some pattern; a part of an algebraic expression that can be variable or constant; for example, $3x + 2y + 6$ has three terms: $3x$, $2y$, and 6.

value of an expression—the number that results from using a number for each variable in an algebraic expression.

value of a function—for any ordered pair (x, y) of a function, y is its value.

variable—a letter, symbol, or other placeholder in a mathematical expression that can serve different purposes. It can represent an unknown value; for example, x in $4x = 12$ represents the number 3. It can represent part of a function rule that changes from stage to stage; for example, in $y = x + 4$, y and x are variables while 4 is a constant. It can represent quantities in formulas; for example, the C and d in $C = \pi d$ are variables. It can be used to represent a general mathematical pattern; for example, in $a + b = b + a$, a and b are variables used to describe the commutative property of addition.

vertical axis—the number line on a coordinate plane that goes up and down; it is usually called the y-axis.

x-axis—see *horizontal axis*

x-coordinate—see *coordinates*

y-axis—see *vertical axis*

y-coordinate—see *coordinates*

Index